Medical Sociologists at Work

Medical Sociologists at Work

Edited by

Ray H. Elling
and
Magdalena Sokołowska

Transaction Books
New Brunswick, New Jersey

Copyright © 1978 by Transaction, Inc.,
New Brunswick, New Jersey 08903

Library of Congress Catalog Number: 76-6204.

ISBN: 0-87855-139-5.

Printed in the United States of America.

Basil Blackwell are agents for the
publications of **Transaction Books** in Great Britain

Library of Congress Cataloging in Publication Data
Main entry under title:

Medical sociologists at work.

    Includes bibliographical references and index.
    1. Social medicine.   2. Sociologists—Biography.
I. Elling, Ray H., 1929–   II. Sokołowska,
Magdalena. ₍DNLM: 1. Sociology—Personal narratives.
2. Medicine—Personal narratives. WZ129 M4866₎
RA418.M512   362.1'092'2 ₍B₎   76-6204
ISBN 0-87855-139-5

Contents

Acknowledgments

The acknowledgments for this book are very brief. It emerged as a work not sponsored by any organization or supported by any grant and was not in any plan of any institution. It was a spontaneous development, quite beyond our increasing ties to and dependence upon formal organizations. Perhaps the real attraction for the contributors was this element of "escape" from routine and control about which they have been critical as sociologists. In any case, as editors we owe our first word of thanks to our contributors who remained interested and involved throughout this long and at times uncertain enterprise.

Although there has been no formal relationship, we express here our appreciation to the Medical Sociology Research Committee of the International Sociological Association for encouraging and mentioning this work in its meetings and newsletter.

Finally, we have to mention a crucial person, Irving Horowitz, thanks to whom we are able to publish this work. His sense for new trends and topics and willingness to support an enterprise of uncertain financial success has been essential for us.

Ray H. Elling
Magdalena Sokołowska
New York City

Introduction

The present volume may serve as scientific material on medical sociology which the reader will find in each chapter. It may also be regarded as a literary creation, or it may be considered simultaneously from both points of view—as a scientific document of literary value. It is written by people deeply involved in medical sociology and it is addressed to anyone interested in it.

BACKGROUND

Origins of This Book

There was opportunity during the Second International Conference on Social Science and Medicine held in August, 1970, in Aberdeen, Scotland, for us, the editors, to discuss possibilities for cross-national collaboration. It seemed at the time that funding for complex survey or other types of cross-national sociological research was at a low ebb. Also, it seemed that medical sociology as a subfield of sociology was coming of age enough in several countries to make it worthwhile to consider some approach to examining the development of the field and its current status in several countries.

Because it would not involve any special funding and would engage colleagues as a matter of intrinsic interest in international collaboration to better understand themselves and their field of work, it seemed feasible to use a work life history approach. The Aberdeen meeting provided a forum in which to discuss this idea. There seemed to be quite general interest and willingness to participate. Following our goal to understand through this work the origins and development of medical sociology, we invited a number of first or early generation medical sociologists present at the meeting to take part. Not all followed through to the point of completing their work. And others were invited subsequently. A few rejected the invitation arguing that they do not like to be "exhibitionists" or that they do not want to create the impression that they think too highly of themselves. All who took part have the common characteristic of belonging to the first or an early generation of medical sociologists in their countries. The authors are of course only part of the world's first generation medical sociologists. The large proportion of American contributors reflects the early and very extensive development of medical sociology in that country. There is no pretense of any kind of having here a representative sample of early contributors to medical sociology in all countries. Obviously, those who began in the field and left it for one reason or another are not included. Further, many notable figures could substitute for several, if not all, of those who have taken part. Thus the final selection included those known well enough to the editors to request this kind of material and individuals invited to participate who were interested enough to see the work through to completion. The fact that the contributions represent the views and experiences only of the authors perhaps requires no comment. There are marked differences in the educational and professional backgrounds as well as in the styles of cultivating medical sociology between the individual authors. There are also significant differences between the editors.

The process of obtaining and publishing these materials in final form was a long one. In addition to the usual problems of international scholarly collaboration, four years passed between the initiation of the process and the point at which publication seemed likely. After acceptance for publication, the scheduling and production process has involved another two years. Thus recent changes in the careers of contributors are not reflected here.

This is a group in constant personal and scientific change. As editors we have joked about making a loose leaf book to which changes could be easily added. But that would not be very feasible. We had to stop someplace. Generally, the contributions are current through 1974.

Relations to Other Work

This book calls to mind another publication of more than ten years ago, Phillip Hammond's *Sociologists at Work*.[1] Both that volume and ours treat the same general, little known theme. The selections in the book by Hammond are chronicles, commentaries, and biographies of well-known sociological studies, written by their authors. Robert Merton once made reference to a huge literature concerned with the ways in which scientists ought to think, feel, and act. But how they actually do think, feel, and act is not known. The essays in *Sociologists at Work* were offered as a partial correction of this lack. According to Hammond, they deal more with the "context of discovery" than with the "context of justification" or a logical program "how to do social research." Most texts on research methods deal exclusively with the latter context while methods related to the former are seldom seen in print. Hammond's focus, however, was different:

> The authors were asked to portray their own research activity as it was experienced during some *specific* investigation. Their instructions were to particularize, not generalize. The suggestion was also made that, in format, the essays be chronologic or ideologic, that is, organized around the sequence of events in time or the sequence of ideas in the mind of the researcher. Happily, both principles are observable, frequently within a single chronicle. Finally—and in defense against anyone who may hold that even a variant of scientific reporting must necessarily be impersonal and dispassionate—the authors were encouraged to write in the first person if they chose, to indicate freely where changes would be made if the research were to be repeated, and generally to let the reader in on the *sub rosa* phases of contemporary social research.[2]

The present book is of a similar character, although it is not mainly a systematic chronicle of some definite sociological study. It is primarily concerned with conserving through memory the beginnings of a given sociological discipline, with a rounded description of the process of its emergence and conditions of development in various geographic settings and social circumstances. The present work began as an attempt to gain insights and information into the development of the new field of medical sociology by contrasting work experiences and the careers of some first or early generation scholars in different settings in several countries. It seems that in order to better understand this new field of work it is important to learn about the ideas, tools, and people and their work settings, about the points of support and resistance. *Medical Sociologists at Work* contains a description of conducted research precisely in the aspects of that "context of discovery," "context of teaching" and, last but not least, "context of action."

The contents of *Medical Sociologists at Work* and *Sociologists at Work* may be considered in the tradition of the sociology of science. They contribute to knowledge of the social and psychological processes of discovery. *Medical Sociologists at Work* lends itself besides to analysis from the viewpoint of the concept "resistance" (or resistances) to discovery and invention in the tradition of Bernhard Stern's work.[3]

We were particularly anxious at the beginning that the theoretical orientation should be to emphasize the invention factor, as expressed in the following passage from an early communication to the contributors:

> The central thrust of each author's account should be on *his or her work as innovation* in or in relation to medicine and public health. Let us examine diffusion of our attempts at innovation, everything surrounding the job activities, the fate of several attempts, changing atmosphere, difficulties, obstacles, resistances, achievements, and, most intriguing, the utilization of new ideas and approaches. Our efforts will resemble Bernhard Stern's. But in this case, instead of the focus being on a biological innovation and resistance and eventual adoption, such as seen in Semmelwise's work, the focus will be on sociological ideas and approaches.
>
> We have some desire to concentrate on sociological innovations related to the organization of the health services. Of interest is the full range of your experience in contributing to plans for new service arrangements, new divisions of labor, new authority systems, new reward systems, new training programs (thus innovations in teaching are relevant), new regional and planning structures, new attacks on pathogenic social conditions, etc.
>
> Each of us will attempt to focus on supports and resistances to innovation and change in medical care services, teaching, and research as represented through the course of his conceptual and actual programs of work in medical sociology.

We then labored under the impression of a new, promising approach to the study of innovative processes and wanted to apply it to the work of our authors. In other words, we desired to establish whether our group was a ground-breaking innovative agent of change, engaged in reorienting the institution of medicine in the society against the resistance to this process from vested interests. The essence of that reorientation was to include in medical endeavors an adequate comprehension of people not only as biological entities but as functional or disabled members of society, and, vis à vis health and other institutions, to create a new set of understandings, alternatives, and definitions of what is health, medical, and health care. But the possibility of conducting such a systematic, rigorous analysis from the viewpoint of innovation turned out to be unreal. Our authors clearly resisted such an "innovation" and were not inclined to follow our suggestions. Their concern was at least as much with contributing to sociology as with reorienting medicine and public health. Moreover, we suspect that this was a major reason for rejection of our invitation by some of our colleagues. They did not seem to like the assumption of being "innovators" as arbitrarily defined by the editors. Those who agreed followed the outline in a general way but appropriately included general impressions of the field which cut across several positions or even their whole experience. This offered the authors a rare possibility to alter the routine of elaborating their writings on the basis of the usual scholarly way of thinking. They could relax, catch their breath, have fun, devote a few hours to summarizing their past, considering the present, and contemplating the future, all of course through the prism of scholarly work in medical sociology, but treated here as a private, personal thing.

It is always possible to consider alternative methods, each with its own advantages and disadvantages. While fully aware of the limitations of life histories, we chose the autobiographical method as economical and practical and likely to produce rich qualitative material. Personal documents (memoirs, reminiscences, autobiographies and other written materials) are a rich source of social reality. Polish-American sociology long ago used this method of public writing inspired by sociologists. It is very strong in Poland today. It was initiated by a contest conducted in 1913 by F. Znaniecki and W. I. Thomas which resulted in their *The Polish Peasant in Europe and in America*.[4] The tradition of contests for writing diaries, memoirs and autobiographies, edited by sociologists, has been preserved in the postwar period in Poland.

The value of personal documents is that they are authentic, spontaneous, free, and unhibited. They mirror men enmeshed in the intricate web of life; and they present not merely one moment but their authors' destinies. We are well aware that in each case there are aspects of the work life itself, the personal life, and the political conditions and contexts of both, about which the authors did not want to write. Some things are left unsaid in any memoir. It is not a problem specific to this book. Who is to say whether the most important determinants of work, careers, and the whole field are not the aspects which are kept quiet. Because we know the contributors well, we have the impression that the important general elements have been brought out in each case, without, however, personalizing disputes and other difficulties since this is not the point of sociological analysis in any case. Nevertheless, we feel a responsibility to alert the reader to the unknown element of unsaid things.

As a literary effort, anyone can collect and edit life histories. But the present volume is devoted to a particular category of man, the medical sociologist. This category has been rarely studied sociologically. As a matter of achieving a better understanding of this category, the present volume seemed to call for sociologists as editors who themselves had lived through, in different ways, the process of becoming sociologists.

Goals

We give primary attention here to the understanding of underlying conditions supportive of the development of medical sociology and to the present status of the field. Some secondary goals are mentioned in the conclusion of this section. For reasons of time and due to some ambivalence because of our roles as contributors as well as editors, we have not succeeded in ordering, summarizing, and assessing the scientific contributions of those included here. We see this as a potentially useful task which remains for others to consider.

Some readers will wish to use the contributions contained herein to understand the conditions and personal responses involved in the development of the new discipline of medical sociology in different countries. Here we will only illustrate how observations of this sort can be drawn from this work by offering a few examples.

There appear to be factors both "external" and "internal" to the discipline in addition to matters of personal make-up and orientation which have been important in the development of medical sociology. Among "external" factors, there is the *Zeitgeist* or climate and conditions of the times. One might have expected the field of medical sociology to blossom in the middle to late 1800s after Virchow, among others, identified medicine itself as a social science. But (and this may be only one of several interpretations) social medicine was largely philosophically and social-welfare oriented, and medicine as a whole became engulfed by the germ theory of disease and sharply oriented its sources of knowledge toward empirical scientific research. At the time, European sociology was largely social philosophical in origin and content and focused on overall societal evolution. The development of specific problem-oriented, empirical sociology occurred first in the climate of American pragmatism. Thus when medicine was ready to once again expand its concerns beyond microbes to the conditions of life of patients and potential patients, and when the increasing popular demands for health care came up against the chaotic system of services in the United States, there was an empirically oriented sociology to which to turn.

People in medicine felt a need to reorient their field and they turned to sociology. But it is interesting to observe in many if not all the life histories collected here that the invitation to sociologists came first from groups in medicine which themselves were struggling to better establish themselves—for example, public health, psychiatry, nursing, and health education. It did not come initially from the most prestigeous and well-established fields of medicine such as internal medicine and surgery.

Other broad societal conditions have had an influence on the development of the field. There appear to be several types of situations and more than one may be interwoven in any particular country. In many countries few qualified people and little work has developed either in sociology or in scientific medicine. In others, scientific medicine may be fairly advanced but there is no base in sociology. In some, scientific medicine is somewhat developed and sociology may be well underway but medicine is rigid and narrowly defined in biological terms and has not turned to nor opened the door to medical sociology. Cross-cutting these situations is the factor of social and political instability which affects the ability of interested and able persons to lend continuity to their work. In some countries, this factor is so evident that neither sense of career nor idea of developing a new field can realistically take hold.

Among the "internal" factors are some of those relating to the development of subspecialties in other fields of work—struggle over definition of domain, access to support and sponsorship, control over and access to favorable recruitment, and efforts to legitimate the field vis à vis the parent discipline of sociology and the content discipline of medicine. Personal factors and orientations will be illustrated in the last section of this introduction which discusses the contributors.

A second goal has been to provide material which would reflect in part the current status of the field and assist in assessing its directions, accomplishments, and shortcomings. Even though the sample is limited as already mentioned, the contributors do present themselves and their work and they reflect a range of medical sociology in a variety of settings. Thus insight into the nature and status of the field are provided. We note, for example, that medical sociologists have in the past and continue to exude a sense of optimism and enthusiasm for their work. This presents us with an interesting contradiction, for only a few if any of the hoped for benefits of the field have actually been realized (or the contributions may have been made but not clearly brought to consciousness and adequately recognized). Concerning contributions to sociology, as suggested by a survey of major textbooks carried out by Frederick Bates some years back for a presentation to the American Sociological Association on the teaching of sociology, little from medical sociology has been incorporated in any of the alternative general theories of sociology. Possibly, sociological theory must be recast so this incorporation can take place; the problem may not be all one way. In the self-conceptions and relations of contributors to sociology proper, we see some of the problematics. Always a certain tension develops between contributing to a theoretical discipline and work in what is seen as a "practical" content area (though this conflict can be more imagined than real). The question remains: How can the work of a subdiscipline be properly recognized and incorporated into a parent discipline? Or is everyone "sociologizing" in his own way—doing his own thing—and thus we should not expect cumulation of framework and understanding? Even if this last alternative is true to a considerable extent, one sees in the approaches represented here, although various and sometimes divergent, a considerable amount of theoretical convergence.

Considering contributions to health, has the field succeeded in reorienting medicine to the betterment of the health of human populations? Many of the contributions suggest what a continuing struggle this is in the face of superspecialization and the technologization of medicine. It is hard to measure success in this sphere of concern—so many factors are involved in the mode of medical work and the level of human health. There is need for a systematic study of changes in medicine attributable to medical sociology and of contributions to or detractions from health.

In any case the field of medical sociology is ripe for serious assessment. It has been accused of being far too establishment oriented, in spite of early concerns and fierce battles to avoid becoming a hand maiden to the medical establishment. With some justification, perhaps as a matter of its early and major development in the United States, the field has also been accused of a certain ethnocentrism and limited world view.[5] It is felt that the chapters here will possibly guide and otherwise contribute to a broad and fundamental assessment of the field. How broadly or narrowly should it be conceived? What should the name of the field be, sociology of health or of medicine? Is its focus most properly on death, disease, disability, discomfort, and dissatisfaction (a broad view of social epidemiology), or is it on the institutions and occupational groups and whole system of health care delivery (a broad view of health care organization)? If both foci are needed, what should be their interrelationship? What methodological improvements are necessary? What working arrangements are called for if the field is to realize its full potential?

A number of other goals were in our minds as we began the work on this volume. We felt it would offer material of didactic teaching value for several types of students at different levels. To a considerable extent, the book could serve as an introductory text.

We hoped also that the book would offer material of theoretical and practical interest to those involved in or interested in further development of medical sociology or the sociology of health and related fields.

Finally, it was our concern to preserve as a matter of historical interest, something of the early stages of this still emerging discipline.

REFLECTIONS ON THE CONTRIBUTORS

Entry into Medical Sociology

The group of contributors represents an interesting mix of people coming into the field from academic sociology as well as from medical or other fields. Although service in World War II interrupted the academic careers of some, and there were other variations in course, most went through undergraduate or European preuniversity work into graduate work in sociology and received their Ph.D.'s. But two received their M.D.'s before doing academic and other work in medical sociology. One entered from a background in economics.

Perhaps it is especially true of a new field of work that people will enter it unconsciously, without deliberately setting course. In any case, the actual entry of the contributors into medical sociology seems in each instance to illustrate well Becker's concept of "side bets" which then take hold and become central parts of a person's long-term behavior.[6] Sometimes with a personal or family experience with illness and/or experience with health personnel as background, sometimes with no apparent prior connection to medicine, those entering from sociology got into some study or work situation with health workers or health content, received some recognition from respected others for this work, and began to build on this experience. The two who entered from medicine had experiences with sick people in poverty or other circumstances of real need and got into an aspect of medicine primarily involving group concepts—occupational health, public health—rather than primarily diseased organs or individual patients, and began searching for the conceptual and methodological tools necessary for work in these areas. Again, for this "side bet" of study in sociology the first "payoff" came in the form of appreciation shown by respected others. Gradually, self-concepts and identities evolved to include if not rest primarily on sociology and medical sociology.

Who Are the Contributors?

Half of the twelve contributors are United States citizens and half are of European or other citizenship. This is probably a fair reflection of the geographic distribution of medical sociologists in the world today. Also, that one-quarter are women may be a fair reflection of sex composition of medical sociology worldwide today. In any case, these proportions are not far off the true mark.

The distribution of contributors by country is as follows: Argentina (Segovia) one; Belgium (Nuyens) one; Israel (Shuval) one; Norway (Løchen) one; Poland (Sokołowska) one; United Kingdom (Jefferys) one; United States (Elinson, Elling, Field, Freidson, Mauksch, Straus) six. Two of the United States group were first citizens of a European country and emigrated at an early age. Several others are from homes in which one or both parents came from a European country and spoke some language other than "American."

As befits a still active group entirely made up of first or early generation medical sociologists in their own countries, ages concentrate as of this writing (October 1975) at fifty years. They range from thirty-six to sixty. Three-fourths of the contributors are married. Four have divorced. None are single. Most have held many positions. Only one or two have been very stable and continuous in a given position or institution. To an overwhelming degree, the work has involved research and teaching in that order. But the careers of most involve some administration and several of the group have been involved in health services development efforts in an active research capacity.

The primary characteristic of the contributors which strikes the reader is an involvement—almost an immersion—of self in the work. They are of course interested in their families and other facets of their lives, but their work is the central part of their lives. Whether or not they are always happy in their work is not the point. They do not work only for money or other concrete material rewards. And their deepest satisfactions and dissatisfactions are experienced in their work. They clearly seem to feel caught up in something larger than themselves.

From what source does this energy, preoccupation with, and devotion to work stem? It is difficult to be sure of any answer. There is not likely a single source. Nor would the authors necessarily consciously recognize and accept what we say here. Certainly they are not bound by it.

In fine sociological tradition, this is a critical group; yet it is a group which seeks respectability, recognition, prestige, and other rewards. Thus the authors show a fundamental ambivalence toward the established orders of their societies and particularly the establishment of medicine within these societies. On the one hand, they present in their writings and life work, however diplomatically or softly this is expressed, a fundamental challenge to "the way things are done" by raising questions about beliefs, assumptions, values, the distribution of resources, and organization of authority. On the other hand, even if some battles with some groups have been tough, and the way seldom simple and often complex, medical sociologists have, on the whole, achieved high recognition, good pay, and other rewards. They have sought to be both in but not of the established order of their societies, particularly the medical establishment.

Every one of our contributors is from a middle-class background. There is a range—from the son of a house painter, partner in a small painting contracting firm to the daughter of a dean of a law school. None is from an upper class family, that is a family with significant capital holdings. Few if any sociologists at all are from such a background. None of the contributors is from a lower class family eking out an existance through unskilled, interim labor, and with little education. Being from the middle class, the contributors are interested in "the good life" (though their definitions of this would differ from more usual middle-class ones). In fact, they are a strong upwardly mobile group. But, somehow, as part of what we might call "the industrial" as distinct from "the postindustrial" generation (this characterization would call for a broader essay but we presume that these terms carry a general meaning for the reader), perhaps through the impact of the Great Depression and the problems of the World War II era, they became imbued with a concern for inequity, the potential for social dissolution, loss of multidimensionality in relationships among men, and the possibility of mistreatment of men in a weakened position by other men in positions of unique authority and power. Thus they did not make their way by going into business, law, or medicine. In some vital and fundamental sense, whether in a highly conscious and deliberate manner or not, the contributors stood outside of or abandoned such traditional and familiar paths to "success;" they stood outside the system; yet they worked their way upward through the system. "What makes Sammy run?" Success striving, but in a very special way.

No doubt there are other sources of the energy and involvement in work that are envinced in this group. These other factors may not be truly independent from the more fundamental ground we have just covered. But one cluster of these related factors deserves special comment. These people are ground breakers, boundary crossers. The attraction of the untried, the unknown has fascinated them and drawn them out from more familiar ground. But in this boardary crossing, it is not a simple matter of survival. These are activists concerned to break untoward boundaries affecting people's health conditions and health. This is true even of the more abstract theoreticians among them, for action as applied to this group is not limited to daily activity such as changing health services arrangements. In a more fundamental way they are concerned with the development and use of knowledge in change and do not limit themselves to contemplation. This boundary crossing also involves curiosity, what W. I. Thomas identified among his four primary wishes, as the wish for new experience. Though each contributor would phrase it differently Hans Mauksch has said it for all:

> As I look back I might have become a sociologist committed to functioning in any of several areas of social concern. One thing I know for sure: I never could have been satisfied to remain confined to the community of my own discipline. Maybe it is my need to discover new questions in real situations; maybe it is my not-so-hidden missionary streak. Maybe it is my, as yet unfulfilled, search for a laboratory in which theoretical knowledge can be tested, and in which sociological experimentation can be undertaken. Maybe—a peculiar personal characteristic—medical sociology offered me a career

where I could always be "one of the few," where I could have all of the titillation of ritualized marginality.

To the editors the work on this book has been most rewarding. It has kept us in contact over several years with our colleagues engaged in what we see as a unique endeavor. We belong to this group. We are medical sociologists first and editors only second.

NOTES

1. Phillip E. Hammond, ed., *Sociologists at Work: Essays on the Craft of Social Research* (New York: Basic Books, 1964).
2. Hammond, *Sociologists at Work*, pp. 3–4.
3. Particularly Bernard Stern, *Social Factors in Medical Progress* (New York: Columbia University Press, 1927).
4. F. Znaniecki and W. I. Thomas, *The Polish Peasant in Europe and in America*, 5 vols. (Chicago: University of Chicago Press, 1918–20).
5. See Manfred Pflanz, "A Critique of Anglo-American Medical Sociology," *International Journal of Health Services* 4, no. 3 (Summer 1974): 565–74.
6. Howard S. Becker, "Notes on the Concept of Commitment," *American Journal of Sociology* 66 (July 1960): 32–40.

Medical Sociologists
at Work

City Slums to Sociosalustics

JACK ELINSON

I was born at home in an apartment in a South Bronx (New York City) tenement. My mother died of tuberculosis (known as "consumption") in 1923 when I was six years old. She had been in and out of hospitals, sanatoria, and "fresh-air" country places where I sometimes accompanied her. For a year or so after her death, I was shunted between grandmothers in Brownsville (Brooklyn) and East Harlem where my older half-sister also lived. (I do not remember where my younger sister was put.) The South Bronx, Brownsville, and East Harlem are currently (1976) regarded as the three worst slum areas in New York City. They were densely populated, lively neighborhoods when I lived there and I did not think they were so bad.

I recall my earliest most frightening experience, a seven-year-old Jewish kid in East Harlem running for dear life back to my home corner on East 107th Street and Park Avenue, chased by a gang of Italian (so I was told) kids who dominated the territory on East 108th Street, one block away.

My father, part of the Russian Jewish migration to the United States in 1904, was twice a widower at age forty. After the usual miscellany of factory employment available to poor immigrants, he had settled on housepainting to earn a living by day, pursuing engineering studies at Cooper Union, a free technical college, by night. With my mother's death, he discontinued his studies and struggled to arrange some kind of home and family life for himself and his children. He took me to the Bronx Zoo, rowing in Central Park, and, when I was old enough, to talks by Norman Thomas, the American socialist leader in the 1920s and 1930s.

To pull the family together, my father purchased a small house in Queens, a half mile past the end of the subway line, where I lived with my aunt (my father's sister and her family) and my paternal grandmother and grandfather. From there I attended the local public elementary school, Boys High School in Brooklyn, (an hour away by subway) and the City College of New York (an hour and a half away by subway) from which I graduated when I was twenty with a bachelor of science degree with majors in chemistry and psychology.

I imagine my father was pleased with my choice of chemistry, so close to his aborted engineering studies. For me science, as against unverifiable religion, was the way to truth and perhaps understanding. At age twelve, I was fascinated by Bertrand Russell and Einstein—a fascination which led to science studies in college. While I relished the theory and method of chemistry, my clumsiness in the laboratory led to classroom disaster. I dropped out of college for a semester and found a five-dollar-a-week job as an apprentice law clerk for a well-known negligence-action lawyer. With the encouragement of my employer, I toyed with the idea of entering the law. In the summer I took some gut courses, government and psychology, and did extremely well in psychology—all brain work, no manual dexterity required. I reentered college, took more work in psychology, continued to do well, and gradually changed my major field of study from chemistry to psychology. If chemistry was the key to life, psychology was the key to living, and a science to boot, albeit a relative newcomer.

At my graduation from CCNY, Mayor La Guardia delivered the commencement address in Lewisohn Stadium where, to earn some spending money, I used to hawk pillows and candy bars for those who were able to afford tickets to the open air concerts. For eight years, between the age of twelve, when I started high school, and the age of twenty, when I finished college, I spent quite a lot of time on the New York subways. The New York subways as a site for extracurricular learning experiences have yet to be exploited by the sociologists of education.

I was a member of that City College generation which was branded "guttersnipes" by the then college president Frederick B. Robinson. Standing in the rain outside Lewisohn Stadium, we had been listening to one of the more radical students drawing an association between the activity of Hitler's Nazis and the behavior and attitude of the college president who happened to be passing by. The enraged college president began to swing his umbrella at the assembled students. The following week a mass meeting was held in the Great Hall of the College with students wearing buttons with the inscription "I am a guttersnipe—I fight fascism!" Addressing the students was the more respected member of the faculty, the philosopher Professor Morris Raphael Cohen. No faculty member was more influential in shaping how I (and thousands of other City College students) should think than Morris R. Cohen. His reasoned faith in logic and liberalism provided lifelong armament against unreason and dogmatism.

My first job after college—it was 1937, and the country was still in economic depression—was as a production records clerk for the Ideal Doll and Toy Company in Long Island City (makers of Shirley Temple and Betsy Wetsy dolls). It was my task to summarize the production of the day before and develop by nine o'clock in the morning an inventory of work-in-progress. There were dozens of operations to be performed in making dolls (spraying cheeks, painting lips, inserting tongues and eyes, buffing seams, preparing layettes, etc.). I got pretty good at hand arithmetic and became adept with all sorts of shortcuts in adding up long columns of figures. When for mental relaxation during lunch hour I tried to do some manual labor by operating some of the machines (buffing heads), I was stopped by the union foreman who explained that it was union work, and that I was a white-collar clerk, which was management. (This was in the fall of 1937 and there was already talk of military conscription.) To show how the impending military draft was regarded, I recall a remark of one of the skilled workman in the doll factory who said he could not be drafted—who would there be to insert tongues in the dolls' heads?

After two months in the doll factory, I accepted an offer of a civil service appointment in Washington, D.C. on the basis of a chemistry examination I had taken while I was still a chemistry major in college two years earlier. The job was to wash laboratory glassware for the analytical chemists in the Food and Drug Administration, then in the United States Department of Agriculture. This was an opportunity to get away from home, which was getting much too crowded—my brother-in-law had moved in with my older sister and I was getting tired of shaking the ashes out of the coal furnace—to get away from New York and its subways for the first time in my life, and to be on my own at $20/week ($1,020 a year).

Washington, D.C. in 1937 to a twenty-year-old New York City College graduate was a southern town—terra incognita. Adult Negroes walking toward him in front of the White House moved quickly to the side, eyes lowered. They sat in the back of the bus. A college teenager who a few years before had cut afternoon chemistry labs to take in the glamerous stage shows in Harlem's Apollo

Theatre, just across St. Nicholas Terrace from City College, found himself the only white person in Washington's Howard Theatre. Alone in a strange city, he sought out more familiar things: enrolled at the George Washington University in evening classes in chemistry (quanititative analysis), and at the Jewish Community Center for the gymnasium and the girls. In New York, he had only read, in his social psychology class dealing with prejudice, about the lynching of southern Negroes; in Washington, he was to hear Billie Holliday sing about it in "Strange Fruit" and see her, emotionally drained, collapse before the audience.

I became a charter member of Group Health, a cooperative, one of the first consumer-owned and managed health plans, forty years later to be known as an HMO (health maintenance organization). Group Health physicians were barred from practice in Washington hospitals by the Medical Society. A suit was entered against the Medical Society, which after a long career in the courts was finally won with the historic decision declaring medicine a trade; and, as any trade, subject to the Sherman Antitrust Act, with the Medical Society declared by the court to be a conspiracy in restraint of trade. Subsequently, Group Health physicians were permitted to practice in Washington's hospitals. All four of my children were delivered by Group Health physicians. My family and I remained members of Group Health for fourteen years, or until the time I left Washington in 1951.

As already noted, my initial job in the federal government was as a minor laboratory apprentice in the Food and Drug Administration. For the next several years I was to hold a series of minor scientific jobs. The next was as a photogrammetric aide tracing drainage patterns on stereoscopic aerial views of the country for the Soil Conservation Service, also in the Department of Agriculture; and the next was as an engineering aide making optical glass at the National Bureau of Standards. This was now 1939; and the Bureau of Standards apparently was already being used as a factory for making optical equipment for bomb sights and other war material.

A year later I was working in the War Department's Personnel Research Section, in the Adjutant General's Office, constructing and analyzing psychological classification tests for soldiers. This post marked my return to psychology and statistics. Here I practiced the psychometric trade, inventing multiple choice items intended to measure and predict performance in one army job or another. Here too I learned (in 1940) to do factor analyses and multiple regressions using, initially, hand, then electrically driven, desk calculating machines. I was able—bleary-eyed—to estimate Pearson product-moment correlation coefficients by eye from scatter plots to within 0.1 or 0.2 of the computed value. My duties included the development of classification (intelligence) tests for the selection and placement of military personnel for training and jobs. I was exposed to the leading quantitative psychologists (psychometricians) in the country, among them Clyde H. Coombs and Thomas W. Harrell, who taught me the mechanics of factor analysis, Wherry-Doolittle regression techniques, item analysis, and related statistical technologies bearing on test development and analysis. A prototype of the technology was J. P. Guilford's *Psychometic Methods*,[1] and there was a heavy influence of the Chicago school of factor analysis: Coombs had been one of Thurstone's students. Most notable among them was Clyde H. Coombs, the measurement theorist, who along with Carl I. Hovland was later to sponsor me as a member of the American Psychological Association.

I spent many hours at the calculating machines figuring commonalities, factor loadings, and regression weights. My diligence and perspicacity was rewarded by a transfer and promotion to the army's Morale Attitude Research Branch, by happenstance. The happenstance was that Margaret Strong (the daughter of E. K. Strong of the Strong Vocational Interest Tests), who had also been working in the A.G.O. Personnel Research Section, was transferred because she married her supervisor, Tom Harrell. It was Margaret's recommendation of me to Samuel A. Stouffer that brought me into the Morale Attitude Research Branch, where I was to seriously continue my unofficial and extrauniversity "graduate" education.

The army's Morale Attitude Research Branch was composed of both military and civilian personnel whose academic backgrounds were primarily in sociology, psychology, and social statistics. Prior to the war they were professors at major universities, who recruited their best graduate students plus a corps of practical survey research people from the world of marketing, advertising, and public opinion polling. I was brought in in 1941 as a civilian junior in the capacity of social research analyst.

In the Morale Attitude Research Branch, I learned about IBM machines and graphic chart presentation from Dean Manheimer, who had been a survey research analyst with the Psychological Corporation in New York. I learned how to "adjust" statistics—how to make margin totals equal to the sums of rows and columns in tables—from Felix E. Moore (a student of Stouffer's at Chicago) who had come from the Bureau of the Census. I learned to compute

standardized rates from A. J. Jaffee (another student of Stouffer's at
Chicago) who also had been recruited from the Bureau of the Census. My knowledge of item analysis and notions of test reliability,
which I had obtained as a student of psychology, were reinforced
by contact with the eminent psychometric consultant, Quinn
McNemar, author of one of the early texts of psychological statistics. I learned about content analysis from L. S. ("Slats") Cottrell,
Jr., who had been professor of sociology at Cornell and a colleague
of Stouffer's at Chicago. I learned most about data analysis from
Sam Stouffer himself, including such esoteric tasks as how to make
an IBM countersorter chase down, usually in the middle of the
night, a stubborn hypothesis buried somewhere in a pack of grimy
punchcards. From Stouffer I also learned the importance of writing
fast and clean, eschewing sociological jargon (he had been a newspaper editor, as well as the first American sociologist to have studied statistics with R. A. Fisher). This skill was most important in
presenting the main findings of a complex statistical analysis in
social psychological research to generals, colonels, and other military decision makers; and equally important, as I discovered later,
to physicians and health service administrators.

I suppose that I learned most about the logic of measurement
from Louis Guttman. From Guttman I learned to question the convenient assumptions of psychometricians and to develop a respect
for manifest data. A heightened consciousness about the rules used
by scientists in the assignment of numerals to observations (S. S.
Stevens's definition of measurement) was developed in me (I may
have been receptive) through seemingly endless, patient, self-
confident (some thought arrogant) explanations by Guttman. Here
was a man who was as prepared in mathematics as any sociologist
(he rivaled Lazarsfeld in this regard), who had published in journals of mathematical statistics, and who saw a utility in applying
mathematical theory to problems of sociological measurement. Attitudes were real! They could be tested for dimensionality. There
were "components" of attitude scale analysis that "flowed" from
mathematical development. I was to become an expert in the second component of scale analysis, "intensity"; the first component
was "content." Indeed, my Ph.D. dissertation, which I completed
after my service with the Department of Defense, was on "attitudinal intensity in relation to personality and status" in which I
showed that the higher the status of an individual in a group (by
any indicator of status), the more intense (certain, convinced, positive) were his attitudes. This explained the rigidity of older persons,

the sophistication of the educated, and the confidence of thuse of higher rank. One of my highpoints of intellectual appraisal was when Guttman said that I knew more about the intensity component than anyone else (this was related to me by Judith Shuval, a colleague of Guttman's in Israel).

I have been asked by Magdalena Sokołowska whether "early political and social interests led me into this problem-solving human service field." I do not know, but I do recall an incident which may shed a little tangential light on this question. At one point all the professionals in the Research Branch subjected themselves to the Kuder Preference Test. This test is designed to reveal a person's interests, presumably with a view toward assisting him in making vocational choices. A profile of scores is derived for variables labeled scientific, persuasive, artistic, social, etc. All the social scientists in the Research Branch rated high on "scientific" interest, but I peculiarly also rated high on "social." I recall being quite self-consious about this at the time; and somewhat bothered about it. I seemed to not be exactly in the mold of the leading social scientists in my immediate vicinity which reaffirmed my marginality at not being from the Chicago sociological group. Something was different (wrong?) about me, and my question was would I ever become a true social scientist? This double interest has perservered, so that while my colleagues in medical sociology may call upon me to write a chapter on "methods of sociomedical research" as I did for Howard Freeman, Sol Levine, and Leo Reeder in the *Handbook of Medical Sociology*,[2] I have found myself for the past twenty years doing research and teaching in a school of public health, a problem-oriented, as well as scientifically oriented, place. I believe this characteristic is also reflected in the kind of graduate program I developed at Columbia, in which half the academic work must be taken in one of the social sciences and the other half at the school of public health, where people like myself (John Colombotos, Eric Josephson) attempt to build bridges between social science and public health, and doctoral students with their dissertations attack public health problems from the point of view of a particular social science discipline which may be anthropology, history, economics, psychology, political science, or sociology.

Am I a sociologist? I am a fellow of the American Sociological Association. I have served on the Council of Medical Sociology of that association.[3] I was trained in wartime in the Research Branch by sociologists (S. A. Stouffer, L. S. Cottrell, Jr., Louis Guttman). I worked side-by-side doing studies of military morale with such fellow sociologists as E. A. Suchman, Shirley A. Star, Robin M. Williams, Jr., Arnold Rose, John A. Clausen, Robert N. Ford, Robert Dubin, Paul Glick, Clarence Glick, A. J. Jaffee, Lionel C. Florant, H. Ashley Weeks, and Paul Wallin. I have published in the *Journal of Health and Human Behavior* (later converted to the *Journal of Health and Social Behavior* under the editorship of Eliot Freidson) and *Social Science and Medicine*, but many of my publications are in professional public health journals.

My college and university training was not in sociology (I have never taken a formal course in the subject), but in psychology; and my doctoral degree from the George Washington University was in social psychology. I am also a "certified psychologist" in New York State.

I entered into medical sociology rather unconsciously, without choice or forethought. It happened during World War II when I was a member of Samuel Stouffer's research group in the United States army.[4] This group was engaged in attitude research whose purpose was to assess the morale of troops and to try to understand the factors that influenced it. The work of the war years was summarized and published in the four volumes of *The American Soldier: Studies in Social Psychology in World War II.*[5]

There was a concern about morale of patients in army hospitals. I was assigned the task of surveying the morale of patients in three army hospitals. It was the custom to keep military patients in hospitals until such time as it was determined that they were either too disabled for further military duty and were to be discharged, or that they would be returned to full military duty (e.g., were able to go on a twenty-mile hike with full field pack). Unexpectedly, my survey showed that, as abhorrent as military service was, patients who would *not* be discharged were next highest in morale. The lowest in morale was the group for whom it had not yet been determined what their fate would be—whether discharge or return to military duty. The uncertainty apparently contributed more to low morale than either severe medical disability or the certain knowledge that indefinite further military service was their lot even though most were unwilling soldiers—men who had been drafted for military duty in the most unpopular service—in the army.

Men in the amputee wards were by far the most cheerful. Legs off, arms off, these men *knew* where they were in relation to their bodily condition and to the prospect of further military service.[6]

My report on morale among army hospital patients earned some attention in the press and among policymakers. A Washington newspaper columnist reported that I was being sent overseas as punishment for uncovering low morale conditions in army hospitals. At a military hearing, where I was sworn to testify, I was cross-examined by colonels and generals. I was twenty-four years old. It was the first time that I had ever been held personally accountable for a piece of social research that I had done. Until then, my superiors had always taken the blame or the credit. Two other impressions derived from the experience were: that the reinforcement of a social psychological notion that personal morale was less a reflection of objective conditions, in this instance of medical disability and military service, than feelings of uncertainty with respect of one's future; and that significant findings of both public policy and sociological interest could be derived from studies in a medical setting—the preserve of white coats, test tubes, thermometers, and bedpans.

I was sent overseas following the military hearings and newspaper publicity to find out whether soldiers felt they were getting enough to eat, whether their laundry was being taken care of, and whether dead bodies were removed from the field quickly enough after combat (sanitary science?)—all functions of the Army Quartermaster Corps.

My next assignment bearing on medical matters occurred in the aftermath of the Battle of the Bulge. Thousands of men in this action in northern Europe in the fall and winter of 1944 had developed "trench foot." Soldiers referred to trench foot as the million dollar disease—a condition which could be severe enough to merit military discharge, yet, if not too severe, would leave no permanent major disability. Trench foot is a circulatory condition in which capillaries are damaged. It can be relatively mild or so severe as to require amputation. It occurs when men are unable to move about in cold and wet trenches. It was said to be preventable by keeping the feet dry through changing of socks which were to be kept dry by body heat under the armpits, and by constantly moving the toes. The feet were to be kept warm and dry as much as possible. Special equipment in the form of shoe-pacs had been issued, but many soldiers had discarded this extra clumsy weight on long marches. The preventability of trench foot under field conditions was under challenge. It was a matter of immediate military concern since General MacArthur's Pacific Command was preparing for the invasion of Japan under climatic conditions similar to those experienced by the European forces. I was asked by the army surgeon general to evaluate the effectiveness of training and equipment in the prevention of trench foot. I designed what I was to learn a decade later was a retrospective epidemiologic study—I matched a thousand men with trench foot with an equal number who had also been in the Battle of the Bulge, and who did not get trench foot, on some eighteen variables of exposure to combat conditions. And by survey research methods, querying both groups, I came to some assessment of the effectiveness of training and preventive measures. (This study was noted by John Gorden, the Harvard epidemiologist, in the United States medical history of World War II.)[7]

This baptism of social survey research in the field of health (hospital care, medical decisions, and epidemiology) may have stuck in the mind of an army Research Branch colleague, Shirley Star, who, in the postwar years, after returning to the University of Chicago to complete her doctoral studies in sociology, had joined the National Opinion Research Center, and who, when NORC was called on to participate in a study of chronic illness, suggested my name as study director to Clyde W. Hart, then director of NORC.

While I was still with the Department of Defense in the postwar years, and before I joined NORC, I had engaged in a major survey, with Ira H. Cisin, of the sexual practices of soldiers in relation to venereal disease. This work drew the attention of A. C. Kinsey. Subsequently, in an experimental evaluation of the effectiveness of venereal disease prevention films designed to affect knowledge, attitudes, and practices of soldiers, we learned that by such educational techniques it was easier to impart knowledge than to affect attitudes and alter behavior.

I really got hooked on medical things when I became study director for NORC for the sociological part of the sociomedical Hunterdon study of *Chronic Illness in a Rural Area*. The Hunterdon study of chronic illness in a rural area (it was to be something more than that) was a ground-breaking study which changed the views of many in the field of public health as to the validity, reliability, and generalizability of methods of estimating morbidity in a population. At the same time, it was this study which forged the bond between my interests and capabilities in social science research and the field of health. Prior to this study, and its companion study in an urban area in Baltimore, Maryland, estimates of morbidity for populations had relied on extrapolations from mortality data, statistics of hospital admission or discharge diagnoses, or household interview surveys like the one carried out on a nonprobability sample in the United States during the economic depression of 1935–36. It was recognized by leading biostatisticians that mortality data, at least in developed countries, were inadequate to assess the morbidity status of a population, that disease registries of reportable diseases provided at best an incomplete picture, and that hospital statistics were necessarily biased since only that part of the diseased population which entered the doors of a hospital was counted. The rural Hunterdon study (and subsequently the urban Baltimore study), with its surprising finding that only one in four clinically diagnosable conditions were picked up in careful, exhaustive, household interview surveys, had substantial impact on subsequent data collection methods in this field. The United States National Health Survey, which was then in the planning stage, developed a strategy to have a personal household interview sample survey to cover certain aspects of morbidity, that is, reported disability arising out of illness, and a health examination sample survey which, though more expensive and more difficult to execute, was the method of choice in estimating clinically diagnosable disease, including disease that was asymptomatic and medically unattended.

Ray E. Trussell was the first physician with whom I collaborated on sociomedical research.[8] Dr. Trussell was the first director of the Hunterdon Medical Center, an experiment in rural medicine.[9]

A national Commission on Chronic Illness had been formed around 1950 to look into the question of chronic illness, its preventability and long-term care. This commission was put together by all the leading national health organizations, including the American Medical Association, the American Hospital Association, and the American Public Health Association, and was initially headed by an epidemiologist, Morton L. Levin. As an epidemiologist, Dr. Levin approached the problem by asking what the prevalence was of chronic illness. It was decided to launch two comprehensive studies, one in a rural area and another in an urban one, to develop methods for answering this question. Dr. Trussell, who had been an associate of Dr. Levin's at the New York State Department of Health and at Albany Medical College, saw an opportunity to serve the commission's purposes and at the same time develop baseline health data for the rural population to be served by the new Hunterdon Medical Center in New Jersey. The National Opinion Research Center was invited to carry out the population surveys, and I was assigned by its director Clyde W. Hart to be the study director for NORC and to work with Dr. Trussell on this study. Thus began a collaboration starting in 1951 which continued after completion of the study with various educational and research endeavors at the

Columbia University School of Public Health and Administrative Medicine. Trussell became director of the School of Public Health in 1955 and I joined him on the faculty as associate professor in the fall of 1956.

Theodore Woolsey, director of the United States National Center for Health Statistics, reviewed the results of the Commission on Chronic Illness Studies most carefully, personally examining and comparing original information obtained from the household interview with that obtained by clinical examination. In the course of his appraisal, he once subjected me to the most grueling scientific cross-examination I have ever received in my life, not excluding the defense of my doctoral dissertation. Woolsey was one of the leading statisticians on the staff of the United States Public Health Service. His principal consultants and friends were Morris Hansen, William Hurwitz,[10] and Harold Nisselson, among the most outstanding sampling statisticians the United States has ever produced, all of whom were then leading officials of the Bureau of the Census. At a dinner at Hansen's house in Washington, D.C., after plying me with drinks, good food, dirty jokes, and assorted banter, the statistical gang of Hansen, Hurwitz, Nisselson, and Woolsey proceeded to question me on the details of the procedures used and the results obtained in this Hunterdon study. After that long and arduous evening of social and scientific discourse, Woolsey, who had been extremely wary of the Hunterdon study since it challenged some of the current assumptions upon which the proposed United States National Health Survey were based, became a respected colleague whose esteem I value highly. The work of the United States National Center for Health Statistics was launched, taking the results of the Commission on Chronic Illness (Hunterdon and Baltimore) studies into serious account.

Over the next decade it was not easy to have both Woolsey and Trussell as intellectual colleagues, but I believe I was able to merit that combination because of the clarifying role the Hunterdon study played with respect to the place of the sociological household interview survey and the medical clinical examination in sorting out the distinct contributions of each in sociomedical and epidemiological understanding. One jury of peers judged the Hunterdon Study to be the best contribution to the sociomedical field to that date.[11]

I think this study helped to make social science researchers respectable in medical and epidemiological eyes—we were not so woolly-headed as they had imagined. It helped find for me a place

in sociomedical science. I was asked, while still a study director at
NORC (this was in 1956) and assistant professor of sociology at the
University of Chicago, to organize and coordinate a summer institute sponsored by the Social Science Research Council on "Social
Surveys in the Field of Health." Some of the participants in that
institute have themselves become well known in medical sociology, among them Peter Kong-Ming New, Robert Eichhorn, Seymour
Bellin, and Edward Hassinger. Others whose research lives we
hope were enriched thereby, even though they did not focus their
careers on medical sociology, were Charles Willie, subsequently
chairman of the Department of Sociology at Syracuse, and James A.
Davis, subsequently director of the National Opinion Research
Center at the University of Chicago, and Irving Ladimer, a lawyer
with the Better Business Bureau and consultant and lecturer on
medical ethics.

One of my presentations of the results of the Hunterdon Study
bore sociomedical fruit in another way,[12] when it was juxtaposed to
a presentation by Lester Breslow, who extolled the virtues of the
household survey in population morbidity measurement at an annual meeting of the American Public Health Association. Breslow
was to corner me at a subsequent invitational meeting of social scientists and preventive medicine practioners sponsored by the Social Science Research Council and the Russell Sage Foundation in
Buck Hill Falls, Pennsylvania. There he asked where he could find
social scientists ("like you," he said) whom he could recruit to
California, where he was then head of the California Department of
Public Health, Division of Chronic Disease. This conversation, directly or indirectly, resulted in the temporary or permanent migration to California of a covey of social scientists, including John Fi-
nan, Ira Cisin, Dean Manheimer, Ray Fink, Joseph Hochstim,
Josephine Williams, and Don Cahalan to sociomedical research and
the establishment of a "human population laboratory" in Alameda
County which continues until this day.[13]

Dr. Trussell joined the Columbia University School of Public
Health and Administrative Medicine where we finished writing the
book on the Hunterdon study.[14] I was appointed associate professor
in the School of Public Health where I headed up a research unit
and took over the teaching of survey research methods, a course
which had been previously taught, more from the literature than
from practice, by George Rosen. Among students subjected to this
course were several who have made important contributions. Mad-
galena Sokołowska became chief, Section of Medical Sociology,

Polish Academy of Sciences, and the leading medical sociologist in
Poland. Samual Wolfe, coauthor with the Canadian medical
sociologist, Robin Badgley, of *The Doctor's Strike*, and *The Family
Doctor*, became professor of Community Medicine and director of
Evaluation at Meharry Medical College. He did a doctoral dissertation with me in social psychological aspects of general practice
published as *Talks with Doctors*.[15] Stamatina Kouvari (alias Mata
Nikias) did a dissertation on social factors in dental care use under
a health insurance plan which led to a book which won a prize
from the insurance industry.[16] She became codirector with me of
the first university program in sociodental research. Jose Nine-Curt
became dean of the School of Public Health in Puerto Rico. Rafaela
R. Robles became head of the behavioral science teaching program
in the same school. Dr. Trussell and I continued collaboration in a
number of studies while he was director of the Columbia University School of Public Health.

One unanticipated (on my part) consequence of the Hunterdon
study was my becoming known as an epidemiologist (an occupation I had not heard of until I became known as one). I was invited
to participate in conferences on the epidemiology of ar-
teriosclerosis with such real epidemiologists as Jeremiah Stamler,
Ancel Keys, Paul Oglesby, Warren Winkelstein, David Spain, and
served for a number of years as a reviewer of grants for the American Heart Association's Council on Epidemiology and Community
Service. It took me several years to realize that an epidemiologist,
even a social epidemiologist, has to know quite a bit about the natural history of a disease in addition to his knowledge of human and
social behavior in order to make a real contribution. I have expressed this conviction in a joint paper with my medical colleague,
Conrad E. A. Herr, entitled "A Sociomedical Response to Edward S.
Rogers's 'Public Health Asks of Sociology . . . .'"[17] Only few
sociologists, I believe, have achieved an adequate knowledge of the
diseases they are investigating to contribute meaningfully to their
epidemiology. Among the most successful of these are Saxon
Graham, whose socioepidemiological studies of cancer, and Leo
Reeder and Leonard Syme, whose socioepidemiologic studies of
cardiovascular disease are well known. Some effort has been made
for social scientists who wish to contribute to this field to take
some postgraduate work in biology (e.g., Kurt Back at Rockefeller
Institute), but I believe this is a greater effort than most social scientists are capable of turning to good account. Accordingly, I gradually left the field of epidemiology to the epidemiologists, although

it is discouraging to observe the simplistic way that epidemiologists generally deal with sociological variables. I have the feeling that only true interdisciplinary training in sociomedical sciences or interdisciplinary collaboration will result in meaningful contributions along these lines. A medical epidemiologist working without social science collaboration, or vice-versa, is not likely, in my judgment, to make sophisticated contributions to social epidemiology. It is possible that my colleagues Mervyn Susser and Zena Stein may eventually show this judgment to be in error. John Cassell and Lawrence Hinkle as epidemiologists have shown a sophisticated assessment of the role of social variables in disease.

At Columbia, with Trussell, I moved quickly into the health services research arena on studies of medical and hospital care in Puerto Rico, where I introduced studies of physicians' and nurses' career attitudes in a general investigation of manpower.[18] I recruited social scientists for Columbia who engaged in studies of the quality of hospital care (June Sachar Enrlich), the utilization of health services under different health insurance plans (Josephine J. Williams), the health of adolescents (Eric Josephson and Ann Brunswick), and physicians' attitudes (John Colombotos).[19]

One of my major activities as research unit head was the development of the Washington Heights Master Sample Survey (one of the early community population laboratories for sociomedical research which were getting underway in the 1960s). I conceived the WHMSS as an instrument which social scientists, social epidemiologists, and health service researchers could use to study problems of their choice without each one having to develop the necessary core staff and structure—sampling, interviewing, data processing, and so on—much in the way physical scientists might make collaborative use of a cyclotron. The WHMSS thrived for a decade until New York City ran out of money for its Health Research Council. It drew and served such notable investigators as Edward A. Suchman, Bruce S. Dohrenwend, and Ernest Gruenberg.[20]

I had been instrumental in recruiting Edward Suchman into medical sociology by recommending him to George James, who was then deputy commissioner of health of New York City for planning and evaluation. Suchman's work with the WHMSS is well known. He used the Washington Heights Master Sample Survey to establish the importance of attitudinal dimensions and ethnicity in the use of health services. Suchman's prodigious energy and productivity led to the widely read and authoritative Russell Sage publications, *Sociology and Public Health* and *Evaluative Research*.[21] The latter book resulted from the seminar which Suchman, James, and I initiated in 1961 at Columbia on the evaluation of health action programs, a seminar which still continues. It remains one of the most satisfying courses that I give at the school, since evaluation has become even more important as social action programs strain the economy. The idea that rigorous social research methods can be applied to social action programs is more accepted now than it was then.

At this point, when I am asked to highlight anything that might be "innovative," I point first to the application of principles derived from social psychology to the study of health problems. The main such principle is the differential perception of phenomena as a function of the perceiver and his orientation. This principle permits consideration of health phenomena in terms other than the legitimate medical concern of whether a clinical diagnosis is "correct" or "incorrect." A nonmedical view of illness is different and not "incorrect." One of my students, Donald Patrick,[22] has recently shown that when nonphysicians appraise the severity of a physical illness (when the factor of prognosis does not enter), the primary factor is limitation of mobility. One wonders now whether the emotional success of the antiinfantile poliomyelitis campaigns might be explainable with this principle.

Physicians are often puzzled that patients do not follow their orders, take medicine as prescribed, and so on.[23] Differential perception of the seriousness of illness may turn out to be an explanatory variable. If so, this should lead to further effort to educate both patients and physicians.

On a macrosystem level, differential perception of the seriousness of illness (as revealed by the United States National Health Survey, for example) due to limitation of mobility versus potential may affect national priorities in allocation of scarce resources. It may be useful to note, in passing, that "restriction of usual activities" indexed by disability days can be laid at the door of the common cold and mild stomach upsets to a larger extent than cancer or heart disease. But disability days does not mean limitation of mobility.

Not only differential perception of health status, but differential perception of health issues lies at the heart of the contrast between profession and community views of health problems. The growth of "adolescent medicine" may derive in part from the differential perception of adolescent health problems by pediatricians and internists, on the one hand, and adolescents themselves, on the other.[24]

A currently debated issue is whether automated multiphasic health testing (AMHT) is acceptable to physicians. One study showed that this aspect of a health care delivery system is more acceptable to general or family physicians than it is to specialists such as internists.[25] Family physicians and internists differentially perceived what AMHT would mean for their practices. For family physicians, AMHT complemented their service to patients and thus enhanced their professional self-image. For internists, AMHT was not only a threat to their economic well being (for many internists already had their own equipment for carrying out tests, or had arrangements with outside laboratories for doing so), but was a source of competition to what they regard as their appropriate professional duties. The introduction and proliferation of AMHT may well alter the hierarchial structure of medical specialties. In the absence of systematic and definitive evaluation which, according to some, will be many years in coming, whether this development will be regarded as "good" or "bad" is clearly also a case of differential perception.

If the notion is adopted that no problem, no health problem, can ever be looked at "whole," but only differentially according to prior orientation, one implication for education on research with respect to health problems is to provide the opportunity for problems to be studied by a useful but limited variety of perceptual orientations. In the social sciences, problems may be examined from the point of view of history, economics, anthropology, political science, sociology, and social psychology. With this notion as a premise, I proposed to the Graduate School at Columbia that a Ph.D. be awarded to those who made a social science contribution to a health problem, no matter which social science was chosen as the perceptual orientation. For the moment this Ph.D. program has been called sociomedical sciences. I agree with George Rosen that the term medical is constraining on the range of health problems that are amenable to study from a social scientific point of view. Rosen has proposed the phrase "sociology of health" to more properly delineate the field. In the search for a single term, I have suggested "sociosalustics."[26]

I have been asked to explain the origins of the neologism "sociosalustics." As medical sociologists we are concerned with the study of public health. We are by now, after a quarter of a century of work, accustomed to the appellation "medical sociology." We recognize the implicit restriction in the adjectival modifier "medical" at the same time that we may bask in the glory associated with the profession of medicine. A number of us have called for a sociology of health (George Rosen,[27] Virginia Olesen). Efforts have been made to change the name of the section on Medical Sociology of the American Sociological Association along such lines but (by 1975) without success. But even "sociology of health" is clumsy—three words, not one. By combining "socio" (society) and "salus" (health) and "ics" (the science of), we can have a single word which means the *science of health in society*. My Greek-born colleague Stamatina Kouvari Nikias and I have conceived a word which would be based entirely on Greek roots, "kenonygeia"; but this turns out to be even more strange to Americans with non-Greek ears. One influence of sociosalustics is the effort to conceive and operationally define the social dimensions of health status.[28]

Over the years the professional and work interests of my wife and myself have moved closer together. Her father, a physician, had owned and operated a convalescent home in Chicago. May grew up living and working in the convalescent home helping with the meal preparation, assisting the nurses, and doing the bookkeeping. She received a bachelor of science from the University of Chicago and currently is a clinical nutritionist at Martland General Hospital in Newark, New Jersey, where she imparts nutritional counsel to poor black and Hispanic women and teaches nutrition to medical students at the New Jersey College of Medicine. She is coauthor of a volume called *Enjoying Your Restricted Diet* designed to make therapeutic diets gastronomically pleasurable.[29] Our joint professional ritual is to attend the annual meeting of the American Public Health Association every fall. We have not worked together; at most I review a manuscript draft of hers. Her orientation is basically clinical, to be of direct help to individuals. Mine is to do research. Clinicians are believers, and scientists doubters.

We have four children, and three grandchildren. May devoted a decade to raising the children; at one time there were four of them under six years of age. The oldest son, Richard, is a scientist, an assistant professor of developmental biology at the University of Toronto, where he is engaged in research on the fertilization process in *rana pipiens*. His wife Lynn, who started out to be a school teacher, is now engaged part-time as a research assistant on an epidemiologic study of breast cancer. Richard and Lynn have two children. Our daughter Elaine has been a journalist for a news service, and has been active in various causes ranging from helping

Ceasar Chavez's struggling farm workers' union to arranging for Jane Fonda and Donald Sutherland to entertain, in their way, United States Army troops in the Far East. Elaine is currently the European representative for the United Farm Workers. She is married to Brian Nicholson, a docker and leader of the London branch of British Transport and General Workers Union, the union whose cooperation was key to the successful boycott of nonunion farm products being shipped from the United States to England. Our son Mitchell is a school teacher, teaching mathematics in a junior high school in the poorest area of the Bronx, near my birthplace. He is married to an Idaho girl who has a masters degree in English literature. They have a son. Our youngest son Robert has been traveling around the country carrying bricks in New Hampshire, working in a gold mine in South Dakota, picking apples in Wisconsin, tangerines in California, and oranges in Florida, and milking cows in North Carolina. He believes in socialism. He has lived on the beach in Oaxaca, Mexico, knows yoga, and is into health foods; he is a great cook. Before all that he studied for several years at Clark University majoring in psychology.

Family acquaintances comment on how disparate seem the lives of our children; they do not seem so to May and me. Each in his or her own way emphasized a set of values we hold dear. Richard, a scientist, with his Ph.D. in biology from Yale at age twenty-five, shot like an arrow to a position it took his father a dozen years more of zig-zagging to achieve. Elaine, a committed fighter for social justice, has been dedicating every fibre of her existence to the struggle her parents have only casually supported in their off-duty free time. Mitchell, using his intelligence in teaching economically poor and intellectually disadvantaged children, is "serving the people" at sacrifice of personal ambition. Robert has most, thus far, rejected material values and is seeking a peaceful, thoughtful existence consciously avoiding any imposition of his way of life on others. Thus we like to think of all of our children as sharing the best values and being at least to some extent like us, only more so.

NOTES

1. J. P. Guilford, *Psychometric Methods* (New York: McGraw-Hill, 1936).

2. Howard Freeman, Sol Levine, and Leo Reeder, eds., *Handbook of Medical Sociology*, 2nd. ed. (Englewood Cliffs, N.J.: Prentice-Hall, 1972).

3. Since completion of this essay I have been voted and served in the chair of the Section on Medical Sociology.

4. This group was known by various names: Research Branch, Information on Education Division, Department of the Army Morale Branch, Attitude Research Branch.

5. S. A. Stouffer et al., *The American Soldier: Studies in Social Psychology in World War II*, 4 vols. (Princeton: Princeton University Press, 1949).

6. U.S., Department of Defense, *Attitudes and Opinions of Enlisted Men Patients at Three Army General Hospitals*, prepared by J. Elinson (Washington, D.C.: Government Printing Office, 1944).

7. U.S., Department of the Army, Health Department, *A History of Medicine in the European Theater of Operations, U.S. Army, 1941–1945*, prepared by J. E. Gordon, Health Department report no. 314.7–1 (Washington, D.C.: Government Printing Office, 1947).

8. My earlier work on trench foot was done at the request of Gilbert Beebe, a noted biostatistician with the army surgeon general's office.

9. See Ray E. Trussell and J. Elinson, *Chronic Illness in the United States* (Cambridge: Harvard University Press, 1959), vol. 3, *Chronic Illness in a Rural Area*.

10. Morris Hansen and William Hurwitz, *Sample Survey Methods and Theory*, 2 vols. (New York: John Wiley and Sons, 1953), 1: 11.

11. Gerald Gordon et al., *Disease, the Individual, and Society: Social-Psychological Aspects of Disease, a Summary and Analysis of a Decade of Research* (New Haven: College and University Press, 1968).

12. J. Elinson and R. Trussell, "Some Factors Relating to Degree of Correspondence for Diagnostic Information as Obtained by Household Interviews and Clinical Examinations," *American Journal of Public Health* 47 (1957): 311–21.

13. J. Hochstim, "Health and Ways of Living: The Alameda County California Population Laboratory," in *The Community as an Epidemiologic Laboratory*. ed. I. Kessler and M. L. Levin (Baltimore: Johns Hopkins Press, 1970).

14. Trussell and Elinson, *Chronic Illness*, vol. 3.

15. Samuel Wolfe and Robin Badgley et al., *The Family Doctor* (Toronto: Macmillan of Canada, 1973). In 1975 Wolfe became head of the Division of Health Administration at the Columbia University School of Public Health and Administrative Medicine.

16. H. H. Avnet and M. K. Nikias, *Insured Dental Care* (New York: Group Health Dental Insurance, 1967).

17. J. Elinson and Conrad E. A. Herr, "A Sociomedical Response to Edward S. Rogers's 'Public Health Asks of Sociology . . .'" (Paper delivered at American Sociological Association annual meeting, San Francisco, 1969).

18. J. Elinson, "The Physician's Dilemma in Puerto Rico," *Journal of Health and Human Behavior* 3 (Spring 1962): 14–21. See also idem, "Career Studies of the Younger Generation of Physicians in Puerto Rico," in

Medical and Hospital Care in Puerto Rico, ed. Ray E. Trussell et al., (San Juan: Department of Health of Puerto Rico, 1962), pp. 141–48.

19. All of these colleagues have published notable works; however, I cite only the following because it treats a seldom-studied problem: Ann Brunswick, "Adolescent Health: Indicators and Determinants for Urban Black Youth" (Ph.D. diss., Columbia University, 1975).

20. C. Gell and J. Elinson, eds., "The Washington Heights Master Sample Survey," *Milbank Memorial Fund Quarterly* 47, part 2 (January 1969, special issue).

21. Edward A. Suchman, *Sociology and the Field of Public Health* (New York: Russell Sage Foundation, 1963); idem, *Evaluative Research: Principles and Practice in Public Service and Social Action Programs* (New York: Russell Sage Foundation, 1967).

22. Donald Patrick, "Measuring Social Preference for Function Levels of Health Status" (Ph.D. diss., Columbia University, 1972).

23. See Milton S. Davis's work on patient compliance, "Variations in Patients' Compliance with Doctors' Advice: An Empirical Analysis of Patterns of Communication," *American Journal of Public Health* 58 (February 1968): 274–88; and work on patient participation by Ray Elling et al., "Patient Participation in a Pediatric Program," *Journal of Health and Human Behavior* 1 (Fall 1960): 183–91.

24. Ann Brunswick and Eric Josephson, "Adolescent Health in Harlem," *American Journal of Public Health* 62 supp. (October 1972, special issue).

25. J. Elinson, J. Colomobotos, and B. Levenson, *Physicians' Acceptance Of Automated Multiphasic Health Testing* (Washington, D.C.: National Center for Health Services Research and Development, 1972).

26. J. Elinson, "Methods of Sociomedical Research," in *Handbook*, ed. Freeman, Levine, and Reeder. See also J. Jago, "Hal—Old Word, New Task: Reflections on the Words 'Health' and 'Medical,'" *Social Science and Medicine* 9 (January 1975): 1–6.

27. George Rosen, "The Evolution of Social Medicine," in *Handbook*, ed. Freeman, Levine, and Reeder.

28. J. Elinson, "Towards Sociomedical Indicators," *Social Indicators Research* 1, no. 1 (1974): 59–71.

29. Margaret B. Salmon et al., *Enjoying Your Restricted Diet* (Springfield, Ill.: Charles C. Thomas for the New Jersey Dietetic Association, 1972).

To Strike a Balance

RAY H. ELLING

INTRODUCTION

Some beginning graduate students might find it useful to consider a prospective approach to recording their work experiences, if doing so would not seem impossibly optimistic. This, however, is a frankly retrospective exercise, subject to an unknown extent, to the distorting effects of self-justification, current interests, available materials, and possibly some efforts which overcompensate for these shortcomings.[1] In this work we are all looking back. None of us has, as far as I know, religiously kept a detailed diary recording support and resistance faced in the process of intellectual and other development of self at work.

As I look back over my work career, I become aware of certain intellectual and emotional tensions which have often motored my work. There are enough concrete instances of recall for me to treat these tensions as realities of the past. In the most general terms, I have often been engaged in striking a balance between the poles of several dimensions of concern—theoretical development versus work on problems of abiding human concern; attachment to my disciplinary base in sociology versus engagement in health institutions; "getting along" versus "standing outside" and "shaking things up" when comfort and conscience would not easily match.

Possibly the most pervasive tension, which was reflected in my earliest intellectual development, was between the search for knowledge and the desire to solve mankind's problems.

EARLY DEVELOPMENT

My father was an immigrant from Sweden; my mother, American born of Swedish parents. My father was a college graduate who sold life insurance. During the Great Depression his company went broke; he lost all his renewals and had to start over. As the youngest of three boys, I remember only some aspects of these "hard times." But my brothers know and it is in "the family culture," otherwise comfortable and middle class.

The dire circumstances I saw in Japan as a seventeen- and eighteen-year-old just after World War II (1946–48) seemed to call for a "saving" of mankind. Thinking it would be through modern technological development that the "saving" would take place, I began my college work at the University of Minnesota in 1948 in chemical engineering. It is ironic that people must still be disabused of such simplistic thinking.[2] But my experiences in Japan showed me many things other than inadequate physical and economic circumstances—things I now understand in quite a different way. Perhaps these experiences triggered in me the need for another kind of knowledge. Concepts of "front" management and "backstage" were unknown to me. My understanding of prestige and reward and authority structures was minimal. At the time, as personal driver and house sergeant of a one-star general who commanded a brigade of occupation troops, I think I felt only moral indignation at the tone of voice and words used about some person when the general discussed him "privately" in the back seat of the car and those he used in face-to-face meetings with the person. I was surrounded by and participated in (though I think uncomfortably) the discrimination against "gooks" and various forms of exploitation, including the sale of cigarettes for fantastic sums on the black market. I also had some unrealistic responsibilities of a supervisory sort with eleven servants in the general's house. Cultural differences had to be overcome but, again, though it was perfectly obvious that language differences were great and ways of life differed markedly, I was unsophisticated regarding culture, social power, and dominance and other concepts which I might use today.

Following discharge from the army, I began my studies in chemical engineering at the University of Minnesota, but the genre of experience in Japan probably contributed to my feeling that it was cut and dried. I realized that the real problems lay elsewhere, although I did not know where. After one year I abandoned chemical engineering and began for the first time to search seriously for ideas, always with a commitment to solving larger human problems.

I was poorly educated and incredibly naive in this search. I recall starting an abstracting and classification system which amounted to an encyclopedia; it had to be abandoned eventually since I had no idea of what I was embarking on.

With no background at all, I set off with two friends to study French in Paris during the summer of 1949. What started as an exciting summer's adventure in Europe turned into a three-year, rich learning experience of study, travel, and encounter with new ideas and people.

After the summer's study in a language school, I took up at the Sorbonne further study of the French language as well as philosophy, political economy, and literature of the eighteenth and nineteenth centuries. I also hitchhiked with a friend through England, Spain, Portugal, southern France, Italy, Holland, Luxembourg, Germany, and Austria.

Through my course of work at the Sorbonne, including some reading of Montesquieu and social-utopian critiques such as Voltaire's *Zadig*, and through cafe conversations about Marxism and capitalism, I began to formulate for myself rather naively the notion of the comparative study of societies as a way toward inventing new forms of human organization which would allow men to solve their problems.

Some time during this marvelous year of study, mostly in Paris, I read Georges Gurvitch's *La Vocation actuelle de la sociologie*. I found it subtle enough, but terribly complex and, I thought, confused. Perhaps there was some influence of the existentialism of the time; in France it was called "le temps du désespoir." People vacillitated between wanting to pick up the pieces and wondering whether it was worth it. Although the encounter with Gurvitch's book was not intellectually satisfying, it was like a clap of thunder alerting me to a discipline—sociology—which was doing what I had, on my own, begun to think needed doing: studying alternative ways of organizing human societies.

On a hitchhiking trip to Austria I met Margit in Salzburg. Telling myself that I was going to Salzburg the next summer to learn German, I renewed contact with her. We spent much time together and decided we were in love and would get married. There were many obstacles—my family; to some extent her family; cultural differences (though she spoke beautiful English with a charming Austrian accent); and no money. When I asked her father for her hand, I cannot recall how I described my prospects to "Herr Direktor," longtime manager of the largest hotel in Salzburg. He appologized that there would be no dowry other than the wedding arrangements, since nearly everything had been lost in the war. Then it became clear: what I really had to offer Margit, his much beloved daughter, was that I could take her to America where she would be safe. Truly a time of reconstruction without great certainty!

I sold my return boat ticket for funds to live on until I could find a job. Somehow, I landed a job in Nuremburg as "inspection reports analyst" in the office of the commanding officer of the United States Armed Forces exchange system in Europe. This involved telephoning or writing installation managers all over Europe to ask them what had been done about deficiencies. I learned a great deal about accounting, inventory losses, grease in snack bar ovens, and writing appropriately worded letters as "the colonel's" reply to the head of the inspection agency. But Margit and I were having difficulty finding housing in the bomb-damaged German economy.

After six months of clandestinely sharing my assigned bachelor's room (much to the chagrin of other bachelors who wanted to bring girls in without the embarassment of a married couple) I asked for a transfer to Austria. We spent the next year and a half in the Austrian Alps in St. Johan im Pongau where, as an area manager, I administered several stores in an Army camp of some 10,000 troops. Later, when I taught organizational theory in a hospital administration program in the Graduate School of Business at Cornell, I could always say, when faced with the test of one's wordly practicality, "I have met a payroll."

At one point, Margit assisted me in the accounting aspects of suddenly announced, frequent inventories in the PX. Sometimes these sessions lasted late into the night, and we would return exhausted to our apartment. The inventories were designed to catch a ring of thieves which, we found, was composed of the head stockroom clerk, two of the four sales clerks, and their soldier boyfriends who would walk out of the store with bags of things covered by false sales slips.

When this problem was resolved, life in St. Johan became very nice. Our apartment had been requisitioned by the occupation forces from the owner of the large general store in St. Johan with whom we became very friendly. In winter, I used to take early morning chair-lift trips to the top of the mountain and ski all the way down to my office. We knew that our time in this kind of life was limited, for we had early reached an understanding that we were doing it simply to "collect ourselves," primarily economically, with the idea that we would go to the United States where I would study for a short time before undertaking some, as yet, undefined life work. The money we were earning, plus the unused part of the GI Bill benefits would provide my schooling. I felt that sociology was the area of study, but at the time I had no notion of earning a living at it. Margit and I simply had an agreement that I was to have a certain period to satisfy my curiosity about the possibility of studying human societies.

I had heard somewhere that the University of Chicago was a great center of sociological studies, so (not knowing the name of the chairman of the department) I wrote to the university admissions office expressing my interest in studying the subject. I received a marvelous letter from Ernest Burgess saying that, although my background did not exactly qualify me for study in the master's program (after all, I had only had one year of college in chemical engineering and a year of study in French language and culture at the Sorbonne), if I took courses in psychology and economics during the summer of 1952, I could enter the program in the fall.

During our time in Chicago, Margit worked in the Billings Hospital accounting office to help support us. I worked in the post office each Christmas season. In addition, with the help of the secretary in the Department of Sociology, I got a fine job driving the weather maps downtown each afternoon. For two years I brought them to Clint Yule at a television station so he could give the evening weather report. I received $5 for each day, requiring only an hour and a half of my time—big money during 1953–55. Finally, for several months, I held a night job counting up car exchanges between the Pennsylvania Railroad and other lines. It was possible to do this job in two hours and then sleep for five or six hours on a couch in the washroom. The other men cooperated in this approach, not only because they knew I needed some sleep in order to go to class in the daytime, but also because they were conscious of the need to preserve "a job." It is something more than a bad pun to identify this as a literal case of featherbedding. In short, even though we had the costs of schooling to meet and we had begun our family with the arrival of our first son, Ronald, in 1953, we lived reasonably well from the several sources of income.

At the same time, our daily life, especially for Margit, was rather uncomfortable and sometimes frightening. While I tended to "stand a bit outside" viewing our surroundings as a sociological laboratory, we lived in considerable turmoil and anxiety because our student housing was in the midst of a "zone of transition." It did not help matters at all for me to announce at home this euphemism (concept?) invented by human ecologists to explain situations such as ours. We still felt the effects of block-busting, racist scare tactics, and the associated aggressions and conflicts, including a significant amount of gunfire and robbery in the neighborhood.

For me these were three very rich years during which the student group (myself as chairman for one year) ran the august Society for the Study of Social Problems. For one of our meetings, we arranged a debate between Phillip Hauser and Nelson Foote on the possibility of cumulating knowledge in the social sciences. The meeting highlighted the factions in the department—the neopositivists, on the one hand, and those who, as Everett Hughes sometimes put it, see sociology as "reporting the big news." The distinction can probably be made in another way between "hard" science and not "soft" but "subtle" science. In the former group I counted Hauser, Bogue, Duncan, to some extent Blau, and Goodman; in the latter group, Hughes, Anselm Strauss, Riesmann, Foote. Obviously these were not hard and fast distinctions. There were commitments to science and understanding on both sides. In any case, a student could learn a great deal in confronting an intellectual issue mixed up in a power struggle.

ENTRY INTO MEDICAL SOCIOLOGY

My first contact with issues of medical organization came in Everett Hughes's seminar on work and professions. Our next door neighbor was an older medical student whose wife came from Vienna. Margit and I found it natural and easy to socialize with them, and I sometimes had protracted discussions with him about his future plans and the way medicine was practiced in the United States. Thus, as a part of the Hughes seminar, I got involved in a study of medical students. This turned out to be the preparation for my master's thesis. The point was to compare seniors and freshmen, assuming that differences represented learning trends (and not simply different cohorts or long-term trends) and to explain senior-freshman differences by studying the prestige-reward structure and students' connections to it—a kind of Bennington study in a medical school setting.[3] The comparisons were focused on issues of "socialized medicine" and "changes" on a modified scale of liberalism-conservatism.[4] Broadly speaking, since I had read Michael Davis's *Medical Care for Tomorrow*,[5] I felt (as I had earlier with regard to society in general) that the big problems lay in the organizational sphere. Although I have learned more detail and more adequate framework since that time, I still hold this view. To the extent that I have been involved in innovation in medicine as a sociologist, it has been more in the sphere of organization of care than in, say, the study of social epidemiology (though I later learned more clearly to link these concerns).

Briefly summarized, my master's thesis work helped me to understand learned orientations toward medical care organization in the following way: seniors in this medical school were more liberal in general and more favorable toward "socialized medicine" than were freshmen. If these differences represented learning through medical school, this seemed to happen by a process of fellow students and faculty granting recognition (friendship choices), prestige (representational choices), and other rewards (e.g., better grades) to liberally oriented students. A concentration of outstanding students was found among the leadership of the local chapter of the now defunct AIMS (Association of Interns and Medical Students). This organization was in its death throes at the time of my study. It was being killed by the influences of the McCarthy period. Specifically, it was put on the attorney general's list, and members who were drafted into the army were made to serve as privates while nonmember physicians served as medical officers. There was also the competition of the SAMA (Student American Medical Association), liberally supported at the national level with a $50,000 grant from the AMA. In spite of these pressures, possibly in part because of them, the emphases represented by AIMS were well recognized and rewarded at the University of Chicago at that time.[6]

It seemed to me that broad political and philosophical influences of a learning environment were being translated into responses of the faculty and students and, from there, into general and specific orientational changes among students. I reasoned that if it happened this way at this level in this school, it could happen in the same way, but in a different direction, in another school under different environmental influences. Newcomb found some rather remarkable persistence in orientations of Bennington students twenty-five years after graduation, apparently because of a persisting pattern of differential associations.[7]

What has happened to those two classes of University of Chicago medical students? I do not know. I have often wished I could find out. One can hypothesize that the dominant form of medical practice in the United States, organized around solo, enterpreneurial medicine, will have taken its toll in weakened opinion toward prepaid group practice, emphasis on prevention, and so forth.

As far as I can tell, my study never had any impact at all beyond its impact on me and my thinking. It was never referred to in *The Boys in White*, a Chicago-generated study,[8] nor in *The Student Physician*.[9] As I analyze supports and resistances to innovations which our work may represent, I must list several possibilities regarding this study.

It may have been bad work—assumptions too large, system of explanation too large, and data too thin to support the whole thing. Even if this were so, there was not much other work of this sort at the time and, at the very least, the study was suggestive of some broad influences on medical education which should have been taken into account more completely in later studies and possibly in the organization of medical education and practice.

Whatever the actual quality of the work, my thesis committee accepted it, but felt it was not worth any special attention, so there was no "sponsorship" or note made of the work in their contacts with faculty colleagues who later pursued studies in this sphere.

Possibly a relatively neutral explanation is the correct one—a sociology department is a bureaucratic organization in which papers are filed and ignored. Or it seems possible that the study was "a sensitive one" and would upset the dean of the medical school, especially in the witch hunt atmosphere to which the university was exposed during that McCarthy period. But probably the biggest handicap was the master's level status itself. Work done at this level was simply not taken seriously in sociology at that time. This level of work is, if anything, ignored even more today.

Since my introduction to medical sociology through the study of medical education, I have added a new dimension to my thinking on this specific part of the field. Besides its impact on students' orientations directly through prestige-reward structures of the school and later through the young physicians' involvement in a certain form of practice, there is probably an additional (perhaps the most important) path through which the larger environment influences the medical student—anticipatory socialization. It seems likely that the student, who is faced with a world of medical practice in which he looks forward to earning his living by fast turnover and discreet treatments in a solo office setting, has considerable difficulty identifying with preventive measures. He tends to ignore, or at best gives lip service to, attempts to understand the patient as a person in a social setting and the functioning of the medical care system beyond the traditional focus on pathophysiology.

By discussing my thoughts as a part of this autobiographical exercise, I want to suggest that this beginning awareness or sensitivity to the larger structuring of society as determining the composition and problems of medicine within it has not been fundamentally revised or abandoned over the years, only deepened. In later work on the flow of support to different types of hospitals, rather than starting with the motivation of individual hospital workers, I formulated the central theme around environmental influences and interactions of internal hospital factors with the environment.

In sum, my earliest conceptions of medical sociology were pretty much limited to concerns with the organization of the medical care system. While this interest has persisted, I have added greater awareness of an interest in the social and environmental causation of disease and disability. I believe that I did not have much awareness or conviction about this other major part of the field as I began. As students, we were deeply immersed in problems of mental illness, Freud, and deviance in general through the Chicago program, but the strong position of symbolic interactionism in the program made me uncertain, even then, of the validity of mental illness labels and etiologic frameworks. It was in my next step into the field, study in a medical sociology program, that my understanding of this sphere as well as that of medical care organization grew.

TRAINING IN MEDICAL SOCIOLOGY

Incredibly naive as this may sound, it had come as a revelation to me during my course of studies at Chicago that one could, as Everett Hughes put it, "play while one works" as a sociologist. In short, I came to know the possibility of "sociologizing" as a way of earning a living, while searching for knowledge to contribute to solutions of problems. I wanted to go on, and Margit agreed, but I did not know what to emphasize. One day, while I talked with Everett Hughes about my desire to go on in sociology, he mentioned a new program in medical sociology. He had received an announcement and request for suggestions of likely candidates from August B. Hollingshead at Yale. Everett Hughes's reference to the Yale program and his statement that "it's good to pursue graduate studies in more than one department anyway" convinced me to apply. Also, it seemed to me that matters of life and death gave to the medical field a more immediate concern with problem solution than might be true in other spheres of sociology. This was attractive to me.

I was accepted along with three others. We made up the first group in the first formal program in medical sociology. The program was supported by a grant from the Commonwealth Fund which provided $1500 per year to the fellows in addition to tuition costs. This support was tremendously important as my G.I. Bill monies had run out. The Yale opportunity offered a new source of support with the luxury of "just studying" and a new place to live. We were very happy.

The support allowed us to go on building our family. A second child was lost at birth in the Grace-New Haven Hospital. This was a bitter experience. Quite aside from what I was learning in the course by studying such researches as the Hollingshead and Redlich study of differential treatment according to social class,[10] it became clear to us in a very personal way that there were stupidities and blind spots in the organization of medical work at the most detailed technical level as well as in the broader arrangements of the system. A chief resident and nursing staff are not well organized when they let a woman lie in labor for twenty-eight long hours without anyone checking progress. However, on November 30, 1956, another son, Gerard, was born in New Haven.

The fellowship was not quite enough to live on, but it allowed Margit to concentrate on raising our children and it allowed me to concentrate on study. In the last year I took a job as janitor in one of the Yale undergraduate dorms cleaning out the trash and sweeping the floors for a short time each morning. With this, plus the fellowship, we got along fine.

There was an element of prestige and promise in attending Yale, even if it was not "the real Yale"—the undergraduate school. This gave a tremendous boost to our hopes and aspirations. I was often reminded of a chant or song I had heard from time to time among boyhood playmates in Minneapolis (in Hennepin County): "I didn't go to Harvard; I didn't go to Yale; so now I'm a sittin' in the Hennepin County Jail."

There were other essential sources of support: a number of key figures in the medical school at Yale—Dr. Senn in pediatrics, Dr. Redlich in psychiatry, Drs. Hiscock and Cohart in public health, Dr. Snoke in hospital administration, and the dean, Dr. Lippard, were all very open and supportive of the students. Of course, the wealth of Yale in terms of library and learning resources generally, including fellow students in different fields, can hardly be overstated.

Curiously enough, the strongest source of opposition seemed to be among other sociology students and, to some extent, faculty. A considerable portion of this opposition was simple jealousy. A group of "seven-day wonders" had been brought in from the outside, while none of the students already in the department was taken into the program as a fellow. When two of the first four fellows who entered failed or withdrew in the first two years, it was a source of some satisfaction and confirmation to others in the department that there was not much very special about these medical sociology fellows after all.

But there were two other components to this opposition, one theoretical and one political. The Yale department, with its roots in Summner's *Folkways* and the social evolutionism of Spencer, had an essentially conservative bent, bolstered by a commitment to the concepts of culture, cultural wholes, and structural functionism (à la Summner's "What the Social Classes Owe to Each Other").[11] The more subtle and fluid possibilities of symbolic interactionism, which I imported from Chicago and which my medical sociology program colleagues seemed to import from elsewhere, was suspect from the beginning. The very title of my thesis, "Family Culture and Patient Participation," was an attempt to disarm the opposition yet focus on social psychological components of self, related to social characteristics and networks.

The element of the program which might allow some day for practical contributions to the solution of deep and abiding human problems probably seemed inherently liberal or radical and drew opposition from the conservatively oriented faculty and student body. It was a very different place, indeed, than the University of Chicago.

I remember being tremendously conscious of this fact when I first faced the examining group for my oral comprehensive, and failed it. This was a shattering experience, but a second chance was offered and, after a two-month period, I had got a firmer hold on defining my thesis problem (around which the examination began) and it went very well—so much so that two or three of the "old guard" faculty even began debating with each other various facets of what I had developed. Among students, this kind of outcome was defined as one of the best. In this success, I owe a great debt to the other surviving fellow, Leonard Syme. Perhaps we helped each other. In any case, the long hours of reading through mounds of books and asking each other sharp questions were of great value to me in organizing my intellectual equipment.

I should not use more space on this stage, but perhaps my thesis work represents as important and lasting a contribution as I have made to the field.[12] While doing some work with Nelson Foote at Chicago on social judgment,[13] as part of the Foote and Cottrell study of family interaction,[14] I was impressed with social participation as a potential way not only to improve personal or microcosmic judgment (get in on things to have the information and

perspective to handle problems), but also to improve the governing
of men. Thus, I had a problem and had done a lot of reading and
thinking about it. I simply combed through the medical field and
local setting for an opportunity to study it.

The medical sociology program introduced me to social medicine, a major source of the historical origins of our field. Perhaps
my European experiences and language competence opened this
area especially wide for me. I read the works of Virchow, Grotjahn,
Rene Sand, Sigerist, and others. The emphasis of this work on the
social causation of disease through direct and indirect conditions
was symbolized by Max von Pettenkofer's reportedly challenging
the germ theory of disease by drinking a glass of cholera baccili in
front of his students and living to tell the story.[15] Works like Beyond the Germ Theory[16] made an important impression, as did
Walter Cannon's "Voodoo Death,"[17] but throughout this learning,
my interest in organizational problems and participation held fast
and grew.

In a statement of Rene Sand I saw a way of merging my interests
in organization and disease. "Health cannot be simply given to
people," he wrote; "it requires their participation." If medical care
or public health efforts (except for impersonal mass measures) are
to have a beneficial impact on health status, the people must be
involved.

It was in Ralph Turner's elaboration of Mead's work on the self
that I located an intervening variable to explain the impacts of
negatively evaluated family and other background on participation
in a medical program.[18] The notion of the reflexive self has recently
been taken up in work on preventive health behavior.[19] Its full implications have not been explored in terms of the participation of
consumers in the governance of medical programs so that they can
be part of or even control the setting of standards by which human
dignity will be recognized. But there are health center experiments
developing in which this line of thought can be further explored.
These developments should be further explored. These developments are to be understood in terms of the struggles of different
interest groups. The point about my thesis work is that it was taken
up to some extent by others and it may have potential for offering
an important part of the theoretical justification for declassé interest groups gaining greater control over the provision of expert services to them. In any case, this line of thought has continued to
guide some of the action-policy suggestions growing out of my research.[20]

There is a kind of irony in this. While my work provided some underpinnings for greater citizen involvement in health affairs, the consumer movement, so much alive today in every field, was not a matter to be reckoned with in medicine in the 1950s. With today's ethical and legal requirement to assure informed consent, it is not certain that I could have pursued my thesis work as freely or in the same way as I did. The interviews in the homes might have proceeded as they did, but how to locate patients' names and addresses in the first place? And what of access to hospital records?

FIRST POSITION IN MEDICAL SOCIOLOGY

Following my work at Yale, two major influences determined that I should spend a year (1957–58) in Germany as a Russell Sage Foundation Postdoctoral Fellow in Medical Sociology. Perhaps the major influence was family, since Margit had not been home to Austria in five years and the possibility of work and study in Germany seemed a good way to satisfy this longing. But the second influence was a growing realization that many of the roots of social medicine as well as sociology were to be found in the works of German scholars. Grotjahn's *Soziale Pathologie* provided both a historical review of social conditions and disease and an introduction current for the time (1915) which was truly enticing.[21] The "German fathers of sociology"—Marx, Weber, Simmel—need only be mentioned adjacent to the names already given for social medicine, to make most interesting the question why these disciplines had never joined forces. Upon reflection, it seems likely that it was essential for sociology to develop an empirical scientific base before it could join with the world of medicine, itself so recently and still uncertainly emerged through scientific observation from vague theories of disease.[22] Empirically based sociological research developed first in the United States,[23] and had only begun after World War II to find its way into the more philosophically oriented European sociology, and German sociology in particular. The two volumes on research methods translated and edited by René Koenig confirmed and stimulated this trend.[24] Still there was nothing in medical sociology. Given the rich background, I was curious to see what potential existed for development of the field. I expressed this interest to Dr. Donald Young of Russell Sage Foundation and received support after I had located a local sponsor in modern-day social medicine, Professor Ewald Gerfeldt, then at the Medical Academy in Duesseldorf.[25]

I undertook two sorts of efforts in attempting to bring about contact between sociology and medicine in West Germany. The first was to plan and pursue a concrete research effort which would itself demonstrate a kind of work in medical sociology. The second was to stimulate the organization of a conference on the subject. Since both efforts were productive, it is worth recording the approaches and results.

Because German social medicine had a tradition of concern with social etiology and epidemiology, and because I felt I had the most to learn in this direction, I decided to focus my research on some problem of this sort, rather than on the organization of health services. As it turned out, the work combined the two interests.

In discussions with Professor Gerfeldt, it developed that my experience in pediatrics at Yale might be usefully directed toward some aspect of the problem of tuberculosis among children, an especially serious problem in the densely settled, highly industrialized Ruhrgebiet and Wuppertal. He put me in touch with Dr. Joern Gleiss, then a docent in pediatrics. After some discussions, I began reading about psychophysiologic aspects of tuberculosis—everything from Thomas Mann's *Magic Mountain* to a large number of medical students' theses in the library of the Medical Academy of Dusseldorf. There were no systematic researches, but there were fascinating stories, suggestions and hypotheses about poverty, bohemian life a la *La Traviata*, social and psychological malaise, the "abandon" of living desperately, sexual excess, personality, and simply succumbing to the disease.

When I felt ready to find a concrete research site and population, Dr. Gleiss put me in touch with Dr. Rudolf Hoppe, Medizinaldirektor, Landesversicherungsanstalt Rheinprovinz, Duesseldorf. Dr. Hoppe, in turn, directed me to Dr. Kurt Simon, Chefarzt, and owner of the Kinderheilstaette in Aprath, a 250-bed institution for children with all types of tuberculosis.

Dr. Simon was most open and helpful. I not only was able to enlist his cooperation and that of the staff in the research, but I seemed also to be accepted more generally so that I could participate in and observe the culture, structure, and functioning of the institution. This was very special. For example, the element of fear of and danger from the disease came out at mealtime in the staff dining room should someone express a lack of appetite or miss a meal. Also, though the nursing personnel in general were without much power and prestige, the chief nurse had considerable power by virtue of her near complete control over nurses' work assignments.

Since the approach and results of the research were published,[26] I need only mention here the central aspects and attempt to assess the implications. With independent evaluation of children's progress according to x-ray pictures separated by at least three months and personal interviews with eighty-three children, the central finding was that children from "disturbed" homes experienced significantly more healing during the time of the study than did those from apparently complete and well-functioning families. This was a startling finding! We could only speculate as to its meaning, but when one put it together with an understanding of the culture of the institution as it bore in upon the patients—strict authoritarian regime with children pressured vigorously to eat all of their meals and some on occasion tied in reclining chairs so they would "rest"—it seemed reasonable to suggest that those from a "normal" home life found the sanatorium very strange and threatening, while those from "disturbed" families found comfort in a predictable, even harsh regime.

While this interpretation might be correct, it was not established. Further, even if it could be established, the psychophysiologic bridges between fear or anxiety and failure of lung tissue to renew itself were far from built and have yet to be built so far as I know. The net assessment of this work is that it had little ultimate impact because it was not pursued to absolutely convincing conclusions, but it seems to me to have had some impact in demonstrating work in medical sociology and in developing an openness in one setting to collaboration between sociologists and physicians. Also, the research itself might yet stimulate some systematic work on socio-psychophysiologic bridges and organization of therapeutic programs in relation to patients' backgrounds.

The second effort was pursued concurrently with the first. This began when I visited Professor René Koenig in October 1957 and discussed medical sociology with him and developments in the field in the United States. He introduced me to Margaret Toennesman, a medical doctor who was pursuing studies in sociology with him. I mentioned that Everett Hughes and August Hollingshead were both expected in West Germany during the year; that I had begun to work with some medical people in Duesseldorf; and that Gerhard Baumert, an able sociologist at DIVO, had some interest in the field and recognized that very little work was being done in West Germany at the time. Professor Koenig referred to work in social psychiatry by Strotzka in Vienna and experiences in the United States of Dr. Thure von Uexkuell, director of the Medical Polyclinic at Justus Liebig University, Giessen. Dr. Toenesmann remarked on some interest in social epidemiology on the part of a young physician, Manfred Pflanz. Professor Koenig agreed that a meeting of available interested persons would be in order and put Dr. Toennesmann in charge of arrangements.

I am sorry not to have recorded the full details of this meeting. It was held in June 1958 in Professor Koenig's institute at the University of Koeln. Professor Koenig served as host and chairman. Sociologists present included Koenig, Everett Hughes, August Hollingshead, Gerhardt Baumert, and myself. These five persons were balanced by medical people more or less sophisticated in sociology: Drs. Joern Gleiss, Rudolf Hoppe, Manfred Pflanz, Kurt Simon, Margaret Toennesmann, and Thure von Uexkuell. There may have been one or two others present, and I apologize if I have missed someone because it was something of an historic occasion.[27] The meeting generally confirmed the importance of the field and the as yet unrealized opportunities. It stimulated and encouraged some original work which later appeared along with republished pieces in one of the first collections in the field.[28]

My contribution was a chapter reviewing work in medical sociology in the United States. On rereading, it seems rather incomplete and inadequate, but whatever the shortcomings of this piece and the collection in general, it went through a second printing in 1961 and seemed to serve as a stimulus to the field.

The large element of self-direction and open exploration of relatively easily exploited opportunities in this fertile but relatively untouched situation may have spoiled me and contributed to my disappointment on my return to the United States.

SECOND POSITION

Before we had decided on the year in Germany, there were several job possibilities to consider. Undoubtedly this reflected the opening up of the field, especially in various medical- or health-related settings (as opposed to departments of sociology). Also, the Yale program had begun to receive recognition. Finally and most important, August Hollingshead, whose groundbreaking work on social class and mental illness had already become recognized, was a key sponsor in opening up opportunities. I felt more ready for and centrally interested in research than in teaching. The most promising position seemed to be in the Harvard University Department of Psychiatry at the Massachusetts General Hospital with Professor Erich Lindemann and his many colleagues in social psychiatry. The position was research associate. Lindemann was a very engaging and impressive person. When he interviewed me before I finished at Yale in the spring of 1957, he penetrated easily, so it seemed to me, my major intellectual and perhaps emotional and family concerns. We discussed his provocative work and ideas on social-psychic "loss" and its relation to ideas of the social self.[29]

When I first spoke with Professor Lindemann, I should have been much more concerned with the specifics of the position and related research, but as soon as he found out that what I really wanted to do was go to Germany for a year with my family, he encouraged me. He said I would be more valuable after the experience and that he would "hold the position open" until my return. After this point in the interview, when a bargain had been struck (without my knowing the specifics), we focused very enjoyably on general ideas and pleasantries. I had been stockpiled. It was a marvelous feeling to have an exciting adventure to look forward to in Germany and such an obviously prestigious and exciting place as Harvard, the Massachusetts General, to return to.

At first the return was exciting. I met the faculty and fellows in social psychiatry at department meetings. Some contacts were of lasting importance to me. Erich Lindemann suggested at an early point that I talk with Dr. John Stoeckle, head of the Medical Outpatient Department at the Massachusetts General. What might have been a courtesy call turned into an exciting exchange which we repeated often during the year. His interest in medical linguistics—"blue shooting pains," etc.—and my concern with conceptions and expressions of self seemed to form a natural match. We discussed events which precipitated persons from the West End or elsewhere coming to the clinic, also the training of medical and nursing personnel and division of labor in caring for "nonorganic" problems which seemed to form the bulk of the experience. Some of his later work with Irving Zola reflects in part a systematic pursuit of the themes of these very rewarding conversations.[30]

The Community Studies Center to which I was assigned as staff sociologist was carrying out a study of some 12,000 persons in the West End who were being displaced by an urban redevelopment project about which the residents had been consulted only after the fact of the decision. The people and ways of life in this area and their concerns over the vast urban development project, the stimulus for the West End study, are excellently portrayed in Herbert Gans's book.[31]

Gans had been with the project only a year and had left shortly before I came. We saw him periodically as he returned to check details for the completion of his manuscript. He had wisely followed his natural bent to work somewhat independently, living in the area of study with his family as a participant-observer. In the sense of being the project sociologist, I was Gans's replacement, though our training and styles were rather different—my own work being oriented much more toward survey research. This seemed appropriate, since the main part of the project was to be a "before-after" survey of the population, growing in part out of Lindemann's work on social-psychic loss and the instances of it stemming from forced relocation and destruction of a familiar social and physical surrounding.

The weekly staff meetings of the studies center were very exciting at first. All kinds of visiting firemen dropped by and tidbits of information from the West End were spun up into more or less appropriate-seeming connections with one grand theory or another. Leonard Duhl, Gerald Kaplan, Benjamin Paul, and Eliot Mischler were among the more frequent visitors.

During this honeymoon period, I had good discussions with the director. He had finished his training as a clinical psychologist in Harvard's Department of Social Relations and was much taken by Parsons's grand theorizing. My training and framework were different. Even though I enjoyed wide-ranging conceptual efforts, I was much more impressed with the need for and requirements of systematic empirical work. However, when this colleague confided to me one day that his real ambition was to develop a theory which would integrate Freud, Durkheim, and Weber, I became uneasy.

Real disillusionment set in when I realized that there was no systematic "before" measure of the West End population's orientations and behavior to compare with their adaptive patterns wherever they located. Among other things, the theorizing and talk had kept the first-wave interviewing from entering the field on time. Further, even though it would not offer a real "before" measure, it seemed to me that, with the surplus of exciting talk, opportunities for recouping on remaining segments of the sample while they were still in the West End were being lost by a not very rigorous or energetic approach to the scheduling of interviews. In addition, when I looked through the interview schedule, it struck me that self-conceptions and the full range of social participation were key spheres either missing or much underdeveloped, given the problem at hand and its conceptualization in terms of significant losses.

After making my concerns known and finding some defensiveness about the whole matter, I decided to follow Gans's relatively independent course in my own way. It must be emphasized here that I was concerned about being submerged in something that did not make good sense to me. I wanted sufficient autonomy to develop and control data which would make sense. It must be admitted that the freedom of my graduate training and the year in Germany as well as my own character did not prepare me for the culture shock of big-time research into which the National Institute of Mental Health and the Harvard Department of Psychiatry, to some extent, were paying money, time, and personnel just to "get into" this complex area. If I had been more mature (or one might say more corrupted) about such matters, I might not have been so insistent about technical details of the research.

The more independent effort was launched with Gustavo Iacono, a social psychologist who, in the time and system of his education at the University of Naples, became a medical doctor in order to study social psychology. We had a truly fine time developing the conceptual framework and the fieldwork for a study of some one hundred first- and second-generation Italian males in the West End of Boston. The big idea was to question whether personality is integrated, as most theories in psychology seem to assume, or whether it develops segmentally in relation to one sphere of social participation or another. Goffman's work suggested the more situational conception of persons.[32] We intended to test this by covering formal and informal participation in all spheres. The interview schedule which we developed and pretested in the North End was directed toward family, friends, church, unions, political clubs, sports, and so forth.[33] The question was: "If a person's participation is low in one of these spheres of life, is it low in all, or only some, or other spheres?" We connected this question with the West End development by viewing the effects of relocation as occurring through impacts on segments of social participation. We reasoned that the family was most central and most transportable—but perhaps not the extended family and *compadre* familiar to many Italians in the area. We realized of course that we would have only a cross-section and would need a prospective panel designed to do more than an exploration of this framework. We completed the sampling and interviewing, Gustavo doing those interviews which had to be done in Italian. We developed the code book and worked out a system for checking reliability of coding. However, with Gustavo's return to Naples, the difficulties of time, cross-ocean correspondence, and divided handling of data soon caught up with us.

We completed a draft paper with certain key cross-tabulations, but it was never fully analyzed and interpreted and remains unpublished. Regarding the main idea, we found a mix of participation types in our sample. The pattern may be correlated with different personalities. We cannot be sure from this research whether personality is an integrated system or a segmentally developed clustering determined by immediate situations of interaction. Thus our central research question remains; to answer it may require another kind of study. To the extent that participation indexes personality, our finding that some persons are high in some spheres of life but low in others suggests that the segmented person is not only a possibility but a fairly frequently occurring phenomenon of our time.

Associated with this effort and other data sources, including the main interview, I developed an inventory of formal organizations (those with a name) including businesses, political clubs, and so on. My interest was to see how removal from the immediate surroundings and destruction of the immediate neighborhood itself affected the survival of the organization. The timing of the work in Boston and the requirements of the research at Cornell to which I was to move made this a second uncompleted and unpublished but nevertheless rewarding bit of work. Some of the conclusions were obvious, but, nonetheless, important to realize through an examination of data. Organizations, seemingly without regard to size, which simply depended on the West End for their physical setting, but had their social interaction only partially in the area or not at all, were able to move and survive: a mail-order house and a philanthropic foundation were among the examples; these organizations were more bureaucratically structured. By contrast, organizations which had their social interaction contained within the West End—corner grocery stores, sports and political clubs, for example—generally did not survive the relocation. Even today, the study of organization-environment relations is an underdeveloped area in sociology.[34] My evolving interest in this problem was an important consideration in my taking the next position at Cornell with Milton Roemer and other colleagues.

The Boston period was my first sharp encounter with disciplinary jealousies and conceptions. Had the director of this large survey effort been an NORC-trained sociologist, I believe I would not have resisted or encountered the resistance I did. This is an oversimplification but, considering the brief tenures of Gans and myself, as well as a Michigan-trained sociologist who followed me and lasted on the project a similarly short time, this interpretation deserves some support. Since Lindeman was very supportive and did not act in a directive hierarchial manner, even though he had overall authority, the experience may be summed up by observing that support for my ideas and concerns came from medically oriented and medically trained colleagues with a direct interest or experience in social aspects of medicine who did not have or exercise hierarchial relations with me. There were basic disagreements and difficulties with the project director which involved authority and jealousy over autonomy of decision making.

THIRD POSITION

As my discontent with the shortcomings of the main West End study grew, I became interested in other possibilities. By this time I had met some of the many talented, but "stockpiled," young academics and intellectuals around Harvard Square who would be a long time moving forward in their own careers, and I had begun to realize I was one of them. I had met Dr. Milton Roemer and was familiar with some of his work.[35] When a letter arrived from him describing a recently funded study of hospital-community relations, I expressed interest. Milton Roemer and Rodney White, a sociologist I had known as a graduate student at Chicago, were, respectively, principal and coprincipal investigators, looking for a project director. After visiting Ithaca and this time learning that the project was in its earliest stages, that I would have plenty of opportunity to contribute to the conceptualization and the gathering, analysis, and interpretation of the data, and that the work was indeed on the organizational unit—the community general hospital—and its relations to the environment, I was quite pleased. In June 1959, I became research associate and director of the Hospital-Community Relations Study, the Sloan Institute of Hospital Administration, Graduate School of Business, Cornell University. In 1960, I was made an assistant professor and taught a course on organization-environment relations to hospital administration students.

The study and related work proved most rewarding and have been reported elsewhere.[36] A key article from the study has been reprinted in readers,[37] and has served as a reference point for further work on organization-environment relationships.[38] Also, it stimulated work on the part of able graduate students, notably Vaughn Blankenship,[39] and later, at Pittsburgh, Ollie Lee[40] and Stan Ingman,[41] and still later, at the University of Connecticut, Joe

Holtzman.[42] And there are indications that organizational competition and conflict over support have begun to be recognized as a central problem in the development of coordinated regional health services systems.[43] Also, the work reconfirmed and deepened my earlier interest in problems of organizing health services and led quite naturally into later work on problems of network organizations, planning, and regionalization of health services.[44]

This period in Ithaca (1959–63) included my first real opportunity to teach and to realize my interest in teaching, particularly in small seminar situations where exchange with students is frequent. There was also the very rewarding opportunity to do review work with Milton Roemer whose historical grasp of medical care and understanding of central problems requiring sociological analysis added relevance to my more technical sociological grasp of the field.[45]

Beginning in 1961, in addition to teaching one course and finishing the write-up of the hospital support study, I assumed the position of field director for the Joint Committee on the Study of Education for Public Health. This brought me into close contact with Dr. William P. Shepard, study director, and other leading figures in public health in the United States.[46] Dr. Shepard was a penetrating, wise, and warm person with whom I enjoyed working and from whom I learned a good deal. He had served as medical director of the Metropolitan Life Insurance Company and had risen to the position of vice president. For many years he was the link between the worlds of private practice, represented by the AMA, and public health, represented by the APHA. In many respects his own field, industrial and occupational medicine, represented this balance. From this vantage point, he had seen and learned to work with the full range of interest groups in the health field and had been instrumental in encouraging a number of people and projects in public health, including the School of Public Health at Berkeley. One could say that sociology was for him only one of the more recent entrants and myself a representative thereof. But he soon went beyond mere tolerance and curiosity to pushing gently but firmly for realization in public health of sociology's potential. Through this experience my conception of health care organization, mainly in terms of complex organizations, progressed to include the struggle of occupational groups as central to this sphere.[47] Regarding conceptual tools, I achieved through this work a much fuller realization of the promise of conflict models of social organization as compared with integrative conceptions.[48] Data from the Joint

Committee study also served as a basis for Jim Walsh's work on social-class orientations of different "professional" groups.[49]

I assess this as the beginning of a productive period with many threads of continuity into later work. An important element of support was Milton Roemer's grasp and use of sociology in his work. He had an understanding and appreciation of the field which provide firmer ground than that which one received from physicians whose appreciation of sociology is limited to lip service or window dressing.[50]

But if my own research and teaching were well supported and reasonably fruitful, a graduate school of business environment was not as supportive as one concerned with human service could wish. Since all the major components of the business school— business, public, and hospital administration—were primarily there to prepare "professionals" for these fields, the battle lines did not form around the issue of academic versus professional emphases, so familiar in other settings. Rather, at issue were the fundamental values of business (that is, profits) versus those of public and health administration (that is, human service). Thus, the tenure of an extremely productive colleague in medical care-medical sociology (both in terms of publication and teaching) was vigorously opposed by the business elements of the school, including the head of the hospital administration program. Support came from research colleagues in the hospital program and from most faculty of the Public Administration Program. It came most powerfully from Robin Williams and others in sociology, from William F. Whyte in industrial and labor relations, and from other parts of the university.

I was as much involved in this struggle as the status of a junior faculty member would allow. My own turn for full realization of the opposition came a year later when I had in hand two firm and attractive job offers, both from good universities, involving promotion and tenure (one was in the position I later took at Pittsburgh in the Graduate School of Public Health with a joint appointment in sociology, and the other was in a department of sociology). I requested the dean to appoint a tenured health person in the program in addition to myself. He agreed only to promotion and tenure for me, but he would not make a firm commitment as to tenure for a health person in addition to myself. Thus the Cornell Business School seemed ready to profit from the Sloan grants and the research and teaching of those involved, but it would not commit itself in any long-term manner to the health field. To this day, if my information is correct, there are one or two faculty contributing to the hospital program, but, should it prove desirable to drop the health field, those who have tenure can be defined in relation to the business area.

In sum, although this was a productive period of considerable personal growth and advancement, when I became vitally identified with the content and goals of the health field and its human service ends, the profit-oriented business setting was not supportive.

FOURTH POSITION

I had become acquainted with Dr. James Crabtree, dean of the Graduate School of Public Health at Pittsburgh, and with Dr. Waldo Treuting, professor and chairman of Public Health Practice, through the Joint Committee study. This had also brought me in touch with Conrad Seipp, a health planner then in Puerto Rico, who was moving to Pittsburgh. In addition, I knew and respected Cecil Shep's work in medical care. Peter New and Paul Geisel, who had joined the Social Science Unit under David Landy's term as head, struck me as promising colleagues. When I learned from Ed Suchman that he was going to Pittsburgh in sociology and would be more than happy to continue his work in public health and medical sociology with a joint appointment in the Social Science Unit, I was strongly attracted to the situation.

When I ruled out remaining at Cornell, it was something of a watershed decision, since the alternatives were to stay deeply involved in the health field, holding a joint appointment in sociology, or to go into "straight sociology." No doubt I could have continued work in medical sociology from the base of a sociology department, but it seemed to me that by virtue of experience and prior investment of self, I was better suited to work primarily in a health setting, contributing to sociology and to its ability to aid in solving problems of deep and abiding human concern in health and health care. This philosophy of attempting to contribute simultaneously to sociology and to the solution of health problems was a key element in what was perhaps the most significant development during my time in Pittsburgh (1963–68)—the establishment of the Ph.D. Training Program in Social Sciences and Community Health Organization.

The actions undertaken to pursue this philosophy and the setting in which they were carried out were of course determinant. It seemed clear to me, and I tried to make it clear to people in public health and sociology, that work in the social sciences in the health field could be no stronger than the strength of the basic disciplinary departments. Thus I expected to play an active role in sociology, attempting to contribute in some essential way to that department. This fitted in well with the policy under Chancellor Litchfield's dynamic leadership by which joint appointments were deliberately encouraged to lend strength to more than one department at a time, building more rapidly from a streetcar-college to a good university. Through integral involvement in the Sociology Department it was possible to involve able sociology graduate students in sociology and anthropology in our work in public health-related research. The School of Public Health in turn had numerous projects going and the medical center generally seemed supportive and open so that the student base, the faculty, and the research training opportunities simply seemed to be waiting there ready for someone to put them together.

The doctoral program, under Edmund Ricci's direction, functions well to this time, January 1975, though vacillating federal support affects it in an unfortunate way as it does other similar programs. I have heard that there was a time after I left Pittsburgh at which there was some resistance developing in sociology from the mathematical group because it appeared that the Community Health Organization Program was "drawing off" the best students. This simply struck me as a measure of the program's success, which by that time could be well defended by those associated with it—above all, the students,

Within the School of Public Health, our unit had responsibility for one of the "core" courses for the M.P.H. and we contributed to other core courses in public health practice and epidemiology. More could be written of these opportunities and responsibilities than there is room for here, but the Social Science Unit impressed me as strong and I had been well treated, being promoted to full professor after just three years. It was a rewarding, happy time.

I could have stayed and been quite content with the teaching and research. The students, especially those in the doctoral program, were good, and working with them offered great rewards. Dr. Treuting involved me in a consultant activity vis-à-vis a community action project in public health in Lexington, Kentucky. Through this, I gained a renewed appreciation of the value and problems of citizen involvement. Perhaps I also gained more of a taste for action which seemed increasingly to be called for by the times.

The problem of balance between knowledge development and the wish to apply that knowledge in problem solving was not just a new-found tension of the times. But certainly the growing momentum of "the movement" generated by the Vietnam War and the concerns of youth, blacks, women, and other minorities contributed to my inclination toward action. Still more of my thought and writing was devoted to problems of planned change in health care organization.[51] The somewhat heretical thought occurred to me that we might never achieve anything other than after-the-fact description (knowledge) of interest centers and groups, their strategies and processes, and the structures they present as we freeze them in a moment or period of study. Perhaps knowledge of change comes only in taking part in change, since it seems possible that the patterns of complexities and subtleties involved in change may make all the difference and may be relatively unique to a set of changes. But this kind of thinking is not a good way to sell sociology. Carried to its extreme, it would leave the politicians, administrators, ad hoc "men of the world," and even some religionists laughing at all contemplative scientists and scholars, sociologists included. This would not do for my concept of self, so I resolved to try to identify key points in the planning and evaluation of change.[52] The comparative research of mental retardation planning programs undertaken with Seipp, Suchman, and others was for me a step in this direction.[53] But, in the United States, public health was not where the action was or was going to be. In 1967, with the university losing support,[54] and some of my closer and more significant colleagues—especially Cecil Sheps and Conrad Seipp—moving on to other places and with Dr. Crabtree's death, the place lost some of its élan.

I believe these developments in thinking and feeling were more fundamental in my move from Pittsburgh than the loss of élan. I reasoned that some form of national health insurance would soon enter upon the scene in the United States. This would be a major marshalling force or central dimension, and we did not know how to approach it. In any case, through the Joint Committee study, I had learned that public health in the United States had long since bowed out of any significant role in personal health services and medical care under cover of Haven Emerson's "basic six" formulated in his disupte with C. E. A. Winslow.[55] The problem was to find an action study base with enough power potential to give the chance to create and test forms of medical care which would bring about a merger of preventive and therapeutic medicine.[56] I am still searching.

FIFTH POSITION

I thought I had found such a setting in the new and (outwardly) very forward-looking medical school in Hartford where social scientists and medical care experts were being included directly in what I thought was the center of power of the medical school—the Department of Clinical Medicine and Health Care. There was also a very significant regional medical program in Connecticut through which one could envision effective approaches to the region. Though I have considered the bases of social power and changing power structure in medicine,[57] an exact calculus for power budgets is lacking and I turned out to be no more shrewd in judging this ephemeral but essential element than the next fellow.

In any case, I was very much attracted to the philosophy and person of James E. C. Walker, the chairman of medicine, and to the promise of the situation. Further, the significant increase in salary was important with a growing family—our third son, Martin, was born in Pittsburgh 2 August 1964, and our oldest son would soon be considering college if the war in Vietnam did not interrupt his life. Thus from 1968 to 1971, I assumed the position of professor of sociology and head of the Social Science Division in the Department of Clinical Medicine and Health Care, University of Connecticut Medical School, and held a joint appointment in sociology on the Storrs Campus. Also in 1967 I had been elected secretary-treasurer of the Medical Sociology Section of the American Sociological Association and served in this capacity during the same period. As the only officer of the section with continuity for three years (chairmen being elected for one year at that time), I found this position very demanding yet rewarding, since there were more than seven hundred members and five very active standing committees.

I was not disturbed by the rather primitive physical surroundings of the old city hospital in which the medical school was forced to bide its time while its new building and hospital were being completed, three or four years behind schedule, out in a rather fancy suburb.[58] This did disturb many of my clinical colleagues used to the standards of Hopkins, Yale, Harvard, and Western Reserve, rightly so from the point of view of simple sanitation, other technical standards, human dignity, and comfort. The resources were not going where the problems were greatest, and it could only be classed as a holding action at the best. They could stand it only as long as they could look forward to nice surroundings and "interesting material" at Farmington. The setting seemed to me to highlight the real problems with which we have to deal. At the very least, teaching by indirection could be excellent in such a setting. At best, it would offer a chance to do something significant about total patient and community care, the kind of merger of therapeutic and preventive teaching and practice one could envision and which seemed so needed. The North End was the obvious place to demonstrate such a program. Even the Hartford power structure and the medical society and other hospitals would have backed or tolerated such an effort, if only as riot insurance.[59]

Again, in this situation it seemed to me that the Social Science Division developed well. Good faculty were recruited—John Glasgow in medical economics; Dorothy Douglas in social psychology; Stan Ingman in political sociology (these area labels do not cover their multiple talents well). A doctoral program in Social Sciences and Health Services similar to the one in Pittsburgh was launched and is functioning very well under Stan Ingman's direction with a steering committee made up of faculty from the Anthropology and Sociology departments at Storrs and, from the Health Center, the Department of Community Medicine and Health Care of the Medical School and Behavioral Sciences, and Community Health of the Dental School. Significant teaching responsibilities were developed in the "Introduction to Clinical Medicine" and in a new "basic science" teaching committee in Social and Behavioral Sciences with eighty-four hours at its disposal in the first year of the medical and dental schools. Colleagues and I were able to launch and complete several researches into the system of medical practice in Hartford as seen from different perspectives,[60] and I completed the editing of a book on national health care.[61] From this narrow perspective, it was a satisfying and perfectly promising situation. Perhaps one should not expect more, but I came to Hartford thinking I would be close to significant action in planning and evaluating new forms of organizing care.

The potential with respect to design and evaluation of promising medical care programs has not yet been realized. Many factors are involved. Some are external, for example, the rough complexities of creating a new school and shortage of resources; but then things are never perfectly smooth and there are never enough resources. There is some opposition in the community and the divisive forces in the medical and welfare system are disturbing, although these might have been overcome with the proposal of a significant community-oriented program. However, the two central, defeating forces are both internal to the medical school, and, if I am correct, I have learned two important lessons; both suggest how really "sick" American medicine is.[62]

The first problem is an entangled mélange of elitist class orientations and seeming worship of superspecialty exotica on the part of the "hottest" clinical teachers. Talk of "interesting" patients! We were surrounded by drug addicts, alcoholics, elderly laboring men and women with hot and swollen joints; but to too many of the clinicians these "cases" were all "junk," "uninteresting," "so familiar," and "besides it's hard to communicate with these people." This attitude prevented our undertaking any really promising new departures. Serving all the people for all their common ills in this "lower-class" black and Puerto Rican area could not even be visualized as the significant thing to do.[63]

It seems to me that to the extent that the medical schools are the value-establishing centers of American medicine, as other analysts have suggested they are, to this extent the implication of this orientation within the medical school is very serious. If prestige and rewards are gained by focusing on the special and exotic, we have and will have a medicine equipped only to handle some facets of care for the few.

The inordinate power of the "basic" science department heads is the second major defeating factor. I had misread the situation: the chairman of medicine did not have real power as he does in most American medical schools today.[64] He was being given a free hand, but when nothing much out of the ordinary happened and when funds for research became short as a part of wartime economy moves, the basic science department heads reared up and broke our department in two, creating the more familiar Department of Community Medicine and a traditional Department of Medicine. When the favored outside candidate turned the offer down in the face of economy moves by a new Republican governor, a new head was recruited from among the most influential "basic" science chairmen. By this means, the basic science chiefs will have more support for their work, since patient research will be tied more closely to laboratory research than to community research. I suspect the state legislature will "find the school out" and tie the purse strings. People will begin to ask what the generally agreed mandate—"excellence"—means. Excellence for what? Microcosmic research? Superspecialists? Or primary practitioners to serve the people? It is hard to say what the impact and meaning will be when the change comes. Already (fall of 1974) public hearings have been held by the legislature investigating the operation of state programs in the University Health Center. In the meantime, things have gone quite traditional regarding the chance to plan, evaluate, and teach a merger of preventive and clinical medicine.

The implications for American medicine of this degree of power for "basic" science departments strike me as serious. One effect is to support the thrust toward the technologically exotic and highly specialized. There is even a tendency for an atmosphere to develop in which training to become a physician who serves people is not as fine as bench research. Finally, there is a dispersal and waste of scientific manpower and other resources by attempting to develop truly creative and productive biological science centers in some one hundred medical schools. A half dozen Rockefeller Institutes would be more efficient and effective.

WHO

With a reorganization of our department underway, budgetary uncertainties growing, and family concerns suggesting "a change of venue" once again to Europe, I was pleased to hear in January 1971 from Albert Wessen that I would be considered to fill his place as chief of the Behavioral Science Unit in the Division of Research in Epidemiology and Communications Sciences (RECS), WHO in Geneva. After a visit to Geneva in March, it seemed to me that Margit would once again enjoy a European atmosphere and profit from being closer to her family. Also, my taking leave for two years from my university post would relieve budgetary pressures and perhaps allow Jim Walker and others in the department a more reflective, quiet new start. My prospective colleagues in the unit, brought on by Al Wessen—Amor Benyoussef, Sherwood Slater, and Jerome Stromberg—seemed very capable, as did many others in RECS. In any case, Margit and I were excited at the prospect and pleased when both the position at WHO and the university's grant of a two-year leave of absence were confirmed.

My time at WHO provided a great learning experience too rich to be detailed here. Through the men in the unit, as well as directly in two instances, I became involved with many of the projects under-way in RECS. Since RECS was composed of units in ecology, epidemiology, mathematics and statistics, and operations research, in addition to social science, and most projects involved someone from each unit, this experience gave me a familarity with the problems and possibilities of large-scale multidisciplinary research involving international sponsorship. In addition, my position as unit chief brought me close to the workings of the organization and matters of diplomacy and protocol as well as decision making within a large-scale, international, political bureaucracy.

I will focus on what seemed to be the central issues regarding sociology and social science in the closing out of RECS,[65] and its merger with OHS (Organization of Health Services) under the title: Division of Strengthening of Health Services (SHS). The rationale of the reorganization was to get rid of disciplinary and professional rigidities and, thereby, have greater flexibility in mobilizing the limited resources of the organization (the overall core budget of WHO was only $105 million or so in 1972) so as to direct them more effectively and efficiently toward the solution of concrete health services problems. Thus, the nursing unit of OHS was broken up, as well as units in RECS. While the goal was worthwhile, the losses involved a dispersal of the relatively fledgling field of social science and certain practices which might reflect lower standards in this field.

For some of my colleagues in RECS, the reorganization meant further politicization and loss of autonomy for their research. Contrary to popular impression, WHO is highly political. This has been well portrayed at the general policy level by Quimby,[66] and specifically for the formation of RECS by the Roses.[67] I have elsewhere offered an initial codification of political influences on research as I learned about them in this situation and through the very sparse literature on the subject,[68] but three other issues were of more concern.

First, though not necessarily first in importance, the reorganization involved an archaic reassertion of medical dominance already strong in the organization. There was a blindness to the "medical mafia" and the "old-boy network" within WHO. Units and therefore unit chief positions were done away with and "programs" were substituted in the new division of SHS. Job specifications called for a physician to head each program so that unit chiefs of disciplines other than medicine became "assistants to" and were left out of policymaking and key decisions.

A second issue was that without unit structure to encourage a sense of identity and colleagueship and to assure quality, social science within the organization was weakened. Even more serious, there was no further mandate to pursue the development of social science within the organization and in countries lacking people with this background in their health research and development efforts.

Finally, and possibly my most central concern, WHO did not seem capable of mounting a continuous, systematic approach to contrasting the ways in which nations organize scarce resources for health. Such work received some initial encouragement.[69] Also, a statement outlining previous work and offering an initial framework and approach appeared as part of a special issue of *Social Science and Medicine* devoted to social science research in WHO.[70] But in the crisis atmosphere of the new division, to do something immediate and noteworthy about the mammoth health services problems of the world, efforts to carry out systematic reconnaisance of the 140 or so natural laboratories found in health systems of the member states seemed either too long term or too politically loaded to receive support.[71] Thus the need for one or more centers for cross-national study of health systems remains, and in one of its most significant documents in recent years WHO itself recognized the need for improved understanding of health systems in relation to their political, socioeconomic, cultural, and epidemiologic environments.[72]

In world health, this prestigious, promising organization is "all the world has," so to speak, and some great and wonderful people and ideas have been associated with it. The purpose in writing this all-too-brief personal account is to add to the impetus to free WHO to realize its potential for improving the health of the peoples of the world.

RETURN

Upon returning to the University of Connecticut in the newly named Department of Community Medicine and Health Care, I found the doctoral program in social sciences and health services going strong under Stan Ingman's direction, with good students interested in working on problems of health services organization. I found that I had matured somewhat regarding teaching of medical students. I was more clear in my conviction of the centrality of my field to the provision of adequate health and medical care.

I found, also, considerable interest on the parts of students, faculty, and administration, in developing work which might eventuate in a Center for Cross-National Study of Health Systems. Although funding is difficult to locate, it has been possible to find ways of sponsoring work along these lines.[73] Work in international health has been taken up by the Division of International Medical Education of the American Association of Medical Colleges as an important part of community medicine.[74] With the anticipated passage of some form of national health insurance,[75] and development of integrated regional health-planning legislation,[76] I look for more encouragement of policy-oriented, group-and-population studies and action programs, including cross-national studies of health systems (CNSHS). With the hope of working toward an interuniversity consortium for CNSHS, and with considerable impetus offered by Manfred Pflanz's presence as visiting professor at the University of Connecticut in 1974–75, a proposal for a New England Program in CNSHS was submitted with Mark Field, Boston University; Dieter Koch-Weser, Harvard; George Silver, Yale; and Albert Wessen, Brown; and Michael Zubroff, Dartmouth. Such studies can add more critical and creative approaches to health services development locally and in the United States as a whole, as well as contribute to similar efforts in other countries. This group is still seeking ways to evolve a program in CNSHS.

The University of Connecticut School of Medicine, now housed in the architecturally impressive center in Farmington, still has the directions and emphases noted earlier. The Department of Community Medicine and Health Care seems to pursue clinical and individual patient interests more than one would expect. This fits with its origins as a department of medicine; yet now there is neither the mandate nor means to play seriously at the clinical game. Instead, there is great need for the Department of Community Medicine and for the school at large—especially in its central decision-making committees—to commit themselves to study and action on group and population units (communities, industries, regions) within which the problems of individual patients can be anticipated, possibly prevented, and, if not, treated and otherwise dealt with.

SUMMARY AND PRESENT CONCEPTION OF THE FIELD

My career can be best summarized, perhaps, as an attempt to strike a balance between development of sociological knowledge and action to solve deep and abiding human problems in health and health care. It would oversimplify matters to say that the balance has gradually moved toward the action end of the spectrum. This has happened, but the concern for action has been a part of my development all along; and I think it a good deal more than a rationalization to suggest that adequate knowledge can be developed only by testing in action. As mentioned earlier, it is even possible

to make the argument that it is more than a question of testing
knowledge in action. It may be that adequate knowledge is developed only in action, but I hope to have some further years before
deciding to accept or reject this idea. For now, I am convinced of
the need for more adequate sociological theory and methods of empirically testing this theory.

It follows for me that medical sociologists must first be concerned with the development of sociology as a theoretical and empirical discipline. Then they must have a commitment to solve
problems in the health field. I believe this conception dissolves the
distinction between sociology "of" and "in" medicine made early
on by Straus.[77] Concerned sociological observers "of" medicine
will not be content simply to report their observations for the development of sociological knowledge. There is an air of irrelevance
and even arrogance in this approach. Such an approach only leads
back to Lynd's question—"knowledge for what?"

A few closing lines cannot deal with the content and organization of the field; but by way of placing myself in the field, I see
medical sociology divided into two broad interrelated spheres:
studies of (1) disease and disability (social epidemiology) and
(2) systems of planning structures, organizations, occupational
groups, and citizens which should be designed to improve the
health of the people. It is in this second sphere that I have concentrated my work.

NOTES

1. The valuable editorial assistance of Janet Turk is hereby gratefully
acknowledged.

2. See Ivan Illich, *Tools for Conviviality* (New York: Harper and Row,
1973).

3. Theodore M. Newcomb, *Personality and Social Change: Attitude
Formation in a Student Community* (New York: Dryden Press, 1943). The
thesis was titled "Outlooks on Medical Organization among a Group of
First and Fourth-Year Medical Students" and was submitted in the spring
of 1955 with Peter Blau and Nelson Foote as my committee.

4. Theodor F. Lentz, *Manual for C-R Opinionaire* (St. Louis: Washington University, Character Research Association, 1935).

5. Michael M. Davis, *Medical Care for Tomorrow* (New York: Harper
and Brothers, 1954).

6. At the time several faculty of the university came under attack from
the McCarthy committee. Public hearings were held in downtown Chicago.
Among them were Ernest Burgess, of all people, and an eminent biologist,

Dr. Anton Carlson. There was great and general support for these men in the university community.

7. Theodore Newcomb et al., *Persistence and Change: A College and Its Students after 25 Years* (New York: Wiley, Drieger, 1967).

8. Howard S. Becker et al., *Boys in White* (Chicago: University of Chicago Press, 1961).

9. Robert K. Merton et al., eds., *The Student Physician* (Cambridge: Harvard University Press, 1957).

10. A. B. Hollingshead and F. C. Redlich, *Social Class and Mental Illness* (New York: Wiley, 1958).

11. William G. Sumner, *What Social Classes Owe to Each Other* (New York: Harper, 1883).

12. Ray H. Elling, "Family Culture and Patient Participation in a Pediatric Program" (Ph.D. diss., Yale University, 1957). See also R. H. Elling, R. Whittemore and M. Green, "Patient Participation in a Pediatric Program," *Journal of Health and Human Behavior* 1 (1960): 183–91.

13. It was a summer research assistantship to do an annotated bibliography. For the earliest conceptual statement of the problem I found, see Graham Wallas, *Social Judgment* (New York: Harcourt, 1935).

14. N. N. Foote and L. S. Cottrell, *Identity and Interpersonal Competence* (Chicago: University of Chicago Press, 1955).

15. Fascinating variations in medical knowledge and treatment in different times and places came through beautifully in a scholarly analysis of the history of this disease presented at the Director-General's Conference of WHO in November, 1972.

16. Iago Galdston, *Beyond the Germ Theory* (New York: Health Education Council, 1954).

17. Walter Cannon, "Voodoo Death," *American Anthropologist* 44 (1942): 169–81. Also *Bodily Changes in Pain, Hunger, Fear, and Rage* (New York: D. Appleton, 1929).

18. Ralph Turner, "Role-Taking, Role Standpoint, and Reference-Group Behavior," *American Journal of Sociology* 61 (1956): 316–28.

19. Lawrence Green, *Status Identity and Preventive Health Behavior*, Pacific Health Education Reports, no. 1 (Berkeley and Honolulu: Universities of California and Hawaii, Schools of Public Health, 1970).

20. For example, most recently, following a survey of disparities in health and health care experienced by "lower-class" urban center residents, we proposed a citizen health action council with its own budget and health planning staff. The proposal failed for lack of power and a variety of contextual reasons. See Ray H. Elling and R. F. Martin, *Health and Health Care for the Urban Poor: A Study of Hartford's North End*, Connecticut Health Services Research Series no. 5 (New Haven, 1974).

21. Alfred Grotjahn, *Soziale Pathologie* (Berlin: August Hirschwald, 1915). See also idem, *Erlebtes and Erstrebtes, Erinnerungen eines sozialistischen Arztes.* (Berlin: F. A. Herbig, 1932). His autobiography closes with

the following "socio-physcho-physiological" observation taken from his grandfather, Heinrich Grotjahn:

> Ein Jeder bemueht sich umsonst,
> Das Raetsel des Lebens zu loesen.
> Ist er des Gruebelns dann satt,
> Loest sich's im Tode von selbst.

22. Erwin H. Ackerknecht, *A Short History of Medicine* (New York: Ronald, 1955).

23. *Encyclopedia of the Social Sciences*, 15 vols. (New York: Macmillan, 1931), s.v. "Sociology."

24. René Koenig, ed., *Das Interview: Praktische Sozialforschung*, vol. I (1957); and *Beobachtung und Experiment in der Sozialforschung: Praktische Sozialforschung*, vol. 2 (Koln: Verlag fuer Politik und Wirtschaft, 1956).

25. As an example of his many works see, Ewald Gerfelt "Von der Individualhygiene zur Gesellschafts-und Kulturhygiene," *Die Medizinische Welt* 20 (December 1951): 1–11.

26. R. H. Elling and K. Simon, "Zusammenhaenge von soziologischen Faktoren und therapeutischem Erfolg bei tuberkulosekranken Kindern und Jugendlichen," *Der Oeffentliche Gesundheitsdienst* 20 (July 1958): 140–45.

27. M. Pflanz, "Die zunehmende Soziologisierung der Medizin," in *Soziologie-Sprache Bezug zur Praxis-Verhaeltnis zu anderen Wissenschaften* (Koeln/Opladen: Westdeutscher Verlag, 1973).

28. René Koenig and Margret Toennesmann, eds., *Probleme der Medizin-Soziologie*. Koelner Zietschrift fuer Soziologie und Sozialpsychologie, Sonderheft–3 (Koeln and Opladen: Westdeutscher Verlag, 1958). The Jaco reader appeared at about the same time in the U.S.: E. Gartley Jaco, ed., *Patients, Physicians, and Illness* (Glencoe, Ill.: Free Press, 1958).

29. Eric Lindemann, "Modification in the Course of Ulcerative Colitis in Relationship to Changes in Life Situations and Reaction Patterns," *Proceedings of the Association for Research in Nervous and Mental Disease* 29 (1950): 706–23. One of the intellectual gains I achieved while working with Lindemann and his colleagues in 1958–59, was a "translation" of "loss" into a view of composition and loss of significant aspects of the social self. I came to see a person's grieving after death of a loved one (or other significant loss) as his effort to reimagine himself without some significant component of the self and thereby recompose himself for social participation on a new basis. Some people manage this "working through" well while others falter with often dire physical and mental consequences.

30. J. D. Stoeckle, I. K. Zola, and G. E. Davidson, "On Going to see the Doctor: The Contributions of the Patient to the Decision to Seek Medical Aid," *Journal of Chronic Diseases* 16 (1963): 975–89. I. K. Zola, "Culture and Symptoms," *American Sociological Review* 31 (October 1966): 615–30.

31. Herbert Gans, *The Urban Villagers* (Glencoe, Ill. and New York: Free

Press, 1963). See also idem, "The Human Implications of Current Redevelopment and Relocation Planning," *Journal of the American Institute of Planners* 25 (1959): 15–25.

32. Erving Goffman, *The Presentation of Self in Everyday Life* (New York: Doubleday and Co., Archor, 1959).

33. For an intimate view of life in this area including gang leadership and other aspects of this "little Italy," see William F. Whyte, *Street Corner Society* (Chicago: University of Chicago Press, 1943). For a delightful study of Italian character and culture emphasizing the dramatic, flowery "front" see Luigi Barzini, *The Italians* (New York: Bantam Books, 1964).

34. D. S. Pugh et al., "The Context of Organization Structures," *Administration Science Quarterly* 14 (1969): 91–114. Also Arthur L. Stinchcombe, "Social Structure and Organizations," in *Handbook of Organizations,* ed. J. G. March (Chicago: Rand McNally, 1965), pp. 142–93.

35. For example I was impressed with his attempt to examine the total organizational make-up of the medical care in a local area (M. I. Roemer and E. A. Wilson, *Organized Health Services in a County of the United States,* United States Public Health Service Publication no. 197 [Washington, D.C.; 1952]).

36. M. I. Roemer and R. F. White, "Community Attitudes toward Hospitals: A Preliminary Report of Research," *Hospital Management* 89 (January 1960): 37–39; ibid. (February 1960): 48 ff; R. Elling, "What Do We Mean by Hospital Support?: A Research Note," *Modern Hospital* 96 (January 1961): 84; R. Elling and M. I. Roemer, "Determinants of Community Support: A Preliminary Analysis," *Hospital Administration* 6 (1961): 17–34; R. Elling and S. Halebsky, "Organizational Differentiation and Support," *Administrative Science Quarterly* 6 (1961): 185–209; R. Elling, "The Hospital Support Game in Urban Center," in *The Hospital in Modern Society,* ed. E. Friedson (New York: Macmillan, 1964), pp. 73–111; and L. V. Blankenship and R. H. Elling, "Organizational Support and Community Power Structure: The Hospital," *Journal of Health and Human Behavior* 3 (Winter 1962): 257–69.

37. Claudine Herzlich, ed., *Médecine, Maladie, et Société* (Paris: Mouton, 1970); M. Zald, ed., *Social Welfare Institutions: A Sociological Reader* (New York: Wiley, 1965); and R. Scott and E. Volkart, eds., *Medical Care: Readings in the Sociology of Medical Institutions* (New York: Wiley, 1966).

38. A. Aiken and J. Hage, "Organizational Interdependence and Intraorganizational Structure," *American Sociological Review* 33 (December 1968): 912–30; W. M. Evan, "The Organization-Set: Toward a Theory of Interorganizational Relations," in *Approaches to Organizational Design,* ed., J. Thompson (Pittsburgh: University of Pittsburgh Press, 1963), pp. 171–91.

39. L. V. Blankenship, "Organizational Support and Community Leadership in Two New York State Communities" (Ph.D. diss., Cornell University, 1962). See also idem, "Power Structure and Organizational Effective-

ness," in *Men at the Top*, ed. R. Presthus (New York: Oxford University Press, 1972).

40. O. J. Lee, "Community Leaders and their Involvement in the Health System of a Metropolitan Community" (Ph.D. diss., University of Pittsburgh, 1968). See also R. Elling and O. J. Lee, "Formal Connections of Community Leadership to the Health System," *Milbank Memorial Fund Quarterly* 44 (1966): 294–306, reprinted in E. G. Jaco, ed., *Patients, Physicians and Illness*, 2nd ed. (New York: Macmillan/Free Press, 1972).

41. S. R. Ingman, "Politics of Health Planning," (Ph.D. diss., University of Pittsburgh, 1971).

42. Joseph Holtzman, "Regional Power Structure and Health Planning," (Ph.D. diss., University of Connecticut, 1975).

43. T. S. Bodenheimer, "Regional Medical Programs: No Road to Regionalization," *Medical Care Review* 26 (December 1969): 1125–66.

44. R. Elling, "Health Planning in International Perspective," *Medical Care* 9 (May-June 1971): 214–34; idem, "Regionalization of Health Services: Sociological Blocks to Realization of an Ideal," in *Topias and Utopias*, ed. S. Ingman and T. Thomas (Chicago: Aldine, 1975), pp. 175–204. Also R. Berfenstam and R. Elling, "Regionalization of Health Services in Sweden: A Social and Medical Problem," *Scandinavian Review* 63 (September 1975, special issue): 40–52. This volume was reissued as *Health Systems of Scandinavia* (Bethesda, Md.: National Institutes of Health, John E. Fogarty Center for Advanced Studies in Medical Sciences, 1976).

45. M. I. Roemer and R. Elling, "Sociological Research on Medical Care," *Journal of Health and Human Behaviour* 4 (Spring, 1963): 49–68.

46. The background, including composition of the joint committee and methods is given along with analysis and recommendations in H. G. Fry, W. P. Shepard, and R. H. Elling, *Education and Manpower for Community Health* (Pittsburgh: University of Pittsburgh Press, 1967).

47. For a sociological view of the meaning of such a "blue ribbon" committee and the "fractionation" of the field into numerous occupational groups which carry on their struggles through "professionalization" and other strategies, see R. Elling, "Occupational Group Striving and Administration in Public Health" in *Administering Health Systems*, ed. M. Arnold, L. V. Blankenship, and J. Hess (Chicago and New York: Aldine-Atherton, 1971): 70–85.

48. For an excellent contrast of these two theoretical approaches, see R. Dahrendorf, *Class and Class Conflict in Industrial Society* (Stanford: Stanford University Press, 1957), chap. 5.

49. J. Walsh and R. Elling, "Professionalism and the Poor: Structural Effects and Professional Behavior," *Journal of Health and Social Behavior* 9 (March 1968): 16–28; reprinted in *Medical Men and Their Work*, ed. E. Friedson and J. Lorber (Chicago and New York: Aldine-Atherton, 1972).

50. See M. I. Roemer, "Social Science and Organized Health Services," *Human Organization* 18 (1969): 75–77.

51. Ray H. Elling, "The Design and Evaluation of Planned Change in

Health Organization," in *Sociology in Action*, ed. A. Shostak (Homewood, Ill.: Dorsey Press, 1966), pp. 292–302; idem, "The Design, Institutionalization, and Evaluation of Planned Change in Colombian Health Services," in "Culture, Disease, and Health Services," ed. R. Badgley, *Milbank Quarterly* 46, part 2 (1968, special issue): 258–73.

52. The notion of central organizing factors is suggested by E. R. Weinerman in "Anchor Points Underlying Planning for Tomorrow's Health Care," *Bulletin of the New York Academy of Medicine* 41 (1965): 1213–36. See also Behice Boran, "Sociology in Retrospect," *American Journal of Sociology* 52 (1947): 312–20.

53. C. Seipp et al., "Coordination, Planning, and Society: Six Case Studies," mimeographed (Pittsburgh: University of Pittsburgh Graduate School of Public Health, 1968).

54. At this writing the university, now a state school, is still paying on the large debt: "Last of $27 Million in Debts to Be Paid by University of Pittsburgh" (*New York Times*, 30 December 1974, p. 18).

55. The call for public health to enter the field of personal health services was sounded by C. E. A. Winslow, "Public Health at the Crossroads," *American Journal of Public Health* 16 (1926): 1075.

56. In this connection see the significant statement by J. N. Morris, "Tomorrow's Community Physician," *Lancet* 18 October 1969, pp. 811–16.

57. "The Shifting Power Structure in Health" in "Dimensions and Determinants of Health Policy" ed. W. Kissick, *Milbank Memorial Fund Quarterly* 46, part 2 (1968): 119–43.

58. Some blacks in Hartford's North End, the area from which the old city hospital drew the bulk of its patients, referred to the Farmington development as "the white palace out in wonderland."

59. There were major riots in the North End four summers in a row; during one of these, some five hundred persons were arrested in a two-day period!

60. Elling and Martin, *Health and Health Care*. Another study examined the system of medicine from the practicing physician's point of view (R. Elling and J. K. Bain, "The System of Medical Practice in Hartford," mimeographed (Storrs: University of Connecticut School of Medicine, Department of Clinical Medicine and Health Care, 1971)). Others in the group studied hospitals and practice in the northwest section of the state (Glasgow); nurse-physician division of labor (Douglas); and consumer involvement and geriatric care (Ingman).

61. Ray H. Elling, ed., *National Health Care: Issues and Problems in Socialized Medicine* (New York and Chicago: Aldine-Atherton, 1971).

62. Senator Edward Kennedy highlights this sickness by pointing out that "health care is the fastest-growing failing business in the nation—a $70 billion industry (1971) that fails to meet the urgent demands of our people. By 1975, we are told, we may be spending $100 billion a year on health and be worse off than we are now in terms of both the quality and

the availability of health care in the nation." (Edward Kennedy, "Changing the Face of American Health," in *Medicine in a Changing Society,* ed. L. Corey, S. E. Saltman, and M. F. Epstein (St. Louis: C. V. Mosby, 1972), p. 105.

63. I must record that there were a number of significant exceptions. There was some promising work with drug addiction both among adults and children. A new nurse-directed screening program was developed in the emergency room. One colleague strove mightily to develop an integrated community-oriented social geriatrics program and joined in coaching a new group of community health aides. Studies of lead poisoning among urban poor children contributed to national attention to this problem. Some important work developed with the Connecticut Regional Medical Program and with consumer groups and the other hospitals. Obviously there were other exceptions. I can only assess general emphases here.

64. Rue Bucher, "Social Process and Power in a Medical School," in *Power in Organizations,* ed. M. Zald (Nashville, Tenn.: Parthenon Press, 1970), pp. 3–47.

65. In French, one of the two official languages of WHO, the research division was "supprimée." This took effect 7 August 1972. To some of us, the closing did not come as a total surprise since a scientific advisory committee meeting on RECS more than a year and a half earlier had been highly critical of the disparate nature of the research program and the lack of a visible product. The executive board, meeting in January 1972, was also highly critical. Yet when the choice was made a year later to "elevate" some of the leadership involved, RECS was declared a great success and its core was identified as operations research defined by the highest authority, and with respect to planning health services as "an objective, scientific way of laying your cards on the table." This is complete nonsense because without a stated guiding framework, operations research allows an examination of whatever is politically expedient and an ignoring of whatever is too sensitive.

66. Freeman H. Quimby, *The Politics of Global Health* (Washington, D.C.: Government Printing Office, 1971).

67. Hilary and Steven Rose, *Science and Society* (Middlesex, England: Penguin, Pelican, 1970).

68. Ray H. Elling, "Political Influences on the Methods of Cross-National Sociomedical Research," in *Methods of Cross-National Sociomedical Research,* ed. M. Pflanz and E. Schach (Stuttgart, W. Germany: Thieme, 1976).

69. United Nations, Official Records, 205, *The Work of WHO, 1972,* pp. 157–58, par. 12.14.

70. Ray H. Elling, "Case Studies of Contrasting Approaches to Organizing for Health: An Introduction to a Framework," *Social Science and Medicine* 8 (1974): 263–70. This article was published in a special issue devoted to social science research in WHO. Members of the Social Science Unit played an important part in assembling and preparing materials for

this issue, but Peter McEwan deserves special thanks and recognition for persevering over many months in the task of seeking official clearance—an especially lengthy process in this case, perhaps because of the reorganization taking place.

71. A WHO/UNICEF joint study was one important effort mounted along these lines (World Health Organization-United Nations International Children's Educational Foundation Joint Committee on Health Policy, *Alternative Approaches to Meeting Basic Health Needs in Developing Countries* [JC20/UNICEF-WHO/75.2], 1975, pp. 4–6). This has now appeared in book form under the editorship of V. Djukanovic and E. P. Mach. Although limited to examining promising approaches, thereby avoiding invidious comparisons with negative experiences, this work on China, Tanzania, Cuba, a project in Venezuela, one in India, citizen involvement in Niger, and certain other cases is quite valuable. It gave me great pleasure in my last months at WHO to work on formulating the approach of this study with Drs. Vojo Djukanovic, John L. Cutler, Edward Mach, and other colleagues. Djukanovic was a particularly engaging and interesting man—one of the great people I met at WHO—former chief medical officer in Tito's army and then minister of health of Yugoslavia. He had done a lot of living and knew about peoples' real needs, politics, and medical care.

72. United Nations, World Health Organization, Official Records, 206, *Organizational Study on Methods of Promoting the Development of Basic Health Services* (annex 11), 1973, p. 110, par. 4.3.1.

73. Ray H. Elling and Henry Kerr, "Selection of Contrasting National Health Systems for In-Depth Study," in "Comparative Health Systems," ed. R. Elling, *Inquiry* 12 (supp. issue, June 1975): 25–40. That special issue was based on papers from the Medical Sociology Research Committee's session on this subject at the International Sociological Association Meetings in Toronto, 18–24 August 1974. Three additional researchers' papers were also included: Peter and Mary New on China, Mikio Yamoto and Junshiro Ohmura on Japan, and Stan Ingman on a family practice in the United Kingdom.

74. Dr. Emanuel Suter, director of DIME, assisted by Wendy Waddell, has formed a planning task force for a core course in international health. Members include Drs. Dieter Koch-Weser, Ned Wallace, Russell Mills, Timothy Baker, Steven Joseph, Milton Roemer, Michael Sterwart, and me. The Fogarty International Center has supported this activity and is represented by Dr. Donald Pitcairn.

75. "[Carl] Albert Says National Health Insurance will Pass in 1975," *New York Times*, 28 November 1974, p. 34.

76. The National Health Policy Planning and Resources Development Act of 1974, Pub. L. No. 93–641 was intended to replace Comprehensive Health Planning, Regional Medical Programs, and to redirect the Hill-Burton Hospital Construction Act.

77. Robert Straus, "The Nature and Status of Medical Sociology," *American Sociological Review* 22 (1957): 200–204.

In the Vineyards of Medical Sociology or How a Jeep Ride in Occupied Germany Changed My Life

MARK G. FIELD

ENTRY INTO MEDICAL SOCIOLOGY

Predisposing Factor

When I slipped behind the wheel of a jeep in occupied Germany sometime in late April 1946, little did I realize that I would not walk again for about six months, and then only on crutches and with great pain. Nor did I imagine (and how could I) that what would happen to me in a few minutes would direct my work (and indeed my life and my career) in the direction of an interest in health institutions and medicine in general. I was at that time serving in the U.S. Army in the town of Ansbach, southwest of Nuremberg. My job was to assist an American colonel supervise an assembly point for displaced persons prior to their repatriation from the American zone of occupation to their homeland, according to the Yalta agreement. I had been selected for this job because of my knowledge of Russian, and I served primarily as an interpreter to Colonel William Dunn, an amiable Coast Artillery career officer. I was almost twenty-three at the time, and had been in the army for about two years, having been drafted in my junior year from Harvard College where I majored in sociology and minored in Slavic.

At the time I was drafted, I was not an American citizen. I was born in Lausanne, Switzerland. My family was either middle class or lower middle class, if one wants to be technical about it. My father was a businessman who owned a photography shop, specializing in portrait work, but also selling cameras and processing film. My mother worked with him in the shop, and I often pitched in, in my free time. I have no brothers or sisters. We lived

in a fairly large, "bourgeois" type apartment, facing Lake Geneva
and the Alps of Savoy. I have, to this day, retained a deep love for
that landscape, and for a more relaxed way of life, which might
explain my frequent trips to Europe. I went to public school and
entered, when I was eleven, the Classical College. This was the
route (via the gymnasium) to the university, although at that time I
had no career or definite occupation in mind. I think my parents
expected that I would take over the shop unless I went into one of
the professions. I certainly was not particularly interested in medicine. In the late thirties, my parents decided to leave Switzerland
and to emigrate to the United States. The official emigration papers
were delivered to us by the American consul in Zurich in October
1939. This was already after World War II had opened with the
invasion of Poland by Nazi Germany in September. These papers
specified that we had to arrive in the United States within three
months, and beyond that time they would not be valid. We left
Lausanne in January 1940 and traveled to Genoa (Italy was still
neutral) where we boarded the *Conte Di Savoia* and landed in New
York on a cold day in February.

We settled in Jackson Heights on Long Island, and I was almost
immediately enrolled in Newtown High School which I attended
from February 1940 to June 1941. I remember taking my final examinations on that day in June when France asked Germany for an
armistice, an event which depressed me immensely. Although I
was brought up and "socialized" in Switzerland, my real "cultural" home was France. Most of the books, the newspapers, and the
magazines we read were French. I can still remember the shock
and sorrow that day in New York when I saw the *New York Post*
headline: "France Gives Up" and the picture of German troops near
the Arch of Triumph.

My parents opened a photo studio in the Times Square area, and
for awhile their business flourished. But after the war, things did
not work out too well for them. In one sense, they never quite
adapted to life in New York.

In the fall of 1941 I entered Hamilton College, a small liberal arts
college in upstate New York which had offered me a scholarship. I
never took to the provincialism and small town parochialism, as
well as the monastic isolation of Hamilton College (including com-
pulsory chapel attendance) and I, therefore, applied for transfer to
Yale and Harvard. I was admitted to both, and entered Harvard as a
sophomore in the fall of 1942, where I studied for almost two years
before I was drafted (in the late spring of 1944).

After basic training in the Georgia swamps in the heat of June and July (and becoming a naturalized American citizen in Macon, Georgia), the army decided that my linguistic abilities might be of some use and I was transferred to Camp Ritchie, Maryland for further training as an interpreter either in French or Russian. At that time, the demand for French interpreters had peaked, so I was assigned to a group of Russian-speaking soldiers and officers. After completing our training at Camp Ritchie, our group was sent to Camp Crowder, Missouri for signal training.

Washington worked on the assumption that since the American and Soviet armies were moving toward each other, some kind of coordination of troop movements would have to be established between the two. In fact, such coordination already existed between American headquarters in Western Europe and the French and the British, and was facilitated by the existence of signal liaison teams. Apparently our mission was to be similar: to be attached to a Soviet headquarters and secure signal traffic between the two armies. As far as I know, three such teams had been formed, and ours was to be attached to Patton's Third Army. When we arrived in Europe, we soon found that we were without a mission. The Soviets had a different conception of coordination. The last thing they wanted was to have a bunch of Americans with signal equipment at their headquarters! After a stint with military government at Rosenheim in Bavaria, our unit was sent to Hof, on the border between the American and Soviet zones of occupation. There we provided liaison and interpretation services for the American unit, most of our work having to do with the transfer of refugees from one zone to the other. And so it was that in the spring of 1945 I was transferred, on temporary and detached duty, to work for Colonel Dunn.

On the day in question, a Saturday afternoon, I was off duty and was going to Nuremberg with a friend of mine who worked for the American Red Cross and had a jeep at his disposal. I volunteered to drive. On the road between Ansbach and Nuremberg we kept a lively conversation. I was looking at my friend, when he suddenly yelled: "Look out!" Out of nowhere, it seemed, a German girl on a bicycle had materialized right in front of the vehicle. To avoid her, I instinctively swung the wheel hard to the left, crossed the road and literally wrapped the front end of the jeep around a large and immovable tree. There were no seat belts in those days. My left knee was thrown into the dashboard, breaking the kneecap and—what was far more serious—the hip cup (acaetabulum). I also suffered facial bruises, chipped teeth, and shock. My friend's leg was broken. From that time on, until I was discharged from the army early the following year to resume my studies as a senior at Harvard College, I lived in a series of military hospitals in Germany and the United States, including the hospital ship that took me from Bremen to Staten Island. A great deal of that time I was in a full body cast and was as helpless as a turtle on its back. And my life, my health, my mobility, indeed my fate hung on the decisions and the actions of medical, nursing, and other personnel. Their awful power impressed and intrigued me. It was most obviously the living of that experience, plus another spell later on in a Veterans Administration hospital (for the same injury), that shaped my initial interest in medical sociology.

Precipitating Factor(s)

Upon my return (still on crutches) to Harvard, early in 1947, I was faced with the necessity of choosing a major. This resulted from the fact that in the years before entering the service, I had accumulated enough credits in sociology and in Slavic so that I could undertake either one. When I had left college, Professor Sorokin was the chairman of the Department of Sociology and held sway. Frankly, I did not relish the idea of going back to the department and to him, and was seriously considering switching to Slavic when I realized that the Sociology Department had now become the Department of Social Relations with Talcott Parsons as its chairman. A friend of mine advised me to give the new department strong consideration, and I decided first to audit and then take for credit Parsons's course on the social structure of the United States. I was fascinated by the course: what Parsons said was eminently clear, interesting, and made sense. Indeed, anyone who has known Parsons only from his writings has missed an experience that only a great university can provide: a man who really professes. It was this course, perhaps more than any other single experience, that kept me in sociology. At that time the Department of Social Relations was an exciting place, what with professors coming back from all corners of the world and with a student body heavily sprinkled with veterans either resuming or beginning their studies.

In the course, Parsons spent a fair amount of time on the role of the professional in modern society, and particularly on physicians. That ignited the spark. This began to stimulate my interest and curiosity aroused by my earlier personal experience as a patient. In addition, at the time I was getting my A.B., the formation of the Russian Research Center gave me the opportunity to combine my work and interest in Slavic and Soviet affairs with that of medicine and health institutions, first as a research assistant, and then as a doctoral candidate. Since the center played such a critical role in supporting my work on Soviet medicine and my career in general, a few words should be said about it.

The first of the so-called regional or area research centers at Harvard, it was founded with a grant from the Carnegie Foundation to try to fill the abysmal gaps in knowledge about Soviet society that existed in the United States at that time. Its first director was a truly "charismatic" figure: Clyde Kluckhohn, one of the world's distinguished cultural anthropologists, and in no way a Russian expert. Indeed, during the war his expertise had been utilized in dealing with the Japanese. But his sensitivity as a human being, his interest in area studies, and his willingness—indeed eagerness—to allow the greatest academic freedom to the members of the center made it an exciting place to be. Indeed, he set the tone, or the "culture," of the center as a place where good people did what interested them with maximum support and understanding. If one went to the center in the evening or on a weekend, one would probably find one or more staff members working. Learning of my interest in Russian and Soviet affairs while I was still an undergraduate and before the center opened its doors, Kluckhohn had himself appointed as a member of my undergraduate honor thesis committee (the others were Parsons and Donald V. McGranahan), and hired me as a research assistant at the center in February 1948. It is also amusing to recall that in those days (late forties and early fifties) the center regularly had its windows smashed by the locals from Cambridge and Somerville who, seeing the words "Russian" and "Harvard" on a sign in front of the building, naturally believed it to be a Communist organization. Twenty years later, that same center was to come under attack, but this time from Harvard students as a tool of the reactionary Washington Establishment. So much for research in politically and ideologically sensitive areas!

In the fall of that year (1948), I also entered the Regional Studies Program on the Soviet Union as a masters candidate. This two-year program (inaugurated in 1947) took about twenty students each year. Although administratively separate from the Russian Research Center, the two were in effect closely intertwined, and prepared students either for an academic career, which they did by switching to a regular department for their doctorate, or for a career in government, business, or journalism. It was also in 1948 that I married Anne Bayard Murray, a Radcliffe student in sociology. We have four children from that union, three boys and one girl, in that order. How tempus fugit! My first son has recently been appointed an assistant professor of economics at Stanford University.

In 1950, after receiving my masters in regional studies, I transferred to the Department of Social Relations to study for my doctorate. When the question of a topic dissertation was raised, Professor Alex Inkeles, my advisor, suggested that I look at the role of the professions in Soviet society, along the lines of Parsons's interest, as well as the increased interest and work in these matters by Robert Merton and his associates at Columbia. The mandate, in my opinion, was too broad and my counter-suggestion was that I begin by looking at one profession, namely medicine. This was accepted not only by Professor Kluckhohn but also by Professor Parsons who, incidentally, had been a member of the center's Executive Committee from the beginning.

When in 1950 a team from the center went to Germany and Austria to interview a sample of displaced persons on what life had been like under Stalin's Russia[1] I was given an opportunity to query them on their experience qua patients with Soviet socialized medicine; I also had the opportunity to interview a group of former Soviet physicians on their professional activities in the Soviet Union. Upon my return to the United States I began an extensive study of library materials, particularly Soviet sources and other publications on Soviet medicine, and from this I obtained enough data of different types to write a doctoral thesis for the Department of Social Relations that eventually was published as a book, *Doctor and Patient in Soviet Russia* (1957).

In those days, there was little interest and even less formal training in the sociology of medicine, so most of what I learned was self-taught, picked up from readings and contacts with colleagues. But I must recognize the people who were interested in my work and the encouragement they gave me. In essence they allowed me full freedom to pursue my interest and the necessary conditions and support to do so. In particular, Professor Parsons was interested in my work, precisely because it provided a comparative dimension to his own theoretical formulation of the role of the physician in American society. In other words, the Russian Research Center provided that all-important reference group that was critical in encouraging and supporting me in the line of research I was following. This interest, I must add, was not widespread.

It will make an interesting exercise in the sociology of knowledge to account why so little concern has been shown in the West, and particularly in the United States, with the Soviet medical system. Was this shying away because of the ideological distate with anything "communistic" and particularly socialized medicine, the bête noire of the American Medical Association? The AMA incidentally maintained in its propaganda that socialized medicine was the entry wedge for socialism (or even communism) in America, an argument that has as much logic as saying that firehouses cause fires. I was once asked by what I presumed was a worried right-wing physician about the authenticity of the oft-used quote, attributed to Lenin: "Socialized medicine is the keystone in the arch of socialist society." Since practically every word that Lenin ever said or wrote has been carefully preserved, recorded, and duly indexed in the Soviet Union, it would have been relatively easy to find it. But it was nowhere to be found, and it must join the ranks of these famous sayings of famous men that were never said! Or is interest in Soviet medicine lacking because medical research has been singularly unimpressive? Perhaps. But if we remain at the "ideological" level for just one more second (as part of the environment of research and work), it should be noted that the partisans of a more liberal medical system, struggling to institute health reforms in the United States, also often saw almost any strictures that I (or anyone) made about Soviet medicine as still another reactionary attempt to discredit the principle of socialized medicine. On the other hand, any positive remark about Soviet medicine (for example, its ability to significantly increase the supply of physicians) was received by the stalwarts of private medicine as a sign of shocking irresponsibility on my part. I derive some kind of satisfaction from the fact that I have been raked over the coals not only by progressive and liberal physicians and professors of medicine, but also by the bigwigs of the American Medical Association, and by the Ministry of Health of the USSR! Perhaps I should have stuck with Elizabethan poetry, or early Slavonic verbs, after all.

In my work on Soviet medicine I had become intrigued with one aspect of the physician: that of the certification of illness (or health, as the case may be) and some of the consequences and implications, within the context of Soviet society, of that function. What became quite clear was that the clinical relationship did not take place on neutral ground, so to speak, but was affected by a series of factors extraneous to the medical system, such as the push toward rapid industrialization and modernization. It also became quite evident that this function (and its implications for the physician's role) was not limited to the Soviet Union but was inherent in the very nature of medical responsibility anywhere, and that it was an important "hinge" between the social and the health system. And furthermore, it seemed to me that the physician was in a critical position to provide really an "in-sight" into many social and motivational processes as these focused upon the individual. What the patient often brought to the doctor was but a microscopic mirror of macroscopic societal phenomena. If patients in the Soviet Union overloaded the physicians' offices seeking medical excuses as a relief from pressures in the larger society, this told us something about these pressures and the way in which the physician's role, as the "natural attorney of the poor" (Virchow), was being seen by the population. Self-inflicted wounds, to take another example, are obviously conditions requiring medical attention and are the symptoms of demands made on the individual that are so overwhelming, and in which he prefers to trade off pain, loss of limb, even crippling rather than something else. From that time on, my work and interest continued in the direction of relating the health system to society. I also suppose that I had a fairly unique advantage in being able to handle Russian-language sources. My work was not limited, however, to the health system but to several aspects of Soviet society, though my central interest remained on that system. And I suppose that for better or for worse, I will remain "that fellow who did some work on the Russian doctor."

ENTRY INTO PROFESSIONAL LIFE AND THE JOB MARKET

First Job
    When I received my doctorate in 1955, regular academic jobs were very scarce, even with a degree from a well-known university. (This was before the educational revolution ushered in by Sputnik.) I was offered a research position in one of the Boston teaching hospitals by the director, a physician who had read some of my work and was interested in medical sociology. He wanted to start some kind of sociomedical research within the hospital, and had obtained a small foundation grant to do a specific piece of research. This was to compare the length of hospital stay of patients with the same conditions before and after the introduction of the "wonder drugs" (this meant comparing all admissions to the hospital for 1932 and 1952), and I was put in charge. The transition from the Russian Research Center, with its research orientation and small but friendly and dedicated staff, to a large, impersonal, general teaching hospital was traumatic. There never was any real specifi-

cation of what I was supposed to do beyond the mentioned project, except some vague generalities about development of a program, and somehow the director and I simply did not hit it off: we were operating on different wavelengths. The expectations were different, and the ambivalence of my role within the hospital made these perhaps the unhappiest years of my life. I felt that I simply did not fit in that structure. We parted company less than two years after I started work at the hospital. This was, however, a learning experience in two important ways. First, as a sociologist within a medical setting I found it difficult to maintain my professional identity. I also found that I was expected to carry out research and work that were of interest to the doctors, but not necessarily to me as a sociologist. And second, I acquired some knowledge and feel about the life and the complex workings of a hospital, as well as better appreciation of the nature of medical work and responsibility. This was hard training, but perhaps—in retrospect—worth its price in unhappiness and dissatisfaction. I found, however, some solace in continuing (in my spare time) my work on Soviet medicine, and even went to the Soviet Union for the first time in 1956 with a medical delegation headed by Boston cardiologist Paul D. White.

I might also add from that experience the personal observation that the different training and responsibilities of physicians and sociologists make cooperative work between them often a problematic area: we do wear different lenses, conceptualize problems differently, see issues divergently. The difference lies probably in the nature of the clinical work and the awesome responsibility the physician bears to the health and life of the patient. As such, he often fails to see the forest for the trees. And the sociologist, so concerned with the forest (groups, communities, classes, societies), often forgets about the individual tree. There is perhaps another observation: physicians, accustomed as they are to call medical consultants as they need them, have the most natural tendency to see sociologists also as consultants. Something is not going well, so let's bring in a sociologist and he will find the answer. This kind of "magical" expectation can often lead to disappointments and falling-outs; or perhaps we simply cannot "deliver the goods"! In addition, and I shall comment on this at greater length later, the "personality" factor plays a critical role in any interdisciplinary endeavor, and in the case I just related, the personalities simply did not mesh.

Perhaps a few words are also in order regarding my first trip to the Soviet Union. It will be remembered that until that time I had never set foot in the USSR, and thus I was eager to see the place. But I did not learn very much that was new. I think a great deal can be learned from the kind of "historical research" we had been doing at the center. What the trip did, however, was to add a capstone of reality to already available knowledge; it humanized the system, made it more meaningful. Even today I still think that a trip there can be most beneficial only to someone who has done a fair amount of preliminary reading and studying. One who goes in cold simply lacks the perspective to interpret what he sees and hears. There is indeed a long tradition of left-leaning Western intellectuals, particularly British and Americans, who have trekked to the Soviet Union and returned, even at the height of Stalinist terror, claiming they had seen a vision of the furure, a society where the imperfections of their own world had been resolved. I sometimes wonder whether the infatuation of certain Westerners with the Peoples' Republic of China and what they profess to see and find there does not bear a strong resemblance to what earlier pilgrims brought back from the Soviet Union.

Second Job

My second job was much more exciting and interesting, in that it took place within a group of colleagues most of whom were social scientists, though my closest associate on that job was a physician, a psychiatrist. The job was a two-year stint as a staff member of a joint commission appointed by Congress to reexamine the treatment and approaches to mental illness in this country, and to prepare recommendations for changes and reforms. In that situation I had a chance to travel a great deal about the United States and Canada, and become acquainted with mental illness as I had become acquainted with somatic illness at the hospital. This was not only research in the academic sense, but it also had policy implications. What I learned came in very handy when I was asked to prepare a paper on approaches to mental illness in the Soviet Union, and I was able to produce more than one such paper, and was also able to include a comparative US-USSR perspective. This was further emphasized when a psychiatrist at the Massachusetts General Hospital began to collaborate with me on such studies, and we went together to the Soviet Union twice (but later than the period I am describing now). However, my desire was to return to my first love and interest, Soviet medicine. As the work of the commission drew to an end, I applied for a Public Health Service grant to devote myself full time to such a study and moved back to the Russian Research Center. I was also asked to teach the course on Soviet Social Institutions in the Department of Social Relations at Harvard.

If in my original work on Soviet medicine I had been interested primarily in the doctor-patient relationship, the next step I felt was to be a more comprehensive examination of the stage on which the relationship took place. In other words, I was interested in a better understanding, description, and analysis of the Soviet health system qua system for the delivery of health services. I spent the next two years happily back onto my own research work, in the library and in an area that was of great interest to me. This is when I began writing my second book, *Soviet Socialized Medicine* (1967).

There is, in every Sovietologist, a comparativist struggling to get out. Implicitly my work had compared, to some extent, the American and the Soviet medical systems, though certainly the emphasis was on the latter if only because it had been so poorly studied and documented. As an example of the issues that one can literally stumble across with a comparative approach, consider this: in the late fifties I was asked by a pharmaceutical journal to prepare a descriptive paper on pharmacies and the pharmaceutical system in the Soviet Union, which I did. Later on, an old friend and former colleague of mine at the center, now a professor at the Harvard Business School, called me up with a problem. He was consulting for one of the large firms in the Boston area. The firm had a contract to study the mounting wave of criticism of the pharmaceutical industry and the high costs of drugs to the patient. My friend had the following idea in mind: if one examined the general critique addressed to the American pharmaceutical industry, and then designed a system ostensibly aimed at removing most of the problem areas, one almost by implication came up with a system that closely resembled the one the Soviets had designed to supply their population with pharmaceuticals. Therefore, if one made the usual allowances and qualifications for different economic levels, one might examine the workings of a system that structurally resembled that which the critics of the American system considered desirable. How did that alternative system perform?

Upon analysis, the answer was not so well. Indeed, most of the criticism addressed at the American system was mirrored, but in just the opposite way, in the Soviet system, as evidenced from an analysis of the Soviet sources. For example, American firms rushed into mass production, perhaps prematurely. In the Soviet Union,

because of the institutional separation between research laboratories and manufacturing plants, tested and licensed new products
often did not get into large-scale production. Managers were unwilling to assume the risks and expenses to retool, particularly in
view of the technical difficulties involved in putting new products
into production and because fixed selling prices by the state made
it difficult, or impossible to recoup start-up costs. Or if new products eventually did get into production, it was after very long de-
lays when the products had already been made obsolete by new
laboratory or clinical research.

Item: American drug firms were criticized for overpromoting
their drugs, and particularly for their use of expensive advertising
campaigns and detail-men who visited physicians and told them
about the products their firm was selling. The costs of these promo-
tional activities are, of course, borne by the consumer. The situation in the Soviet Union, it turned out, was just the opposite, and
produced its own negative results: the underpromotion (or non-
promotion) of drugs meant that busy physicians did not learn of the
existence of new and more effective products in the pharmacies.
These products, the results of a long and expensive process, simply
lay on the shelves, unsold. The whole investment in these drugs
was wasted. The Soviet sources suggested one possible solution:
pharmacists should come to the clinics and give talks to physicians, informing them of what was available in the pharmacies. A
detail-man by any other name. . .!

Item: American drugs were available but too expensive. Soviet
drugs were sold relatively cheaply, but often were not available at
all. Item: American firms often produced drugs that were in small
demand in order to promote their entire line and earn the goodwill
of physicians. The Soviets often did not produce items in small
demand. Item: American drug firms contributed to the proliferation
of preparations that were simply combinations of items, rather than
new preparations. Soviet complaint: there were not enough pre-
compounded items, and pharmacists lost valuable time compound-
ing them by hand. The list of these items could easily be extended.
Such an analysis almost suggests a dialectical synthesis: by selecting the best aspects of the two systems and dropping the worst, one
might devise a better system that would better fit the needs and the
pocketbooks of people in the two societies. For example, retain the
aggressive and innovative and dynamic features of the American
system, with the more equalitarian and financially fairer system of
the Soviets. Perhaps the federal government should use detail-men

to orally inform physicians of what is new. Perhaps the patient should receive a subsidy so as to be able to easily afford those drugs whose development costs have to be recouped somewhere along the line. And so on!

On a more sociological level, there remained in the back of my mind an interest with the comparative study of the health systems in different societies and cultural settings. I questioned the degree to which the hypothesis of *Industrial Man* (by Inkeles) and the general idea of a "convergence" of industrial societies would hold for the health systems of these societies: would they also exhibit some type of convergence? To some degree these ideas and hypotheses were further stimulated by my auditing another of Parsons's courses on institutional structure in the early sixties. He spoke at great length about the evolution of social systems and the trend toward their increased internal differentiation that multiplied or augmented their adaptive capacities. This was the beginning of my conceptualization of the nature, internal structure, and functions of health systems in general, but of modern industrial societies in particular. I reasoned that if the hypothesis of convergence and differentiation were correct, then the health systems of the most advanced industrial societies would constitute the further point empirically available in the evolution and differentiation of health systems. I also assumed that in their essential lines the health systems of less-developed or developing societies would essentially follow the more developed ones.

Third Job

When in 1961 I was offered a job as associate professor of sociology at the University of Illinois, I accepted it as my first full-time, tenured, academic position. Until then, I had gone from one research position to another, without the security or the perspective of a fairly constant attachment and environment. The Department of Sociology at Illinois rolled out the red carpet, met all my demands, and I became a professor for the first time. (I had never been an instructor or an assistant professor.) The department, furthermore, encouraged me to continue my work and my research, and I took my grant to the corn and wheat fields of central Illinois. Although the atmosphere was most pleasant and supportive for me, the same could not be said for my family, and particularly my wife, a born New Englander who regarded the Middle West as some kind of American Siberia. It was symbolic that we had not sold our house outside of Boston but had rented it, "just in case." During

one of my periodic trips to the East Coast, I mentioned to a friend
and colleague who was chairman of the Department of Sociology at
Boston University how my family felt about the situation, and he
later invited me to join his department, which I did. This proved to
be an extremely pleasant arrangement; we took back the threads of
our previous life; my renewed affiliation with the center continued
to provide me with the research atmosphere, and particularly with
the matchless research and library facilities it had accumulated. In
addition, a courtesy appointment with the Department of
Psychiatry at the Massachusetts General Hospital enabled me to
keep pace with my interest in psychiatry.

PRESENT JOB AND CONTEMPORARY
PROFESSIONAL CONCERNS

As I returned to the Boston area and became professor of sociology at Boston University, I continued to address myself to the description of the Soviet health system at the macrosociological level.
I eventually completed a manuscript which I regarded (and entitled) as an "Introduction to Soviet Socialized Medicine," mentioned earlier. I fully intended to follow this with a more complete,
detailed, and minute description of that system, a sort of magnum
opus that would permit me to write *finis* to my involvement with
Soviet medicine. My only chagrin was that there was no intellectual heir, so to speak, to this interest of mine, a student or colleague
to whom this interest could be passed on. There had been, and still
are, graduate students and a few physicians who from time to time
had evinced some curiosity in that area of work, but very few, almost none who followed it through systematically. I was thus enjoying a kind of monopoly, again as "that fellow who had done
work on Soviet medicine," and often called upon to lecture on it to
many audiences, but a monopoly can also be an awfully lonely position. The only other person in the West whose interests are
somewhat parallel to mine is Dr. Heinz Müller-Dietz of the Ost-
Europa Institut at the Free University of Berlin, and I had met him
several times, worked at his institute, and shared ideas on the subject. At one time, we even contemplated collaborating on a book,
but nothing came of it. This is not to deny that this field has totally
been neglected by Western scholars and observers, though it has
been by sociologists. I am thinking, in particular, of such persons
as Milton Roemer, Victor Sidel, and Patrick Storey, but the list is
small. Honesty would compel me to admit that the Soviet health

system is hardly one that has mobilized great interest (particularly when compared with the British National Health Service, for example), whether this interest be among Soviet or medical scholars.

On this subject, I must acknowledge the support, in the form of grants, I received from 1959 on from the Public Health Service which permitted me to carry on my work, particularly during the summers. I suppose that the completion of the introduction marked a definite cutting off point, and from that time on, I began to grow increasingly restive (or bored) with Soviet medicine.

I then began to seek a way of broadening my interests, particularly in the comparative direction. I thus began to work on developing what I hoped would be an adequate theoretical approach to the conceptualization of the health system that would eventually permit me to branch off from the exclusive concerns with the Soviet (and the American) systems to a multiplicity of such systems, and tease out general principles. In this respect, another research opportunity was to be decisive. I was approached in the late sixties by the Program on Technology and Society at Harvard (funded by IBM) to participate in a research seminar on the impact of technology on medicine. The seminar, chaired by Seymour Kety of the Massachusetts General Hospital, also included such distinguished persons as Louis Lasagna (then at Johns Hopkins), and John Knowles (recently appointed the president of the Rockefeller Foundation, but then general director of the Massachusetts General Hospital) Everett Mendelsohn, (professor of the history of science at Harvard), Stanley Reiser (now at Harvard Medical School), and Judith Swazey (at Boston University Medical School).

It is in the course of this work that I began to apply a "systemic" approach to the conceptualization of the health enterprise of modern society, using, as a departure model, that of the United States. I felt that such an approach should be carried out at the macrosociological level with the nation-state representing the unit of analysis and of comparison. I further reasoned that the concept of internal differentiation of societies could be applied, among others, to their health system. That health system should be seen as a differentiated, identifiable, and bounded subsystem of the society, evolving from a state of relative simplicity to that of increased complexity. It was also reasonable to assume then that we were dealing with a historically evolving societal and cultural mechanism dealing primarily with the problems and consequences posed by morbidity and premature mortality for the society, and that this evolution was the result of certain forces impinging both on the society and on its health system. An attempt to identify these forces was facilitated by the deliberations of the group in the Program on Technology and Society. It seemed that it was the impact of science, knowledge, and technology that constituted a major qualitative influence on the health system, as well as faith in their efficacy, as recently pointed out by Powle. One only had to look at the modern, highly instrumented, research-oriented teaching medical center of today and compare it with the hospital of a mere fifty years ago to realize the magnitude of the transformation, a transformation that had indeed begun in the nineteenth century when the scientific approach percolated into the art of medicine. The other major influence was the sheer quantitative impact of increased effective demand for health services backed by ideological, political, and functional-economic considerations. From this vantage point, curiosity about how other health systems in other nations were developing, and whether they would show the same kind of evolutionary trend became irresistible.

In order to obtain support for this kind of research, I again turned to the Public Health Service with a grant application, requesting that the funding begin at the time that my grant on Soviet medicine and medical organization came to an end. In my application, although I emphasized the heavily theoretical orientation of my work, I also suggested the utility and the relevance of examining the health systems of other societies that were not in their basic structural features (i.e., industrial, urban, mechanized, etc.) fundamentally very different from the United States. I also reasoned that if the convergence hypothesis were borne out, i.e., if we could show that the options available to industrial societies for the structuring, management, and financing of their health services were fairly limited, and tended with time, and because of universal technological and demand constraints, to converge toward roughly similar patterns, this certainly would make the job of planning an appropriate health services delivery system for the United States easier and more rational. The research proposal contained budgetary allowances for foreign travel. I had decided to limit myself to six or seven countries, including the United States, the Soviet Union, Japan, Great Britain, France, Sweden, possibly Norway, and a Latin American country (either Chile or Columbia). Although the request was granted, I later received notification from Washington asking me to reduce my budget by about 15 percent to 20 percent, and I decided to give up (at least for the time being) Latin America.

In 1970 I visited all the above-named countries (with the exception of the Soviet Union whose health system I knew and which I had visited earlier on four occasions). My plan was not to generate research in the countries I visited, but rather to take an inventory of what was available in terms of data and figures and to speak to persons who had a broad view of the health system who might supply additional insights into the processes I was interested in. Briefly, my approach could be described as an input-output scheme, in which structural resources (personnel, facilities, knowledge, legitimacy) are channeled into the health subsystem. These inputs are "generalized" resources; they are transformed or metabolized by the health system into specialized outputs or services of functional significance to the social system and its members. As mentioned earlier, the approach is, at the minimum: (1) macrosociological; (2) structural-functional; (3) historical-evolutionary; (4) dynamic; and (5) (hopefully) relevant. I will discuss the question of relevance in greater detail below.

At the present time, I am trying to "operationalize" the above scheme, i.e., to give it more than hunches or hypotheses, to supply actual figures and other supportive data to see whether the basic departure points are correct, and whether the different health systems in my sample are evolving and converging toward a common pattern, in spite of widely different cultural, historical, and traditional backgrounds. Preliminary data seem to bear this out, although one should not rule out the possibility of coincidence over convergence.

Inevitably and inexorably, however, I feel myself brought back full-circle again to the very question that had interested me as a graduate student: the doctor-patient relationship, and particularly the nontechnical, supportive aspects of that relationship. It seems quite significant that, if medical care in the dual etymological sense of "treatment" and "love for the patient" consists of two elements related to physiology and psychology, that the latter has, increasingly tended to be squeezed out both by the technical complexity of medicine and by the accompanying ever increasing division of medical labor, its fragmentation, and the ensuing alienation of the patient. This often leads to a Kafka-like medicine of the absurb where biomedical abundance and therapeutic poverty inhabit simultaneously the modern house of medicine.

As my interest in the Soviet health system began to be slowly superseded or complemented by a comparative dimension, I became increasingly involved in international activities. There was first, my attending the International Conference on Social Science and Medicine at Aberdeen in 1968. I was then asked to join the International Medical Sociology Committee, Medical Sociology Section of the American Sociological Association, as well as the International Medical Care Committee, Medical Care Section of the American Public Health Association. There I was able to interact with colleagues who had had research experiences in a variety of countries, and to learn from them the many issues and difficulties in this area. A stint as a consultant to the Behaviour Science Unit of the Division on Research in Epidemiology and Communicative Sciences at the World Health Organization in Geneva (1969) brought to my attention the wealth of accumulated data on international health available there, as well as a chance to work closely with Milton Roemer who has, for years, also been interested in international health and comparative systems. Attendance at the Asilomar Workshop early in the fall of 1969 brought me into close contact with other colleagues in the same general area, and particularly with Richard Weinerman who was, shortly thereafter, to tragically lose his life in the bombing of a plane in Switzerland. In 1970, in addition to the travel on my grant mentioned earlier, I also attended the Second International Conference on Social Science and Medicine at Aberdeen, as well as the Seventh Congress of the International Sociological Association at Varna where I was elected chairman of the Research Committee on Medical Sociology of the association, succeeding, in that position, Eliot Freidson. In December of that year, I was invited to deliver a paper before the Société de Sociologie et Démographie Médicales in Paris, where I compared the structural evolution of the medical professions in the United States and the Soviet Union between 1910 and 1970.

More recently my attention has been drawn to the health systems of developing nations, particularly in Asia, when I attended a comparative conference organized by the Wenner-Gren Foundation in Austria in the summer of 1971 and where I got a rare inkling of the meaning and functions performed by traditional medicine in the countries of that continent, particularly Arabic, Ayruvedic, and Chinese medicine. Exposure to the health systems of developing nations, particularly Asia and Southeast Asia, led me to a better appreciation of the fact that "scientific" medicine is Western medicine, and thus an often culturally alien phenomenon outside of the West. I find, for example, the coexistence of two medical streams and traditions in China (Western and traditional) particularly fascinating when contrasted to the Soviet medical development. I had an opportunity to explore this at greater length at a conference on Chinese medicine at the University of Washington early in 1974, where I speculated that the alienated patient in the West had his counterpart in the Eastern patient who distrusted the cold (and often inhuman though sometimes effective) ministrations of Western physicians and Western medicine. And perhaps these phenomena are part and parcel of the price that society pays as it moves from a Gemeinschaft to a Gesellschaft form, from a primary group to the secondary group society, from the traditional to the modern, urban, and industrial order. It is that alienation that goes with size, complexity, rationality, science, technology, efficiency, formal organization, and the division of labor. It is met on the assembly line, in the huge offices where people shuffle bits of paper, in the hyperefficient supermarket where the housewife shops swiftly but without exchanging a word with anyone, in the highly instrumented, technological, computerized medical center where the patient's body is "processed" and "monitored" and handled by a multiplicity of specialists, superspecialists, technicians, aides, and "upper left nostril specialists." The *Castle* has been turned into *The Hospital!*

In the summer of 1972, I participated in the Third International Conference on Social Science and Medicine, held that time in Elsinore, Denmark. I presented a position paper in which I summarized my work and ideas on the health system up to that point. Early in September of that year I chaired a symposium on the Social Consequences of Modernization in Communist Societies at Salzburg. This was sponsored by the American Council of Learned Societies and its Planning Group on Comparative Communist Studies. The basic question posed at the symposium was whether one could detect major differences in the structural consequences of a modernization process carried out in a conscious and deliberate way by an agency such as the Communist Party and the same consequences flowing from a more spontaneous, lengthier, nondirected process as had taken place in the West and in Japan. At that symposium, I presented a paper on the Soviet and American health systems, cautiously trying to see the degree to which, in spite of their many organizational differences, there were common and convergent elements. In May of 1973, I attended a round table on Prospects for Comparative Studies organized under the auspices of the International Social Science Research Council at Cologne, and read a paper presenting statistical materials on the seven national health systems I was comparing. Later on that year, I attended a

conference at Warsaw held under the sponsorship of our Research
Committee and organized by Magda Sokołowska. There I emphasized the concept of the health system as only one of a multiplicity of other subsystems in society, each one performing a complementary task, and each one again competing for scarce resources
of all types. My attempt there was to counter the understandable
tendency of those concerned with health to place that area at the
center of their societal universe, often ignoring the equally valid
claims of other subsystems in the society. In the spring of 1974 I
attended (and had the honor to preside over) a seminar on Methods
in Cross-national Sociomedical Research, also sponsored by our research committee, and organized by Manfred Pflanz. At that seminar, my paper attempted to outline the major "pay-offs" or "utili-
ties" of cross-national (rather than simply comparative) studies in
health. All these papers, of course, had at their conceptual center
the approach I have outlined earlier (and which I will detail below), but each paper embodied (at least I hope it did) not only some
small progress over the preceding one, but also it tried to accen-
tuate that specific aspect that would fit with the theme of the conference or the seminar where it was being presented.

The Yugoslav Evaluation Study

Between 1971 and 1973, I had another most interesting and fruitful experience related to the health field. The Office of International Health of the Department of Health, Education and Welfare
circulated, in May of 1971, a request for a proposal to evaluate the
impact of its Excess Currency Program in Yugoslavia. This requires
some explanation. As a result of the sale by the United States in the
post–World War II period of primarily agricultural surpluses to
several nations, the United States accumulated large amounts of
"excess" local currencies that, by mutual agreement, were not con-
vertible into dollars. The monies remained in the country and were
utilized at the discretion of and appropriation by Congress, to
either meet United States obligations, or to fund mutually agreed
upon programs.

Since the early sixties, a fairly extensive cooperative health program had been mounted in Yugloslavia from these funds (sometimes called P.L. 480 monies) including such activities as laboratory research, epidemiological surveys, exchanges of medical students, translations programs, critical reviews and international conferences. What the department wanted was an evaluative study of
the impact of the program on the health of the people of the United
States and of the host country.

Dr. Dieter Koch-Weser, associate dean for international affairs at the medical school, Professor Ralph E. Berry, Jr. of the Department of Health Services Administration at Harvard, and I constituted ourselves into a team, wrote a proposal, and had it accepted. This was the beginning of a pleasant cooperation between a physician (Koch-Weser), an economist (Berry), and myself. Later on Dr. John Karefa-Smart, former assistant to the director general of the World Health Organization, and Mark Thompson, then a doctoral student at the Kennedy School of Government at Harvard, also joined our team, which was augmented by several consultants and staff members. The major part of our work consisted in developing a metric for impact evaluation and then applying it to the 113 projects funded under the program. One often hears about the desirability of multidisciplinary research and teams. The team worked extremely well together, and I suspect again that the members liked working together both at the personal and the professional level. I think this was reflected in the final report (written by Professor Berry) which will soon be published as a book by D. C. Heath in their Lexington book series.

At this point, I would like to add a few notes on the life of the professor as I personally experience it now.

When I was an undergraduate at Harvard, every time I went to the Widener library, I saw a man, with a green eye shade, sitting at one of the long tables with a pile of books before him. He read and made notes. This was the year (1944), incidentally, when Gunnar Myrdal's *An American Dilemma* was published, a book that had impressed me by its scope, scholarship, comprehensiveness, and massiveness. I had some fantasy that this was Myrdal, the patient, thorough scholar, going through the literature and preparing another equally impressive contribution. This is perhaps when I decided to pursue an academic career. This career was wrapped, in my mind, in a triangular cocoon of assumptions about what the academic life was: the library and its quiet strata of books (and despair of course, expressed by Thomas Wolfe about our ability to read but a minute fraction of them in our lifetime); the classroom where one "professed" to those seeking knowledge and understanding; and the study, where one secluded oneself, read and particularly wrote. Having drawn this idyllic picture, I might want to contrast this with the life of the professor at Boston University (or, I suppose, at any major university), a life dominated by the clock, the endless deadlines, the multiplicity of phone calls, the obligations, the nitpicking details to attend to, the mail that must be answered, and the myriad of other interruptions and frustrating activities that have but peripheral relevance to the scholarly pursuits. In those days, many years ago, I was also blissfully unaware of the modern version of Chinese torture called the "meeting," whether it be department, committee, or faculty, where in so many instances the unimportant is endlessly trivialized into nothingness.

A footnote on Gunnar Myrdal. In January 1964, on my way home from Moscow, I was asked by a colleague who was spending a year at the Wenner-Gren Institute in Stockholm to stop there for lunch. My friend asked me whether I wanted to meet the "old man" who was then director of the institute. So twenty years after I had so admired his book, I finally met Myrdal. He was not, of course, anything like my role model at Widener!

CONCEPTUALIZATION OF THE FIELD

The house of medical sociology has many chambers. What I would like to do is to briefly recapitulate the manner in which I conceptualize the field, and some of the basic underlying assumptions that have and are guiding my research efforts.

My focus remains on the sociological approach to medicine and health care as a basic commitment to the application of sociological insight and knowledge to one important sector of society. I believe, furthermore, that a correct theoretical formulation will, in the long run, have more beneficial and thus "relevant" consequences than a direct plunging into the issues and problems and the search for instant and hasty solutions and reforms. This does not mean, however, that I am not interested nor committed to the solution of the "health crisis" either in the United States or elsewhere. I simply want to limit my contribution to as correct and valid an analysis of the aspects of that crisis as I am able to so that, in the future, reasonably intelligent programs may be proposed and attempted. Second, my focus remains at the macrosociological level rather than the microsociological. This happens to be a personal preference that does not downgrade the importance of community and other similar types of conceptual levels. But I am interested in the broader cultural currents and forces that are at work in the total society on the assumption that these set the framework and the conditions for the local situations and problems. With this approach in mind, I think I am also better able to conceptualize the health system in its proper place within the societal system, rather than (as I said earlier) the center of the societal universe, a view that professional health advocates are more likely (and for understandable reasons) to adopt. In other words, I see the health system as competing with other systems (education, housing, welfare, capital investments, and so on) for scarce structural supports, and I try to visualize the unstable equilibrium represented by these systems in a rapidly changing society. Not that I pretend that I (or anyone for that matter) will ever be able to conceptualize and computerize the complexities of the social system and, with that, of the different segments that are differentiated and provide services or other outputs. Since my approach is so clearly structural-functional, let me try to specify this at greater length.

My departure point is a basic functional need of society: the ability of its members to act in the variety of their institutionalized social roles within the social structure. I thus posit that the social system is dependent, to a large degree, on the statistical probability of institutionalized actions on the part of social actors, and that, given the biological and psychological nature of these actors, disease, disability, and premature death present functional threats of critical importance to the social system. Thus, from the viewpoint of that system, health is a fundamental resource (second to life itself) quite apart from the individual's suffering, and the anxiety caused by illness and trauma and their association with dependency and death. I thus see medicine, the rise of medical-therapeutic roles, and the emergence of a medical culture (or lore, as the case may be) as sociocultural responses to the threat of disability. As such, modern society, as it becomes increasingly internationally differentiated, gives rise to a fully identifiable "health system" separate from other differentiated subsystems, whether these be the economy, the family, the general (but not the medical) educational system, religion, the polity, and so on. I posit that we can draw a net around the health system and that we can define its boundaries with a fair degree of accuracy, assuming again that there are certain grey areas or definitional questions that can be resolved in a more or less arbitrary manner. For example, are the American drugstore and pharmacist part of the health system—to which I answer only insofar as they are concerned with the provision of prescriptions ordered by a physician or the furnishing of certain implements such as crutches or bedside supplies, again as ordered by the physician or other health personnel. The selling of the hundreds of notions (including cigarettes) and other supplies commonly available in American drugstores is not a part of the health system. I think it is important to come to these definitions, for otherwise the concept of the system may be carried to absurd levels if we assume that everything is connected to everything else. This might lead us to state, for example, that the relativity theory is the result of the work of the farmer(s) who grew the food that kept Einstein's body functioning and permitted his brain to elaborate the theory! Once we have identified the health system (or the health systems which, in their aggregate, can be said to constitute the health system of a society), the next conceptual question is to examine the kinds of inputs or supports the specialized health system needs in order to be able to function since it is not (indeed it cannot be) completely self-supporting, i.e., it cannot usually generate its own resources. I have earlier identified (and later I will try to quantify) these resources, and I need not detail them here. Since these resources are essentially scarce, any sudden increase in the demand for these resources by any one of these systems must perforce lead to dislocations and reallocations, and to the establishment of some kind of balance or equilibrium. Indeed, I feel that one important element of the crisis of American medicine is precisely the increased demands for resources on the part of the health system at a rate that increases faster than the general increase of the gross national product, forcing, so to speak, the society to begin to reappraise its priority categories. Such allocation of resources is also often challenged *within* the health system, for example, in the mix between research, services, and education. Or one might put it more dramatically by comparing the opportunity costs in personnel and facilities and funds necessary to perform very delicate operations for a very few people to the utilization of the same amount of resources to provide more routine services to many more persons who suffer from more benign afflictions.

Thus, a dynamic approach to the health system leads us to an examination of the changes in the health system, and indeed its evolution, again over fairly long periods of time. Empirically then, today's health system is different from what it was yesterday and more visibly from what it was ten or fifty years ago, and is different from what it will be tomorrow, ten years hence, a hundred years from now. However, I would maintain (at least from the historical evidence) that the health system(s) will continue to provide society at any stage with the basic functional services (but in probably a quite different guise) that it has traditionally done, since disease, injury, and premature mortality seem to be a constant element of the human condition. One might also, in that context, speak of changes in certain aspects of the mandate of medicine, either toward a narrowing of that mandate (let us say toward physiological needs alone) or more likely toward a broadening of that mandate, toward problems of living and so on. It is precisely at this point that the comparative international approach is, to me at least, exciting and generative of ideas, insights, and hypotheses. If, on the one hand, the health concern is truly a universal societal concern, and if the factors that impinge on the health system are also universal or fairly similar from society to society, will these elements shape health systems everywhere toward a kind of universal pattern (convergence), or is the particularistic strength of cultures, traditions, national identities, etc., so strong that in the future the health systems of different nations will continue to exhibit the amazing diversity we are now witnessing? The likely answer probably lies between these two formulations. The question is where.

As I look back upon my work and career, I find it difficult to identify specific sources of encouragement and support. I should mention, first, my experience at Harvard after I returned from the service, and particularly the encouragement and assistance of such men as Professors Kluckhohn and Parsons, and later Inkeles, as well as the presence of an atmosphere of research and inquiry. They gave the kind of approval, i.e., they in a sense "legitimized" my area of inquiry by saying, "Go ahead!" At the same time, the presence of the center provided that logistic backup at the time when I was an unknown graduate student and when foundation and other external funding might have been difficult to secure. Furthermore, the center, much more indeed than the Department of Social Relations, was my reference group, with its critical mass of colleagues that provided a rare combination of professional and personal supports. Here again I must mention Professor Alex Inkeles, who indeed served as a role-model for me both as a splendid teacher in the classroom and as a researcher and writer. I admired and respected Alex then, and a quarter century later my feelings for him have not changed. I also very much want to acknowledge a debt of gratitude to the members of the different study and advisory groups that, over the years, recommended support for my research work to the Public Health Service.

What of the future? I would like to help establish a university-based research center on comparative health systems (I even have a memo dated 1959 when I first expressed the idea). Obviously what I have in mind is an organization patterned along the lines of the Russian Research Center, with a small permanent staff and a fairly active group of graduate students and research fellows. Until now I have been too busy keeping my head above water to undertake

planning such a center. But my work in the last few years, and
particularly my research and my chairmanship of the Sociology of
Medicine Committee of the International Sociological Association,
have convinced me that this is worth a try. If such a center would
turn out to be anything like the center with which I was affiliated
in the early part of my career, the vineyards of medical sociology
will be carefully tended and should yield a wine rich in theoretical
bouquet and practical aroma.

NOTES

1. This became known as the Harvard Refugee Interview Project on the
Soviet System. Using political refugees as sources of information was, of
course, a major methodological challenge and there was considerable ob-
jection to this kind of research. It should be remembered that in the early
fifties access to Soviet society was out of the question, and that displaced
persons were the only living eyewitnesses we had of what life had been
like under Soviet conditions. I believe that most of these objections were
met by careful staff work, and the use of information from different
sources. My own philosophical approach could be formulated as follows:
"If one person had survived from Elizabethan England, would one not talk
to that person and ask about life then, even though the sample was biased
due to the fact that other members of that society have been dead for a few
hundred years?" There was enough internal evidence from the responses
we obtained to see that the refugees did not systematically attempt to
present a distorted picture (there was for instance a great deal of consistency in the responses given by members of different socioeconomic
strata). In my own work, for example, I administered questionnaires to two
groups of refugees from the Soviet Union, one in Germany, and the other
in the United States. To the question, "Which system of medical care do
you prefer, the Soviet or the German/American?" an overwhelming majority of the German sample answered that they preferred the German over the
Soviet system. A just as overwhelming majority of the respondents queried
in the United States preferred the *Soviet* over the American system. This
could be interpreted as follows: The Soviet system as a blueprint satisfied
these people, but the German *Krankenkasse* system delivered better what
the Soviet system had led them to expect. In the American situation, what
these people were in effect saying was: "What good is that system if I
cannot afford to pay for it and have no claim to get it as a right?"

The Development of Design by Accident

ELIOT FREIDSON

In considering how my work in medical sociology developed, it seems to me that the only way I can make sense of it is by seeing it as a process by which I have responded to a series of historical accidents within the framework of the institutions to which I had become economically, socially, and psychologically committed. My entrance into the field was entirely by accident and without prior interest or intent. My progress in the field was partly a function of commitments established by my initial work in it, and partly a function of my idiosyncratic response to opportunities which happened to be offered to me at a time when I happened to be free to take them. Thus, insofar as my publications have been coherent and systematic, showing design, they do not reflect their origin in accident. Rather, they reflect my struggle to produce writings which follow the rhetorical rules of science and scholarship and which cover up the disorder of the life and career of the scholar. In this paper I wish to discuss the interaction between the accidents of career and the designs of intellectual production.

BIOGRAPHY AND STYLE

The rules of scholarly discourse are such that intellectual production can be discussed and evaluated solely on the grounds of the work itself—the grounds of logical consistency and compatibility with the evidence available. Such grounds are not the source of the work so much as the rules one follows in creating and evaluating it. They may be considered quite separately from the individual who produces the work, and the historical period in which he produces it. Nonetheless, other elements are involved in intellectual production which are not so timeless as the rules of logic and of evidence. The substantive approach to a topic—that is, one's selectivity, em-

115

phasis, and style—may be understood far better by its concrete historical and biographical context than by its methodological quality. Thus, some elements of my work—at least the substantive emphasis, or style—can be found only in my personal biography. Therefore, while I shall not attempt to make connections between my work and my personal life, it does seem necessary to provide some minimal biographical information so that the reader may at least consider the possibility of such connections.

This is not an occasion on which I care to indulge in personal confessions, but there are some basic facts of my life which seem appropriate to mention. I was born in what was then a respectable, white-collar, Jewish neighborhood of the Dorchester section of Boston. I was the third child, but the first and—as it turned out—only son. (A third sister was born when I was eight.) My father was a shoe jobber with little formal education, having emigrated from Russia to the United States when he was twelve. My mother was an émigré at an earlier age, with a high school education, and was the daughter of a fairly well-to-do small manufacturer of clothing who was a pillar of the local orthodox Jewish community. Both of my parents drifted away from orthodox Judaism during the course of their lives, however, and finally became active in a Reform synagogue in the suburbs.

As the fortunes of my father's shoe business improved, my parents bought a house in Brookline, then an upper-middle-class suburb of Boston. For me, at age ten, it was a move from a fairly homogeneous protective Jewish neighborhood to a place in which Boston "Yankee" norms, including its politely condescending version of anti-Semitism, were dominant. Perhaps because of the minority position I found myself in when I transferred to the sixth grade of an elementary school in Brookline, I came to feel rather detached from the conventional world. By the time I was in high school I felt little identification with either Yankee or Jewish institutions and questioned the authority and virtue of both. My aspiration was to avoid the conventional, both to refuse to "take over" my father's business and to refuse the other respectable options for children of the 1930s, which was to become a doctor or a lawyer. I wanted to be a poet. Only later did I discover that sociology, too, could sustain a position of critical detachment from conventional institutions.

In high school I did little work in my courses, read a great deal, and associated with the "wild" adolescents who drove automobiles too fast and drank too much. In consequence, I did rather badly academically, and was not able to graduate at the end of the normal period of four years. After a fifth year at a boarding school in Maine, I was graduated and entered the University of Maine. There, I continued to read widely and unselectively, to write plays, poems, and short stories, and to do little work in my courses. Finding little at Maine to be attractive save for a sympathetic English professor, and doing poorly except in English composition, I thought of transferring elsewhere, but my grades were poor. Hearing that the University of Chicago gave its own entrance examination without reference to high school or college grades, I took the examination and entered the College of the University of Chicago the following year. For six months I read more, wrote more plays, poems, and short stories, and then entered the Army.

In 1946, after three years in the army, half of that time overseas in Italy, I returned to the College of the University of Chicago, still without any definite aim or purpose except "to write." But I did have rather more concern with doing better at college than merely scraping by. I received little encouragement from instructors in the humanities, but a great deal from David Riesman, who was one of my social science teachers in the college at the time. Nonetheless, I did not become committed to social science in a positive sense at the time. The only conscious decision I made was a negative one, which was that I would not take graduate training in English or comparative literature. I was beginning to doubt my literary abilities, but I felt that if I could not write good literature, I did not want to spend my life writing about good literature. I wished to create, not analyze others' creations. And since the likelihood of my being able to create literature had come to seem slender, it seemed better to go into an entirely different field where I might be able to create something else—what turned out to be sociology.

EARLY SCHOLARLY CAREER

Exactly how I entered graduate study is entirely obscure in my memory. Part of the reason for entrance lay in the rejection of literature, part in the encouragement to work in social science which I received in the college, and part in the positive excitement I felt when I began to read the work of Robert Park. But I drifted into sociology; I did not choose it. Indeed, even while "in" sociology I remained somewhat outside of it: as a graduate student I did much work with Robert Redfield in anthropology, and with W. Lloyd Warner, who was in sociology, anthropology, and an interdisciplinary program in "human development."

As a graduate student in sociology at the University of Chicago, I

became involved in exploring the problem of understanding the
effect of mass communications on audiences, and the social character of language and symbolism. By the time I collected my data and
looked for a job, however, those topics were singularly without any
academic market value. The academic marketplace was in a very
depressed state and neither I nor many of my classmates had any
professorial prospects. When I received an offer of a year's job as
research assistant to a project on language and symbolism connected with the Department of Philosophy of the University of
Michigan, therefore, I leapt at it. My first wife—a graduate student
in medieval history—and I moved up to Ann Arbor for the year.
During that year I finished writing my dissertation, went down to
Chicago to defend it, received my degree *in absentia*, and set about
looking for a job for the next year.

Academic appointments continuing to be scarce, I took a two-
year postdoctoral research fellowship in the Department of Psychology at the University of Illinois in Urbana. Blessed by free
time, I devoted myself to writing articles from my dissertation and
doing exploratory work in language and symbolism. I studied
changes in the speech characteristics of patients undergoing
psychotherapy (with O. H. Mowrer), the grammatical characteristics of the speech of children and hospitalized schizophrenics,
and, finally, a study of the character of the social process leading
mothers up to the point of seeking help for their children at a psychological clinic. The last study, never written up, turned out to be
a very important proving-ground for the ideas I developed later in
my study of ambulatory patients in the Family Health Maintenance
Demonstration.

At the expiration of my postdoctoral fellowship in the summer of
1954 I was again without a job, so I moved up to Chicago in September to look for one. Several months later I got a one-year research job in Philadelphia to do a study of student government in
American colleges. I found the college an absorbing institution to
study, and attempted to find some way of gaining support for a
participant-observer study of a small college. Russell Sage Foundation indicated interest in supporting me to do such a study, and I
obtained official access to an appropriate college. At the last moment, however, in September 1955, access was withdrawn. This
left me without a project for which a foundation would support me,
and without a job again.

It was precisely this situation which led me fortuitously into
medical sociology. Knowing I had no job prospects at all in the fall,

a helpful staff member of the Russell Sage Foundation suggested that I might find something interesting to look at in an experimental program at Montefiore Hospital. A foundation-supported "Social Science Residency," designed to expose sociologists to professional fields like medicine, law, and social work, was open at Montefiore Hospital. It was a one-year appointment, paying a sum of money on which my family and I could live, though hardly luxuriously.

It might be well to mention at this point that while both my master's thesis and doctoral dissertation were on the topic of symbolism and mass communication, I did maintain a continuing interest in occupations. During the second year of my postdoctoral fellowship at the University of Illinois, my friend and colleague Howard S. Becker joined the program down there, and while he and James Carper did their interviews of students in biochemistry, physiology, and engineering, Becker and I were collaborating on a paper on occupations which, unfortunately, was never finished. I cannot recall the details of my interest at the time, but apparently I did have some latent interest in occupations even though I was concerned with studying other things. It was this latent interest which was stimulated by my visit to the Family Health Maintenance Demonstration at Montefiore Hospital.

FIRST WORK IN MEDICAL SOCIOLOGY

On the recommendation of the foundation officer, I visited Dr. George Silver at his office at Montefiore Hospital. I had read literature he had sent me about the composition and functioning of the professional teams of the Family Health Maintenance Demonstration, and I felt quite skeptical that services could be organized in quite the way they were described in print—namely, as a democratic team of psychiatric social workers, public health nurses, pediatricians, and internists, with a psychiatrist as a consultant. When I met Dr. Silver, I found him to be extremely enthusiastic and open, filled with interest in what sociologists were doing. And instead of being upset by my skepticism that the demonstration in fact worked the way it was described in the literature, he expressed enthusiasm for my finding out whether or not it did work that way. His very open, encouraging, and literate manner made me warm to him fairly quickly, and I decided that I would accept the residency in order to do a study of the professional teams of the demonstration.

After a month or so commuting between Philadelphia and New York, my family and I moved up to the Bronx so that I could be on the site fairly continuously and study the interaction of the various professional members of the treatment teams. However, I quickly found that while I could do such a study, I could never be entirely sure how much of the interaction among the team members was a matter of the individual characteristics of the persons involved, and how much a matter of their professional characteristics. Furthermore, I began to worry about how I could possibly report the results of my study without identifying the individuals involved, for some of my material would embarrass or even damage those described if they could be identified. Finally, I began to pay close attention to the fact that the members of the teams kept complaining about the degree to which patients were or were not very receptive to their roles as therapeutic agents. Slowly, it came to seem to me that much of the behavior of the members of the team was as much if not more a function of what patients expected and demanded of them than of their professional aims, and so it seemed necessary to examine the patients' views of the various professionals involved. To focus on the patients' views not only emphasized an underattended phenomenon in the literature, but also had the advantage of avoiding identification of individual professionals.

And so it was that by the winter of that year, 1956, I began an intensive interviewing program in which I drove around the Bronx virtually every evening of the week visiting the homes of various patients, and interviewing both husbands and wives about their response to the Family Health Maintenance Demonstration. Those interviews themselves opened up new areas of interest which widened the scope of the study even more. In attempting to explain their opinions, the patients kept referring to the difference between the demonstration and their previous experience with the personal physicians whom they had in childhood, or before they enrolled in the insurance plan of the medical group, and referred also to their experience in the medical group within which the demonstration was operating. Exposure to the patients' own ways of making sense of their experience with a special medical program led to the adoption of their own comparative view of various kinds of practice, and so allowed systematic exploration of their responses. It also led to a shift from the patients' views of the interprofessional teams, to the patients' views of the various modes of practice which they experienced.

The Russell Sage residency lasted for a period of only one year, like most of the positions I had up until then. Luckily, however, I obtained an academic job at the City College of New York by the spring of 1956 and began teaching in the fall. During that first year of teaching, when I was desperately trying to find time to prepare courses which I had never taught before, I also attempted to continue my study of the patients of the demonstration. It came to seem appropriate to add to the small survey I did at the time of my residency, a follow-up survey of the same panel a year later, and, finally, a baseline comparison survey of a sample of subscribers to HIP, of which Montefiore Medical Group was a member. Slowly, the data began to accumulate, and I began to find patterns emerging from it which seemed useful to report.

Initially reading much of the library of Dr. Silver, which included a great deal of historical material, and later exploring the library both of Montefiore Hospital and of the New York Academy of Medicine, I began to feel that my study, while limited empirically to a small number of people in a borough of New York City, nonetheless had relevance for more general issues of medical care. In part to gain access to the data of an extensive national survey, and to digest it as a test of and foil for my own parochial study, I took a partial leave of absence from my academic job in 1958 and worked part time at the Health Information Foundation. There, I had an opportunity to learn a good deal more about survey methodology than I knew before, and to test my Bronx data against national data. With Jacob Feldman, who directed the NORC survey itself, I wrote up selected segments of the data which were published by Health Information Foundation, and worked on other data, particularly a study of physicians, which were never published. Given the material I had access to, I felt more and more that the Bronx experience was relevant both to national policy and to generic issues in the study of such professionals as physicians and such clients as the patients in the Bronx.

THE DEVELOPMENT OF A SOCIOLOGY OF MEDICINE

Given the work that I had done on patients, work which was concerned with how patients conceived of professionals, and what implications those conceptions had for the work of those professionals, I became more and more interested in studying the professionals themselves. By 1960, when I had written "Specialties Without Roots" and "Client Control and Medical Practice," both of which, in somewhat more refined form, appeared as chapters of my

book *Patients' Views of Medical Practice* (1961), I became committed to studying physicians, and particularly to studying physicians
in the prepaid medical groups which were supposed to be the wave
of the future in American medical policy. I applied to the federal
government for support of a fairly substantial grant. After some negotiation with staff, I cut the request down to a modest proposal for
an exploratory study, and I received the grant.

On leave from my academic job again, I spent the next two years
doing a field study of one large medical group. In association with
my colleague, Buford Rhea, I became deeply involved in interviewing, eavesdropping, and all the other activities of field work. All
during that time I came to feel I was developing a fairly accurate
and intimate notion of what physicians were like as people, and
what their problems were in performing like physicians. After having formulated a national survey to follow up the field study, I accepted a position at New York University, and had to devote a great
deal of my time developing my new duties there, and withdraw
energy for analyzing and writing up the materials from that study
of group practice. Indeed, what with one thing or another, it has
taken me ten years to begin to do the qualitative material justice.

Another fortuitous event occurring in the early 1960s was the
signing of a contract to write a textbook in medical sociology. At
that time, there was only one textbook in existence—by Norman
Hawkins. I began to work on the textbook while developing a graduate course on medical sociology at New York University. Sustained by the earlier work I did for *Current Sociology*, on developing a review of the field up to 1961 and an annotated bibliography,
I could develop both the course and, initially, my plans for a
textbook. Consonant with the emphasis of the 1950s, my first
course emphasized epidemiology, psychosomatic medicine, and
stress. In addition, I used my own work, and that of others like
Koos, Feldman, Saunders, and Suchman, to build up concepts of
patient behavior, the seeking of medical care, and the utilization of
services.

Initially, given the fact that so little was to be found in the empirical literature, the course placed little emphasis on the materials
related to physicians and the organization of medical care. During
the early sixties, however, given my own study of physicians, my
preexistent interest in occupations and professions, and my steady
loss of interest in psychological variables, I became more and more
preoccupied with issues of social organization in general and the
nature of occupations and professions in particular. Consonant

with the emphasis on referral structures in my study of patients' views of professional services, I began to shift more and more to an emphasis on the way the services themselves channel the alternatives open to people, no matter what they may think and no matter how they might be psychologically motivated. It helped clarify my thinking to be commissioned to write a paper on the organization of medical practice for the *Handbook of Medical Sociology.*

By the middle of the 1960s, I had come to devote virtually all of my attention to learning all that I could from published material, historical and otherwise, about the organization of health services, and in particular the organization of medical services. By then, I was teaching one course on the sociology of illness, and a separate one on the sociology of medicine, with less and less interest in continuing to teach a course in the sociology of illness as such. It was, again, a wholly fortuitous event which led to a renewal of my interest in illness.

By that time the work of Howard S. Becker had become very well known in American sociology. The main thrust of his book *Outsiders* was to assert that people believed to be criminals or otherwise deviant were believed to be so not because of what they have done, or because of what they are, but rather because of the existence of rules or norms which define what they have done or what they are as deviant. In this sense, Becker points to the fact that human behavior assumes meaning by virtue of human interaction and human symbolism, and has no a priori meaning in and of itself. Why could this not also be so of illness, I reasoned?

This question arose in my mind due to the fact that I was invited to attend a conference on disability—the invitation having as much to do with the people I knew who were involved in the project as anything else, since I had never at any time paid any attention to disability or physical handicaps. I accepted the invitation to prepare a paper in order to gain an excuse to read and gain some command over the literature on deviance in other areas in sociology—juvenile delinquency, mental illness, and the like. It was from the review of that literature that I wrote a paper which led me to be quite interested in illness all over again, but from a different point of view—that is to say, conceiving of illness as a social meaning created by professionals who assume an official position in society itself. It allowed me to break away from medical conceptions of illness and to develop a specifically sociological conception.

Bringing that paper together with Parson's famous analysis of the sick role soon led me to a reformulation of Parsons, as well as to a more elaborate use of some of Parsons's own theoretical variables in defining various types of illness. Thus formulation was consciously made while avoiding the assumption that there was anything necessarily real to illness which stood apart from social activity. It allowed me to be liberated from any reliance upon medicine as authoritative guide to the ultimate character of illness. Medicine became simply the profession which was accepted as the authority about illness in a given society. Thus, it became possible to compare illness all over the world, and the human behaviors surrounding the imputation of illness, without being concerned with what was "true" or not. And the authority of modern medicine could be relativized.

At that point in my thinking, it became clear that what began as a textbook had become something quite different. Rooted almost entirely within sociology through the concepts of profession and deviance, what had emerged could no longer be considered a review of the field as a majority of practitioners view it. It became a theoretical work, and it became almost impossible to keep it within the limits of what might responsibly be called a textbook. By 1967, when the largest part of the book was in first or second draft, I had to face the fact that I had not written a textbook, and began revising accordingly. However, traces of the "review of the literature" still remain in the book, which was published in 1970 with the title *Profession of Medicine*.

At the same time, I began to become more and more clear about the connection of the "labeling" theory of deviance to the old established field of the sociology of knowledge. While I was not unaware of the connection, by the time Berger and Luckman's book on the sociology of knowledge appeared, I began looking at illness as a particular meaning ascribed by a physician and at health as a kind of ideology asserted by an organized profession, looking at both as problems in the sociology of knowledge. Similarly, I began to use Mannheim's idea of "mentality" as a way of beginning to grapple with the essential normative elements involved in the way physicians behave. Also, given the work of Scheff and others, I could address the question of why physicians' concepts of disease are as they are. The latter question, of course, had been raised many times by historians concerned with the fact that quite selective attention is given to human illness in various periods of history.

And so it was that in the final revision of the erstwhile textbook, faultily at times, and with obvious seams and awkwardness at various points, I attempted to produce a book which treated medicine as an occupation with special characteristics, including a special location in the social structure, a special self-justifying ideology as well as evangelistic view of health, and an unusual amount of autonomy. The human as well as the analytical problem lay in the extent to which the claims of the profession (through its ideology) were in fact being realized. These issues required analysis of the character of the profession's "knowledge" as well as of its self-regulating mechanisms. By adopting the approach of the sociology of knowledge, I could reject the use of the criteria ordinarily used by sociologists in addressing the professions. From the point of view of the sociology of knowledge, both the knowledge and the ethicality of the profession became ideologies which were problematic and which had to be evaluated by the sociologist as one who stands outside the system. In this sense, I deliberately chose the stance of the outsider rather than the stance of the collaborator. It is also a stance compatible with my biography.

Developing slowly at the same time was yet another idea. This idea stemmed from my study of and thinking about the role of the social worker and public health nurse in the original Family Health Maintenance Demonstration team. I was skeptical that those teams were in fact democratic. I produced evidence that the patients themselves virtually forced subordination upon some of the workers and superordination on others. I also knew that the physicians had the prerogatives which neither nurse nor social worker could possibly claim, and that those prerogatives had priority in the case of patients. These distinctions became useful in attempting to deal with, though hardly settle, the definitional question of professions, and by the same token suggested that one need not look at occupations in isolation, that in fact one must look at occupations in their structured relations to each other.

On this foundation did the idea of the social organization of the division of labor begin to develop during the latter half of the 1960s, allowing me to visualize the possibility of tracing much of the orderliness of work in the field of health by reference to the stable and legally defined relationships of occupations to each other. These relationships could be conceived of not merely as a matter of differentiation of function or task, but also as a matter of *authority*, specifically the authority of expertise. This principle of authority could be seen as wholly different from the authority of office, and in fact an alternative source of organization and coordination in human activities. While reality is hardly simple, merely to develop this logical alternative would allow, to my mind, a fresh view. Health institutions have been dominated too long by what I believe has become a rather stale way of thinking about them, largely in administrative and bureaucratic terms. If we are to have flexible and creative services in the future, it seems to me that we must try new ways of thinking.

"RESISTANCE" TO "INNOVATION"

At the time I entered medical sociology in the 1950s, the major works which the neophyte was urged to read were the pioneering book by Simons and Wolff, *Social Science and Medicine*, which emphasized the psychosomatic (nonbiological) element in illness and thereby indicated the importance of social variables in illness; the excellent collection of papers on cultural change edited by Benjamin D. Paul, which emphasized the importance of cultural difference in patients' orientations toward modern medicine; the classic work of Koos, *Health of Regionville*, which again emphasized differences between the attitudes of patients of varied social class levels in a rural community, and those expected by modern medical men; and the still useful work on Mexican Americans by Lyle Saunders. It was of course no accident that most of these books were published by Russell Sage Foundation, which pioneered in supporting and publicizing the work of social scientists in medicine. If one can characterize all of these works together without too great distortion and bias, however, I think one can say with reasonable accuracy that neither the idea of social structure nor the idea of formal, administrative organization was very prominent. Preoccupation was largely with the fact that patients had characteristics which led them to constitute problems of management to modern physicians. The strategy was to show physicians that social science could help them to better understand and manage their patients.

In my response to these orientations, I was probably influenced most strongly by my training with Robert Redfield, who, along with other colleagues in anthropology at the University of Chicago, was more preoccupied with issues of social structure than American anthropologists elsewhere, who emphasized culture. The images used by Redfield in his own work, particularly in his examination of peasant society, combined emphasis on differences in culture with stress on differences in location in the social structure. This stress on the importance of differential location in a social structure was not merely one on location as such, but also on the extent to which location provides access to a particular kind of "knowledge" or "culture." As such, it was rather different in its implications than the orientation which stressed cultural differences alone. It implied that change was not so easily accomplished and in fact that inherent conflict exists between the client and the professional. It suggested that the perfectly sincere interests of medicine and medical personnel are not synonymous with the interests of humanity, except insofar as one accepts medicine as the arbiter of the interests of humanity.

This orientation justified my standing outside of medicine in my work, rather than collaborating with medicine in the task which it had defined for itself. Furthermore, it encouraged me to evaluate medicine by criteria which stand above it. Indeed, I could not help but see myself as a sociologist first, and someone interested in medicine as an object of study second. While opportunities to work in medical settings on a full-time basis did arise during my career, there was never any question in my mind about wanting to stay in a department of sociology and to avoid, even at serious financial handicap, working on a full-time basis in a medical school, hospital, or whatever. Indeed, I have never been employed by a medical institution. The studies I did of patients and group practice were, first, as a fellow of a foundation, and later as someone with a tenured academic appointment who has gone on a leave of absence to do a study in a medical setting.

One's relation to the setting he wishes to study is an important issue for the kind of work one can do. On one occasion, a powerful—but to me personally a quite generous, open, and encouraging—medical man offered me complete freedom to work as I would in his institution if I were to take a post there. He did so in complete good faith, and so he was upset by my refusal and by my assertion that I could not have complete freedom. "What," I asked, "if I decided to study lawyers, or priests, and what if I attended history but not public health association meetings?" My interest has always been in sociological concepts which I wanted to be free to follow as their pursuit led me. Sociological concepts, like others, abstract reality in such a way that when they are applied to a concrete field like medicine, the concrete field loses its uniqueness and its intellectual authority.

To study medicine sociologically is to be drawn to study it comparatively, exploring the ramifications of its membership in a more general class defined by a concept. By the nature of the case, as Everett Hughes has argued, to study medicine in such a fashion requires the study of other occupations. And it requires concern with other sociological concepts. My presence in a sociology department gave me access to colleagues working in a variety of areas—deviance, methodology, general theory, the sociology of knowledge, and the like—which could stimulate me to think in abstract ways about medicine. Colleagues who have no particular interest in medicine as such are extremely valuable resources for reinforcing and expanding one's interest in sociological concepts and one's continued concern with treating medicine as a sociological object rather than something in and of itself. Furthermore, teaching general sociology and being *continuously* in contact with students (as is surely not the case for someone who comes in to teach "a course") also reinforces and nurtures the approach. In such a setting, the questions raised are not only substantively different than would be the case for questions raised within medical settings, but also, because they are abstract, they are critically detached from medicine itself.

I think it would take an extraordinary person to be able to work full time in a medical setting and at the same time define his problems sociologically rather than medically. He would also have to be rather amoral, since he would have to resist the moral obligation to be of some help to those around him, help which they define by their own practical capacities and needs. It is easy to see how in such a setting one's energies would be constantly drained by having to answer these legitimate requests for help. Only an inhuman or amoral person could refuse them in order to be able to concentrate on work which is *not* defined by the setting.

There is still another price one seems to have to pay by working in medical settings, and this is the cost of treating that peculiar social disease pandemic among those in professional schools of health-related personnel—"conferencitis." I gather that about one-third of one's working time is spent in a state of relapse attending conferences. Conferences are of great value and I do not mean to deprecate them in reasonable dosage. Whatever else they do, they communicate the usefulness of particular ideas and programs and develop a sense of community among their participants. In this they are far more effective than printed materials, if only because most of the people who attend those conferences do so at the expense of so much time that I rather doubt they have any time left to read! Everyone has the problem of deciding how much time to devote to one activity rather than another. My own choice, probably for reasons related to my own character and not principle, was to attend rather few meetings, and to devote myself primarily to teaching, reading, thinking, and writing. I do not think such a choice could be made easily were I to work in a medical setting where conferencing is greatly valued.

That the ideas and orientations I developed in the course of my work in the sociology of medicine are innovations is a matter of evaluation and judgment. I should rather speak of them as products, products in which words and ideas are embedded, the ideas and perhaps phrases conceivably being innovations in the eyes of the readers. That any of the ideas are genuinely new, in the sense of never having been used before, is highly unlikely. Perhaps even more than the ideas can we speak of the words and phrases being new and in that sense innovative.

I strongly suspect that what is most important to innovation in most disciplines is one's writing ability, including the stylistic capacity to express ideas with catchy phrases that stick in peoples' minds. As catchy phrases they can be used almost as slogans, tokens passed from conversation to conversation and into the written literature, acknowledged by a footnote reference to the author. Eventually, the most successful of such catch-phrases become absorbed into the professional and even the lay language without the necessity of citing, or even remembering the original source of the phrase. No one bothers to footnote the word charisma any more, or to refer to Weber. This is a sign of his success—the fact that his phrases have passed into the language while he himself may be forgotten as the author of it.

This may seem to be a digression in that I was speaking of the question of innovation, and addressing the editors' interest in resistance to innovation. It is not a digression, however, because I want to make the point that insofar as one produces ideas and words alone, particularly of an abstract sort, it is very difficult to tell whether one can legitimately speak of resistance without at the same time claiming that the innovative value of the ideas or words is so great that a problem could be seen in the failure of people to adopt them. The innovation may in fact be rather indifferent, in which case to speak of resistance is rather foolish. All I can do in this context is to write of the circumstances surrounding the development of my own work, and to indicate which of the circumstances seemed to help me and which might have made it rather more difficult for me to produce my writing. The acceptance of the writing by others is a different matter which I find myself obliged to avoid evaluating. While it is difficult to speak of resistance to innovation as such, then, it is quite possible to speak of the way different kinds of ideas and orientations are antithetical to and incompatible with others.

I think it is possible to delineate two orientations common in medicine which tend to be antipathic to the orientation I have developed in my work. One is the kind of orientation implied by what I have written about "the clinical mentality." That mentality is carried by men who, like physicians, are deeply involved in the practical issues of day-to-day consultative work. By the nature of the case, these men must rely on their individual judgment on the spur-of-the-moment, without being able to wait for a careful and complete evaluation of whatever facts may be available in some library, and they must rely on their subjective evaluation of the situation in which they must make decisions. This kind of mentality exists quite independently of any prior scientific training. It is grounded essentially in the necessity of undertaking practical action, a necessity which is made psychologically bearable by perceiving actions to be successful not by virtue of mere chance but rather by virtue of special insight, knowledge, skill, and judgment. Success is due directly to deliberate action, while failure, when it is actually perceived as failure, is due to chance, anomalous conditions, and the like.

People with this particular mentality are suspicious of all that lies outside the purview of their own first-hand experience. They suspect both abstractions and generalizations (a generalization, of course, being an abstraction). They scorn statistics. They rely primarily upon their own subjective sense of the world, and their own personal experience with the world, conceding rather little authority to ideas in general and abstract ideas in particular. Ultimately, their final arbiter is themselves and their own view of the world; this they are inclined to consider "wisdom." Neither systematically collected data which surpass personal experience, nor the force of logic which stands independent of experience, has very much strength in influencing such people, and so they are inclined to deny the authority of ideas based upon scholarly and discursive activity. Given their commitment to their own experience, and their conception of themselves as active, independent individuals, they are likely to resist the idea of social structure and to think in terms of such variables as native intelligence, will-power, individual personality, and the like.

Another kind of mentality might be called "the administrative mentality," which is common among high-level executives and policymakers with an interest in planning. These people typically assume that there is a structure which constrains human behavior, but they are inclined to believe that this structure is something that can be created and sustained independently of the participants—a formal administrative structure. They are prone to assume that if they plan a model system and enact it into law, or organize a given enterprise, the system will work the way they intended because the people they order will fit themselves into the requirements of the administrative system itself. In a rough kind of way, enough occurs according to their expectations that they cannot feel that their orientation is false. The many failures of such formal planned systems and their degeneration into what very often becomes a scandal in a few years does not dissuade people with such an orientation from thinking in their rational, administrative manner. In the case of failure they find blame not in the system, but in the people who carry it out—as if a system could be viable without people! They do not adapt system designs to people so much as expect people to adapt to the design, and when they do not they blame the people rather than the administrative design. So they, too, like everyone else, sociologists included, have a way of discounting failure and maintaining their commitment to their special way of thinking about and acting toward the world.

I suppose I could discuss other kinds of orientations, but these seem to be the ones which are most important in the health services. Because my own orientation is rather different, I should expect resistance from those with the other orientations. My own orientation uses the idea of social organization as a way of referring to the fact that there is a world of other people around the individual, and that those other people's reactions have a great deal to do with what the individual is himself able to do. This tends to violate the assumptions of the clinical mentality. But, contrary to the administrative mentality, neither the individual nor those around him are mere passive creatures of social structure. Rather, all are engaged in continuously working-out their activities and relationships. One does not merely set up a collection of positions on a hierarchy and assume that the individuals will fill them in the expected way, and with the same assumptions and interests as those who created them in the first place. In this sense, while one may speak of social organization as a conceptual device which helps one analyze human affairs on a given level of generality, one would be hopelessly naive to assume that it is a faithful reflection, rather than a convenient abstraction, of human activity as such. Indeed, in the planning of a system of, for example, the delivery of health services, to do so without accounting for the clinical mentalities of the practical participants is to invite catastrophe and failure. These peoples' way of seeing their lives must be taken into account in designing the structures which can be imposed on them, or the structures will fail. Social organization is, in this orientation, a useful abstraction, but an abstraction which does not represent all of what goes on which is significant. Social organization both creates and is being continuously created by its participants; it is not something which some legislation or set of administrative directives can create on anything other than paper—surely not on human beings.

It should be clear from these characterizations that I believe that the characteristic orientations of medical practitioners and policy-makers are antithetical to the approach that I adopt, each antithetical for different reasons. In this sense, I suspect that my work might be considered "interesting" by some subscribers to such orientations, but I suspect also that very few could seriously consider it as an important way of approaching or evaluating his own activities. This suspicion, of course, is the self-congratulatory paranoia of any author, and may be discounted by the reader.

A FUTURE TO MEDICAL SOCIOLOGY?

Finally, I may say a few things about the present state of medical sociology as a field. Assuming that medical sociology should not be considered a collection of people who happen to be interested in vaguely "social" elements of health, but rather a particular discipline rooted in sociology, it seems to me that medical sociology as a field is in decline, and may even vanish. I believe this is a possibility because the trend seems to be for less and less medical sociology to be undertaken in academic departments of sociology, and more and more in professional schools. Indeed, there seems to have been a deliberate policy on the part of the United States government to increase its support of training programs for the application of social science to health affairs in professional schools, and to reduce or even eliminate support for training programs in academic departments.

Some of the rationale underlying this policy seems to be purely a matter of official manpower statistics; it is said, rightly or wrongly, that academic Ph.D.'s will soon be in greater number than demand justifies. The Ph.D. is more often given in an academic department than in a professional school. Second, the thrust of policy is to produce more practitioners in the field of health. Given that intention, the reasoning behind training-program support on the part of the federal government is that to support a graduate student in sociology to study medical sociology and to take a Ph.D. degree is to support someone who may not join the ranks of the health practitioners which policy is aimed to increase. But on the other hand, people trained in "medical sociology" in a professional school, and who obtain a professional degree, have no other choice but to stay in the field and increase the total sum of "health manpower."

From the point of view of increasing the number of people who can be counted in censuses of health manpower, this apparent policy is of course sensible. But if the concern is with developing special kinds of knowledge, including that kind which is comparatively abstract, and perhaps, therefore, a better source of projecting future trends than the mere passive reflection of what happened the day before yesterday, then it would seem that such a policy is designed to reduce the amount of "innovation" in ideas, and of scholarly research in the area. It may very well be that all we need are bodies and not ideas or scholarship, but it is important for me as a scholar not to believe this.

Serendipity: An Autobiographical Account of the Career of a Medical Sociologist in Britain

MARGOT JEFFERYS

I contribute to this volume with a good deal of ambivalence. Since I started professional life as a would-be social historian I should welcome—as indeed I do—the opportunity to put on record my interpretation of the factors which influenced the early development in Britain of sociology applied to medicine. As a participant in that development my interpretation of it does at least have a phenomenological value bound to be welcome in some quarter or other of the sociological field, even if it is refuted by some for its philosophical naiveté. And again, since the invitation to contribute suggested that I try to examine the process by which I personally became associated with this field of inquiry, I was provided with a license to undertake what in prospect seemed a desirable cathartic experience of self-analysis—an experience in which until now I have not indulged.

Having once accepted the invitation, however, the exercise has given me more pain than pleasure. I have a poor memory for events, for people, and for books: I live very much in the present and have simply forgotten far too much of the past to be a reliable reporter. Moreover, documents which might have acted as aide-memoires have been jettisoned in successive house moves. It has therefore been more of an effort to recall events and significant encounters than I had contemplated. Furthermore, the present has intruded in another way into my efforts to make sense of the past and to trace changes which led to the growth of my and other sociologists' interest in medicine as a field for sociological study. Current commitments to colleagues, to students, to research sponsors, and to family and friends have not only taken precedence over autobiography; they have also dictated that the time I have had to

chase a reference or follow up the vague recollection has been severely limited. Time has had to be snatched for writing in half-
hours or hours rather than in full days.

I assume that in describing this situation I am also not only portraying my own problems but those of my fellow contributors to
this volume and most social science professors today. Hence I
apologize for my craven attempt to curry favor and indulgence
from readers. I hope they will not judge me as harshly as I judge
myself for this floundering attempt to make sense of my own career
and of the field in which it has taken place.

While my main concern in this essay is to account for the way in
which medical sociology developed in Britain during the 1950s
and 1960s, I think readers elsewhere and, indeed, social scientists
born since the end of the Second World War in Britain may find it
easier to understand that development if they are aware of the intellectual climate in Britain in the interwar years, the decades when I
was growing up and at university. Indeed, they may find it interesting to know something about the social setting in which I was
reared, for although that experience was not all that common even
then, it certainly has no real counterpart today. So I start the exercise by painting a picture of the antecedent factors which I think
influenced my entry into the sociology of medicine. I begin with
my childhood in the years between the two world wars and the
ways in which it helped to form my earliest assumptions about the
nature of the social world. I then describe what being a student at
the London School of Economics in the years just before the Second World War meant for me and the effect the war and its aftermath had on the development of applied sociology and on the careers of social scientists, including my own. Finally, I describe how
.medical sociology, from a slow and shaky start in the 1950s expanded in the 1960s and 1970s. Interwoven with this historical
sketch is the story of my own career and how it was influenced by
my marriage and predilection for tackling problems with an eclectic empiricism.

EARLY INFLUENCES

I was born into the English professional middle class in the middle of World War I, but my family was somewhat shielded from
that experience since my father worked in India. The great subcon-
tinent was then part of the British Empire.[1] My father was principal
of the Law College in Madras. Although part of the alien adminis-

tration of the British raj, he, like some other expatriate civil servants, was an advocate of Indian independence. He admired Ghandi and felt that the British government was hypocritical in its assertion that it was working towards such independence while making the excuse that the time was not yet ripe for the British to withdraw. In other words, he was a liberal who, in his personal conduct as well as his political stances, tried to overcome the snobbish segregationist behavior of the British raj. My mother, although loyal and proud of him in most respects, found his unconventional, nonconformist views a trifle uncomfortable. She had too developed a sense of propriety to be quite comfortable with someone so willing to defy the public opinion of her class. Nevertheless she battled bravely to overcome the prejudice she had acquired in her childhood, prejudices against Indians, Jews, working-class people and even against those who made money in commerce. At the end of her life she called herself a Christian Socialist and deplored her lack of courage in defending her views when confronted with those of most of her middle-class relatives and friends.

It was customary in the 1920s for English children whose parents worked in tropical countries to be sent back to Britain when they were ready to start full-time schooling. The tropics, I can vaguely remember, were thought to be unsuitable for whites but suitable for those with dark skins. Moreover, even if this had not been so, most reasonably well-to-do middle class parents assumed that their sons should have a boarding school education, paradoxically called public schooling since nothing could be more private. In keeping with the times, parents were not so insistent on an equivalent education for their daughters; most questioned the desirability of sending girls off to boarding schools at least at the tender age of eight, even if they thought it right to do so later.

My older brother and sister were taken to England by my mother when I was four, and I and a younger sister were left in the charge of my father and a governess, and when I was five, accompanied by our governess, we rejoined them in England. In my youth, the governess took over from the less-educated nanny (or mother's substitute) the formal education of those for whom no suitable academy for young ladies was available. As an occupational category the governess has, I believe, almost wholly disappeared. There were only a few of her species left in 1971 according to the census of that year for England and Wales. In the Britain of the 1920s she was most likely to be an impecunious spinster doomed to failure in the marriage stakes since there were over a million more women than men in the age bracket fifteen to forty-four. As the sex ratio swung towards unity due to changing mortality and migration patterns so has the sea of unmarried women receded; that change, along with others hastened by World War II, has also reduced to a tiny fraction the numbers of individuals once employed or retained directly by middle- and upper-class families to undertake their domestic and child-rearing duties and care for their elderly dependents.

I can remember very little of my life up to this point and, not having had the time, money and, more important, the inclination to reconstruct the past and bring it to the level of present consciousness, I am not sure whether I then bore or now bear the traces of maternal separation or deprivation. If I felt mad with my parents for their various repeated desertions I have forgotten it. It is for others, less involved than I, to posit a causal sequential relationship between the kind of life enjoyed or endured by the children of British middle-class expatriates who were lords in one country and quite ordinary professional folk in their own, and their sociopolitical ideologies or career patterns. It is likely, however, that the particular form of maternal and paternal deprivation which we underwent was not as disadvantaging to us as others have been to less affluent children. After all it was a deliberate choice undertaken in favorable economic circumstances by our conscientious parents, not the outcome of poverty, ill health, physical violence or marital discord.

My first recollection of anything approaching a sociological thought occurred when I was about nine years old—at the time of the 1926 General Strike in Britain. Nearly all organized labor came out in support of the miners who had been locked out by their employers in a war of attrition aimed to starve them into submission. Most of my school fellows in the middle class semisuburb of London where we lived took their cue from their well-to-do parents and condemned the strikers.[2] Although the latter were woefully ill-prepared for the struggle and decisive sections of them only too easily persuaded to retreat from a confrontation with the power of the state, they were seen by most of the comfortably-off men and women in my neighborhood as devils incarnate, probably led from Moscow. My parents, on the other hand, supported the strikers and taught me that there was nothing sacrosanct about a social structure which resulted in a high level of malnutrition, low income, and unemployment for at least a third of the population.

As the economic crisis developed—the Wall Street crash in 1929 precipitating a series of panic moves in this country which greatly increased unemployment and poverty—so did the politicalization of many of my middle class contemporaries. The world was manifestly less secure, less programmed for inevitable progress than children had been led by their parents to expect. Moreover, the war to end all wars had manifestly not succeeded in doing that. In the 1930s, the world picture was one of high unemployment, of victory for fascism in Italy, Germany, Japan, and Spain, and of escalation towards a second global war.

It was in this atmosphere that I returned in 1935 from a year spent living with a Swiss family, much more politically aware than I had been, and anxious to switch from my intended course in physical education to one which would better equip me to understand the world forces which seemed to be shaping my future and that of my contemporaries. Incidentally, a year in Europe, learning a foreign language, was almost mandatory for upper-middle-class girls at the time. Professional parents sent their daughters to comparable families in France, Germany, or Switzerland; more aristocratic girls, those destined to be presented at Court—the debutantes—were likely to end up in fashionable finishing schools rather than in families.

ALMA MATER

The London School of Economics where I was a student from 1935 until the outbreak of war in 1939 had a reputation for political radicalism which was only partly deserved. There were, it is true, few representatives among staff and students of the far right in politics, such as you might find in most universities; but the majority of the economists were not socialists. At the risk of oversimplifying their position, it seems true to say that insofar as they were concerned with political economy and not with narrower market analyses they were proponents of conservative policies. The prevailing orthodoxy of London School economists suggested that government should seek its way out of depression by increasing the profitability of private enterprise, which entailed a reduction in taxation and government controls. There was resistance to the Keynesian thesis expressed in the *General Theory of Employment* when it appeared in 1936, which postulated an expansionist government policy to reinflate the economy.[3]

At the other end of the political spectrum among the staff of the school was Harold Laski, probably the best known figure outside the school and largely responsible for its radical reputation.[4] He was on the left-wing of the Labour Party of which he was an active member, and his analysis of the ways in which the organs of the state were devised to support existing class interests were manna to the rapt audiences of students who attended his weekly lectures on British government—lectures he delivered without notes or hesitation, heavily loaded with irony.

The sociologists at the school with a reputation—Morris Ginsberg, T. H. Marshall and Karl Mannheim—were not, as far as I know, actively involved in political argument at either college or national level. Indeed, they and the small group of students they taught were much less likely to be identified with the radical left than were the political scientists and historians. However, I did no more at that time than attend one or two of their lectures and give myself a nodding acquaintance with the theoretical propositions of the founding fathers through my interest in nineteenth century economic and social history. I am not, therefore, a good witness of their influence on the intellectual and political pursuits of the students they taught.

After a preliminary year in which I was introduced to the elements of economic theory, political science, economic and social history, and research method, I decided to specialize in modern economic history. The economic historians were, in the main, democratic socialists and eclectic in their approach to their subject matter. With hindsight, I see Eileen Power as a meticulous chronicler, trying to reconstruct what she thought important about the economic life of medieval society and avoiding argument about the catalysts of societal changes. R. H. Tawney also eschewed grand theory;[5] but his ideas, particularly those expressed in *Religion and the Rise of Capitalism*, were sufficiently close to a Marxist interpretation of the historical relationship between ideology and the material self-interest of particular social classes to win grudging approval for his historical work from left-wing students of which I was by then one. His weakness in our eyes was his refusal to see contemporary Soviet Communism as a welcome stage in the inevitable progress towards the abolition of all classes.

The most stimulating member of the History Department to the radicals within it at the time was undoubtedly H. L. Beales.[6] He is difficult to label now as then, and there is little in the way of published work to guide us in a final appraisal of his role. There is no doubt, however, that he put many hundreds of undergraduate and postgraduate students everlastingly in his debt by spending countless hours provoking them into thinking for themselves, inviting them to check their grand theories with detailed empirical studies

and insisting that they look critically at all secondary sources and
at the conventional wisdom of the pundits. We were constantly encouraged to go back to original documents and other forms of evidence before reaching conclusions.

I suppose it is common for middle-aged academics to look back
upon their student years with nostalgia; certainly when I now meet
those who shared my experience then we tend to view the period
as a halcyon one despite the constant exposure to poverty and distress at home and unrestrained fascist advance abroad. Clearly we
were sustained by our certainty that we knew what the right solutions were at national and international level. We were not sceptical; we were committed and optimistic. We thought that, even if
fascism was temporarily ascendant, socialism had proved itself to
be a viable form of political economy. It only required world peace
in our view to shed its obvious but excusable brutalities as manifested in the Soviet Union.

For most of those on the left, political activity and academic
work did not conflict with each other for our time and allegiance. I
felt I was using Marx's dialectical materialism both to interpret the
social and economic history of the nineteenth century and to explain the contemporary crisis. The politically active did not drop or
flunk out. It was a matter of pride with us that we were the most
assiduous workers, the most vocal in seminars, and the most likely
to do well in the examinations.

It is difficult to estimate the lasting effect of my four heady years
at the London School of Economics, but there are several ways in
which my experience there seems to have influenced the way I still
think and work. For example, I am sure that I have been influenced
by the fact that I took a degree in the social sciences rather than
sociology and that I joined a department committed to a developmental approach to society rather than to the exegesis of the contributions made by different schools of sociological thought to an
understanding of contemporary social structures. I am still more
likely to view a contemporary health service as the outcome of a
long development shaped by many different factors rather than as a
system of social transactions in which the individual actors negotiate the resulting order. In short my academic lens is a wide-angle
rather than a telescopic one zooming in on the details of the transactions.

My tendency to adopt a macroscopic rather than a microscopic
perspective was probably further reinforced by the absence of any
introduction to social psychology. I certainly do not undervalue the

work of those who have chosen to use sociological concepts such as power, authority, control, labeling, and stigma to explain the nature of relationships and behavior in small groups such as the family or in face-to-face dyadic situations such as the doctor-patient consultation. However, I still cannot help feeling that their concerns are of less moment than are those of sociologists who work on a broader canvas and borrow unashamedly from many disciplines in their attempts to explain social change.

THE WAR, ITS AFTERMATH, AND MY DOMESTIC LIFE

The outbreak of war in September 1939 put a stop to my postgraduate studies. After a brief period as organizer for the left-wing University Labour Federation, I married and joined my husband in Coventry, the centre of the British aircraft and motor car industries and consequently a target for German bombers. I spent most of the war years there working in a factory as a lathe operator during the day and teaching labor history or current affairs to Workers' Education Association groups comprised of miners and engineers in the evening.

I found the factory work extremely dull. I wanted as much variety as possible in a routinized job and so took on work assignments which lasted for a day or so rather than a month or more, a course which cost me quite a bit in piecework earnings. I chose to work at the bench instead of in the personnel department of a factory or other administrative job on ideological grounds. I wanted to share the experience of the "ordinary worker" rather than accept a position of authority. On the other hand, outside working hours, I accepted the role of teacher and enjoyed my evening classes and the challenge of interesting and informing workers who had had little in the way of formal education about the history of their trade unions or about issues underlying such blueprints for the future as the Beveridge plan for a comprehensive social security system.

Early in 1944 my husband, who had also worked as a factory hand while awaiting a call-up which never came, was summoned to the Ministry of Aircraft Production in London to assist in writing its history. I was pregnant at the time and went to live with my sister and her year-old son in a primitive cottage some thirty miles from London. We had to fetch all our water from a well at least a hundred yards from the cottage, excrete and urinate in a chemical pail in a hut in the garden, and bury the results in a trench in nearby woods. We cooked on a wood fire or spirit stove and burned kerosene lamps at night. My first son was born two days before D-day, the opening of the second front in Europe. When the guided missiles—fondly called doodle bugs—had almost ceased to fall on London I returned to the city, but beat a hasty retreat when the long range rockets began to fall, and I was back in the primitive cottage with my infant son and pregnant with another when the war in Europe ended. Apart from baby-minding, I kept myself intellectually alive by acting as unpaid research assistant and editor to my husband who, in his spare time, was writing a history of the major British Engineering Union.[7]

I suppose the encouragement given to women to work during the war and the provision of facilities for them to do so, however young their children, reinforced my unquestioning assumption that I would work as well as rear my family. I anticipated that interruptions would be short and that there would be little difficulty in the new liberalized climate of opinion in making suitable communal arrangements for the day care of my children. No one in the immediate aftermath of the war was telling me that I would be irresponsible to leave my children in the care of others, that my duty and my salvation lay in fulfilling merely the role of mother and housewife. Moreover, graduates, especially those in the social sciences, were in great demand in the expanding civil service, and I was not made to feel guilty when I took a full-time job in research in the Chief Scientific Adviser's Division of the Ministry of Works, then responsible for housing development.[8] My youngest son was then eighteen months old. I was lucky enough when my children were young both to share accommodation with others at a similar stage of the life cycle and to find a domestic helper who continued to work for me until my younger son left school at seventeen. Clearly she contributed a great deal to my capacity to emulate on relatively equal terms the work habits of my male colleagues.

It was only after I was relatively well established in work and confident that I could cope with it that mothers in Britain began to be subjected to considerable social pressures to stay in the home. Day nurseries were closed and the few available places given only to the children of mothers whose income was the family's sole support. John Bowlby, the Freudian psychiatrist had a book published in 1952, *Maternal Care and Mental Health* which was widely used to imply that the mother who worked was effectively deserting her children and depriving them of maternal love. The consequences, we gathered, were the likelihood that her children would become as delinquent or psychopathic as the institutionalized children Bowlby had studied. At the same time, the press, the radio, and television seemed to make a concerted attempt to persuade women that they could find their major satisfactions in life in serving their men as glamorised sexual objects and assistants in the rat race to keep up with the Joneses.[9]

Many of my contemporaries were affected by these pervasive admonishments, by the prejudices they encountered at work, or by the very real difficulties they found in making satisfactory arrangements for their children while they worked. It was an awareness of the difficulties faced by many of them which made me undertake a mailed inquiry into the domestic situation of the few married women who had reached the higher ranks of the civil service.[10]

In my civil service job I had the task of analyzing the structure of the building and building materials industries and estimating their capacity to deliver the goods in short supply. I worked largely from information collected and returned routinely or from time to time by business firms; but some inquiries involved visiting firms and interviewing representatives of both workers and management and I began to acquire some idea of the problems involved in social survey work. All the same, I was minimally qualified in social survey research techniques when I became a research fellow in 1950 at Bedford College, one of the constituent institutions of the University of London, charged with the responsibility of conducting a survey into labor mobility.[11] I not only had to learn how to collect and analyze data, but to teach others how to do it as well. Fortunately, there were relatively few people in Britain with the expertise and experience to criticize me destructively and I was able to make many mistakes without being crucified for them. I was lucky enough during this time to be a member of the Sociology Department then headed by Barbara Wootton. Iconoclastic, clear-headed, and coldly witty she has had less influence on British social policy and less of a reputation on the other side of the Atlantic than Richard Titmuss who was ten years or so her junior but who predeceased her.[12] In my opinion, however, she was a more brilliant social analyst than he. Several of her books and particularly the The Social Foundations of Wage Policy (1954) and Social Science and Social Pathology (1959) broke new ground in the analysis of social policies and deserve to survive.[13]

One of the teaching assignments I undertook in 1952 set me on the road which brought me finally into the sociology of medicine. I was asked by a friend, a pediatrician, to find out how many of the mothers, delivered in a maternity hospital in a working-class area of South London, where he worked, continued to breast feed their babies after their discharge. Taking me and my students into the homes of mothers with young babies, this small study roused my interest in health and health services. It also resulted in my being asked in 1953 to join the Public Health Department of the London School of Hygiene and Tropical Medicine as lecturer in the social aspects of public health and research associate in a study of the health problems and behavior of a population of Londoners who were being rehoused in a new estate on the outskirts of the city.

I could at the time have stayed in the field of industrial sociology; but in 1953 I thought that any research in that field likely to attract finance was also likely to further the aims of management and not those of labor. I saw in the health field an opportunity to contribute directly or indirectly to an improvement in the welfare of disadvantaged people. Moreover, by that time I was thirty-six years old and my wider experience, including motherhood, had convinced me that those responsible for planning and delivering health services needed a greater understanding of the social context in which people sought help from them. I was filled still with a quasimissionary zeal, a desire to bring the enlightenment stemming from a knowledge of the social sciences to those who I felt were narrow technical experts.

FIRST YEARS IN MEDICAL SOCIOLOGY

When I joined the staff of the London School of Hygiene in 1953, neither that institution nor I had a clear conception of my role. I was expected to lecture a class of sixty or so doctors taking a diploma in public health on the development of social services and their contemporary problems against a background of the social structure of modern Britain. I was also expected to tutor a small group of doctors and senior public health nurses through a research exercise in a health related problem. Finally, I was part of a research team investigating various health and health delivery problems of a population of working-class Londoners settled in a new estate outside the metropolis.[14]

My approach to my subject matter at this time was eclectic and largely atheoretical. In my teaching, I described recent developments in the health and related social welfare fields and the policies pursued by governments of different political complexion to deal with contemporary problems. I suggested the existence of relationships between observed phenomena emphasizing those between technological and social service development on the one hand and changes in the class and demographic structure of British society on the other. I stressed the importance of culture in determining the responses of subgroups within our own society to health service provision; implicitly rather than explicitly I hinted that changes in such provision could be explained largely in terms of the interplay of the perceived self-interest of pressure groups in and outside the health professions. In seeking reasons for the continued disparity between the health status of social classes as measured by mortality and morbidity indexes, I emphasized the continued presence and uneven distribution of adverse environmental factors and the probable effects of social distance on the capacity of different social groups to profit from the activities of the medical profession.[15]

In research I was content to describe at a simple level and to associate two variables, for example, social class membership and the use of the infant welfare clinic, or a mother's work status and reported self-medication. The main research problems seemed to me to be drawing an unbiased sample; ensuring the accuracy of the information collected from informants; phrasing questions in such a way that they were unambiguous, not misunderstood, and provided a standard stimulus to all informants; training interviewers to empathize while remaining detached; recording objectively; reducing the refusal rate in order to prevent unknown biases creeping in; and finally, speculating on those relationships between variables which, on analysis, were shown to have reached at least a 5 percent level of statistical significance. I learned a great deal about the craftsmanship of these research procedures from Ann Cartwright, who was then one of my colleagues in the research team and already had a great grasp of survey work.[16]

In 1954, Talcott Parsons was a visiting professor at Cambridge, England and we invited him to a staff seminar at the London School of Hygiene. I had come upon his work indirectly through reading a child's guide to *The Social System* written by W. J. H. Sprott.[17] Parsons's structural-functionalist approach to role theory applied to the doctor-patient relationship was intellectually fascinating, but all the same I was critical of what I then saw as its intrinsic conservatism, its underlying assumption of consensus values and shared perceptions of function, and its apparent lack of interest in change or in social distance as factors influencing the conduct and outcome of doctor-patient interactions. The reaction of my medical colleagues to what Parsons had to say at this meeting was predictable. He made no concessions in explaining his theoretical propositions. He did it in terms with which they were totally unfamiliar. They failed entirely to see its connection to their own work and summarily dismissed him as irrelevant.

SOCIOLOGY IN MEDICINE IN THE 1950s

During the 1950s few medical educators or research workers in Britain were interested in health behavior or in the structure and functioning of health care systems. Besides the London School of Hygiene, only Edinburgh University's Department of Public Health, and three Medical Research Council units—Social Obstetrics, Social Medicine and Social Psychiatry—together with Maxwell Jones at Belmont Hospital had opened their door to let in a few sociologists.

There are, I believe, several explanations for the coolness of medical educators and research workers to social scientists in Britain at this time compared to the more positive response found in many medical institutions in the United States.[18] The first is to be found in the relative state of sociology in the two countries. In the United States sociology had already begun to boom and a synthesis was being effected between the theorists and the empiricists. In the United Kingdom sociology departments were small in number, in size, and in influence in academia; the theorists were still concerned predominantly with philosophical questions while the empiricists had no interest in theory and were concerned primarily with social mapping. There was little interest among either group in health status or behavior as general social variables or in health care units as social systems. Insofar as there was any specialization of sociologists in a particular substantive field, education, industry, urban development, and poverty seemed best to exemplify the age-old concerns of social scientists with social differentiation and inequality and thus to attract more interest from neophytes.

The second reason was that in the United Kingdom epidemiology and medical statistics were more firmly entrenched in medical circles than in the United States, and had had signal successes in investigating some of the social dimensions of disease.[19] In their use of survey methods, epidemiologists were as sophisticated as most sociologists and saw little reason to draw the latter into their investigations. In the United States, on the other hand, sociologists often possessed more knowledge of epidemiological research methods than did physicians and were hired by the latter for such expertise rather than for their command of sociological theory. Third, the advent of the National Health Service, instead of fostering the idea that social research was required for planning, encouraged the belief that the major problems of social equity in access and utilization had been solved with the passage of the 1946 act. In the United States, on the other hand, the patent inequalities in the provision and uptake of health care fostered inquiry into the social components of health behavior. Finally, in the United Kingdom, available resources for research had to be extracted from a country impoverished by war; service rather than research development took priority. In the United States increasing wealth made it possible to devote considerable resources to research.

Nevertheless, there came a time when the Medical Research Council showed itself willing to consider a more substantial investment in social research. In 1955, on the initiative of the then secretary of the Medical Research Council, Sir Harold Himsworth, a meeting was called to consider the part which the Medical Research Council itself should play in encouraging social scientists to participate in medical research. Those invited included three distinguished professors of social anthropology, Raymond Firth, Meyer Fortes and Max Gluckman.[20] The rest of the social science contingent were sociologists or anthropologists who, like myself, were in comparatively junior research posts in medical institutions. The medical representatives, on the other hand, were mostly eminent professors of public health, social medicine, social obstetrics, and social psychiatry and directors of Medical Research Council units in these fields. Some of them were eager to draw social scientists more into their work; others were sceptical and reserved their judgment; and a few were hostile.

From the standpoint of those of us who wanted to see a greater commitment on the part of the Medical Research Council, the meeting was pretty disastrous. It was dominanted by Max Gluckman and Meyer Fortes who were not themselves seeking resources from the Medical Research Council to extend their research or provide work for their students. They lectured the gathering didactically and condescendingly and ignored requests from the epidemiologists to say how they would deal with questions of measurement and inference in the small scale, intensive, observational studies they advocated. Raymond Firth who had worked with doctors and shared a joint anthropology-public health postgraduate seminar with me in London was, I believe, deeply upset by his colleagues' failure to understand or deal with the questions raised by the medical men which he saw as legitimate ones in an intellectual discourse. So were those of us who had already committed ourselves to working within medical institutions alongside the medically qualified. This latter group included George Brown, Raymond Illsley and Fred Martin.[21] Although our own academic positions were, by then, secure, we felt, and subsequent events have confirmed our judgment that the Medical Research Council was persuaded by the encounter at the meeting not to take active steps to encourage social scientists to work in the medical field, even if it did nothing to discourage those already in it.

The Medical Research Council was willing, nevertheless, to support the small band of sociologists already at work in medical settings by financing periodic meetings at which they could discuss their work. These meetings, which continued for two or three years, had an instrumental purpose. They gave us an opportunity to discuss our research work and our approach to teaching. They were also important at the symbolic level, in that they allowed us to develop a sense of identity, that is, to distinguish ourselves from both mainstream sociologists and those medically qualified doctors who had turned from clinical medicine to one or other aspect of social medicine. We developed as a result of these meetings a sense of solidarity and comradeship which has still survived.

All the same, until the mid-1960s the general climate in Britain remained relatively unfavorable to the development of medical sociology. While those of us who had joined medical faculties or research units began to secure some recognition from colleagues who found us provocative and stimulating, most of us also found our paths blocked to more senior posts within these institutions. Furthermore, young sociologists were hired for their skills in interviewing or data analysis, but were not given opportunities to participate in the design of inquiries let alone to develop genuine sociological perspectives. Given the lack of autonomy and career prospects, it was not surprising that most left after a year or two in the field. Those of us who stayed on often witnessed the frustrating if not humiliating experience of seeing less able people promoted over our heads to professorial status by virtue simply of possessing a medical qualification. Not unexpectedly, there was little growth in thin ranks as people drifted back, often with great reluctance, into mainstream social science departments or into research in other fields where they could secure greater recognition.

Until the early 1960s, perhaps because I had internalized some of the "fear of success" traits allegedly common among professional members of my sex, I accepted my situation rather more philosophically than my male colleagues. Moreover, unlike most of them, I was not prepared to be a "spiralist" that is, to move out of London in pursuit of my career.[22] My reason was not that of many other married women, namely that to move would have meant ending their marriage. By the 1960s, my own had ended and I was free to move if I had wanted to; but I loved London and thought then, as I do now, that I could not make a permanent home elsewhere. This coupled with the affection I felt for many of my medical colleagues made me less impatient to leave the medical school setting than were most of my male social scientist colleagues.

In 1963, however, on my return from a tour of the United States during which I visited most of the American schools of public health to see what role social scientists were playing in them, I became more frustrated and consequently more aggressive. I tried to get the London School of Hygiene to establish a medical sociology unit independent of the Public Health Department whose reputation at that point in time was deservedly at a low ebb. I hoped that an independent unit with several career posts and a postgraduate studentship program would encourage able graduates to enter a field which I personally had found intellectually rewarding. I was unsuccessful at least partly because the London School of Hygiene as an institution had signally failed to respond to the challenge of the changing spectrum of health and disease in industrial countries and was providing no leadership to those responsible for the administration of the public health services.

Consequently, although I was fully committed to work in the field of medicine and health services, it was becoming clear to me that I was unlikely to obtain the degree of autonomy I needed as long as I stayed at the London School of Hygiene. I began to consider seriously the possibilities of moving out of a medical institution, and in 1965 accepted an invitation to become director of a newly formed Social Research Unit at another of the University of London's federated institutions—Bedford College.

In the twelve years I spent at the London School of Hygiene, as I have already implied, there was little growth in medical sociology in Britain. Those of us who worked in Research Council establishments or university departments headed by medically qualified men remained few in number and we tended to work within the pragmatic empirically based research model of the able epidemiologists and on problems seen by the latter as important. Our contribution tended to lie in our greater knowledge of the complexity of such well-used indicators of status as social class or of the problems of obtaining reliable data from informants in home interviews. We were particularly good at describing the distribution of specific social traits in populations and relating them in two-by-two tables to a number of health outcome variables such as smoking, the utilization of health services, and the taking of self-prescribed medicines. By and large, we did not seek to understand the processes by which a social attribute of an individual made him more likely to behave in a certain way. We were curiously incurious about how to interpret—theorise—about the nature of the relationship between two statistically associated variables.

The explanation for what in retrospect appears to be a comparatively pedestrian approach to social factors operating in the field of medicine, is not a simple one. It cannot be ascribed entirely, for example, to the fact that we worked in medical settings and not in sociology departments and were therefore forced to investigate phenomena which were seen as problematic and research-worthy by the medically qualified. For if this had been so, we might have seen a more sociological approach adopted by those working on health issues from academic departments of sociology; but this was not the case. There was little work on health service issues coming from such departments in any case; but, more important, the empirical work undertaken in mainstream departments on education, urban society, poverty, crime, stratification, and industry tended to be equally pragmatic and cast in an epidemiological type mold. Although paying lip service to the necessity of a holistic view of man and his institutions, sociologists in their own research were likely to use a simple unidimensional model. This consisted in seeing how far each of a range of input variables (usually personal traits or social circumstances) were independently associated with a variety of outcome variables which could take the form either of a disease, or a behavioral manifestation such as the use of a particular health service. In short, the sociology of medicine in Britain at that time was cast in very much the same mold as the sociology of education, social stratification, and so on.

RETURN TO THE FOLD

I am sometimes tempted to ask myself what effect my decision to move from a school of public health to a sociology department in a small multifaculty college had on my subsequent work. It is, of course, an unanswerable question in the sense that the move was only one among a number of other events taking place around the same time which could account for the changes which have taken place subsequently in what I do, how I do it, and what I think about it. And since these other events have been important in the development of medical sociology generally and not simply in my personal experience of that development, it is with them that I shall be mainly concerned; but I believe the move itself was important for me in at least two respects.

When I moved I did so in the anticipation that it would allow me greater freedom to plan my own research and teaching; but I also thought I might have more difficulty than I had had in the past in gaining access to health service institutions. My expectation of greater freedom was undoubtedly met; and, in addition, I am certain that I would not have achieved full professorial status if I had stayed in a medical setting. On the other hand, my fears that I might have sacrificed some opportunities for research within medical institutions were not confirmed. When I was seen by those responsible for health services to be independent of an academic department which had been losing its reputation for research leadership over the years, I had many unsolicited requests to engage in independent or collaborative research and offers of access to information. The years I spent in a medical institution have also, I believe, stood me in good stead. The knowledge I was then able to build up about the various forms of medical enterprise has since been useful both for teaching other social scientists, and for making health service workers feel confident in my ability to understand them.

The increased facilities for research which I experienced were, however, mainly the result of a marked change in the climate of opinion in the United Kingdom in the middle and late 1960s about social research in general and research in the health services in particular. Until the 1960s British politicians and senior civil servants had been sceptical of the value of social research. The information required for decision making was not thought to be complicated; it was generally assumed that it could be obtained largely from analyses of data routinely obtained by social service agencies about their expenditure, their manpower or their clientele, supplemented by the decennial population censuses or an occasional ad hoc sample survey. When the conventional wisdom or commonsense assumptions of existing policy were challenged the appropriate mechanism was seen to be the appointment, depending upon the political importance of the problem, of a royal commission, committee of inquiry, or working party to take evidence from interested parties, deliberate, report, and recommend. This device had the added virtue of reducing the political pressure for immediate action on the part of the government of the day; the latter could always argue that it was awaiting the commission's report.

Faith in these traditional ways of equipping governments for policymaking in the social service field began to falter in the 1960s. Some independently conducted surveys threw doubt on the complacent assumptions made about the levels of poverty among old people and children and indicated that the mere existence of a range of statutory benefits did not imply their uptake by those entitled to them.[23] Human behavior was at last seen to be more complicated and problematic than it had appeared to be to administrators in the past. The gaps between the expected and the observed were also more apparent when it became fashionable to think in terms of planning the use of scarce resources of manpower and capital in the health and social services. A case seemed to have been made out by the social scientist for more investment in both problem-oriented and basic research into social behavior and social institutions.

In this kind of climate, the Social Science Research Council was established in 1965 with the object of promoting postgraduate training in research methods and of financing projects in which the major disciplinary inputs would be from the social sciences.[24] Simultaneously, the Ministry of Health (now the Department of Health and Social Security) set up a research division with the power to finance research done in university departments and elsewhere. These developments meant that social research workers interested in health-related behavior were no longer solely dependent as they had been in the past on private research funding. My own unit was able to profit from these developments, particularly as my own interests lay in trying to throw light on issues which were already perceived by administrators as problems. For example, I was financed to undertake studies into the problems of identifying and servicing disadvantaged groups like the elderly and the handicapped, or into the issues surrounding the organization of primary medical care services and the interface between them and other service agencies such as the hospital and the social service department of the local authority.[25] Sociologists who were more interested in using research funds to answer theoretical problems which they set themselves rather than those perceived as relevant by administrators, although better served after than before the establishment of the Social Science Research Council, were rather less likely to obtain all the support they sought.

Yet another factor influencing the social research scene was the government's swing to the left in the second half of the 1960s. The Conservatives' thirteen years run in office was broken in 1964. The Labour Party was committed to a policy of increasing welfare benefits and of reducing persistent social inequalities. They were also committed to expanding the tertiary sector in education, and teenagers in increasing numbers were opting to study the human sciences, including sociology. Those of us who had left-wing political ideologies felt that we had the opportunity to contribute to an improvement in the quality of life of the underprivileged by studying the way in which the services worked and who benefited or failed to benefit from them.

The late 1960s, then, was a period of optimism among social research workers, an optimism warranted by the considerable expansion of resources available to university social science departments for both teaching and research. As yet, however, comparatively few of the increasing number of sociologists were seeking work in the field of medical sociology. The most able were more interested in the age-old concerns of sociology, social class and social stratification. In particular, destroying the widespread belief that the educational system was a vehicle for producing greater equality of opportunity, greater equity in the distribution of income or privilege, or the S'embourgeoisiement of the workers was probably the most attractive field for empirical studies. Beginning to chase it in the popularity poll, especially after the militancy of the student movement in 1968 and the increasing use by young people of illegal forms of mind-altering substances, was the sociology of deviance. This in itself was a form of protest, in which the villains were seen as the agents of social control who, obligingly, labeled as deviant individuals whose activities threatened existing values and structures of society.

In this climate, the sociology of medicine did not immediately attract the most able young sociologists. It was still seen, perhaps, as a field in which it was only possible to work if you shared the implicit objectives of those with power in the health services, that is, the medical profession or the government. To this extent, those who did work within it were seen as overwilling to accept research objectives of administrators or the dominant professional group without examining their legitimacy from the standpoint of others involved in the services.

Of course those of us who chose to work in the field v ere aware of the problems of perspective and bias. We were not naive enough to argue that our research was value free; but we felt that it was not only permissible but desirable to associate ourselves with some of the explicit objectives of both governments and the medical profession, and with this intent we were prepared to work with them. All the same, we always felt free to conclude, if we were convinced by the evidence, that improvements in health or a reduction in pain and discomfort could be achieved by modifying the behavior of governments or professionals rather than that of patients.

Given this ideological stance, I have seen nothing inconsistent in my decision to accept research funds from government-sponsored bodies, or to collaborate with medically qualified colleagues. I do not think the result of my work has been to increase the power of the government or professions to manipulate in their own interests less powerful groups or individuals. Indeed, I would hope that if my research or teaching has had any effect at all on the behavior of powerful professional workers, it has been to reduce not increase their capacity and their willingness to act against the interests of less privileged people.

During the 1970s, the climate of opinion in Britain and the position of sociological research has again changed. Medicine, as a field for research, is now attracting more young sociology graduates. The reasons are mixed. The market for research staff in this field has expanded steadily if not spectacularly while the demand in other substantive fields has comparatively speaking contracted. Since medicine is concerned with what Parsons has described as a central value of most social systems, the health of its members, it attracts social scientists who want to use their knowledge to "do good" for others. However, in addition, there appears to be a shift in the interests of left-wing social scientists following the political militancy of the late 1960s. Then, targets for the radical protesters were right-wing politicians and exponents of blatant racist or elitist policies. In the 1970s, invective has been turned on professional workers and particularly on those whose popular as well as whose self-image is one of caring. Sociologists have been delighted to emphasize the way in which the professions have been drawn into self-seeking collective forms of action and social control functions which principally, if not entirely, benefit existing powerful groups. As protagonists of underprivileged groups and, perhaps subconsciously, envious of the status and rewards accorded to the established profession of medicine or of the income won by social workers in recent years, they wanted to expose the machinations of professional groups.

These preoccupations of many of the students applying to our unit for postgraduate work undoubtedly reflects what is going on in the teaching of sociology to undergraduates at the present time. We cannot but applaud the scepticism underlying these preoccupations with the covert as well as the overt objectives of social interaction; scepticism, after all, is a necessary state of mind in a social scientist. On the other hand, scepticism is often only partial. It does not usually extend to consideration of the *methods* by which generalizations relating to such matters as professional behavior have been established. I have the strong impression, furthermore, that insofar as any sociological theory or method is critically evaluated, the criticism is one sided. A process of derogatory labeling is applied to theories which are not in favor in order summarily to dismiss them. This stigmatization only too often appears to provide a respectable excuse for avoiding serious study.

Enough said on this theme. I am only too aware that I can be accused of echoing sentiments expressed by many aging professors who are liable to deplore the slovenliness of the young generation and who defend stoutly their own theoretical stances against innovative ideas of any sort. In practice, I am grateful to many younger colleagues for persuading me not to abandon but rather to extend the basic eclecticism with which I have approached both research and teaching problems. I must also acknowledge a steadily increasing debt to many sociologists on both sides of the Atlantic, including many of the contributors to this volume, who have provided me with so much of my store of intellectual fodder and so much of my wealth of friendship.

A FINAL, PERSONAL NOTE

When I worked as a research assistant, I was often critical of the administrative skills of those responsible for directing a team of research workers. Now as director of a small research unit, I am more aware of the difficulties of research management. There must somewhere be a nice balance between letting research workers take the bit between their own teeth and keeping a tight enough rein on those who lack experience; but it is extraordinarily difficult to find. I veer inappropriately between the two extremes, sometimes leaving too much to the initiative of those who are looking for more leadership, and at other times clamping down with destructive criticism which can destroy self-esteem. I suppose there are those who successfully direct units with a substantial number of research workers; but I now subscribe to the view that most good research is done where the principal investigator has only one or two strings to his bow and is engaged on a day-to-day basis in the planning and execution of the project. If this desirable state is to be achieved, the investigator must have the strength to resist pressures from both research initiators and actual or aspirant research workers to expand his activities. To my own detriment I have always found it difficult to say no. I envy those with the capacity to recognize the point at which their own is stretched to or beyond its limit, and to call a halt.

If the pressures were limited to those of research alone they would be more tolerable; they include, however, teaching responsibilities and the varied professional chores which go with being one of the few long-standing and therefore better known medical sociologists in Britain, that small offshore European island.

The situation will be familiar to most of those who have reached similar positions in their field of work, particularly if the field is a newly developing one. Succumbing to a mixture of cajolery and flattery you are persuaded or persuade yourself that, for the good of your discipline rather than yourself, you should begin a new course, join an investigating or grant-giving body, address a multi-disciplinary conference, act as rapporteur to a WHO expert committee. You know in your heart of hearts that you cannot take on another commitment without incurring excessive cost—a cost which may be paid vicariously, that is, by those you are forced comparatively to neglect, your students, your academic colleagues, your friends and your family; but you allow yourself to be fooled because there are real benefits which are likely to accrue to you personally. In return for the short-lived agony of finally producing the paper you blithely agreed to write six months earlier or of reviewing the grant request, you meet new and interesting people, travel to various parts of the world, experience new sensations, hear fresh ideas, and renew old friendships.

Moreover, extended commitments make it almost possible to continue the self-deception, the might-have-been image of self. By that I mean the view you have of yourself as someone who might have made a major contribution to scholarship if only it had been possible to escape the excessive and inescapable demands made upon you. Unfortunately, comfort derived in this way is not long tenable. A more plausible explanation of frenetic butterfly behavior is that it provides the excuse presumably still needed to cover intellectual nakedness. All I can hope is that my peers will not count all butterfly behavior as valueless and therefore condemn mine out-of-hand. I like to comfort myself by thinking that along my flight path some of the individuals I have met may have had some pleasure from the contact and even been helped thereby to achieve something which they and the various referees of academic work may consider valuable.

For my part, I count myself as one of the most fortunate women ever to have lived. I was born at a time and in a country where it was possible for at least some women both to have satisfying and well-remunerated work in academia and to enjoy the delights of motherhood. Within that context, I was one of those lucky enough to possess the requisite characteristics for the privileged positions: enough intelligence to pass, enough physical and psychic energy to survive the undoubted schizoid-like strains of the dual maternal / professional role; enough emotional stability to weather the acute anguish and chronic distress of a broken marriage and to find compensation for the loss of an intimate relationship in a wealth of firm affectionate friendships with men and women of every age and nationality; enough money in my family of origin and a tenured position in the last twenty-five years to prevent me from feeling afraid for the future or deprived of material comfort in the present. These were the factors to which I attribute my good fortune. Born earlier or later I might not have been so lucky. Earlier, even by as little as ten years, I would have probably had to choose between marriage and motherhood on the one hand and an academic career on the other. Born later, I would have had to face greater competition for promotion and recognition in the academic world from well-qualified social scientists who are no longer as scarce on the ground as they were when I was on the bottom rung of my career ladder.

Moreover, there has been a serendipity in the specific area in which I have worked. I did not consciously seek or prepare myself for work in the sociology of medicine; it was a series of chance factors which brought me into it. However, I have never for one moment found the sociological issues that are posed by health-related activities and institutions dull or intellectually unrewarding. On the contrary, they have offered and will continue to offer many exciting challenges. The relationships and institutions which are formed around health issues may not be the most crucial ones in determining the distribution of power and resources within any given society; but the part played by health services in sustaining or undermining the economic and social structure of a society and its normative values has been of fundamental interest to me because I see myself not only in the business of changing the world by political action. I would also like to have played some part in persuading my fellow men and women to modify in my lifetime those aspects of their behavior which bring unhappiness to those dependent on them.

NOTES

1. There has recently been a revival in Britain of interest in the days of the British rule in India. Recollections of those who worked there in the administration, army, or commerce and of their wives and children have recently been published. See Charles Allen, ed., *Plain Tales from the Raj* (London: Andre Deutsch, 1975). The classical novel portraying the interface between the rulers and the ruled is, of course, E. M. Forster's *A Passage to India*.

2. One of the best source books on interwar Britain, including the General Strike is C. L. Mowat, *Britain between the Wars* (London: Methuen, 1955; rev. ed. 1956).

3. John Maynard Keynes, *The General Theory of Employment, Interest, and Money* (London: Macmillan & Co., 1936).

4. See Kingsley Martin, *Harold Laski: A Biography* (London: Johnathan Cape, paper ed., 1969).

5. R. H. Tawney, *Religion and the Rise of Capitalism: An Historical Study* (London: Murray, 1929). Also see *Equality* (London: Allen & Unwin, 1931).

6. Two of H. L. Beales's books give the flavor of his style: *The Industrial Revolution* (London: Longman, 1934; new ed., 1958); and *The Early English Socialists* (London: Hamish Hamilton, 1933).

7. James B. Jefferys, *The Story of the Engineers, 1800–1945* (London: Lawrence & Wishart, 1946).

8. A good history of women in Britain covering the period 1910 to 1975 is by Ruth Adam, *A Woman's Place: 1910–1975* (London: Chatto & Windus, 1975).

9. Two friends of mine, themselves victims of prejudice, wrote on the trivialisation of women a year or so before Freidan tackled the same theme. Nan Berger and Joan Maizels, *Woman: Fancy or Free?* (London: Mills & Boon, 1962).

10. Margot Jefferys, "Married Women in the Civil Service," *British Journal of Sociology* 3 (1952): 361–71.

11. Margot Jefferys, *Mobility in the Labour Market* (London: Routledge & Kegan Paul, 1954).

12. The work of Richard M. Titmuss is well known in the United States, particularly *Essays on the Welfare State* (London: Allen & Unwin, 1958; rev. ed. 1963, 1970). Also, idem, *The Gift Relationship: From Human Blood to Social Policy* (London: Allen & Unwin, 1958).

13. See particularly Barbara Wootton, *The Social Foundations of Wages Policy* (London: Allen & Unwin, 1954); idem, *Social Science and Social-Pathology* (London: Allen & Unwin, 1959).

14. This research project resulted in a considerable number of publications among which I was associated with the following: Margot Jefferys, "Londoners in Hertfordshire," in *London: Aspects of Change*, ed. M. Jefferys (London: MacGibbon and Kee for the Center for Urban Studies, 1964); idem, "Married Women Who Work: Their Own and Their Children's Health," *British Journal of Preventive and Social Medicine* 12 (1958): 159–71; and idem, "Consumption of Medicines on a Working Class Housing Estate," *British Journal of Preventive and Social Medicine* 14 (1960): 44–76.

15. The paper I wrote was largely speculative but makes interesting reading today in light of empirical work since published in both the United Kingdom and the United States (Margot Jeffreys, "Social Class and Health Promotion," *Health Education Journal* 7 [1957]: 109–17).

16. Ann Cartwright's national surveys of particular sections of the public on issues of contemporary importance to health services provide the most reliable sources of information about doctors and patients in Britain in the 1960s and 1970s. See particularly her *Human Relations and Hospital Care* (London: Routledge and Kegan Paul, 1964); *Patients and Their Doctors* (London: Routledge and Kegan Paul, 1967); *Life Before Death* (London: Routledge and Kegan Paul, 1973); and Karen Dunnell and Ann Cartwright, *Medicine-Takers, Prescribers, and Hoarders* (London: Routledge and Kegan Paul, 1972).

17. W. J. H. Sprott, "Principia Sociologica," *British Journal of Sociology* 3 (1953): 203–21.

18. R. Badgley and S. W. Bloom, "Behavioral Sciences and Medical Education: The Case of Sociology," *Social Science and Medicine* 7 (1973). 927–41.

19. Particularly important in this regard was the work of Richard Doll connecting smoking with lung cancer, and of J. N. Morris and his colleagues on infant mortality and coronary heart disease. See Richard Doll and A. Bradford Hill, "A Study of the Aetiology of Carcinoma of the Lung," *British Medical Journal* 2 (1952): 1271–76; and J. A. Heady, et al., "Social and Biological Factors in Infant Mortality: The Independent Effects of Social Class, Region, the Mother's Age and Her Parity," Lancet 1 (1955): 499–507.

20. They held respectively chairs in the following universities: London, Cambridge, and Manchester, England.

21. An amusing account of this meeting and the uneasy relationship between doctors and sociologists at the time has been written by Fred Martin

in his "Comment" in *Seminars in Community Medicine*, vol. 1, *Sociology*, ed. Roy M. Acheson and Lesley Aird (London: Oxford University Press, 1976), pp. 16–19. Others who have written about the period from firsthand knowledge of it are Raymond Illsley and John Brotherston. Derek Gill is also, I understand, researching this period in the development of medical sociology in Britain.

22. I believe I am right in attributing the term "spiralist" to Bill Watson, an irreverent social anthropologist who used to work in Manchester, and who coauthored *Sociology in Medicine*, with Mervyn W. Susser (London: Oxford University Press, 1962; 2nd rev. ed., 1971).

23. Among the most important surveys: Peter Townsend and Dorothy Wedderburn, *The Aged in the Welfare State*, Occasional Papers in Social Administration Series no. 14 (London: Bell, London School of Economics, 1964); and Brian Abel-Smith and Peter Townsend, *The Poor and the Poorest*, Occasional Papers in Social Administration Series no. 17 (London: Bell, London School of Economics, 1965).

24. The Social Science Research Council Newsletter no. 29 (November 1975) is a tenth anniversary issue in which its successive chairmen review its work since its inception.

25. A mimeographed account of the work of the Social Research Unit from 1965 to 1975 which contains a list of publications of its members is available on request at a small charge to cover cost of production and postage. Inquiries should be sent together with £ 2.00 or $5.00 (USA) to the secretary, Social Research Unit, Regents Park, London. N.W.1, England.

Disciplined Protest and Academic Work: The Emergence of a Professional Identity

YNGVAR LØCHEN

INTRODUCTION

The purpose of this project is to increase the understanding of medical sociology. The point is not only an intellectual clarification of the substantive issues constituting the field. It is also to elucidate some of the dilemmas in the role of the medical sociologist. The method is to compare the main experience of professional people actually working in medical sociology. This cannot be done successfully unless some kind of standardized procedure is pursued in the presentation of these experiences. However, since traditions, training programs, professional roles, and the stage of sociology as a discipline vary a great deal from country to country, every author cannot follow exactly the same path. Modern medicine too, which is the target of our sociological activities, is far from similar in the countries from which we come. In Norway medicine rests its work on a rather encompassing and inclusive concept of illness. Medical services are largely publicly financed, but we do not have socialized medicine in the sense that all doctors have a fixed salary or are employed by public authorities. Sociology is increasingly becoming, and to some extent always has been, a critical discipline, a trend that naturally influences medical sociology as well. Sometimes I feel that I am just as much a general sociologist trying to view medicine as an alternative way of handling and often successfully solving human problems in modern society as I am a medical sociologist, especially when a medical sociologist is perceived as a person with a main and exclusive purpose of implementing new medical programs or making old ones better. I find myself increasingly unhappy about a narrow etiquette of medical sociologists and I have often wanted to cut the word medical out of my title. At the same time, though, I also like being close to the medical profession because it is action oriented. I am discontent with the wide discrepancy between words and action in sociology. My ambivalence probably indicates a broader dillemma in the medical sociologists' roles as professional people.

ENTRY INTO MEDICAL SOCIOLOGY

Medicine in Norway, as in other countries, is a highly esteemed profession, and a medical degree almost automatically elicits a deferential response from the lay public. The teacher, the clergyman, and the doctor have historically constituted a famous and powerful triumvirate in the Norwegian local community. This, of course, is changing. The medical profession is often criticized now, and the public increasingly refuses to grant the medical profession an entirely autonomous position in society. However, some years ago the Norwegian Gallup Institute asked a sample of the population for their best advice to a young person not knowing what occupation to choose. The absolutely most frequent advice was: become a doctor.

In 1950 I also considered studying medicine. However, it was then and still is very difficult to become a medical student in one of our two medical schools.[1] The required qualifications are hard to attain, and I was never quite convinced that medicine was my first choice. When I did not qualify, the problem was solved. Having a typical upper-middle-class background, I found it quite natural to enter the university and seek higher education. I believed that the university education could lead to a richer and probably nobler life.

Sociology became a university discipline in Oslo in 1949. When I started sociology in 1950, I had only some vague notions about it. I wanted to understand why social relations had become distant and one-dimensional, and I wanted to know why human values seemed to be so unevenly distributed. I wondered why some people apparently were not included in a secure and supportive collectivity. The middle-class generation I belonged to after the war was largely preoccupied with such questions, rather than such issues as class-struggle and other dividing conflicts. This attitude was probably a reflection of an underlying feeling of cohesion after the war which it was important to try to preserve. We were more concerned with human emotions than with ideologies, and we were not so much engaged in political activities. We looked inward and towards social relations. Psychoanalysis, psychotherapy, and sociology absorbed much of the radical motivation in the middle and upper classes. However, we were—including myself—upset about the Norwegian entry into NATO in 1949. This point of view was at variance with the majority position in Norway. We strongly feared that atomic weapons would be placed in Norway. If we had started our academic careers today, it is not unlikely that we would have become active Marxists involved in more direct and organized political action.

The resolution to study sociology was probably more basic, but not more rational, than the process by which I became a medical sociologist. Medical sociology was a totally undeveloped field in Norway in the fifties. There were no courses or programs to follow. In a way I *became* a medical sociologist rather than actually choosing it. Medical sociology gradually symbolized and constituted a happy compromise between a host of personal, professional, and intellectual concerns. It was a probable avenue to respectability, and a medical institution was a target for disciplined protest. Medicine also conveyed a host of sociological concerns like the organization of professional work, deviance and control, voluntary association, and so forth; thus it represented a scene for studying important social processes related to the issues and themes which led me to sociology in the first place. It somehow also brought me a little closer to a field where knowledge eventually could be used, hopefully for the right purposes.

In 1953 Kaspar D. Naegele visited the sociological institute in Oslo. He talked affectionately and brilliantly about such important and easily recognizable social distinctions as those between young and old, poor and rich, black and white, man and woman, and he showed how such distinctions were interrelated. He also brought in the rather arbitrary yet powerful and consequential dichotomy between ill and well, and he discussed how the changing content of that dichotomy was a part of a wider social reality. He had a lot to say about the role of medicine in society, and he saw the medical institution as much more than the pure application of rational devices to control and cure sickness.[2] He was a true sociologist who in a tremendously inspiring way asked questions about apparently simple but in fact very complex matters that were seldom questioned. Although his respect for medicine was great, he looked for magic and ritual in medical practice and he questioned the validity of basic medical concepts. His intellectual inquiry, also covering the sociology of medicine, always proceeded with the "instruments" of passion and distance, respect and doubt.

In 1954 I read *The Mental Hospital* by Stanton and Schwartz.[3]

This book impressed me significantly. For a few years I had played with the idea of making a study of a mental hospital. Somehow, I had always felt that the mental hospital operated on the basis of and was legitimated by rather questionable distinctions and categories. Stanton and Schwartz convinced me that the mental hospital represented a "strategic place" to learn much about central social processes in human life. Before I left the university in 1956, I read about medical matters and tried to get acquainted with the emerging field of medical sociology. There were no other students deeply interested in the field. I wrote my dissertation about psychosomatic disorders among refugees in Norway. Refugees who came to Norway after the war and married there had more psychosomatic problems than, for example, refugees who were brought to Norway by the Germans as prisoners of war and decided to stay in Norway after the war.

There was no strong reason to be more worried about a future in medical sociology than in any other sociological field. Of course, it was a risk in any case to become a sociologist in a small country with a very limited number of jobs for sociologists, and where law and economics always have been the important professions in government. I established contact with the director of a mental hospital before I left the university. This was Dikemark Hospital which is the municipal mental hospital in Oslo. The director was Harald Frøshaug. We applied to the Norwegian Research Council for a grant. Harald Frøshaug's support can not be overestimated, and it went beyond the intellectual exchange of words and ideas. The papers in this book will probably show that this form of recruitment into medical sociology is fairly common. Anthropologists tell me that it resembles the way in which a social anthropologist can be adopted by the chief in a simple society.

We got the grant, and I started my work at Dikemark in 1956, as a research fellow under the Norwegian Research Council. I was not expected to be directly responsible to the hospital, and my job was to do a study of the mental hospital system and learn what could be learned about the daily life of patients in the wards.

There were also other important events of my life. I married in 1956. My wife—Vivi—is a kindergarten teacher. She is also from Oslo. We lived a rich social life in Oslo until we moved to Tromsø in 1971. My relationship to Dikemark lasted for many years, although it had a rather intermittent character. I had some form of connection with Dikemark until 1965. In the meantime, however, I have been abroad and also made another study in a somewhat different field.

FIRST WORK EXPERIENCE: THE DIKEMARK STUDY

Dikemark Hospital is the largest mental hospital in Norway, and in 1956 when I came there it had about 900 to 1000 patients, mainly psychotics. The hospital was progressive and treatment oriented. There was some psychotherapy, and it was already influenced and to some extent modeled by the therapeutic community. Occupational therapy was used extensively. It is still regarded by younger psychiatrists as a desirable training center.

When I started the study in 1956, the hospital was undergoing major ideological changes. A new philosophy of equality and closeness affected the staff's relations to each other and to the patients. We wanted to take a closer look at what would happen when such a philosophy was launched in a mental hospital.

Considerable attention was given to the problem of selecting a method, which was rather troublesome since no research hypotheses and problems were precisely defined.

The following considerations justified the final choice. It was generally agreed that the study should be, and had to be exploratory. It was also felt that it was crucial to gain some knowledge about the intimate sides of the hospital, the medical world, and its reservoir of strains and rewards.

Thus it was decided that I should attend all meetings in the hospital—clinical meetings, administrative, formal and informal, and observe on wards. I should be a participant observer. Rather than looking for data, I would be looking for a problem.

Two major concerns dictated the thinking about my role: the research aims and how they could be approached, and the necessity of not disturbing the hospital in its everyday functioning. My role would essentially be a compromise between these two goals which, I thought, could under certain circumstances be in conflict.

With this mandate I was let loose, with keys in my hand and dressed in a white coat. In order to give full justice to the white coat as a well-meant expression of generosity and hospitality and to give recognition to what it meant to staff, I should note that it was argued by the staff that the patients would be confused by a "civilian" walking around on the wards. Nevertheless, it had the definite function of placing me in a role. To the patients, I was now one of "the others," and to the staff I was presumably one of "them."

I listened rather than participated. I took notes. Occasionally I raised questions but contributed very little to the understanding of the themes being discussed. I believed that others would, after a while, get used to this form of passive behavior and that my pres-ence would be unnoticed.

At this time the nicknames given to me were of a particular na-ture and reflected to some extent the image others had of me. I was given such labels as a stranger, the institutional superego, the spy, the one nobody understands. These labels were symptomatic of the fact that to the staff I was a diffuse person who never gave any signs which would facilitate the assessment of what I was really doing there.

The staff's conceptions of what constitutes work were not wide enough to incorporate my activities and lack of therapeutic respon-sibilities. As a researcher I was different from the clinician who has to fight against time. Time was for me, I argued, an irrelevant con-cern which a scientist ideally ought not be restricted by. And that I apparently, in their eyes, was not overly oriented towards possible therapeutic applications also worried them. It was accepted that my ambition was not to treat and cure. But, an egoistic scientific goal was not enough either.

The reactions to the observer became more differentiated. One reaction was open hostility. A second reaction, more pleasant but probably less honest, was represented by some who offered friend-ship. A function of such an arrangement was to entangle me in relationships where my obligations could be defined in terms of loyalty and solidarity rather than in terms of what factual findings would tell me. A third reaction was a skeptical one. It was frank and realistic, stating in effect, "Let's see what comes out of this. It is too early to form an opinion."

However, the basic reaction was personal and particularistic rather than oriented towards possible contributions and perform-ances. Although I wanted it differently, my motives were fre-quently questioned. I was not evaluated as a researcher and a sociologist. Since my role was not formally defined, my personal behavior seemed to be the main clue to understand what was ac-tually going on.

Personally, I felt more and more lonely. I did not have a feeling of accomplishment and could enjoy few rewards. The fact that the position of the observer is basically different, in spite of polite at-tempts to make it look otherwise, became clearer to me.

Having nowhere else to go, I found it hard to resist the tempta-tion to become involved with the patients in a sort of conspiring and semisecret therapy. The patients liked coming to my office where they could speak about things seldom discussed elsewhere with nonpatients. The discrepancy between long-term and vaguely-defined scientific goals and what could be done in the more immediate sense, thus became one of the more serious dilemmas.

I adopted the patients' outlook, responded to their applause, and perceived the hospital as a cruel and mean place. I became committed to their demands, contrary to the idealized conception of a research role. Patients soon learned that I shared their views. They called me their best friend, sent me gifts, and invited me to secret parties at the wards.

At the same time I became associated with the radical part of the staff which consisted of some psychologists and young doctors and a few nurses. It was hard to maintain a relaxed and unstrained relationship with the rest of the staff. I felt morally impelled to let the staff know how the patients in my opinion were mortified by the institutional procedures. This I did with a considerable amount of worry and also with guilt feelings since I departed violently from the neutral research role.

To my great surprise my fears and attacks were respected. Rather than meeting rejection, I met relief. For the first time it was understood that I shared a concern for mental health.

Gradually I became more and more interested in the dilemma between treating the patient as a "case" or as a "person." I got more and more concerned with the pressure in the direction of impersonal relations, which could be documented by interviews, ward observations, and some reactions to my dealings with the patients. I could also make inferences from my own feelings. What were the functions of impersonal relations? Was it true that distance between patients and staff allowed a smoother functioning and operation of the ward system, as well as providing a form of protection against the emotional problems of the kind I experienced being close to patients? And why did the various professional groups find it so difficult to find room for their professional ideals?

As this interest grew stronger and stronger, my days were spent in a somewhat more meaningful way. The satisfactions I got from my work increased. Very clearly I was in a transition. The frequency of congenial interactions with staff increased. My dealings with the patients became more distant but not worse. I made myself less dependent upon them and could resist their demands with less trouble.

What corresponding changes took place in my outlook? I understood what it must be like to work in a hospital where a substantial portion of the one thousand patients remind one of failure, of inadequate means of healing, of the unknown, of our impotence as scientists and practitioners. I felt that as a society the hospital is a strange one; the successes move out of it; the failures—and there are plenty—remain unchanged and some of them die. There is no room for surprise when we see that in such a society anxiety mounts. The nature of the mental hospital, I thought, is victimizing—not only are patients victims, but also the staff.

There was not less doubt about my professional identity and there was more interaction. For the first time we saw that we were different yet basically the same. I was given more responsibility, asked to give lectures, consulted on questions in research, was invited to be on a committee formulating some ideas concerning the structure of a new ward, and so forth. I had several discussions about what others had regarded as unfortunate events in the past. I administered a questionnaire investigation among the nursing staff to obtain some quantitative data, after I had been away for a couple of years. That was not easy, and considerable resistance had to be overcome. In 1965, I published a book about Dikemark, *Ideals and Realities in a Mental Hospital.*[4]

Looking back, a certain pattern emerges. A sequence of several consecutive and overlapping stages evolved, each stage with its own characteristics and dynamics and some representing approximations of, others departures from, a neutral research role. First, there is a stage of latency, relatively neutral, commencing at the entry to the hospital, and which has no definite finality. Second, a phase of loneliness with subsequent underdog identifications, and in which a severe deviation from a research role takes place. Third, a phase of transition in which the researcher emerges from obscurity to increasing clarification. Fourth, a final stage characterized by an "identification with the whole hospital," one in which the role of the observer is accepted by himself and others, and in which the observer is associated with a profession. This whole process took about two years. This sequence is probably not atypical for sociologists working in mental hospitals. It also resembles a pattern that evolved in other treatment organizations and total institutions.[5]

The "errors" of the first stages provided the various parties with an opportunity to get close. First feelings, motives, emotions, and values had to be dealt with. After a while a realistic detachment was established. Is it true, then, that we do not achieve an adequate combination of distance and concern which can become the basis for working together in the common undertaking of doing sociological research before we first come close or show face?

Is it also true that the observer, as he becomes defined in a role, gains personal and professional identity? He becomes a participant and acts according to the needs of a sociological enterprise.

And now we ask: What does the sequence of closeness and subsequent distance reflect of the institution? Why is it so important to know the observer before he can be trusted?

The mental hospital highlights some general orientations concerning how we deal with people who are both unfortunate and different. In it, an ideology of equality is gaining stronger foothold, yet there are obvious differences which can never be overlooked. We believe that personal relations are important for therapy, yet the institution demands a certain proportion of impersonal relations. If the organization is to maintain itself as a society, some of the patients' needs must be categorized—a process that the patients most likely will resent. But because of this, staff and others are forced to make personal, moral compromises and to do things they cannot easily justify. They face unresolvable existential conflicts which research in the hospital unveils. Some have already learned to live with these problems; others are in the painful process of deciding what to become. There is very little which could be more threatening than to be watched while trying to resolve such problems, and little which could be easier for an "outsider" to misunderstand and not take seriously enough. This, I believe, explains the patterns seen above.

There is another component in the explanation. Although the pattern described above may have some general implications concerning what fears and reactions are regularly evoked in sociological research, it is significant that this was the first study of a medical organization in this country. The support I finally got in the hospital from the medical staff had to be won. There was no knowledge about sociology in medicine, so support could not be gained by staying in close conformity to a neutral and traditional research role. Some of my frustrations stemmed from my need to conform to that role, a fact that isolated me and fabricated suspicions and fears. Only by departing from that role could the various parties get acquainted and do the job. This was obviously important since the study also took a somewhat different course than the staff had expected. Initially they did not perceive how sociology could bridge the gap between subjective personal experiences and a diffusely understood social structure.

Ideas and instruments from the Dikemark study are often used in

other studies in Scandinavia. It must be fair to say that it helped to
define the role of the medical sociologist, for it is not uncommon
now for various treatment organizations to want a sociologist to
describe relevant social processes. Of course, this may have come
more in spite of than because of what I have done. Nevertheless,
the book will soon be printed in its fifth edition.

The Dikemark study has not led to the implementation of new
practical programs at Dikemark, but that was not the intention of
the study. It did perhaps widen the psychiatrists' insight into their
social situation and the administration of patients. This point has
been related to me several times by psychiatrists both from Dikemark and other hospitals. Although my contacts with Dikemark
were not numerous after the book was published, I have constantly
lectured to psychiatrists and other groups about the inner life and
social processes of a mental hospital. The book has apparently influenced the thinking about mental institutions in Norway, and it is
well known in other Scandinavian countries. The basic thoughts
and concepts are well integrated into Norwegian psychiatry. The
psychiatrist is not alien to sociological questioning concerning the
applicability of his own medical and other models. A particularly
important point in the book was a discussion of how a diagnostic
culture could be used for repressive purposes by removing the attention from actual social conflicts and instead placing it on internal psychodynamic problems.

The climate may be changing somewhat. My book was a rather
stubborn effort to understand and even sympathize with the personal problems of psychiatrists who were forced to apply the irrelevant ideals and professional models they were taught in school
within the restrictive social structure of the mental hospital. It was
not, however, a forceful and explicit attack on the moral and political legitimacy of the hospital and the role of the psychiatrist in
society.

The book became, several years after it was first published, absorbed in the radical criticism of psychiatric work, and it has been
used as a foothold in the argumentation that the mental hospital—
and psychiatry—in its present form is repressive. This perspective
is evidently provocative, but it falls outside the value system on the
basis of which this particular piece of sociological work was accepted and given a status of respectability.

Thus the position of the book is somewhat altered; now it is used
by both sides in the modern debate on the social role of psychiatry.
Still, almost ten years after the book was first published, I receive

invitations from psychiatric societies around the world to talk about the inner workings of a mental hospital. Somehow I feel very discontent when I go to such meetings. In a way, I have become a radical alibi proving that a psychiatric establishment is occupied with social conflicts and struggles. But the main issue now should be how to bring psychiatry out into society and find some new ways of dealing with—or preferably preventing—human problems. There is a clear tendency to extend psychiatric thinking and role patterns to situations outside the hospital without questioning the assumptions underlying this development. Therefore I feel that my job is to point out that today ideals and realities do not match and that my initial problem has a general validity beyond the segregated world of the mental hospital. One has to ask what functions the extension of psychiatric services might have and whether this trend may partly be supported by forces which are alien to the ideal goals of psychiatry.

There were a few important breaks in the Dikemark project. I was in Canada and the United States from 1958 until 1960. I was back in Oslo in 1960 and got a job at the Institute of Sociology, University of Oslo. In 1962, a physician and I did a study of decision making in a social welfare program. We found that irrelevant factors not related to the condition of the client clearly entered the decision-making process. That study was financially supported by the government. It met tremendous resistance from the "top-dogs" in social welfare administration, and it was very well received by those in the lower echelons. It was one of the first studies of the microdynamics of the welfare state, and it may have had some significance for the emergence of a social science of the welfare state.

A SOCIOLOGIST IN THE MEDICAL FACULTY

In 1965 I took a position in the medical faculty at the University of Oslo. The position, which was located in the Institute of Social Medicine, is probably comparable with an assistant professorship in an American university. It was—and still is—the only full-time position for a social scientist in the whole medical faculty. In 1965 when the book about Dikemark was published, I received my Norwegian doctoral degree. Immediately afterward I received a promotion within the occupational category of assistant professorship. The institute urged me to study some of the factors responsible for the uneven geographical and occupational distribution of Norwegian physicians. The structure of the medical profession in

Norway resembles the structure of any other medical profession in a modern industrialized nation. In spite of the often expressed and official consensus of the profession concerning the great need for general practitioners or "frontline" doctors, there is a marked tendency in the direction of specialization and hospital work. The structure is not well suited for the problems of the population, and it is very different from what the profession itself thinks it should be. In spite of the fact that general practitioners are heavily overworked and that the university had taken little interest in them, they cooperated nicely with the research staff.

During 1967–68 I was a visiting scientist at the Institute of Mental Health, Bethesda, Maryland (as I also had been during 1959–60). There I pursued my interest in the role of the sociologist which could now be approached in a comparative perspective. I tried to analyze the strain between the values involved in the traditional sociological scientific enterprise on the one hand and in the politically engaged and inspired sociological activities on the other.

In 1969 I was asked by the government to take on the leadership of a study of poverty and the operation of various welfare schemes in a community outside Oslo undergoing major and rapid changes in the economic and occupational structure. This study has become rather large and comprehensive, and it deals with the functions of an expansive social policy within a welfare state. This study is now finished, and published.

In 1970 I published a book on the role of the sociologist,[6] and in 1970 another on problems of health and healing.[7] In 1969 I became a member of a public committee which was established in order to analyze and suggest reforms in Norwegian social policy. This committee finished its work in 1971. I ran into trouble because I strongly objected that the committee refused to take a stand on the Common Market issue. I was very much against a Norwegian entry into the EEC which would—in my opinion—release destructive forces in society thereby producing more social problems.

Recognition came from outside and from my friends and colleagues within the institute. I was also a chairman of a committee under the Norwegian Research Council. This committee was established in order to construct an organizational basis for the development of a science of the "welfare state." This would also include medical sociology. But the medical faculty cared little about sociology, and after awhile it was quite clear that there would be few opportunities for promotion and for developing a social science unit within the faculty. (Lately some plans have been drawn up, but apparently there will be no top positions for sociologists.) The faculty had no particular or systematic expectations concerning the use of social science, and there was small reason to be very optimistic. Since I enjoyed a fairly nice reputation outside the medical faculty, a rather strong dimension in the total situation was status inconsistency.

My experiences at the Institute of Social Medicine were not bad. I had friends and good colleagues. I found peace and was not unproductive. But in a larger perspective there were obvious problems.

Sociologists share some not too encouraging experiences in relation to the medical schools. Some do not get in there at all. And those who get in, find it hard to progress. Sociologists often become mired in the lower and powerless echelons. It is doubtless a legitimate expectation to have a fair chance of promotion within the system in which one works, especially in the university where evaluation is based on certain rigid (yet often irrelevant) criteria. We may of course not be good enough, but nevertheless it is true that for sociologists, academic performance does not lead to academic recognition and increased influence, as it so often does for others in the medical school. There is, however, much more involved here than pure occupational interests. What is at stake is the possibility of ever getting one's message across, and of being able to establish the validity and relevance of a new mode of thinking. The possible anonymity of the sociologist may be advantageous for him in one basic sense. He is free. He does not have to explain and defend his research, and at the same time he is not taking part in the destructive and energy-consuming rivalries and conflicts of his own discipline. But thus he is not really supported either, and he does not enjoy the full satisfactions of close, stimulating cooperation. Then certain paths or lines of adjustment are naturally available to the sociologist. He may turn sour and bitter, employing a whole armory of protective devices. He may become a moral reminder of how poorly he is treated.

He may even choose the very unproductive solution of becoming a semidoctor forgetting his own professional identity and competence. He may be flattered, wearing a white coat, enjoying the deference shown him by other less prestigious occupational groups. He may spend his time teaching the niceties of good communication between doctor and patient. Or he may become belligerent, forming alliances with progressive students.

I am fully aware of the fact that sociologists are not the only ones having difficulties within medical schools. The part of medicine, in

my country called social medicine, studying the relationship between social factors and disease, is regularly faced with strong resistance. It may be too much to expect that social medicine, being
itself such a relatively weak specialty within the medical family,
should carry the heavy burden of introducing and defending sociology in the medical system. But social medicine is also after all
defined as a medical discipline within the medical professional
structure, and it is basing its activities to a large extent on medical
concepts. Sociology functions somewhat differently. Sociology
questions the concept of disease and the systems of privileges and
obligations being attached to it. Social medicine is often imperialis-
tic on behalf of medicine, and it expands the concept of illness to
make it cover conditions that at the moment fall outside the medical domain. This imperialism of course is questioned by a
sociologist. However, it would be a strategic disaster to overlook
the fact that we do have allies within medicine. In spite of the differences between social medicine and sociology, in many connections they belong to the same party. The problem, obviously, is to
find a productive place for both these disciplines within or close to
the medical schools that still base their work on traditions formed
in times when these traditions apparently were far more relevant
and promising than now. And this is a part of a much larger issue:
What—if any—is the place of our disciplines in medical schools
that obviously find it extremely hard to change appropriately to
human suffering? And a most important question: What vested interests and gratifying experiences explain the resistance to change?
Why is it so difficult? These are probably the most important
sociological questions to be asked. In a way, I would even, as far as
sociology is concerned, ask the very negativistic question of
whether it really is worth the effort—What is the point of being a
medical sociologist in a traditional medical school that is not receptive to sociology? Do we become tokens—good to have when
radical students demand a more socially relevant curriculum? Is
the effective teaching of sociology and maintenance of the sociological identity dependent upon a widened view of the goals of medical education?[8]

PRESENT POSITION

A new university was recently established in Tromsø. Tromsø is
far north in the country, and some two thousand kilometers from
Oslo. The university was intended by the political authorities to
become one of the means to include the northern region of Norway

as a fully developed district into the whole nation. Many professional groups found this political decision rather arbitrary and unacceptable, and especially within medicine the opposition has been strong. In order to fulfill its goal, the university has to be integrated into the surrounding society. It will have to direct its intellectual attention to the problems of the north. It is impossible to do so without disciplinary integration, which to some extent has to be obtained at the expense of old traditions. Obviously there is a different dilemma here. Social science has taken a great interest in this new golden opportunity, and there is now an institute of social science at this university which also includes history and philosophy. The whole institute has approximately forty positions. The social science part is divided in five major problem areas in which research and teaching will be done: minorities, school and educational systems, isolated communities, fishing economy, and social politics and medical sociology. In each of these areas there will be representatives of different disciplines. Medical sociology and the study of social policy have been institutionalized. This area has now approximately ten positions. My present position is within this group as a full professor. I have been chairman of the institute, and have represented the institute in the main council of the university.

The university aims at several forms of integration: of disciplines, of levels of influence, and of theory and practice. It represents a very important event in Norwegian academic life. The goals of the medical school are progressive. It is explicitly stated that the idea is to create a "relevant doctor," or a new kind of physician educated for the problems of our times. Accordingly social science has a broad base and constitutes one of the three bodies of knowledge constituting the medical curriculum: the biological sciences, the clinical sciences, and all social sciences ranging from psychiatry to sociology. The medical committee which was responsible for these plans did an impressive job; indeed, it opened the way for fruitful collaboration between medicine and social science.

Heavy demands are placed upon the social science institute. We try to educate our own experts in social science while we also participate in a very interesting educational experiment in medicine. The group in medical sociology is in a particularly strategic position between social science and medicine. The cooperation between medicine and social science has so far been very stimulating. Of course we are not so naive that we expect everything to be perfect. We have already encountered some problems.

In the process of planning the participation of social scientists in the medical school, we have met a rather clear-cut demand for concrete knowledge. Doctors want knowledge that can improve their ability to cure and heal. The more lofty speculations of social scientists do not impress medical men as particularly precise and applicable.

Doctors want specified results easily transformable into practical activities. Polemically one could say that they want cogent answers to questions like how many hours of psychology is necessary for a medical student to become a good doctor? It is almost like a confrontation between a pragmatic culture stressing the importance of action and having things done and another contemplative culture being maybe overly preoccupied with problems. The underlying issue is perhaps that medical education is so strongly directed towards an occupation. The medical school must guarantee the quality of the doctor, and this creates a fairly strong need for an organized school system.

Doctors and sociologists do not think alike.[9] If they conform to the characteristic structures of the thinking processes in their respective fields and stay within the typical "mind-spaces" of their professions, problems of communications are likely to occur. A doctor basically views an illness as an individual problem. It is a process that can be located within the organism of the individual person, and the illness develops through time and space. Needless to say, this model has provided mankind with enormously valuable methods for curing diseases. But medical men have a tendency to go a step further, and they often explain social behavior within the same perspective. The medical man often perceives deviance, even poverty, as a medical problem. The implication is that treatment or some form of disablement pension is the correct solution. Poverty is the result of mental or other handicaps.

A sociologist does not think exactly like this. He is perhaps biased in his own way. He is not unlike other professionals in this respect. An expert and specialist is granted the right to overlook certain distracting and disturbing facts that may impress others, and he may proceed in his own professional doings. As sociologists we tend to view social behavior as expressions of social situations. Deviance is explained by class structures and blocked opportunity systems. Differential access to the centres of influence in society maintains social differences. Thus we tend to view the human personality as rather flexible.

Doctors and sociologists represent two different conceptions of man. Sociologists believe man is socialized to his present form of behavior. Behavior is understandable in terms of the social situation in which the actor finds himself. The medical man believes man does what he does because he is healthy or ill, getting older or somehow reacting to the changes in his biological organism. One very important aim of teaching sociology in the medical school is to confront the student with an alternative mode of thinking. The student ought to be acquainted with a larger intellectual universe.

Medical men are worried about the discrepancy between the models of positivistic science and the actual performance of sociology. It does not seem easy for medical doctors to accept that sociology does scientific and systematic work within completely different scientific traditions. Many of them discard the notion of a phenomenological or humanistic sociology. At the same time sociologists—probably in increasing numbers—reject the whole concept of a positivistic science of society.

We are in other words confronted with expectations of becoming natural scientists: social phenomena ought to be studied with the methods of natural science. Certainly this is difficult, and the sociologist finds this scope too limiting. I have met such pressure from medical students. They want us to become "real" scientists who conform to the wider ideals of the natural sciences. Prestige is accorded on such a basis in the medical school. I must admit that this impresses me as rather contradictory; doctors do not hestitate to make vital decisions for their patients and base these decisions upon empirical material collected by intuition and purely humanistic methods. Psychiatry does this constantly. And the most cherished concept of "the art of medicine" is meaningless without a full share of humanism. Somehow sociologists are less worthy if they employ the same kind of scientific equipment.

One of the most difficult and important tasks is to define the sociological contribution. Sociology has factual information to provide and offer. Definitely sociology must continue to do research and establish cumulative knowledge in several separate content areas. I do not reject the positivistic model of social science, though the political purpose and spirit of the researcher matter more. There are few questions more important for the radical student of society to study than rates of (occupational) diseases in certain types of industry and under different life conditions.

A main contribution of sociology is to assist the physician in becoming more reflective about his own medical and social role in various settings. When I worked in the mental hospital I have already referred to, I observed that the psychiatrists had a definite tendency, when they were threatened, to employ diagnostic categories and procedures rather indiscriminately. Several types of individual and social phenomena were put into diagnostic categories. A diagnostic culture emerged. This diagnostic culture became a means of controling the patient and of solving the doctor's dilemma. When patients placed legitimate demands on the psychiatrists which could not be met because of scarce resources, an easy way out was to interpret the demands in diagnostic, therefore ideosyncratic categories. The demands were seen as expressions of subjective conflicts. This is misuse of power, and a dangerous one since it is shrouded in respectable medical concepts. The doctor must become more conscious about the social forces impinging upon him when action is expected. This is one of the aims of sociology, and the teaching of this kind of sociology is far from easy, partly because the medical man believes that he is a man of action who hopefully should be in control of the situation. The whole idea suggests that the teaching of sociology is not only a technical delivery of cumulative knowledge. Sociology has also an intellectual substance which requires that the student mature emotionally and socially as he learns it. The production of insight is a primary goal.

Doctors and medical personnel in general ought to understand that some of their personal frustrations may actually be produced by the social system of which they are members. This insight may potentially mobilize the frustrations and transform the unreleased energy into meaningful action. Sociology is a means of breaking down the barriers against reciprocal identification and of enlarging the understanding of the problems of other groups. I remember from my mental hospital study that psychiatrists perceived their patients and other groups in the hospital in a too limited perspective, neglecting how social forces and strains call for surprising actions.

This approach leads to the simple sociological idea that all things are interrelated. This is not a terribly precise statement. Nevertheless, the social system idea may be the basic wisdom of sociology. This idea suggests that even treatment programs that are beneficial for patients may have some harmful consequences for others. The therapeutic community in psychiatry exposes the ward personnel to marked stress. The system idea may also imply that the system "requires" harmful ways of dealing with patients. One aim of teaching sociology is to enhance the understanding of the full consequences of medical activities within a social system.

The next step is to ask the same questions about the total medical institution: What part does it play in society? What does the expansion of the concept of illness really mean? Why does society accept a much broader use of medical concepts than ever before? Is it only because medicine has so much more to offer? What does it mean to call upon an expert—and a medical expert—for a wide variety of human problems? Can medicine also be used for repressive purposes? And how are medical services distributed? In other words, what kind of society does the present structure of the medical institution grow out of and support?

And then there is no way around the basic question of what kind of society we actually have. This, it seems to me, is another basic and medically relevant theme in sociology. I do not have to say that sociology should be taught in the form of Marxism. It is sufficient to say that it should teach how things interrelate in society, and that there is a tremendous gap between official descriptions of society and its realities. It is a difficult point to get across because medicine is fairly smoothly integrated in the present society. It is a problem when the macroperspective on society should be taught. Students easily get scared, probably less than the faculty members, and political sociology may be rejected if it is taught in the first year of the medical curriculum. However, we teach macrosociology in Tromsø in the first year of the medical study.

My view of the contributions of sociology does not automatically include a congenial cooperation between sociology and medicine. It would be a lot nicer, and more comfortable, if the sociologist willingly entered and stayed within the role of an uncritical expert on questionnaires and methods. But that solution does not reach the full potential of sociology.

I have experienced rather dramatically the forceful reactions from medicine against the critical kind of medical sociology, even in Tromsø. Internists and surgeons react, and some even believe our form of teaching is simply a revenge for the fact that no medical school accepted my application to become a medical student back in 1950. A few months after I got my position in Tromsø, I was interviewed in the Scandinavian medical journal (Nordisk Medicin), and the first question I got was this: "Is it true what is said about you, that you hate physicians?" Several people have commented upon the interview—both favorably and unfavorably—in the journal afterwards.

The location of sociologists at our university has been a difficult issue. The group in medical sociology was originally established at

costs that ran over the budget in medicine, and it was quite understandable that several persons in medicine wanted the positions to
be located in a medical institute. It was not so easy to solve the
problem, and the answer to this organizational question is not necessarily the same for all types of possible sociological contributions. It is perhaps meaningful and correct to locate a sociologist
participating in an integrated research project on social class and
coronary disease within the medical school if that is the home base
of the project. In Tromsø we have gathered the social scientists in
one Institute of Social Science, and there is a formalized cooperation between this institute and the medical school. For some of us
it is important that the critical content of sociology might be better
developed in this way. We are fully aware of the problem of relevance in teaching and research. In building up a new university
with scarce resources, we are afraid that a dispersion of very few
sociologists in various settings would make them anonymous and
weak.

Medicine is an essential part and one of the political foundations
of this university. There has always been a shortage of doctors in
northern Norway, and medicine was what people wanted. Medicine can put great strength behind their demands, and its political
bargaining position is strong. The medical men in charge are also
very competent. They will have a new hospital. It is hard to understand how we can succeed in producing a new physician with
more humble attitudes towards himself and others when he costs
many times as much as any other student.

SUMMARY

An autobiography must be self-centered. I may have blurred the
fact that I entered medical sociology when this discipline was
emerging. With a less personal approach it would probably have
been a lot easier to see that medical sociology has been growing
fairly, not entirely, independently of my participation in it. In any
case, medical sociology is now a discipline, also in Norway. But
medical sociology here is not exclusively centering its attention on
the medical institution alone, and another discipline has emerged
as a Siamese twin. Medical sociology is clearly related to the study
of the so-called welfare state which is natural because the medical
profession is so intimately connected to the welfare system.

Medical sociology is now attracting the interests of several researchers in Oslo, Bergen, Trondheim and Tromsø. Research on so-

cial political matters also expands, and, at the University of Bergen, there has recently been established a new professorship in Social Policy and Social Administration. It is of great importance that the Department of Social Affairs of the Norwegian government has a budget to support this kind of research. The development has not been rapid, but recently much work has begun. Also physicians seem to become increasingly interested in the institutions of health and cure, and there are conferences being held attended by both physicians and social scientists.

Two major themes cut across the different intellectual enterprises in which I have been involved. First, I have tried to show and analyze why there seems to be such a distance between ideals and realities in medical and sociological work. My thinking about this all started at Dikemark Hospital where this line of inquiry was developed. The project turned out to be an analysis of the difficulties associated with the realization of various professional models and human values. The study of decision-making processes in a welfare program was a continuation of the same line. It showed that decisions were frequently made in a way that drastically deviated from the ideals of rationality and justice. It was also difficult to establish the kind of cooperation necessary for the solution of the problems of the clients. The theme was brought up again in the study of the structure of the medical profession. The purpose was to explain some of the factors contributing to the uneven geographical and occupational distribution of physicians. The same idea is also represented in the large study of poverty in a community outside Oslo. The basic purpose was to describe the actual distribution of economic as well as other human resources in a modern, productive society where the expressed political and social ideals favor equality and a shared responsibility for the solution of social problems.

The other main theme is the role of the sociologist. I have also been concerned with the degrees of freedom in sociological research. My honest opinion is that sociology is not problematic in medicine as long as it stays within the limits of tolerance and lends moral legitimacy to medical work and concepts. I have become increasingly interested in the great distance between theory and practice in sociology and social science. Hopefully sociology could become something more than the theoretical production of words. It should develop an emphasis on the transformation of knowledge into action. Accordingly, I have progressively become interested in practical activities, outside the domain of medicine, and we have tried to define alternative ways of dealing with social and human problems. This form of sociology—action research—is perhaps the most controversial sociological enterprise. This theme—the role of the sociologist—has been broadened a good deal, and now I am working on some issues related to the roles of science in society. I am now chairman of the Central Committee for Norwegian Research, the purpose of which is to advise the government on issues in science policy.

These themes may not seem to be related. But they are. There is a kind of progression. I view medical sociology as a way of analyzing and questioning medical concepts and medical ways of handling human problems. Sociology in medicine becomes less interesting to me as time goes by. I am personally much more concerned with trying to develop a strong and critical sociology of medicine. Of course, one has to be compassionate and possess knowledge about medical methods and work. But sociology must contribute to the destruction of the unnecessary myths surrounding medical work. The clients of sociology must be taught to be honest, realistic and independent. Medical sociology is in principle not different from general sociology. Medical sociology, then, becomes the conscious utilization of the critical potential in sociology for medical matters. And it ought to be interested in finding practical methods for meeting needs of people falling outside the proper limits of illness.

However, the fact that medical sociology has significant contributions to make to the direct practice of medicine ought not to be repressed. This will be a practical project aiming at more suitable ways of dealing with the problem. Obviously there is a wide range of problems solidly resting within the domain of medicine which ought to be dealt with. Results from such work might indeed contribute to make medicine more humane, personal and relevant, and might help to explain the behavior of patients and sick persons. Obviously this brand of medical sociology is often strongly resisted. But it is basically not a vital threat to the principles of medicine. It defines itself as a discipline in cooperation with medicine, and it is not really questioning the premises of medical work. It does seek to find new ways of healing people suffering from disease and of delivering medical services. It will definitely broaden the perspective of medicine as well as the actual content of medical relationship.

I am personally tempted to place the emphasis of medical sociology somewhere else. An important task for medical sociology is to confront medicine with the full register of social consequences of medical concepts and medical work. Medicine must be seen as a social institution. The underlying and varying concept of the distinction between ill and well ought to be seen as an expression of a social and political structure. It might become clear that although the modern and inclusive concept of illness definitely has enormously positive consequences for those who thus can be covered by a medical reaction, it also has the function of "diagnosing" a socially and politically relevant problem. In my country it would be important to study how the responsibility for the solution of a variety of medical and social problems is progressively defined as a public matter. Citizenship involves a contract between the state (or other relevant official authorities) and the individual. This contract is released when medical and social services are needed. Medicine has become an integral part of the welfare ideology. It has a pervasive impact on the thinking about social problems and their underlying causes.

Medical sociology ought to invest work and energy in trying to understand one of the great and basic paradoxes of today's medicine. The dominant pattern of medicine still develops in a technical, specialized and natural science-oriented direction. The general practitioner disappears, and the hospital system is growing. Pharmacological treatment is widely used. At the same time there is much evidence to support the belief that the public increasingly suffers from nervous and sociomedical problems which must be dealt with in personal and human terms. Apparently it is difficult to swing medical attention to such problems, which, to a large extent, are the problems of poor and powerless people. And, of course, society plays a considerable part in producing these problems. Good medicine should work for a better society. Why does medicine resist change? What forces are preventing a new and more modern orientation? Is one of the answers the difficulty in abolishing and leaving behind medical traditions which have been effective in controlling some of the major and most threatening diseases? Is the phenomenon a reflection of the fact that medicine is a fairly autonomous institution with its own power structure directing attention, thoughts, research, and teaching in the old direction? Or is the basic structure of thought in medicine alien to these problems? I do not know. In my opinion medical sociology should not be too clearly separated from general sociology. Although much is to be gained by letting it become an independent specialty, we might then lose sight of what medicine really is as an institution in society with a whole range of interconnections and functions in it. Medicine can be studied as a branch of a scientific institution whose knowledge to a large extent is applied in society, in cooperation with the sociologist. Medicine should attempt to strike a balance between words and action, emotion and clear thoughts, politics and academic work, and with sociology should form a sort of productive disciplined protest.

NOTES

1. A third medical school is now established in Tromsø, and the first students arrived in the fall of 1973.

2. Some of Kaspar Naegele's papers were compiled and edited after his death by Elaine Cumming in *Health and Healing* (San Francisco: Jossey-Bass, 1970).

3. Alfred H. Stanton and Morris S. Schwartz, *The Mental Hospital* (New York: Basic Books, 1954).

4. Yngvar Løchen, *Idealer og realiteter i et psykiatrisk sykehus (Ideals and Realities in a Mental Hospital)* (Oslo: Universitelsforlaget, 1965).

5. Renée Fox, *Experiment Perilous* (Glencoe, Ill.: Free Press, 1959).

6. Yngvar Løchen, *Sosiologens dilemma (The Dilemma of the Sociologist)* (Oslo: Gyldendal, 1970).

7. Yngvar Løchen, *Behandlingssamfunnet (The Treatment Society)* (Oslo: Gyldendal, 1971).

8. These last pages are prepared from my paper "Sociology and Medicine," *Acta Socio-medica Scandinavia* 3 (1971): 161–68.

9. Also the following pages are more or less directly taken from my "Sociology and Medicine."

A Few Ideas and Many Opportunities: A Career in Medical Sociology

HANS O. MAUKSCH

The invitation to contribute to a volume on the origins of medical sociology forces me to face my own views of the label with which I have now been associated for about twenty-five years. There are times when I feel that our generation was privileged not to be burdened by a speciality designation as we went about doing sociology in the health field. Like all processes of institutionalization, the emergence of medical sociology as a speciality has brought gains and costs. Like all institutions, once established, medical sociology has to be defended, justified, and managed as a social enterprise. If, in my earlier years, my relationship to the sociology of the health field was reminiscent of courtship, I seem to have now been caught in all of the rituals, obligations and issues of domain associated with marriage.

I became involved in medical sociology without intending to discover or to develop a new area of specialization within my discipline. Actually what attracted me to these areas of inquiry looks very different in retrospect, than it did when I first made my decisions and utilized available opportunities. I felt comfortable in locating an environment permitting me to combine a variety of activities which I enjoyed and which I was moved to pursue. I was not fully aware at the time that my continuing theoretical interests in the interface between sociological theories could be so fruitfully pursued in a setting which is highly institutionalized, and in which continuous, around-the-clock operations and crisis management place role behavior under the spotlight. This environment offered me an opportunity to do what I have enjoyed so much all my life: to transmit and to interpret knowledge to those who could use it in addressing themselves to social needs and who could test the relevance of sociological precepts in real life settings.

It was almost coincidental when, looking for part-time employment, my first opportunity to teach surfaced in two hospital schools of nursing. The appeal of this environment for teaching and research was particularly persuasive since it felt like the discovery of a new world in which my barely acquired new academic skills seemed excitingly appropriate.

As I look back I might have become a sociologist committed to functioning in any of several areas of social concern. One thing I know for sure: I never could have been satisfied to remain confined to the community of my own discipline. Maybe it is my need to discover new questions in real situations; maybe it is my not-so-hidden missionary streak. Maybe it is my, as yet unfulfilled, search for a laboratory in which theoretical knowledge can be tested, and in which sociological experimentation can be undertaken. Maybe—a peculiar personal characteristic—medical sociology offered me a career where I could always be "one of the few," where I could have all of the titillation of ritualized marginality.

None of this was evident to me when, in the fall of 1946, I was admitted to graduate study at the University of Chicago. I had emigrated to the United States in 1938, leaving my native Vienna after the annexation of Austria by Germany in March of that year. After an initial period of several short-lived menial jobs, I spent four years in the retail business selling ladies' clothing and shoes. World War II represented the real turning point for me. Trained as a specialist in military intelligence, I became involved in teaching, innovation, and in carving out an unusual military career for myself. I had the opportunity to develop and to administer new large scale training programs. This was a crucial moment for me. The refugee who had nearly abandoned any ambitious dreams for his future discovered an area of excitement and experienced success. I wanted to teach, I wanted to explore the powers of education. When I left the army, the GI Bill made it possible to pursue these goals.

When I entered the University of Chicago, my interests, therefore, were in learning about education. I was particularly interested in discovering how teaching could affect social change and how it functioned as a "helping occupation." After being enrolled in the Department of Education for three academic quarters, I switched to sociology. I discovered that it is difficult to gain understanding of a social phenomenon by immersing oneself into the midst of it. Rather than learning how to become an educator, I wanted to find out how education functioned. Sociology seemed to offer a more promising approach. The stance of sociology helped me to conceptualize my interests in terms of careers, occupations, and institutions.

In the course of my studies, Everett Hughes introduced me to the sociological potential of the health field. His preference for examples from medicine and nursing piqued my interest. Nevertheless, I might have pursued my earlier intentions and joined a group of graduate students in studying teachers, if coincidence had not intervened.

Most diploma schools of nursing contained in their curriculum a course in sociology. These were taught by a variety of personnel including nurses, social workers and, occasionally, graduate sociology students or sociology faculty. At the Presbyterian Hospital School of Nursing a rather impressive sequence of sociologists had taught this course. Joseph Lohman, Earl Johnson, and Maurice Schwartz had preceded Morris Janowitz, who, wishing to terminate his teaching at the hospital, asked me in the fall of 1948 whether I was interested in taking over. It was a job, and also, I needed an opportunity to gain teaching experience. Even though I was graciously accepted, and like my predecessors was a valued symbol, it was evident that the sociology instructor came, taught, and left. The definition of the "welcome outsider" with emphasis on both words was clear. Yet, the job was satisfying and, during the spring of 1949, I discovered the gratification which can come from bringing sociology to those who neither know, nor asked to know, what sociology is about.

The experience at Presbyterian Hospital School of Nursing might have remained but a stimulating interlude if, six months later, a second door into the world of health had not opened. Using it for deeper penetration was made possible by my being legitimated through my relationship to one of the influential members of the "ingroup." My wife is a nurse, and throughout our married life she has been fully active in her profession. During recent years, this career has resulted in her achieving national eminence as teacher, author, administrator, and practitioner and has been a matter of choice and commitment. However, during my graduate student days, my wife's occupational activities were necessitated by my need to live "by the sweat of the frau." In 1949, she had accepted the position of chief nursing arts instructor at St. Luke's Hospital School of Nursing. In this position she was one of the senior members of the faculty, in charge of several other teachers, and responsible for the initiation of the novice into the rites and the procedures of nursing.

The sociology course at St. Luke's Hospital School of Nursing had been taught by a social worker who left in the summer of 1949. I was asked whether I might be interested in teaching the course, and I accepted. Thus, beginning with the fall of 1949, I was responsible for the sociology courses at Presbyterian Hospital School of Nursing and at St. Luke's Hospital School of Nursing. In contrast with my role at Presbyterian School of Nursing, I became a real member of the faculty at St. Luke's Hospital. The combination of teacher and of spouse of one of the senior faculty members provided a peculiar role basis for inclusion and involvement. As a new part-time instructor, I was a very junior member of the faculty; yet, as spouse of one of the senior members, I enjoyed visibility and status by contagion. This position opened communications and observations to me which the novice "male nonnurse" could otherwise have sought in vain for a long time. My interest in the world of nursing was stimulated by the observation that it approximated a closed social system, making it possible to combine my interests in institutions and in roles.

I still do not understand why I chose not to use this newly discovered territory for my master's thesis. Perhaps it was my sense of not being ready, but I also did not choose my previous topic of interest—teachers. My interest in occupations and careers led me to undertake a study of career lines of the members of the Seventy-sixth United States Congress (1940). Although it was a great experience, this work has since rested in the oblivion which it deserves.

I was privileged to be at the University of Chicago. Great teachers and significant scholars provided a marvelous learning environment. I feel special indebtedness to certain faculty members for the seeds they planted although they are not the only ones who left their mark on my career. To Everett Hughes I am indebted for learning how to ask questions and for assuming the stance of curiosity and irreverence vis-à-vis the world of everyday experiences. Herbert Blumer taught me to view process and interaction as reality and to approach manifest data with caution. Earl Johnson is the man who supported and enhanced my commitment to teaching, while Edward Shils symbolized the drive for conceptual rigor. Louis Wirth demonstrated that academic pursuits are compatible with elegance and that the ultimate purposes of knowledge are its social consequences and its application to human needs.

It was a mixture of these influences which made the study of nurses increasingly fascinating to me. Here, I could pursue my initial interest in occupations devoted to service and their legitimation in a success- and acquisition-oriented society. At the same time, I saw a laboratory for the study of relationships between institutional and service processes, between ingroup and intergroup realities and between the plot of the play and the experiences of the actors.

In order to initiate data gathering I planned to start collecting observations in the patient care areas of the hospital. Since I was going to do this at St. Luke's Hospital, I requested permission from the director of nursing. She consented, but felt it necessary to send a memorandum to all head nurses in preparation for my appearance in the wards. Rather than announcing the sociology instructor, the memo introduced, "Hans Mauksch, a male nonnurse." The ambivalence and ambiguity of my status surfaced differently at the annual School of Nursing dinner, where the director of nursing herself showed faculty members to their tables. She, the assistant directors, the hospital administrator, and two physicians were scheduled to sit at the speakers' table. When my wife and I entered the dining room, the Director of Nursing first directed us towards an appropriate table, then, looking at me, corrected herself and invited us to join the speakers' table. Although my wife's position was by far more senior than mine, the male sex seemed to warrant special treatment.

After starting data gathering in the hospital, I realized that my status in the School of Nursing did not automatically transfer into the patient areas, and that new definitions were required as I changed place of operation. This served as an initial stimulation for my dissatisfaction with formal institutional analysis and with traditional role theory. It was so evident that new settings created new rules but that previous situations gave rise to claims. My observations in the hospital underscored this sense of continuing negotiation and maneuvering. I recall the impact on me as novice when I observed that the nursing students, who had been known to me as sheltered, protected, and controlled young girls within the School of Nursing, were expected to behave as "adults" in the domain of patient care. The same girls to whom no one in the School of Nursing could speak about the facts of life, were expected to stand by while patients died, cried, or shared their most innermost secrets because, "you are a nurse and you will understand."

Although by 1952 I had clarified the general outlines of my research interests and felt I could begin the development of a dissertation proposal, I was not destined to take the avenue of pure scholarship. My first opportunity in institutional development and experimentation occurred when a new director of nursing took over St. Luke's Hospital School of Nursing in the fall of 1953. She was a very energetic, astute, and innovative woman, who was intent on implementing changes throughout her domain. It became obvious that I was a useful ally; we started to work closely together in initiating change. I became involved in all kinds of committees and served as advisor to the director. In the building of a new curriculum I was one of the main architects. This also helped the growth of the social sciences in the teaching program. It grew from 36 hours in 1952 to 120 hours in 1953. In that year I organized a Social Sciences Department, which by 1955 included five sociologists and psychologists.

Less and less was I viewed as an outsider within the school of nursing. I had become accepted and my sex was either overlooked or I was defined as a safe, captive male. This had not been so prior to 1953. When the freshman class in 1952 voted to choose me as their class advisor, the previous director of nursing felt that she had to check with the Board of Directors to determine whether a man could be trusted as an advisor to a class of young women. By 1954 I had become an institutionalized recipient of confidences from all sides.

This increasing intimacy with the world of nursing not only took much of my time, but it challenged the theoretical foundation of my initial plans for my dissertation. I had learned by then that I had previously barely scratched the surface, and that the interaction between the socialization of nurses and the institution within which this process occurred, could not be understood without understanding the institution itself. The methodological and theoretical debate over the advantages of rigorous, imposed research design against the deep, intimate type of knowledge derived from full participation became a keen concern for me. I have since resolved to my satisfaction that—like in so many of the debates in the history of sociology—the question should not be posed as a contest between right and wrong. Appropriate modes of inquiry are determined by the objectives of the research and the type of knowledge sought. Since I was concerned with the interface between individual careers and institutional functions and processes, I had to resort to a combination of methodologies. To understand the nursing population as a possibly distinct group I employed aggregate quantitative data gathering methods which provided the capability to impose a systematic theoretical scheme for purposes of group analysis. Yet, the meaning of these findings and their consequence in day-to-day behaviors emerged from observation, participation, listening and sharing. Merging and matching findings with hypotheses made during participation provided intellectual excitement and a sense of being intimate with one's own data.

This approach to my research interests essentially confirmed my long-range commitment to the sociology of the health field. Getting close to my data gave me meaning and depth; it also forced new questions upon me and led me to incorporate contextual issues into my sphere of interest. The network of roles, agencies, and functions within which nurses have to be understood made me wish to study the subcultural content of this occupation. The discovery of the fascination and complexity of the hospital and its inhabitants made specialization merely appear as the choice of the laboratory for the study of many issues.

Early in 1954 I had two opportunities to present to nursing audiences my initial findings about the dilemmas inherent in the role of the head nurse. The findings which I reported may have been supportive of the interests and needs of my audience. Possibly I had learned by my intense involvement in the world of nursing to communicate effectively in the language of my audience. Whatever the reason, I was extremely well received and, within six months, began a long career of speechmaking in conferences, meetings and workshops.

Looking back at my career, this preoccupation with oral communication is not an insignificant aspect of role development and self-presentation. It occurred to me in later years that, possibly, the choice of preferred mode of communication has its own sociology of knowledge, its own interdependent relationship with the role of the scholar. The culture of the "scholarly paper," the traditionally read presentation of written language at the typical scholarly meetings suggests caution, reserve, and the speaker's preoccupation with the subject matter. The translation of knowledge into primarily spoken communications brings with it a sense of timing and of drama, of priorities, and of pedagogy. It forces the speaker to relate to audiences and to learn how to use himself as an integral part of the communication itself.

I was fortunate by starting early on the lecture circuit. By having acquired a mode of speaking without notes, I was able to use my speeches not merely as means for communication, but as conceptual explorations helping me understand my data while addressing an audience. It was in one of these speeches that I formulated the distinction between "cure" and "care," a scheme which has since become part of the literature as a way of sorting the flow of authority and function originating from the physician from processes consistent with the mandate of the hospital itself.[1]

During that time I began to differentiate among the roles of sociology within the health field. It became apparent that in the selection from the body of knowledge called sociology that which was useful and relevant to the practice of nursing and to the politics of the profession was not synonymous with the accretion of data about nursing and its functions.[2]

I began to learn then what has more recently become an accepted paradigm for the teaching of behavioral sciences in medical schools: to be effective for students in the health professions, the subject matter of sociology has to be organized as deductive and synthesis-oriented material related to the real issues of professional practice and professional role. Even Max Weber's "Essay on Bureaucracy" could be made meaningful to nursing students, once they had experienced and learned to evaluate the conditions under which their own role unfolded in the hospital.

I continued my triple life as teacher, as researcher, and as observant participant in the hierarchy of the nursing department and of the school of nursing. I delved into various experimentations as part of my participation in policymaking and innovation. Yet, many theoretically seminal ideas emerged from my immersion in real life. My interest in territoriality as a sociological concern was stimulated when I discovered that changes in the physical layout of nurses' stations did, actually, increase communication between physicians and nurses.

I learned to see the world of patient care through the eyes of nurses. I became intrigued with an occupation which had institutionalized restraints upon itself; at times, I referred to it as the "occupation of not-quite." Almost the healer, almost the manager, almost the mother or the sweetheart to the client, the nurse fascinated me not only as an occupation but as a peculiar mixture of the pedestal and the suppression which characterizes the female role. When I recently looked at some notes, assembled during the fifties, I found that, while observing nurses, I anticipated the assertions currently made by the women's liberation movement.

Among all minority groups, the place of woman has continued to fascinate me, partly because it is crucial to an understanding of the structures and strains of the health care system and, partly, because I am attracted by the complexity of woman's minority status. It is unique in that sex is clearly a means of differentiation, subordination, and discrimination, but also provides a fundamental, biosocially rooted attraction between the "castes." This immensely complicates and modifies the network of relationships, power, and symbolic behaviors.

In the hospital I found the most extreme forms of male dominance and exploitation. The powerful forces of labeling and expectations, at best assured a woman that she was "half again as bright as girls are meant to be."[3] The potential of sociology to utilize cognitive dissonance as a device for social change has continued to intrigue me. The development of militancy or, at least, the need to modify ongoing arrangements frequently is related to the discovery of the incompatibility of coexisting ideologies previously not consciously experienced as conflict. By reporting the covert accommodations to a submissive, subservient female role, the sociologist makes a previously suppressed arrangement cognitively apparent and, thus, intolerable as conflicting with the professional role.

The middle fifties saw the emergence of medical sociology as an identity and as a speciality within the discipline. I have two overriding impressions as I remember the first meetings of medical sociologists during the sociological conventions. One was the attempt by a significant segment of this group to seek approval from the medical profession and their apparent preoccupation with acceptance by physicians. The other, possibly a more idiosyncractic feeling, was that sociologists who worked with physicians looked down on sociologists who worked with nurses. I recall that, at first, I felt insecure and marginal and then became fascinated with the power of contagion which the object of inquiry has for the status of the observer. I must confess that I, too, having absorbed from my host environment, the nurses' resentment of the physician, at times felt this resentment. It is important to remember that those who chose the window of medicine to look at the hospital saw indeed a somewhat different spectacle from the one I had observed from the vantage point of nursing. I am still preoccupied with the epistemology of simultaneous, multiple truths as a problem, especially relevant to sociology. Our discipline must always acknowledge the link between the answer and the locus of the question and the method. Complex social settings require complex, pluralistic research designs.

I began to feel the need to find a platform not primarily identified with nursing. Since I had accepted that in studying "real world" phenomena there was no scientifically neutral corner, I decided to switch to the point of institutional output, that is, the patient's care as the location for the sociologists's lens. In this I received encouragement from Dr. Lester Evans of the Commonwealth Fund. A grant from this foundation enabled me to initiate a project in 1968 designed to study the patient's perception of patienthood. This grant included the provision establishing a Department of Patient

Care Research as an independent unit within the hospital. This arrangement gave me a new and significantly independent basis of operations.

In the meantime, the institution in which I was working had undergone profound changes. Early in 1956, the boards of directors of Presbyterian Hospital and of St. Luke's Hospital initiated the merger of these two institutions which was consummated in the fall of that year. I regret that my ongoing research prevented me from systematically studying the process of merger. Two institutions with long-standing traditions and loyalties do not merge easily. There was a clear distinction between the balance of power in the relative position of the two corporate bodies and the mosaic of power struggles which occurred between the different departments and sections of the two hospitals. In the area of nursing, it was immediately clear that nursing at St. Luke's Hospital was assuming control over the merged departments and the joint school. This new school of nursing, thereby, became one of the largest diploma schools in the United States. While all department and section chiefs were meeting with their counterparts in the other hospital, I was in the unique position of having held for years the comparable position in both institutions, although with a different degree of involvement.

In a peculiar way the reorganization of the department of nursing and of the school of nursing provided certain strategic advantages to the social sciences. The need to negotiate with counterparts in the other hospital absorbed time, energy, and degrees of freedom for most segments within the nursing system. This provided greater latitude to my unit since I had no concern with my counterpart in the merger. I was able to become more directly involved in certain aspects of the experimental design associated with the development of the new curriculum. We were able to develop a curriculum which, although structured within the framework of "diploma" education, represented a systematic move towards a single-purpose academic program, somewhat along the line of previous patterns in law, engineering, and medicine.

Having been interested in professional education not only as socialization but also as a form of occupational claim and manifesto, I had become concerned during those years with the peculiar transition of nursing education from the hospital-based diploma programs to the college-based degree education. Unlike other professions, except possibly education, the emerging undergraduate curricula in nursing were a mixture between liberal arts and professional content, thus representing much academic compromise and dilution. Granting all of the dangers of educational blinkers of single-purpose curricula in engineering or in medicine, nursing did not have an educational laboratory which it controlled for its own purposes, either in the hospital or in the college.

Considering the size of our merged school of nursing, it would have been possible to experiment with an autonomous, undergraduate educational institution, oriented toward occupational preparation and capable of developing for nursing the potentials of research and experimentation. This experimental development never fully materialized. The groundwork was well done, an academic organization was developed providing for a full mobilization of the natural sciences, the social sciences, and the humanities. Also the curriculum which evolved seems, even today, favorably comparable to many collegiate nursing programs. Yet survival is usually more a matter of politics than of merit. For reasons of institutional pressures, the ultimate step of changing identity and claiming academic status through incorporation and charter was never taken. The experimental program at Presbyterian–St. Luke's School of Nursing, like so many other diploma programs, closed its doors in 1968.

In the development of research in medical sociology and in the experimentation with the role of the medical sociologist, this was an important period. Instead of being tolerated and having to justify one's existence, our group of sociologists and psychologists had become not only accepted, but fashionable. The rapid expansion of our space within the curriculum and our involvement in institutional changes created a situation where our research findings and even pilot data became immediately marketable and demanded. In those days I found ample support for my belief that my discipline can make a difference and that the translation of intuitive and experiential insights into systematic sociological knowledge provides not only a basis for developing further research but for the application of sociology to practice. Science represents a conceptualization of given phenomena at such a distance from reality that its content can be comprehended and manipulated. The natural sciences do so by formulating concepts which bring knowledge from the distance of total ignorance. This natural science method is erronously felt to be more important and consequential than the process of the social sciences which, at the same conceptual distance, organizes knowledge fetched from such experiential proximity that it was too close for precision, comprehension or manageability. In the continuous struggle and maneuvering which characterize the health professions, this contribution of sociology makes the difference in playing the game, in understanding the plot, and in effecting the outcome.

I was fortunate in attracting a number of excellent young social scientists to join me, first in the social sciences department in the school of nursing, and then also in the newly created hospital department of patient care research. Of these, Wolf Heydebrand, James Skipper, and Daisy Tagliacozzo deserve special mention because their professional work and subsequent scholarly products were influenced by their association with Presbyterian–St. Luke's Hospital. Daisy Tagliacozzo, my colleague in the program in patient care research contributed significantly to my own development.

Between 1957 and 1962 these activities progressed to include a variety of conceptual interests. I continued to explore the hospital as a laboratory for the interface between the sociopsychological processes of socialization and role behavior and the social organizational factors of power, structure, status, and function. This general thrust of inquiry was primarily carried on in the department of patient care research, with major emphasis on the patient, on nursing, and on hospital organization and administration. Relatively little work was done with physicians. As part of our involvement in the education of nurses, we came face to face with the wealth of sociological contributions to clinical practice and to the relationship between illness and sociological variables. Exploratory studies of patients and subsequent experimental changes of nurses' behavior suggested the potential worth of a real life laboratory setting which, typically, is denied the sociologist. This led to the development of a proposal which would have established an experimental patient care unit designed to be the site of research and experimentation in the organization and process of patient care. This project was to simultaneously produce benefits to sociological theory and professional and administrative means of improving care. I found considerable interest in this idea among officials of the public health service, but, when I proposed this plan to the administrative officers of Presbyterian–St. Luke's Hospital in 1961, I did not find them willing to make such a major commitment.

Our grant from the Commonwealth Fund terminated in the fall of 1962. To obtain additional research support I would have had to demonstrate continuing financial and organizational commitment on the part of the hospital administration. This was not adequately forthcoming. Although I could have, in other ways, continued to be active at Presbyterian–St. Luke's Hospital, I decided to leave, having gained during my thirteen years of association with this institution a great deal of experience, a career, and a set of long-range questions to be answered. The social sciences department in the School of Nursing continued to function for the remainder of the existence of the school. The department of patient care research was essentially discontinued.

Among the number of positions which became available to me, I chose the one which seemed, at first glance, to be the most complete turning away from my career, and which demanded an apparently impossible task. I accepted the position of dean of liberal arts at Illinois Institute of Technology (IIT). This institution which had been primarily an educational training ground for engineers, sought to develop its program in the liberal arts. I was partly attracted to this position because of my interest in educational development and experimentation, and partly because I enjoyed the creative potential of academic administration. However, I was also attracted because I felt that an immersion in the world of engineers would provide a new type of in depth view of professional socialization and role creation. My methodological predilection for observant participation made this opportunity very palatable to me. I spent nearly six years in that position, gaining great satisfaction from the development of programs in the biological sciences, social sciences, and the humanities. From the point of view of this essay, my continuing career in medical sociology was maintained in a number of ways. I managed to produce some published results of my previous research in the hospital, and I continued to be active on the speaker's platform. I tried to organize an institutionwide center for health-related research, and I established relationships with several hospitals in the vicinity of the institute. In seeking to establish an institutional inventory of health-related research it was amazing to discover how many members of the faculty in various departments were conducting such studies. It was equally fascinating to discover that faculty members in neighboring departments did not know about each other's overlapping research interests. This was true in engineering, as it was true in biological and social sciences.

My contact with engineers and engineering students provided a new perspective to my previous research with nurses. I was impressed with the similarities between these two occupations. Both of them had placed their educational socialization on the prebac-

calaureate level. The literature of both occupations seemed preoccupied with their concern and insecurity about "professional"
status. Both seemed an avenue for upward mobility and appeared
to recruit a large proportion of young people who wanted to rise
under reasonably structured and secure conditions. I was also impressed that in the conceptualization of engineering students, I
found the same identification of their chosen career with their sex
role, just as I had found a large proportion of nurses identifying
nursing with an institutionalized female role. In both occupations
one detects an ethos of not being accountable for the full impact
and consequence of one's activities. Even though this is more generally substantiated in the reality of nursing, it is a mood which
prevails in both occupations. What to the nurse is the physician's
authority, the corporation appears to be to the engineer.

The office of an academic dean is a sociological laboratory. I
learned a great deal about interdisciplinary communications, about
academic and occupational territoriality, and about the utility of
sociology in solving real problems. Here, too, I was impressed with
the simultaneous validity of several coexisting truths, protected
from each other by cognitive compartmentalization or by in-
trainstitutional myopia. The university as an institution which has
features of a formal structure, of a federation of competing disciplinary domains, of a contractual base for an aggregate of individual
contractors is, to the dean, frequently a dichotomized world of faculty and administration. All these perspectives are valid and they
have implications for the methodology of organizational analysis.

The decision to leave the dean's chair and to return to full involvement in medical sociology was precipitated by my having become involved in a preliminary planning group which was exploring the feasibility of a new medical school jointly sponsored by IIT
and Michael Reese Hospital. I served as the representative of IIT on
this committee and, together with another faculty member, joined
two physicians from Michael Reese Hospital in exploring medical
education and the role of the medical school. The development of
this school could have been an exciting one and, had it come to
pass, might have changed my career. However, the directors of both
institutions did not wish to assume the scope of fund raising and
the type of commitments which a medical school required, even
though one potential major donor had been active in stimulating
our explorations. The large gift, which thus was not earned, was
finally given to the University of Chicago School of Medicine after
Michael Reese Hospital had established a relationship with that
university.

This involvement with medical education during 1966 and 1967 provided the leverage in my decision to return to academic sociology and to become involved in the education of physicians, and in research associated with medicine. I had, by now, gained experience in interpreting sociology to nurses, engineers, hospital administrators, and the military. In terms of impact and consequence I felt most challenged to try my luck in medical education. At the same time I was interested in organizational experimentation. My experiences as dean had convinced me that the traditional departmental organization of universities is inadequate and frequently serves as an obstacle to educational and to scholarly functions. I saw the inadequacy of programmatic arrangements between departments if it was accompanied by the protection of the domain and claims of the participating departments. I also became keenly aware of the tender issues associated with the subordination of basic sciences departments to professional academic bodies. Just as medical schools frequently incorporate and dominate departments of basic biological sciences, so the College of Engineering at IIT included the physical sciences. My jurisdiction as dean of liberal arts did not include them and was confined to the biological and social sciences and the humanities. There were many times when I was involved in delicate explorations about the possibility of "liberating" the physical sciences.

To leave the dean's chair and to return to an academic position seems, in retrospect, to have occurred almost as a smooth, natural progression. Yet, there were some factors which influenced the actual timing of this move. Becoming involved again in the health field strengthened my continuing perception of myself as having only detoured through a dean's office without ever abandoning my image as an academic. Yet, I felt my competence was fading and I foresaw the crossroads of no return. At that time, I happened to receive several invitations to become a candidate for positions of college president. I turned all of them down without giving them consideration. One morning, I was awakened at 7:00 a.m. by a telephone call, essentially offering me a position of university provost. I declined immediately and turned to my wife to announce that my own behavior indicated that I was ready to leave administration since I had rejected all opportunities for advancement in administration. My wife agreed and on that day I called three trusted friends to tell them about my availability.

I explored a number of positions. I was surprised to discover that I would be able to match my dean's salary in professional positions, particularly if associated with a medical school. I was seeking an opportunity to experiment with organizational arrangements which would provide an effective bridge between the social sciences and the world of medicine, providing the fullest mutual involvement without diminishing the integrity of the participating disciplines. Such an opportunity appeared to exist at the University of Missouri. At Missouri I found in the person of Vernon Wilson (then dean of the medical school), someone who seemed willing to fully support the development of the social science experiment academically, administratively, and structurally. I also felt that the faculty in the School of Medicine provided a favorable environment, with initial development of a behavioral science course having been already undertaken.

The Sociology Department at the University of Missouri seemed an equally hospitable environment. I felt exceedingly welcome and felt assured that activities linking sociology to the School of Medicine would be supported. This was essential, particularly since joint appointments and extra departmental activities do not enjoy favorable reception in many academic quarters.

I joined the University of Missouri in February 1968. The years since then have made all my previous experiences seem like gentle rehearsals for the real effort. Although I feel justified in claiming significant areas of success, I neither feel that they are as yet secure or fully developed in their own potential. From the point of view of program, I can subdivide the development of these last seven years into the following activity spheres: the education of medical students; experimentation in organizational and administrative arrangements; education of graduate students in the sociology of health and health care; research; the development of new programs; and the role of the change agent.

THE EDUCATION OF MEDICAL STUDENTS

If I had become confident about my ability to interpret sociology and the social sciences to the students in the health professions, trying to do so to medical students proved to be an unsettling experience designed to shake any sense of accomplishment which I might have had in the beginning. We came face to face with a set of attitudes which combined lack of respect and understanding for the social sciences with a subtle but powerful status problem, in which the medical students as future physicians tended to define all others as subordinate and auxiliary to medicine. Our experiences tend to replicate those of most of my colleagues engaged in similar pursuits.

The problems are, however, quite complex and are linked to the whole nature of the medical curriculum and the changing priorities in the practice of medicine. The content of the social sciences moves the physician from the apparent certainty of the technology of disease control to the probabilistic, and only partially controllable factors of human behavior, human relationships, and the constellations of human environment around issues of health and illness. In transferring attention from microscopes, social sciences seems simultaneously less scientific and more threatening. Somehow the microbial contagion which the physician can bring into the examining room seems scientifically respectable and acceptable. The contagion of the physician's behavior by his cultural and personal background and the differential treatment of patients by age, sex, appearance, and social class are interpreted as unprovable and unwarranted attacks on medicine.

During these years our behavioral sciences courses have become more accepted and, by at least a significant segment of students, are seen as relevant and important to their careers. There has been, if only by precedent, acceptance that these courses are part of the curriculum. Rewards and gratification have increasingly come our way, particularly from students who visit during their clinical years to tell us that it was only then that the significance of our teaching had become apparent. Medical students now seek us out to explore their views of their own careers and to share with us their concern about health care. Occasionally one even has the privilege of feeling that a student's career and priorities have been influenced by one of us.

Probably I have learned more in these five years than many of the students whom I taught. I have rediscovered the tremendous difficulty in organizing a teaching program around issues and problems, and in seeking to maintain rigor in the process of selecting teaching content aimed at fostering synthesis rather than analysis. I have rediscovered what I had learned many years ago during my short sojourn in the Department of Education at the University of Chicago: a clear and explicit formulation of educational objectives is a prerequisite for curriculum development and for teaching.

Among the several available target areas which could link the social sciences and medicine, we chose several to serve as organizing principles for selecting course content. Thus, the choice of objectives derived from the confrontation between physician and client enabled us to relate sociological knowledge about role behavior to an understanding of the physician, the patient, and of his community as a network of social processes which have a direct bearing on the effectiveness of medical practice. The training in interviewing as a syndrome of skills and behaviors and the inclusion of the topics stigma, sex, and death as special issues affecting the physician's relationships provide depth and drama to our educational plans. The relationship of medicine to health services and health care needs, the role of the physician among other health professions, and the relationship between health and human behavior are other target areas which we chose to develop as educational units within the sequence of the behavioral sciences courses.

Quite beyond the scope of teaching content and teaching technique are other factors which, in my view, are integral aspects of the process of medical sociology and the success or failure of our mission. It is a correct use of the meaning of science to expect that the content of sociology is distinct from the sociologist and independent of his behavior. This applies within the community of sociologists and within the process of contributing to sociological theory and concepts. Manifestly, this notion is an inadequate definition in situations which involve innovation, demonstration, and social change. Only the future will show whether I was right or wrong in seeking to articulate vis-à-vis medical students, not only knowledge, but also behavior appropriate to the social scientist. It was not easy to withstand the temptation to join the competitive pressures imposed on students in the school of medicine. Notwithstanding the students' preoccupation with immediate survival in courses,[4] our teaching seeks to focus on future role problems. In relating to medical students our staff has continued to encourage interaction and negotiation. Even in the face of disparagement and insult, we sought to demonstrate to medical students how, in a professional relationship, one can take a stand against attack and yet accept positively the person whose message is rejected.

I feel that we have just begun. The current mode of teaching the behavioral sciences is but an intermediate platform on the road to continuous presence of the social sciences in the process and structure of medical education. Initially, it will need to be the social scientist who must become involved in the translation of didactic content to the practice situation, be it at the patient's bedside, the community health center, or the marketplace of health-oriented policies. In the near future, I foresee an increased number of physicians whose disciplinary competence will be within the social sciences, just as many physicians today are experts and researchers in one of the biological sciences. They will, hopefully, serve as demonstrators, translators and innovators.

EXPERIMENTATION IN ORGANIZATIONAL AND
ADMINISTRATIVE ARRANGEMENTS

The presence of social scientists in medical schools takes on a variety of administrative patterns. This ranges from the isolated social scientist located in clinical or in basic science departments, to the presence of full-fledged departments of behavioral sciences. I might have sought the latter route if I had joined a school of medicine which was physically distant from the arts and sciences campus. However, I had deliberately picked the University of Missouri because of the proximity of the two. I opted for the development of a behavioral sciences section which, although organizationally within the Department of Community Health and Medical Practice, is able to function quite autonomously. I felt that as members of a section we could develop informal relationships more easily with all areas within the Medical Center, as well as with a number of departments in the College of Arts and Sciences. This has worked out very well.

The absence of formal interdepartmental obligations has permitted us to approach relationships casually, to prepare the ground for the relationships between social scientists, physicians and others, before engaging in the substance of the relationship itself. The behavioral sciences unit serves as an organizational basis for social scientists within the Medical Center, but it also serves as a bridge between the health professions and the arts and sciences. This unit serves as a facilitating agent in bringing other social scientists into the health area for purposes of research, planning, or to augment teaching. Conversely, physicians, medical students, and others in the Medical Center are assisted in locating and using resources on the general campus which otherwise might not be available to them.

Whether it is my personal style and my own preference for the politics of ambiguity, or whether it is the practical application of the theoretical position identified as "negotiated order," I like the current arrangement which minimizes structure and maximizes flexibility although with a degree of risk. Fundamentally, however, I feel that our organizational arrangement is a move in the direction which academic organizations must take to accommodate scientific, political, and educational needs. The current organization of the university equates disciplinary organization with societal or conceptual issues, thus creating proprietary relationships between academic disciplines or professions and social issues. Health

should not be the sole property of the biological sciences and
neither should technology be exclusively the domain of the physical sciences. A matrix university organization would provide an
academic home to all according to areas of disciplinary competence
by maintaining departments as they are, but would open up functional and substantive associations by severing the "colleges" and
their concerns from the departments. Thus everyone would have an
academic and one or more functional homes.

EDUCATION OF GRADUATE STUDENTS IN THE SOCIOLOGY
OF HEALTH AND HEALTH CARE

It was my intention from the beginning that the sociological laboratory which we were developing in the Medical Center had to be
made available to graduate students in sociology; an area of
specialization within the doctoral curriculum in sociology was developed. The faculty of the sociology department supported this
development. Having assembled a promising group of medical sociology faculty, we were fortunate to be awarded a training grant to
underwrite this development.

It was not without ambivalence that I spearheaded this development. I have deep concern about sectarian splintering within my
discipline, and I maintain the conviction that the sociologist who
applies his knowledge in a field of practice and application must,
above all, be a competent scholar, committed to his discipline. Yet,
at the same time, I was moved by the recognition that the development of an expansion of the role of the sociologist into fields of
application and practice, and into domains of experimentation and
social change must be accompanied by more comprehensive
socialization than provided by the traditional, limited focus of doctoral education in the arts and sciences. I must emphasize that I
have never felt that sociologists specializing in the fields of health
are people who only export and apply sociology in a quasiservice
function. I am deeply committed to the proposition that the growth
of sociological knowledge and the maturing of our discipline cannot occur unless an effective involvement with the vast range of
real issues of social concern occurs, whereby sociological propositions are submitted to test, and whereby new questions for sociology are raised, pursued, and added to the core of sociological
theory. The sociologist who functions in a practice setting should
see his relationship as one of reciprocity; sociology gives and gains
by the appropriate involvement. Whether we will succeed in edu-

cating students to accept the duality of sociological outreach and sociological accretion remains to be seen. Clearly, a variety of role models is possible.

RESEARCH

Neither the education of medical students, nor the education of graduate students can be effective without an ongoing program of research and inquiry. It is probably in this area where, in retrospect, I feel I have paid the price for the career choices I made. The administrator, the organizer can find time to teach; however, the consistent time commitment required by research is hard to combine with management. In developing a unit with educational-, research-, and policy-influencing components, I had to spread myself thin in terms of commitments. I could, personally, be least directly involved in research. I was fortunate to be able to continue a small output of publications. Some of them had been started before I moved to Missouri,[5] others represented continuation of my previous work with nursing.[6] Some of my articles over the recent years reveal my search for conceptual directions.[7] My publications in the last few years reflect only two of my more recent areas of interest— the dying patient and family health.[8]

One function of an innovative organizer, particularly in a host environment can be that of research initiation and sponsorship. Like giving birth, it has its pleasures and its hurts. Formulating, initiating, and planning a project which must be turned over to junior associates, if it is to prosper, provides considerable satisfaction and attainment of objectives. Yet, having to become a stranger to one's own creation if it is to succeed requires the management of feelings. The quality of one's colleagues makes all the difference. In this I have been very fortunate. The studies initiated in our unit range from social corollaries of illness to career decisions of medical students, from studies of patient care to evaluation of community health programs. The continuing growth of the research program, and the development of a research base which increases the links between the medical center and the arts and science departments is a priority of my current agenda. The involvement of students is crucial. Research participation serves as training ground for the graduate students in sociology and as a crucial opportunity to experience the significance and the relevance of sociology to the participating medical student.

THE DEVELOPMENT OF NEW PROGRAMS

As outgrowth of my experiences, I see a number of practical developments which need to be explored and tested. One of these is the use of the teaching program in the social sciences as a meeting ground for students in a variety of health professions. The current pattern of segregated socialization for health professionals, although taught in the same building, effectively plants the seed for subsequent strains, hostilities, and the inability to communicate. I should like to explore the possibility of using our program as a common experience and as an opportunity to develop mutual respect and understanding, and awareness of the common and of the different objectives which characterize the occupations devoted to health services.

Another new program which I should like to explore would be designed to meet the needs of those who, although committed to a career in direct health services wish to attain competence in the social sciences for purposes of practice or evaluation. The currently available route of doctoral education in sociology or one of the other social sciences is really not appropriate to this career interest. There is a need for an advanced program deliberately oriented towards the practice and integration of social science knowledge in the health field. This is a difficult undertaking if it is to be a program of excellence and rigor. Selectivity and application has all too frequently been associated with dilution and superficiality. The need for personnel trained this way exists among physicians, nurses, and other health professionals.

THE ROLE OF THE CHANGE AGENT

Throughout the previous comments one can see that the presence of the medical sociologist within the health field, at least at this time, is not confined to the role of researcher or teacher. As part of the negotiated raison d'etre, the newcomer in an institutional environment must sell and demonstrate his own role definitions, and cope with the latent expectations which attend his appearance. This applies whether one has asked permission to enter, or whether one has been invited to join. At this time medicine is subject to public criticisms and pressures; the profession is seeking to expand its concern to include not only illness, but also health, and to assume responsibility not only for the technical availability of resources, but for their allocation and application. In being invited to join, the social scientist frequently is expected to serve as the point of the arrow. His role is to conceptualize, legitimize, and to facilitate the changes with which the health field seems to be churning and, sometimes, to absorb the friction or impact. I have sought to conceptualize a model which avoids the traditional retreat into scientific neutrality and objectivity but which also protects the social scientist from the trap of becoming a king maker, short-lived hero or, perhaps, the "fall guy." Our teaching and our research are in fact tools of social change. Our concerns for social process and for the human component of technological performance do alter scope and priorities in the performance of those who listen. Our participation in the scenes where services are delivered serve as leverage behavior.

This recogition of the nonacademic and nonscientific aspect which can be part of the role of the medical sociologist seems an appropriate transition to the concluding comments of this essay. I hope I succeeded in communicating that I see my career as an integrated, but by no means as a homogeneous process. I have felt comfortable in unifying among my life goals my commitments to sociology as a science and as a pursuit of researchable knowledge. My love of teaching has been important to me. At the same time I have felt the need to make a difference in the quality of the services provided by the enterprise to which I have become attached. I care about the excitement of new ideas and new propositions; I care about my students as human beings and as colleagues; and I care about the care received by the clients of those whom I teach and whom I study.

These areas of involvement are not a prescription for success in medical sociology. Among my most successful colleagues are some who have chosen to cast their lot primarily as scientists and others who concentrated on being agents of social change and policymaking. However, I do wish to offer this formula: Innovation demands a toll in energy, self-management and the friction associated with all penetrations. If one cares about something, this price may well be worth while. William Graham Sumner once defined an institution as consisting of a concept and structure; I would suggest that, if my life involved innovative activities, innovation can be characterized as the synthesis of concerns with opportunities.

NOTES

1. In developing these concepts, I am indebted to Harvey L. Smith, "Two Lines of Authority Are One Too Many," *The Modern Hospital* 83 (March 1955): 59–64.

2. The classic statement of this issue is Robert Straus, "The Nature and Status of Medical Sociology," *American Sociological Review* 22 (1957): 200–204.

3. From the "Soliloquy," a song from the musical *Carousel*. This song is one of the most complete condensations of stereotypes about the male and female roles.

4. See Howard S. Becker et al., *Boys in White: Student Culture in a Medical School* (Chicago: University of Chicago Press, 1961).

5. Daisy M. Tagliacozzo and Hans O. Mauksch, "The Patient's View of the Patient Role," in *Patients, Physicians and Illness*, 2d ed, ed. E. Gartly Jaco (New York: Free Press of Glencoe, 1972).

6. Hans O. Mauksch, "Nursing: Churning for Change?" *Handbook of Medical Sociology*, 2d ed., ed. Howard E. Freeman, Sol Levine, and Leo G. Reeder (Englewood Cliffs, N.J.: Prentice Hall, 1972).

7. Based on my earlier report on nursing in the hospital ("Organizational Context of Nursing Practice," in *The Nursing Profession*, ed. Fred Davis [New York: John Wiley and Sons, 1966]), I sought to add additional dimensions to the analysis of the hospital, first in a contributed paper ("Patient Care as a Perspective for Hospital Organization Research," in *Organization Research on Health Institutions*, ed. Basil S. Georgopoulos [Ann Arbor: University of Michigan, Institute for Social Research, 1972]), then in an article ("Ideology, Interaction, and Patient Care in Hospitals," *Social Science and Medicine* 7 [October 1973]: 817–30.

8. Hans O. Mauksch, Review of *The Dying Patient* by Orville Brim, Jr. et al., eds., *Life Threatening Behavior* 1, no. 4 (1971): 272–82; idem, "The Organizational Context of Dying," in *Death: The Final Stage of Growth*, ed. Elisabeth Kuebler Ross (Englewood Cliffs, N.J.: Prentice-Hall, 1975); idem, "A Social Science Basis for Conceptualizing Family Health," *Social Science and Medicine* 8 (October 1974): 521–28.

Medical Sociologist without a Chateau?

YVO NUYENS

INTRODUCTORY NOTE

It took me a long time to decide to write this paper because I had to fight considerable personal resistance against participating in this project. I never liked autobiographies very much, and this for various reasons. First of all, autobiographies to me always suggest a kind of intellectual striptease. And although striptease may be characterized by high technical quality and professional expertise, intellectual striptease speaks of a kind of self-consciousness and self-complacency hardly in harmony with the scientist's ability of objectivity and his sense for relativity. Then, I have this objectionable habit of associating autobiographies with testaments; before dying, physically or socially, the "wise old man" offers some very profound reflections and statements for the next generation to orient itself for the following years. At thirty-five with not even a decade's experience in the field of medical sociology, I feel no need whatsoever to write a testament, neither do I feel capable of writing one; it was only recently that I discovered the possibilities and challenges of the subject and I feel that I still have a whole process to go through. Finally, my participation in this international project would earn me my admission to the establishment of medical sociology. Daily confronted with the obnoxious effects of the medical establishment, I have developed over the years an aversion to every form of establishment because of the closed, assertive and repressive nature of this social phenomenon. Moreover, as a sociologist, one cannot afford to be identified both with the establishment and the mafia.

Why, then, did I finally participate? As is often the case in sociology, coincidence, or a certain wonder was at the base of this change of course. In 1973 and 1974, I was fortunate enough to meet Renée C. Fox twice in a row, and discussed with her at length the most diverse topics. American sociologists will presumably associate Fox's name primarily with two excellent publications in the field of medical sociology: *Experiment Perilous* in 1959, and recently in 1974 *The Courage to Fail*. For non-Americans, and Belgians in particular, the name Renée C. Fox also, and perhaps chiefly, refers to an American sociologist who in 1962 made a keen and critical analysis of the way in which various social, cultural, and historical factors affect clinical medical research and research careers in Belgium; she reported this in two articles, "Journal intime Belge / Intiem Belgisch dagboek" and "Medical Scientists in a Chateau.[1]"

The latter article, particularly, provoked a wave of protests, controversies and emotional reactions, both within the medical setting and before the forum of public opinion. Fox had dared to analyze the structure of clinical medical research in Belgium, its particularism, its pluralism, its centralization and decentralization, and to reveal its negative effects on the development of research and research careers.

In Belgium, this cannot be done with impunity. While at the Jablonna conference on medical sociology in August 1973, I presented a paper on the development of a training program in medical sociology in Belgium, Fox pointed out to me how this development could possibly be explained from the frame of reference she had drawn. A little irritated and challenged by this remark, I decided to reread both articles of my American colleague carefully. This reading confronted me with two surprising observations. First, I found to my astonishment that Fox's remarks on the social structure of clinical medical research in Belgium were, fifteen years later, still as up to date, relevant and applicable as ever, so that social change in Belgium must be extremely slow. Second, I had the impression that Fox's explanatory scheme for clinical medical research could be expanded to match scientific research in general, and sociological and medical sociological research in particular. In other words, while Fox saw the Belgian medical scientists symbolically operating in various chateaux, I became suddenly aware that medical sociology too, was drifting almost unobservedly, into a similar development and that certain of my initiatives in the two last years were meant, probably unconsciously, to escape this development.

There I found a concrete point of contact and a frame of reference sufficient to abandon my personal resistance against an autobiography and to allow me to contribute to this international project. Keeping in mind, however, my original resistance, this paper has no other aim but to report and systematize some impressions, experiences, and insights acquired in a relatively short period of time, concerning an extremely fascinating but also different subject, that is, health care in Belgium, which has been qualified by certain observers as one of the most liberal systems in the world. Instead of a testament speaking with maturity and completion, this paper aims at being a kind of testimony of a phase in a process of development—not only on a professional level—which is by no means concluded or anchored in fixed channels or patterns.

ENTRY INTO MEDICAL SOCIOLOGY

Looking over my first experiences which led toward my interest in medical sociology, I find in the period 1964–68 four independent points of reference which determined my entry into medical sociology.

Research Interests

After having obtained a master's degree in sociology at the Catholic University of Leuven in 1961—at that time the only university in Belgium with graduate training in sociology, but where there was no trace yet of medical sociology—I was granted a four year research fellowship by the National Council of Scientific Research. This council annually offers a limited number of such fellowships in order to enable further specialization and a rapid preparation of a doctoral thesis.

My "patron" at that time explicitly requested me to do political sociological research,[2] since this would enable me to develop this field of sociology with respect to research as well as teaching in the Department of Sociology at the University of Leuven. To an outsider this may appear very naive and conceited, but listen first to what Fox observed about appointment procedures at Belgian universities. "Furthermore, especially in certain university milieus, such particularistic considerations as the political, ethnic, linguistic, philosophical, religious, class, and family affiliations of candidates play as important a role as their scientific competence in determining whether or not they will be named to an available university position. Indeed, this state of affairs is quasiinstitutionalized in that each university represents a distinct political, ethnic, linguistic, and religious-philosophical cluster and that almost all faculty appointees are chosen from among the graduates of the university in question."[3]

My credits at that moment were very favorable so that my

academic career was guaranteed even before I had obtained my doctor's degree. So I started a political sociological research project. Following American political scientists such as Key, Lipset, and Truman, I made an exploratory investigation of the phenomenon of pressure groups in the Belgian political system. On the basis of three case studies, that is on a professional, an economic, and a cultural pressure group, I tried to measure the share of pressure groups in political decision making and describe some consequences for policy in a so-called democratic system. When I was drawing up my final report on this research in 1964, an important event occured in Belgium, closely related to my research topic. An open conflict arose between the government, particularly the minister of public health, and the Belgian Medical Association, finally resulting in a three week strike, the famous doctors' strike that put Belgium for some weeks in the international spotlight. What struck me the most in this strike was the enormous, almost absolute power with which a limited part of the population was able to impose its so-called moral, but actually financial, interests against the government and public opinion. If Eliot Friedson had been in Belgium at that time, he might have written his *Professional Dominance* five years earlier.[4] My first reaction to this strike was certainly not emotional, but rather of an intellectual curiosity: What factors were at the base of this unrestricted, excessive power of the medical profession? I then decided to work out a new research project, centered around two main themes: the process of ideological compartmentalization, rapidly developing within the medical corps on the occasion of this strike; and the impact of the various medical groups on the outline of and decision making in health care.

Although this research project has never been realized—for the remarkable reason that no agency could be found to finance it—this medical strike was a first point of contact with the problem of health care and stimulated my entry into medical sociology.

Teaching Assignment

Immediately after obtaining my Ph.D. in sociology, I received, somewhat by chance, an academic appointment at the University of Leuven. By chance my "patron" unexpectedly decided to abandon a number of courses, which were then assigned almost automatically to me, his first dauphin. In 1965 I suddenly found myself in care of, first, an introductory course in social problems for undergraduate students in social sciences and, second, a general introduction to sociology for the master's degree program in the department of hospital administration and medical care organization of a school of public health. Due to the abandoning of my plans concerning political sociology, for reasons irrelevant in this context, and my stimulated interest in problems of health care policy, this department of hospital administration constituted a new point of contact with medical sociology. Training future hospital and medical care administrators in sociology meant to me first of all that I had to familiarize myself with the problems of health care, and thus with medical sociology.

International Collaborative Study

In the same year, 1965, the Geel Foster Family Care Research Project was started. This was an international research project jointly set up by an American university and Leuven University, but chiefly financed by American foundations. The project studied various aspects of the system of family care for mental patients which has been functioning in the Belgian town of Geel for a couple of centuries. Since the department of hospital administration participated as one of the main Leuven partners, I was invited as the only sociologist in this department to participate in this project. My acceptance of the invitation was a third contact with medical sociological activity.

Personal Life Events

My mother died as a cancer patient at the age of forty-three. Although this happened more than twenty years ago, I have never been able to entirely cope with this early confrontation with death. In other words, the problem of death and care for the dying have constantly fascinated and occupied me. When during the period, 1965–68, I was confronted in a very short time with some six deaths in my immediate family circle, my former interest was actualized and reinforced. However, a new dimension was added. The dramatic circumstances in which some of these deaths took place, for example, in academic hospitals, and the inhuman way in which the medical setting structured the death situation, both for the terminal patient and his relatives, shocked me deeply. This emotional experience was so strong that I decided to do something about these problems professionally. What I was to do exactly was not yet decided, but the problem of death and dying constituted a last port to the field of medical sociology. Contrary to the previous points of contact, the latter had nothing to do with professional interest or career considerations, but relied exclusively on personal experiences and emotional feelings.

Summarizing, I may say that my entry into medical sociology was not the result of a consciously planned professional choice, but rather the consequence of coincidence. Research interest, incidently manifested in the problem of health care, a fortuitous teaching assignment for health professionals, an incidental invitation to participate in an international research project on mental health care, and several personal life situations and experiences first confronted me with medical sociology and also determined my permanent entry into the field. I should not neglect to mention that at the time of these first contacts, medical sociology did not at all exist as a discipline in Belgium. Perhaps to me this was an additional intellectual challenge and motivation to start building a new chateau in Belgian social research. Only afterwards would it become clear what dysfunctional effects such a chateau may have for the position of medical sociology in a changing society.

TRAINING IN MEDICAL SOCIOLOGY

This part of my autobiography will be extremely brief, for the obvious reason that at the moment of my entry into the field there was no formal training program in medical sociology in Belgium. The only actual, professional basis on which I could rely was my graduate training in general sociology which had allowed me to acquire the basic elements of sociological theory and sociological research techniques. For specialization in the field of health care, I was, as I presume most of my non-American colleagues were, dependent on an informal, self-directed training.

Yet, I must say that in this initial period I was offered, through a school of public health, a fellowship in the United States for specialization in medical sociology. I declined this offer, partly on the advice of several colleagues from the Department of Sociology, mainly for the following two reasons. Career perspectives in medical sociology at that moment were still very vague and scarcely structured, so that the output of such an investment seemed insufficiently assured. Also, I was convinced that such a specialization could only yield an optimum turnover if one could start with concrete questions concerning the field. The theoretical as well as social questions I still had to discover and formulate for myself.

So my training for medical sociology became a weakly structured, self-directed program in which socialization with the field of health care was done primarily through the following channels. First there was the traditional way of reading and studying medical sociological literature (handbooks, reviews, research reports) at that time in full expansion and chiefly "made in U.S.A." In connection with this, I became an ardent reader of professional newsletters of national associations of doctors, nurses, hospitals, and the like. Finally, I began to familiarize myself with all kinds of official policy documents about health care in Belgium. This channel provided me with a number of conceptual frameworks and approaches in medical sociology, as well as a rather detailed factual knowledge about the morphological structure of health care in Belgium. These two components may be considered of crucial importance for any training program in medical sociology.

A second channel for socialization was offered me by the teaching assignments. Originally I was only involved in a degree program in hospital administration and medical care organization; soon new assignments followed in nursing schools, schools for social workers, and finally also medical schools. In addition, I cooperated with several thematic courses within the framework of a postgraduate education program for practicing hospital administrators. This confrontation, within a didactic context, with a main professional group in health care provided an excellent opportunity to constantly compare the acquired theoretical knowledge in medical sociology with the factual reality of Belgian health care. I also gained important additional insights and experience concerning the value and norm patterns, ideological positions, and conflicting interests of the professional participants in health care.

I finally became somewhat familiar with the health care setting through active participation in a large number of councils and advisory committees which raised all kinds of problems of health care such as training, research, policy, planning, and evaluation. My access to these committees was facilitated by the fact that at that time a sociologist showing interest in health care was still considered a curiosity, somewhat like a new species at the zoo, a modern gadget one should show off to both supporters and opponents. My participation in those committees was situated originally only at the intrauniversity level; it then expanded into various professional groups in the field of health care, and, most recently, also penetrated into the national policy level. Looking back, and evaluating this third channel, I wish to stress here its enormous importance for the restructuring of medical sociology into what Bloom defined as "an evolution towards a consulting profession."[5]

Through these three channels I tried to compensate for my lack of formal training in medical sociology. As the absence of formal training possibilities was in my opinion a serious set-back for the development and professionalization of a discipline, the creation of a formal training program in medical sociology for sociologists would obtain high priority in the objectives which I wanted to realize. When in 1970 a survey revealed the same situation in most countries of the European community, with the exception of England, this acted as an additional stimulus.[6] As for my training in medical sociology, I wish to make one more observation: the informal and self-directed nature of my training enabled me to systematically explore various theoretical approaches. This provided me with the knowledge, not very startling indeed, that medical sociological activity supposes a pluralism of scientific paradigms or models. In other words, depending on working context and concrete professional assignments, the medical sociologist should be able to rely on a score of paradigms or approaches. I might exemplify this pluralism by indicating that in the period of intensive involvement with hospital problems, I found many references to the system approach as developed by Field, Buckley and Georgopolos. The interdisciplinary research project on the rehabilitation of haemophiliac patients, which I will discuss later, led me to the interactional approach of Mechanic, Goffman and Becker. Freidson's structural approach, finally, offered a valid frame of reference in my permanent confrontation with the medical profession. Translated in terms of training, this means that a training program in medical sociology should allow the student to become acquainted with these various approaches and not force him in the shackles of one single approach, as is still mostly the case. In our own developing training program, an attempt is made to develop such polyparadigm training in medical sociology.

WORK EXPERIENCES IN MEDICAL SOCIOLOGY

Looking back to my rather limited experience in medical sociology, at least as far as time is concerned, I can nevertheless perceive three clearly distinct periods by which to systematize and rank these various experiences. The transition from the first to the second period was accompanied by a rather fundamental change of social position and work setting which was much less the case for the transition from the second to the third period. In identifying these periods, I am boldly extending Renée Fox's metaphor.

Visiting a Chateau

I had my first work experiences in medical sociology in a school of public health, more specifically in the department of hospital administration and medical care organization of this school. The main activities of this department were: a degree program in hospital administration, a postgraduate program for practising hospital administrators, and research in hospital administration and medical care organization. The departmental staff was chiefly composed of medical doctors, jurists, economists, and several research assistants. In Fox's terms, the leading persons of this department, an oligarchic nucleus of four, undeniably belonged to the "jeunes" in 1959–61 (the time of her investigation). But in a short time they had been able to work themselves up to important "patrons." One of the characteristics of these patrons was that they "spent a good deal of their potentially creative time and energy simply in coping with the burdensome administrative responsibilities that running a department or an institute entails. . . . Above all, these professors are engaged in what they refer to as the *chasse aux subsides* (the hunt for subsidies). This hunt involves them in a complicated, time-consuming, never-ending process of writing eloquent, inquiring, imploring, demanding, grateful letters; of making formal and informal visits to strategic officials; and of sitting on numerous commissions."[7] Through a clever system of double appointments, within the university structure and within the main policy centers in health care such as the ministries of public health and social affairs, the Federation of Hospitals, and so on, these particular patrons had found a very efficient way of dealing with the search for subsidies. So grants, funds and money were never a problem for them. Their system of double appointments put these patrons moreover in a strategic position from which they were able to influence and control to a high degree the national health care policy.

This may be exemplified by the fact that relations with the various departments of the WHO were almost exclusively controlled and dominated by this group. So when I define this department as a chateau, I am referring to two different things. First of all, I want to stress the closed and oligarchic nature of this institution, which, from a gradually conquered position of power and expertise, controlled an important part of government research and policy advice in the field of health care. Newcomers and visitors in such closed strongholds are tolerated on the periphery, but very rarely have access to the hall, let alone the treasury. Like medieval lords who usually had only a very selective perception of the surrounding social reality, these patrons were notorious for an analogous selectivity concerning the problems of health care. This was true from two points of view: on the one hand, they reduced the problem of health care to the hospital problem, ignoring the problems of primary care, mental health care and preventive care. On the other hand, they applied exclusively bureaucratic managerial standards, ignoring the client's prerogatives in health care.

In such a chateau I would, as a sociologist, play the role of visitor. This role was in the first place forced on me by the "lords" themselves, since they saw in my presence an excellent opportunity to add a little color to their interdisciplinary blazon. I felt that my presence was particularly valued at business lunches with American colleagues. On the other hand, my academic and social position was so unimpressive at that time that my admission into the oligarchy could by no means be considered. So I should be a visitor. Looking at the things after the event, I see that I reinforced this role concept myself by moving through the chateau with detached concern, at the same time keeping up my relations with the Department of Sociology at the university where I had a small teaching assignment.

What was essentially expected from me in this period and what were my own initial concepts of the field? The expectations I found excellently illustrated in a recent paper by M. Pflanz, in which he thoroughly analyzed the relationship between social scientists, physicians, and medical organizations in health research:

> When one applies the social sciences within medical institutions and organizations, one accepts in general the high value which society accords to health. . . . The task of the sociologist is therefore clearly defined. It is to adjust human behavior to demands which derive from the values accorded to health. . . . The social scientist has not only to accept the values of medicine, but he must adapt himself to them and, as far as possible, submit himself to them. . . . Medicine, being an activist science, will be particularly prone to make pragmatic demands in respect of the uses of sociology within medical organizations. The average physician is unlikely to consider basic research in medical sociology to be as relevant as basic scientific research. In this way the sociologist is forced in the direction of applied research, whose usefulness for the organization can be clearly demonstrated, by the very nature of the tasks imposed upon him.[8]

Pflanz is right in pointing out how sociologists active in health care

are almost always confronted with preestablished medical standards which should not or cannot be questioned, a preestablished problem definition whose essence he can change only very little. As a consequence, the sociologist will be expected to give only those data, information, and advice actually contributing directly to a more efficient realization of a policy determined without him. If he produces this material—the sociologist will primarily be invited for his research technical skill—he gives an excellent example of justification research or, as Pflanz states: "Seduced by the magic spell of medicine, involved in the medicalization of society and of sociology itself, he becomes, whether he likes it or not, the public relations man of the medical organization in which and for which he works." If, however, he refuses to prostitute himself in this way and wants nevertheless to develop his own problem definition and approach, his advice and contribution may be dispensed with at any time, as Ray Elling has clearly demonstrated in a case study on the development of sociology within the World Health Organization.[9]

It is remarkable, however, that, whereas these role expectations and task descriptions of the sociologist are commonly known and widespread as far as the clinical medical setting is concerned, exactly the same pattern manifested itself with equal intensity in an institution primarily oriented towards hospital administration and medical care organization. Although not so much dominated by medical prerogatives, this institution confronted the sociologist in the same degree with preestablished standards—in this case of a bureaucratic managerial nature—and with preestablished problem definitions hermetically locked for any possible reformulation by a sociologist's point of view. In other words, the door was wide open to the reproach which Freidson makes to the greater part of present-day medical sociology: "Medical sociology has focused on the areas that the medical practitioner himself has considered problematic, adopting the conception of what is problematic from the profession itself without raising questions about the perspective from which the problem is defined."[10] Probably more through intuition than systematic insight at that time, I considered it the prime task of the sociologist "to formulate a consistent way of thinking and ordering data that is independent of the institution studied"; in other words, to make on the basis of systematically acquired knowledge, an emancipating contribution to the process of societal problem definition and redefinition of health care. That such a conception or development of a specific sociological problem definition was not given much of a chance can be easily illustrated by means of a few concrete cases.

Teaching Hospital Administrators

As I indicated above, I was intensively involved in teaching the degree program in hospital administration as well as the post-graduate program for practicing hospital administrators. From the very start I made it my main teaching objective to develop a structural approach to the hospital "approaching the organization by following out the implications of its frequently conflicting goals, the social requirements of the technical tasks being performed within it, and the hospitals' sources of support."[11] This approach enabled me to counteract the human relations approach which at that moment was becoming very popular in Belgian hospitals. This approach also enabled me to break through the closed-system attitude of this important group of health professionals who were only capable of establishing an internal problem definition around the hospital while ignoring social questions and forces outside the hospital. This approach, however, was not welcomed with great enthusiasm and certainly did not correspond with the health professionals' expectations about the sociologist's contribution to the outlined training programs. Rather they preferred that the principles of personnel management and scientific management be taught: how to motivate one's personnel, how to improve communication, how to control possible labor conflicts, and so on. Because of my persistance in my "sociological infatuation" they decided a couple of years later to introduce two new courses: management techniques and management principles, to be taught by the patrons themselves. Thus an attempt at conceptual change failed because no translation in concrete program work was made.

Participating in Interdisciplinary Research

As I indicated above, my entry into medical sociology was stimulated largely by the possibility of participating in the international and interdisciplinary foster family care research project. A full discussion of this long-term project, and especially of the way in which sociologists were consumed in it, would require and perhaps also deserves an extensive study, but I must limit myself here to a few general remarks. My colleagues from the sociology of the family and sociology of religion sections, who were originally involved in the project too, soon found out as I did that it seemed to be quite difficult if not impossible to have a specific sociological problem conception and definition inserted into the research design. Rather we were confronted with the task of data collection concerning a problem definition on which we ourselves had little or no control or impact. More specifically as far as my own part of the project was concerned, my research interest in an analysis of the decision making in this system of family care and a study of the power structure within it was given little chance of realization, officially because "these matters [were] too hot and critical to be treated in this phase of the project." Actually I was charged with investigating the industrialization of the area and its possible impact on family care, a rather neutral assignment which would allow me to demonstrate the sociologists' well-known occupational disease of using the survey questionnaire. After reporting this first assignment I was given as my next assignment the collection of new data on employment rates, labor force, housing, number of farms, bathrooms, telephones, and so forth. I declined the offer—something my two colleagues had already done much earlier.

Advising in Policy Research

The patrons of the department were at the moment of my visit to their chateau closely involved in the planning of a new academic hospital in substitution for the old one. In connection with this, they were given a research assignment to design, by means of system analysis in nursing, a more rational use of nursing abilities in light of an increasing interfacing of nursing with other care and service functions. More particularly the project was to prepare a system of unit management which,[12] after first being tested and evaluated in the hospital for children, would be applied generally in the new academic hospital. *After* the research design was entirely outlined, defined and agreed upon, a sociologist was invited to the table and asked to conduct an investigation measuring the satisfaction of the nursing staff with the existing and the new system. The same sociologist suggested that new management directives could and should also be evaluated as to their impact on the evaluations of the clients, that is, the hospital patients. It is indeed possible that certain measures are both functional to the staff and dysfunctional to the clients or vice versa, so that new management options have to be taken. Thus, a redefinition of the research assignment was proposed. After a few more meetings, probably held out of courtesy, further invitations for participating in the project failed to appear. The conclusion was obvious.

Summing up this first period, I may say in all objectivity that my impact as a sociologist on changes and innovations related to the organization of health services was extremely limited if not nil. Although there was a supply of conceptual work, in the sense of the development of new concepts and frameworks, these had no practical consequences because they did not result in concrete program work, for example in the form of training programs or research efforts. This may have been due to the following factors: my highly isolated position within an established department, where I had to make my debut as the first and sole representative of the behavioral scientist's approach; the absence of any power, such as might have stemmed from close affiliation with a department of sociology, which caused me to participate as a weak party in the bargaining process concerning teaching and research; the closed and oligarchic nature of the department, strongly discouraging actual participation from the beginning; and the dominance of bureaucratic managerial standards within the department, requiring from a sociological approach only a justification and defining an autonomous sociological approach as a threat to the standards applied.

Anyway it is clear that my psychiatrist, after having analyzed me for some years, will discover for this period a number of traumata, some undigested disillusionments, and probably also a kind of Jerry Lewis complex. I didn't have any particular aversion to the name Lewis, but it was the "Jerry" that haunted me. So I decided secretly to end my visit to the chateau.

Building a Chateau

The opportunity to do this was presented to me rather fortuitously at the end of 1968. Two factors were of crucial importance. First I was given, mainly with the help of a colleague from the section of sociology of the family, the possibility to participate in an interdisciplinary research project on the rehabilitation problem of haemophiliac patients. This project was started within the medical school and required, in addition to the cooperation of doctors, psychologists, educationists, social workers and nurses, one full-time sociological researcher. It was remarkable that the medical team directed its demand to a sociological research institute, where there was no trace of medical sociology at that moment, instead of to the school of public health, where medical sociology was present under the above-mentioned conditions. This was more than a *fait divers* since in my opinion it clearly illustrates the clinical medical research unit's reluctance to cooperate with schools of public health. For disciplines like medical sociology, this has important implications: if they place and develop themselves exclusively within schools of public health, they meet a structurally implied hindrance to relationships with medical schools and clinical medicine. After a thorough discussion with colleague sociologists, we decided to do the sociological part of the haemophilia project neither in the medical school nor in the school of public health, but rather within the sociological research institute. This institute had made substantial efforts in recent years to centralize all sociological research done at the university, so that the decision was in line with its overall policy. That is why in 1968 the Group for Medical Sociology was established with two collaborators within the sociological research institute.

The second important factor was at the teaching level. Important curriculum modifications were being made at that time in the Faculty of Social Sciences and the Department of Sociology. With the active support of colleagues from general sociology and sociology of the family, I was granted important new teaching assignments in the framework of these modifications, concerning training programs for undergraduate and graduate students in sociology. A basic course in medical sociology (sixty hours) was introduced as optional at that moment, but was exclusively designed for graduate students in sociology.

Both factors together offered sufficient guarantees for me to change my work setting without too much risk, even though I did not have too much to lose then either. This new work setting consisted of the Sociological Research Institute for my research activities and the Department of Sociology, closely linked with the former, for my teaching assignments.

As I have placed this second period under the heading "Building a Chateau," I want to indicate several things with it: From my new position of *patron*, partly ascribed partly achieved, I was confronted with the possibility (but at the same time the necessity) of constructing an identity of my own, in view of the typical structure of the Belgian university system. Through a relatively successful participation in the *"chasse aux subsides"* a new research structure (chateau) was organized. It was actualized in eight more or less substantial research projects and an expansion of the professional staff to seven full-time sociologists working in medical sociology. The gradual development of the basic course into a more or less complete training program in medical sociology for graduate students in sociology was another important component in the building process of a chateau. Finally the term "chateau" indicates how in this phase the medical sociological unit remained primarily defined in academic terms of training and research and the dialectical link with the social world of health care remained underdeveloped.

Since the directives for this autobiographical paper urge me "to focus on supports and resistances to innovation and change in medical care services, teaching and research as represented through the course of conceptual and program work in medical sociology," I select from this period the three most relevant cases. But first it should be noted that in this period we started to publish rather intensively, mostly conceptual papers on various aspects of health care, such as primary care, mental hospitals, social epidemiology, structure of health care, drugs, illness behavior, and, of course, death and dying.[14] Right from the start we published both in specialized professional journals and in popular general magazines, to which we will return later. In this way, Belgian society discovered medical sociology, leading to an important side effect of more and more frequent invitations to symposia, congresses, and conferences of all kinds of organizations, ranging from honorable medical associations to equally honorable feminist groups.

Interdisciplinary Research Project on Haemophilia Patients

This project actually was a meeting of a unidisciplinary (sociological) team with a medical team constituted of various disciplines.[15] To the latter, the heamophilia problem was defined in more or less clear categories of diagnosis and treatment. One of the aims of the interdisciplinary consultation was to systematize these categories into more precise instruments for diagnosis and treatment of haemophilia. It was exactly this expectation concerning the imputation of a social dimension which acted as a catalyst.

In becoming acquainted with the haemophiliac group and the social studies concerning it, as well as in designing a less stereotyped questionnaire concept of research, we became aware that, concerning the haemophiliac population, a social dimension should not be "imputed" but rather "extracted". The social problems concerning the haemophiliac population seemed sufficiently specified, but insufficiently generalized. We tried to bring about a redefinition of the haemophiliac problem, suggesting the possibility of developing a different approach from what had been evident in the framework of this problem, that is, a sociological approach taking into account the positional diversity of those concerned by indicating the general social context in which both haemophiliac patients and doctors act. The question concerning us was: Is sociology, by broadening the existing perspectives, able to encourage a better, more efficient, more comprehensive health care service? We tried to answer the question in the following way.

It is sufficiently known that the medical profession is dominated by a clinical perspective, which means that at the time of diagnosis and therapy the patient and his illness are situated, for the most part, in the family. Attention to more remote factors possibly influencing the case, for example, recognition of the patient's behavior as partly determined by sociological structures and sociocultural evaluations, is almost completely lacking. This is no reproach, but it might in certain ways adversely affect an otherwise excellent treatment. The sociological team applied quite a bit of energy to convince the clinical team that many people have seen a lot less, read less, know less, do not want, or are not able to change their habits even though this might be required from a medical point of view. Many patients cannot be convinced by rational arguments, have emotional responses to straight medical facts, hold back important data for diagnosis and therapy because they are considered irrelevant in their milieu, and so on—the list is endless. It is important, however, that all these characteristics are not distributed at random over the population but rather according to distinctions much more refined than "upper," "middle," and "lower" class. We attempted to enlighten the physician's clinical blindness a little by sensitizing him to the diversity in social and cultural backgrounds of the patients consulting him. This brings up a crucial issue in the project, which was already indicated by H. Bynder[16], namely the differences in evaluation concerning the possible usage of the knowledge gathered by sociologists. On the importance of the problems investigated, medical men and sociologists can easily agree, but on the practical importance of the results, opinions often diverge. Physicians too often expect cut and dried material for solving their problems, whereas medical sociological research, as any other scientific research, may also lead to new questions which complicate rather than simplify the problem. Sociological studies about illness and illness behavior are more easily evaluated as important by the medical world if they can be translated in traditional individualized therapeutic terms or if they can set the illness in a psychosomatic frame. If the sociologist adds information to the individual case, he will be welcomed with open arms, but there is less openness for information in the field of the functioning and organization of certain services within health care, the uncovering of implicitly applied social presumptions, or the sociocultural conditioning of the illness process. That such insights might be useful in preventing, controlling and treating illnesses is only moderately valued. Particularly the dominating position of the physician with respect to almost all aspects of the illness prevents the use of sociological findings in health care and impedes a socialization of health care. That is why this haemophilia project primarily led to innovations on the conceptual level concerning the future orientation of medical sociological work. If medical sociologists wish to be socially relevant at all, they should not limit themselves to further analyses of the well-known "social behavior surrounding disease," but should aim as well at testing alternative forms of cooperation in the sector of health care.[17] That such innovations cannot as yet be actualized in concrete program work is primarily due to the contrary expectations of the medical and the sociological team concerning the sociologist's share as well as the slanted balance of power of both partners in the decision making process.

Training Program in Medical Sociology for Graduate
Students in Sociology

While discussing my training in medical sociology above, I pointed out the lack of formal training in medical sociology in Belgium as well as most countries of the European community. From the very start I have considered this void as a serious impediment in the development and professionalization of medical sociology. This impression was confirmed in the survey which I made on the status and orientation of medical sociology in several countries of the European community. People like M. Pflanz, M. Jefferys, M. Sokołowska and C. Herzlich affirmed to me the high priority which should be given to such a training program. That is why the concrete realization of a training program in medical sociology was at the top of my list of objectives to be realized in my new chateau. On the basis of the existing basic course in medical sociology, a first concept of such a program was realized gradually, over a period of three years. Schematically and formally this two-year course may be represented as follows.[18] (see next page)

The training program in medical sociology is part of an overall graduate program in sociology, in which the students are also familiarized with the historical background of sociology, contemporary theories, and research methods. The above scheme only considers subjects directly connected with medical sociology. The scheme distinguishes between professional tasks (of the medical

OBJECTIVES

TASKS	KNOWLEDGE	SKILLS	ATTITUDES
RESEARCH	Teaching course (60h)	Seminar I (60 h) Seminar II (60h) Memoir	Seminar in medical sociology & medical psychology (30h)
SOCIAL ENGINEERING	Teaching course (60h)	Seminar I Seminar II	Practical training

sociologist) and teaching objectives (in medical sociology). In the professional role of the (medical) sociologist three essential dimensions are usually distinguished: research (including both basic and applied research), teaching (also to various categories of health professionals), and social engineering (or problem solving sociology, a theory of practice of socially effective action).[19] The teaching task is not included in the scheme because there is a special training program for graduate students in teaching sociology. The teaching objectives are traditionally broken up in knowledge, skills and attitudes. It should be noted that attitudes are given a particular importance, especially with respect to the socialization of sociologists with the health care and medical subculture. This socialization, if it exists at all, remains restricted to knowledge and skills, while the aspect of attitudes is left, in our opinion unduly, to personal imagination and improvisation. An important role is played by the seminar course in medical sociology and medical psychology, in which both graduate students in medical sociology and medical students participate in the form of discussions concerning social aspects of medicine and health care. Practical training too, in the form of a kind of internship program, plays an important part in the formation of this attitude.

Whereas the seminars offer a training in medical sociological research methods and techniques as well as exercises in problem solving sociology, the teaching course is primarily oriented towards the different concepts and theoretical approaches in medical sociology. The different approaches are described in comparison to one another and their essential differences are indicated. Suggestions are made as to what approach is most likely to be successful for a specific type of problem and also to what extent one approach implies another.

This program is certainly not a finished product, but rather a first draft which will be modified in the near future. For example, the social engineering dimension will be further developed, since we are still searching rather unsystematically and experimentally for adequate form and contents.

The concrete output of this program has been a limited number of graduates in medical sociology who have found professional positions in various sectors of Belgian health care where they are primarily charged with research and management duties and in this way will probably help to start social change processes in health care.

In trying to trace back the sources of support in the development of this program, I see four main factors. The presence of a complete graduate program in sociology, in which some specialization tendencies were already developed (family, religion, industry) and which provided an excellent opportunity to introduce and develop a specialization in medical sociology. Second, the traditional structure of the Belgian university system gives an additional stimulus to the frequent establishment of chateaux, hence also a chateau in medical sociology. The presence and relatively strong growth of the medical sociological research in our research unit facilitated its extension into a training program; And finally, the active support of several colleague sociologists from the Department of Sociology also favorably affected the development of this program.

Specific sources of opposition I cannot recall, not even from medical schools or schools of public health, even though the entire program was designed without their advice or cooperation.

Project on the Belgian General Practitioner

All over the world the problem of primary care has drawn much attention lately. This is also true in Belgium, where the system of general practice in particular has been characterized by crisis as well as renewed attention.[20] The crisis has been promoted by the prevailing system of free demand by patients, that is direct access to specialized medicine, and free supply of services by the general practitioner, entailing competition between G.P. and specialist. If one considers that a large majority of G.P.'s still organize their practice in a traditional, almost medieval fashion (solo practice, fee for service, absence of paramedical or technical collaborators), one may imagine the crisis of general practice in a system of health care characterized by increasing specialization and organization. Gradually there has grown some reaction by G.P.'s who have started looking for a specific function and a specific place in the health care system. Sociologically speaking, Belgian general practice combines a process of deprofessionalization and reprofessionalization. Against this background, our unit started an investigation of the problem of general practice in Belgium. A sample of some four hundred general practitioners was interviewed, with special attention—besides morphological information about structure of practice and the morbidity treated—to the subjective component of the problem defined above. In this way systematic knowledge was gained about the way G.P.'s themselves define the problems of their professional situation and the policy measures which they advocate for solving them. These measures concerned: a special specific and new function in health care defined in terms of continuous, comprehensive, and personal care; specific training channels and curricula; a formal and legal task delimitation between G.P.'s and specialists; a wavering option for a more group-oriented development of the system of primary care; and reintegration of a large part of preventive health care in general practice.

These results were presented in detail to the official policymakers as well as the medical associations concerned. Although an exact measurement of the effects of a research project on social change is always very delicate, our investigation yielded the following results. First, it promoted the fact that the social problem of general practice in Belgium was more readily considered as a policy problem (acceleration effect). Also, the emotional and controversial debates about this problem were to a large extent made objective and relative by our research results (objectivity effect). Finally, the investigation resulted in a stronger awareness and sensitization effect. Moreover, the investigation also resulted in close contacts and relations with an important professional groups in Belgian health care, which afterwards proved to be useful.

As opposed to the first period, this second period resulted in a few concrete realizations. In a relatively short span, our own chateau was built, in which, for the first time in Belgium, a teaching structure in the field of medical sociology came about, structurally independent from the medical setting. Within its limits were developed both conceptual and program work in medical sociology. Its effect on concrete changes and innovations in health care remained in our opinion limited, since the walls erected in academic terms of training and research obstructed the view on society and completely blocked a dialectic relationship with society. However exquisite life in a chateau may be, its occupants' experience after some time a certain nostalgia for the reality outside its walls. So we pass on to a third and for the time being last period.

LEAVING A CHATEAU

Whereas the transition from the first to the second period implied a rather fundamental change of professional position as well as work setting, this was not the case in the transition to this third period. The newly-built chateau was further extended and fortified, in other words the *"chasse aux subsides"* was successfully continued, so that research assignments and professional staff continued to expand and the training program in medical sociology was further developed. The latter concerned primarily the quality of training, which was enhanced by inviting visiting professors of medical sociology, from Poland and France, not without a favorable effect on the academic prestige of the medical sociological discipline. The only main structural change was not compensatory but rather complementary with respect to the previous position and work setting. In a newly established university in Antwerp I was appointed extraordinary professor, that is part-time for half a day a week, with a twofold assignment: teaching a basic course in medical sociology for graduate students in medical sociology, and a very concise introduction to medical sociology (ten hours) as an obligatory course in the clinical part of the medical curriculum. The latter course was at that moment an innovation in medical training in Belgium where behavioral sciences in medical schools had been highly underdeveloped if not absent. Presumably this innovation had some connection with the conceptual and program work which we had done in the field of medical sociology, for it was particularly the association of G.P.'s which had insisted on the introduction of medical sociology in the medical curriculum. That in teaching this course to medical students I experienced some frustrations and disillusionments cannot be called an innovation, but was rather a confirmation of an international and almost traditional stereotype.

When I placed this period under the heading "Leaving a Chateau" I did not mean to say that the recently built chateau would be pulled down again or left to new lords, but rather that the number of exits was greatly increased. This would constantly invite and enable us to leave the chateau and visit the surrounding society, and enter into a more or less permanent dialogue with it. Moreover, society would thus be able to give us advice and directions as to the architecture and functioning of the chateau, something for which the occupants experienced an ever increasing need. Indeed, it became more and more clear that medical sociology if exclusively conceived in terms of teaching and research and mainly concerned with giving (to whom?) theoretical conceptions and empirically verified research results—however important and essential these functions might be—must remain sterile as far as social impact and effective aid in processes of social change are concerned. Gouldner goes even one step further when he says: "The social sciences (such as medical sociology) increasingly become a well-financed technological basis for the Welfare State's effort to solve the problems of its industrial society."[21]

The relationship between sociology and policy may often result in a concept of sociology in which the latter, through so-called justification research, only supplies advice for modifications and thus directly or indirectly contributes to a continuation of an existing system of policy. If, however, the sociologist does not want to restrict himself to a secure background activity in aid of adaptation to a certain policy which itself is not questioned, the alternative is not necessarily to become oneself an actor in the policymaking—a step which many critical and radical sociologists make, in our opinion, wrongly—but rather to search for a dialectically positioned and operating sociology.

In this view, the sociologist's task may be defined as the extension into policy of social evaluations crystallized at the basis of society, as well as the provocation of social evaluations by pointing out unnoticed consequences of certain policies. The dialectical element lies in the fact that sociology acts as an externalizing agent in the extension of the policy into action, as well as in the translation of action for certain policy channels. One of our staff members formulated this dialectical element in a recent paper:

> This sociology cannot ignore the process of problem definition and redefinition in society, in other words the societal problem classification and disposition process.... However, the acquired knowledge must then be reflected towards the social problem (re)definition process, where the sociologist finds a permanent touchstone for his knowledge. In this manner, sociological knowledge will influence the societal process of problem definition and redefinition. With respect to health care, the dialectical process between sociological

knowledge and societal problem classification and disposition takes place on various levels, on which not only specific problem areas are situated but also the societal problem definition process takes concrete form. Thus, medical sociology may be assigned a problem defining task on the levels of the patient, the professions, and the policy.[22]

This centering on the societal problem definition process and the feedback of acquired sociological knowledge to the social contexts involved protects the sociologist from "sociologizing" society and prevents a technocratic conception of his activity. On the contrary, this method will oblige him to compare his acquired knowledge with that of other disciplines and social evaluations. This confrontation and dialogue helps society to become more conscious of its problem and may lead to collective policymaking action. How this new approach is actualized will be illustrated by means of a few cases. First, however, I would like to make two remarks.

This new and more policy-oriented approach is conceived and developed as complementary to the existing approach as outlined in academic terms of research and teaching. To what extent this new approach will ever replace the existing one cannot for the time being be decided. As this new approach was started only recently, the cases below will certainly bear the marks of it. These cases are still in full development so that more or less objective statements about the importance and impact of these processes are still very difficult to make.

Since health care may roughly be divided into three problem levels—those of patient, professions, and policy—the cases were selected according to this key.

The Patient Level
In this last decade much research on patient problems and evaluations has become available, particularly from the medical sociology perspective. It is, however, important to note that this research is usually communicated exclusively to the policymakers, without any feedback of the acquired knowledge to the consumers of health care. Yet, this feedback is an essential contribution to the development of the societal problem definition process. To fill this need our unit decided to produce a brochure on health care in Belgium which was to meet essentially two criteria: it should outline and analyze health care problems through various scientific approaches and focus exclusively on the basis of the observed needs and desires of the patient; and it should strip this scientific knowledge

from its traditional jargon and communicate it to the patients in colloquial language. A core of medical sociologists involved a number of psychiatrists, general practitioners, psychologists, and social workers in the project and it proved not too hard at all to find a publisher willing to see to it for a small price. In this way, the brochure was produced quite rapidly, discussing in eight sections important aspects or sectors of the Belgian health care system.[23] The first section is devoted to the multidimensional meaning of the concepts "health" and "illness" in the affluent society. Then two main actors in the health care system are discussed, the patient (problems of inequality in health care, participation of consumers) and the physician (inadequate training, doctor-patient relationship). The next sections deal with the patient in the hospital and the possibilities (and limitations) of home care programs. Then extra- and intramural mental health care is discussed, as well as the social services system.

The final section discourses upon the problem of terminal patients and death guidance. The brochure concludes with statements about and possibilities for a more patient-oriented health care policy. Moreover, at the end of each section a few concrete questions are formulated to stimulate critical reflection and facilitate group discussions about the information supplied. Besides its wide distribution, the main observation to be made concerning this brochure is that it enabled us to make contact with all kinds of sociocultural organizations—adult education groups, labor unions, women's organizations, informal and critical action groups—all of which actually contributed to the process of socialization of health care. This may be exemplified by the fact that the weekly magazine of the country's largest labor union reprinted for a few months entire sections from the brochure and invited its readers' comments on the articles. A few weeks later a selection from the letters was published in the magazine, which started a communication. Thus, medical sociology made a direct and concrete contribution to a process of growing consciousness around problems of health care in society, meeting the measures Zola thinks of as necessary to counteract medical power: continuous investigation of the premises on the basis of which medical and other experts act; open discussion of the viability of certain rights: what we do with our bodies and our minds, the right to live, as well as the right to die; a renewed investigation of all prerogatives of the expert, the treatment which he alone should be allowed to apply, and how and in whose name he organizes his schedule and services; and sharing of information and common decision making instead of technocracy and oligarchy.[24]

Finally, it is important to note that negative and sometimes hostile reactions to the brochure came chiefly from policymakers and certain medical associations. Needless to say, these reactions made abundant use of labels and stigmata denouncing us as "Marxists."

The Professions Level

Above we indicated how general practitioners in Belgium in recent years became involved in a process of deprofessionalization and reprofessionalization, resulting from technological as well as structural developments within health care. One of the side effects of the investigation conducted by our unit on this problem was the establishment of many formal and informal contacts with the group of G.P.'s in general and one G.P. in particular. The latter may be considered the most active participant in the process of reprofessionalization of the G.P. group, in that it makes an effort both among the G.P.'s themselves and with various policymaking authorities to introduce the notion of a new and specific G.P. function (continuous, comprehensive, and personal medical care), together with its implications for training and health care structure. These contacts finally resulted in a more solid and institutionalized cooperation between this group and our research unit (with one of our staff members taking an advisory function in the monthly executive meetings and the various committees of the group). This enabled a permanent feedback of the acquired sociological knowledge to an important professional group and perhaps also indirectly had an influence on social changes within health care. The opportunity was all the better since the areas in which the sociologist was to operate were not determined in advance. This also developed gradually and the cooperation certainly has opened up new areas. At present, sociology contributes in the realms discussed below.

The Role of the Future General Practitioners

In the new medical curriculum prepared particularly under the impulse of this group, a considerable share of the training is devoted to behavioral sciences which is an important innovation in medical training in Belgium. In the national in-service training program designed by the Ministry of Public Health in aid of the G.P.'s, a considerable share of behavioral sciences was included, largely as a result of this group. Primarily under the influence of the sociologist, a start has been made in altering the structure of health care by beginning to situate primary medical care within the more general framework of overall primary care.

The Development of Scientific Research

Whereas the scientific research of the group used to be limited to the narrow medical-clinical field, there has been a constantly growing interest in behavioral science research on and with general practitioners. At present, an integrated project by G.P.'s and sociologists is being prepared, in which physicians will work under the direction of a sociologist. In this connection Pflanz's remarks are relevant: "It will ... be necessary to keep the role of physicians in these institutions under close observation. Will they attempt to adjust to the thinking and the idiom of the sociologist? Will they find their own solution to the conflict between the dominant value system of sociological methodology and those values in society towards which their training has oriented them? Will there be for them an alliance of the two disciplines even in terms of power?"[25]

Organizational Problems

Finally, the sociologist also contributes to the internal and external organization of the group, paying special attention to the internal communication between base and top (and vice versa) and attempting to be more open-minded with respect to other professional groups in health care.

In spite of the scantiness of our experience in this cooperation experiment, the following observation may already be made. The general awareness of the dominance of narrow medical thinking within general practice first of all led to the stressing of psychological and social factors in health and health care. However, the emergence from narrow medical thinking and the integration of somatic, psychological, and social dimensions have led to a new situation—G.P.'s also want to include these three dimensions in their therapeutic activity, assuming new roles such as family counselor, and thus stepping up medical power and control. This newly acquired insight now leads to a better setting of the new G.P. function within the overall social welfare system, cooperating and splitting responsibilities with other experts. This case also illustrates how sociological knowledge progresses through the continuous interaction with societal dynamics.

The Policy Level

In discussing the policy level, we will limit ourselves to the mac-

rolevel of the hospital sector. As is presumably the case in most
developed countries, health care in Belgium developed the last decades strongly in the direction of hospital-based health care, to the
extent that it became practically entirely organized on the basis of
the hospital. Two characteristics of the Belgian hospital system are
relevant in this connection. Hospitals in Belgium are characterized
first by a system of compartmentalization. Public hospitals and private (Catholic) hospitals are organized in two separate compart-
ments, each having its own chateau with its specific structures and
ideologies. Next, these hospitals, both public and catholic, in their
recent development conformed primarily if not exclusively to medical and economic organizational criteria, to the extent that medical
technical quality and organizational efficiency obtained most of
their attention.

The latter feature in particular led in the beginning of the seven-
ties to a movement for the humanization of the hospitals. Chiefly
expressed was dissatisfaction over the fact that the human and social dimensions were not organized in hospital structures and service. Our unit participated actively by means of articles, lectures,
and research in this movement for a more patient-oriented hospital.
This drive finally resulted in the establishment on the national
level, both in the public and the private sectors, of special committees discussing the problems of humanization and preparing policy
advice in this matter. One of our staff members was closely involved from the very beginning in the initiative of the public sector
as a member of the executive committee. The private Catholic sector, controlled by the patrons of my first period, called in the help
of a colleague of mine, a sociologist of religion. This added another
affiliation and also tended to confirm the above-mentioned thesis of
Renée Fox.

Our participation in this project provided new opportunities to
test and actualize the dialectic interaction between sociology and
social processes. As this third case too is still in its first experimental phase, only a limited number of preliminary observations
can be made. The humanization of the hospital is now considered a
policy problem and a start has been made to solve it on the policy
level. The sociological share focused on the following topics: stimulating problem definitions and solutions concerning humanization in the hospitals themselves; starting up regional consultation
between hospitals, consciously aiming at pulling down and bridg-
ing the compartmentalization in the hospital sector; gradually developing a comprehensive program of humanization, jointly from
both chateaux, so as to present this as a program to the national

policy level and have it realized by means of legal measures; and finally, designing an option and a strategy for a better integration of consumers in the problem-definition and decision-making proc esses in health care in general and hospital care in particular. By concentrating on these topics we might have sociological knowledge to contribute to the societal process of problem definition and disposition. Against this "sociological power," we oppose society which must seek to clarify itself—a process to which the sociologist may make an important contribution.

SUMMARY

According to the instructions of the editors, I should add here a more or less extensive summary, bringing together the pervasive innovative efforts throughout this autobiographical story and my present conception of medical sociology. Due to lack of time and space and other academic sophisms, I have to omit this. Besides, I think I have sufficiently said and illustrated, particularly in the third section ("Leaving the Chateau"), what I feel to be the present and future task of medical sociology. To state it once more: to enter into a dialogue with the reality of health care means to the sociologist to take a position in the magnetic field between policy and society, continuous confrontation with and choice between problems already defined and problems yet to be defined. On the basis of value-implying criteria, medical sociology will have to choose what pole it wants to stimulate and to guide processes of change. A sociology which takes a dialectic position cannot escape this choice.

Also I wish to state that the opportunity to develop a discipline about which there was no tradition or knowledge at all in Belgium has been an extremely fascinating task and a challenge.

Involuntarily this brings to my mind the image of the old-time missionary in underdeveloped countries. After a period in which the missionary was considered a curiosity, some unearthly being, there usually followed a period in which souls were being saved, a mission house was built and the missionary's power and prestige increased. History shows, however, how at the same time resistance increased: mission houses were nationalized, souls became unfaithful, and missionaries were exiled primarily because of a deficient or insufficient integration of the missionary system in the surrounding society. It is in order to prevent the latter that we have left our chateau in time and made it open to the public.

Although this autobiography does remind me of a testament, I

find it nevertheless too early for me to die and let Albert Hammond
sing "He is looking young for his age. . . ."

NOTES

1. Renée C. Fox, "Medical Scientists in a Chateau," *Science* 136
(Spring 1962): 476–83. Fox made a sophisticated analysis of the ways in
which social, cultural and, historical factors affect clinical medical research and research careers.

2. The term "patron" is borrowed from R. C. Fox, who uses it in the
following sense: "Research units are typically headed by one full professor,
with all of the authority and responsibility of a patron. Generally, the other
members of the research staff are junior to him and greatly subordinate in
status" ("Medical Scientists" p. 477).

3. Fox, "Medical Scientists" p. 476.

4. Eliot Freidson, *Professional Dominance: The Social Structure of
Medical Care* (New York: Atherton Press, 1970).

5. S. Bloom, "From Learned Profession to Policy Science" (Paper
presented at the Conference on the Sociology of Medicine, Warsaw, 1973).

6. Yvo Nuyens. *Medical Sociology in Europe; A Report to WHO/EURO*
(Copenhagen: European Regional Office of WHO, 1970).

7. Fox, "Medical Scientists," p. 481.

8. M. Pflanz, "Relations between Social Scientists, Physicians and
Medical Organizations in Health Research" (Paper prepared for the Fourth
International Conference on Social Science and Medicine, Elsinore, 1974).

9. Ray H. Elling, "Political Influence on the Methods of Cross-National
Socio-medical Research," in *Methods in Cross-National Socio-Medical Research*, ed. M. Pflanz and E. Schach (Stuttgart: Thieme, 1976), pp. 144–55.

10. Freidson, Professional Dominance, p. 48.

11. Ibid., p. 23.

12. R. Jelinek, et al., *Sum-service Unit Management*, W. K. Kellogg
Foundation Study Report (Battle Creek, Mich. 1971), p. 114.

13. For a survey of these projects see Sociological Research Institute
K.U.L., Group for Medical Sociology, Quinquennial Report, Van
Evenstraat, 2 B (3000 Leuven, Belgium, 1968–73).

14. In 1969 we published an introductory manual in medical sociology,
the first in Dutch-speaking territory, which was frequently used in all sorts
of training programs for health professionals such as nurses, social workers, and doctors.

15. For an extensive description see R. Cref, "Medisch-Sociologisch on-
derzoek" ("Screening of Medical Sociological Research") in *Sociologische
Verkenningen (Explorations in Medical Sociology)*, ed. Y. Nuyens et al.
(Leuven: Universitaire Pers, 1974), pp. 47–76.

16. H. Bynder, "Sociology in a Hospital: A Case Study in Frustration,"

in *Sociology in Action,* ed. A. Shostak (Chicago: Dorsey Press, 1966), pp. 61–70.

17. This idea has been developed further by Ray H. Elling, "The Design and Evaluation of Planned Change in Health Organizations," in *Sociology in Action,* ed. Shostak, pp. 292–302.

18. For a complete description of the program see Y. Nuyens, "Teaching Medical Sociology to Graduate Students in Sociology" (Paper prepared for the Warsaw Conference on Medical Sociology, August 1973).

19. M. Sokołowska, "On the scope of social sciences in medical education," mimeographed (Warsaw 1969).

20. M. Bracke, "Huisartsgeneeskunde: naar een nieuw toekomst" ("The General Practitioner: Towards a New Future," in *Explorations,* ed. Nuyens, et al., pp. 89–102.

21. Alvin Gouldner, *The Coming Crisis of Western Sociology* (London: Heinemann Educational Books, 1970), p. 43.

22. L. Vermost, "Counteracting Medical Power: The Sociologist's Task" (Paper prepared for the Fourth International Conference on Social Science and Medicine, Elsinore, 1974), pp. 12–16.

23. A Ampe et al., *Zeg maar "a" tegen je dokter* (Antwerp: De Nederlandse Boekhandel, 1973), p. 64.

24. I. Zola, "De medische macht: De invloed van de gezondheidszorg op de maatschappij" ("Medical power: The influence of medicine on society") (Boom: Meppel, 1973), p. 132.

25. M. Pflanz, "Relations between Social Scientists," p. 9.

From Medicine and Public Health to Medical Sociology in Argentina

JORGE SEGOVIA

I was born in Martínez, a suburban residential town in the north of greater Buenos Aires. My father owned a drug store. He was a "practicing pharmacist," a sort of special license that was given when he was young, because of a shortage of college pharmacists. He immigrated to Argentina from the nearby country of Uruguay. My mother was a housewife, a second-generation Argentinian in a family of Spanish emigrants. I have a younger sister, and we have been always very close since our family, in the rigid Spanish tradition, had very few friends outside the extended family. We had a common education, first at a public elementary school and later at an unpretentious private high school, moving up as our family was incorporating middle-class values.

I was the first one in the family to attempt to have a university education; consequently, I was faced with the problem of having to make my own way, without the benefit of the experience and help of relatives or friends, something that was common among most of my fellow students at the University of Buenos Aires. It is very difficult for me to offer an explanation of why I chose medicine as my career, aside from the fact that in those years, most people restricted themselves to three traditional careers: law, engineering, and medicine. I started medical school in 1952 and finished in 1959. Those seven years were quite different from the experience of an American student. The University of Buenos Aires (UBA) has one of the biggest medical schools in Latin America, in terms of student enrollment.[1] One policy of the university—reinforced by Perón's populist ideology—was an "open university." It was common to have more than two thousand students admitted to the first year of medical school in any single year.

Under such circumstances, medical education became more a matter of chance and personal effort from the student than a result of an organized program. Many laboratory sessions were, in fact, theoretical, due to lack of equipment and material; many instructors were themselves students, selected by their high grades or through a primitive theoretical examination. Often to get into a classroom was a matter of luck and force, since the number of students was several times the number of seats. In many subjects, the students themselves tried to find more opportunities to learn outside the regular lectures and labs. In the clinical years, one of the most popular methods to gain clinical experience was to become a member of an emergency service at the municipal hospitals of the city of Buenos Aires, or at nearby towns.[2]

Despite all these shortcomings, most of the students were dedicated and responsible. Working together with the best instructors, it was possible to learn first the basic sciences, and later to acquire clinical knowledge and experience. During the clinical years—there was not a very clear-cut differentiation from the basic science years—the students were divided among several departments (cátedras) for each subject or speciality; in fact, after third year, the school was divided into several clinical schools, using the wards of many municipal hospitals, in addition to the old Hospital de Clinicas, at that time the university hospital.[3] In consequence, to a large extent each student was able to shape his last years to his aspirations, choosing the best places and the best professors; for that, it was necessary to have good grades and also, in some cases, a helping hand in the form of a timely note from a relative or friend with the proper connections. In my case, my grades were quite good and I was fortunate to be in the right place at the right time.

Those years were years of turmoil because the organized student movement was one of the main forces against Perón. The faculty was forced to show its loyalty, and several professors were ousted for various reasons, for example, for refusing to sign a letter of support—among them, a man holding the Nobel Prize in medicine. Many students were jailed. My participation in those struggles was nil; my group of friends had very well internalized that supreme value of Argentine middle class: "Do not get involved, especially in politics." Of course, all these things contributed a great deal to an inadequate education.[4]

In 1957, following the example of most of my friends, I became the youngest member of an emergency service at the nearby town of Boulogne. There, in addition to a fine group of friends from medical school, I met a physician—a surgeon—who later became instrumental in my shift toward public health, Dr. Simón Feld.

Boulogne was mainly a working-class town, and, also, the site of several large shanty towns (*villas miseria* in the local term). Suddenly, and through my many ambulance trips, I came in contact with poverty and need, and for the first time, I saw patients in their environment, outside a hospital bed.

When I finished medical school in 1959, I went straight into a common pattern of practice: an honorary appointment at a public hospital during morning hours, and a private office in the afternoons. No money came from the honorary appointment and very little from my practice, so I was still maintained primarily by my father at this time. None of my friends, or myself, went into a residency program; residency was just starting, and very few openings were available.

The honorary appointment was at an internal medicine ward at the San Isidro Hospital. The chief of the ward was Professor Francisco Secco, one of the last clinicians not wholly dependent on technology to study a patient. He had an incredible capacity to use his hands and ears and always beat us at diagnosing, although many times, and against his advice, we took a peek at x-rays and tests before examining the patient. From him I learned an important lesson: to listen to the patient first, not only out of concern for a proper technical approach, but of a genuine concern for the patient's needs as a human being.

During my first months as a physician I felt comfortable only on a ward, or in the emergency service at Boulogne, of which I had become the attending physician. I found very little challenge in solo private practice. I suppose that I was looking for something that I did not know how to define or search for: a program of training in clinical medicine, with a scientific approach to it, and without the elements of an entrepreneurial approach to the profession. To build a private practice was beginning to be difficult, since the number of physicians in the greater Buenos Aires area was increasing in accordance with the number of students of medicine.[5] This competition for patients was difficult for me to accept.[6]

Just when I was realizing that I did not like the future ahead very much, I again met my friend from Boulogne, Simón Feld. He was now practicing surgery in a small town in the northwest of the country, in the province of San Juan. We talked about that town—maybe a dozen blocks of mud-brick houses, around a central square—and he told me that a new program of maternal and child health was about to start, and that there was a shortage of physicians for it. I grabbed that opportunity. I wrote a letter first, and

then made a trip to talk with the local secretary of health. Before I
could realize what was happening, I was appointed as a medical
officer for maternal and child health in the town of Jachal, in September 1959.

I had suddenly become the head of a pediatric ward of thirty
beds, the chief and organizer of a Maternal and Child Health
Center, and the visiting physician for three small health posts located in the rural section of the valley. A typical day would be like
this: a round to the ward; a trip in an open jeep on twenty miles of
dusty roads to a health post with up to thirty children to care for;
back to the "city," to the outpatient clinic of the hospital and thirty
more children; another round to the ward; and if there was a call, a
visit to the ward in the evening. I also had my private office—since
I was paid by the province for only four hours a day, following the
usual pattern in those jobs—but, again, I did not pay much attention to it. In fact, I worked very much as a full-time physician, although nobody, even myself, realized that.

Of course, all this was too much responsibility for a young and
inexperienced physician. I was very concerned about this, and I
discussed the problem several times with my only professional
mentor at Jachal, Dr. Feld. We always reached the same conclusion:
at least the children did have some services, and the most widespread illnesses—malnutrition, infectious diseases—could be better
controlled, since their diagnosis and management was a matter of
very simple knowledge and techniques.

I had several problems at Jachal in addition to my inexperience.
Maybe the most troublesome was my relations with the group of
local physicians. There were six other physicians, not counting
Feld and myself—for a region with less than twenty thousand people. Their reception toward us was, at best, cool. We were un-
wanted competition for the few private patients in town. In addition—and this was especially true for me, as an officer for a new
program—we had different duties, and the preventive activities of
the Maternal and Child Health Center were strange and distasteful
for them. I believe that the program was the first organized attempt
by the secretary of health of the province to get involved in the
medical care of an important group of the population—mothers and
children—and to do it with some degree of comprehensiveness. As
most physicians in any country with an important private sector,
the local physicians practiced, probably unconsciously, a double
standard of care: one for poor patients at the hospital, the other for
paying patients at their offices. Although I was incapable of a

sophisticated analysis, it was clear that I was an agent of change, and that these changes were against the physicians' interests and traditions. It should be clear that I do not want to blame them personally; they were the consequence of a system of training and thinking—shaped more by the circumstances and modalities of their medical practice than by their deliberate personal motives or even their formal education—that set them against "state medicine." For them, public medical care was anathema; and at this point, I was, rather unwittingly, the devil preaching it. The consequence of all this is that during the twenty-odd months that I resided at Jachal, I was the subject of a constant, although muffled and even polite, resistance.

My second problem was with the people in general. Here, I had a somehow stratified experience. With the low-class people, the ones I saw at the clinics and the hospital, I got along very well after a period of initial distrust. I will always remember—and I think this is one of my few legitimate self-prides—one day when I arrived late at one of the health posts, and found the mothers in turmoil because they were energetically refusing to be seen by the local physician instead of myself. But at the same time, my contacts and communications with the local people were restricted to medical matters. I knew almost nothing about their living and working patterns and the like.

With the middle and upper class I had a mixed reaction. I was well received by many members of the middle class, especially if they were also outsiders or had some university training. Soon I made a fine group of friends among them. The upper class—a small number of families, living at Jachal for many generations—I can say that I never met, save for a few casual encounters. The fact that I was single, and a member of the small group of "intellectuals" of the town, made me quite far from their idea of a "proper physician."

In all, these were very happy months. I learned to manage my own life, outside the restrictions and care of a traditional family setting. I gained, for the first time, a group of friends with which to interact freely, and not only at work or study hours. Despite the problems with the local physicians, I was learning an important lesson about the importance of an area that was entirely new for me: public health. The province of San Juan was a testing ground—through the energetic actions of the secretary of health—for many public health activities that were new to the country (or had been forgotten). I came into contact with several advisors from

the Pan American Health Organization—PAHO—and realized that
there was a lot to learn about what I was attempting to do through
trial and error in the organization and management of my programs.

Soon I became aware that I liked administrative and planning
duties at the small health center very much. I had also some
glimpses of the activities at the central level, and I began to sense
that it is possible to receive great satisfaction from the performance
of administrative and organizational duties without even touching
a patient. I have answered this question many times, about how I
feel being a physician and not helping people directly on a one-to-
one basis by attempting to cure them. My answer is that a public
health physician *is* helping people, because someone has to take
care for the budget, the supplies, the personnel, and so on. Further,
there is more to helping than treating problems after the fact of the
disease's occurrence.

One important component of my experience was to be a distant
witness of the political maneuvering behind the health plan for the
province. The secretary of health was acting very fast, aware of the
instability of political positions in the country, and counting on the
fact that the governor of the province was himself a physician with
a great deal of interest in public health. It was a muted but fierce
battle, between a handful of people with interest in public health,
and the majority of the physicians organized in the local medical
society. It was what I later learned to call a power game played out
between different and more or less organized interest groups. One
important element was the drafting of a bill for a civil service career for physicians. Gradually, it became clear that the medical society would be able to coopt the original project, and to change it
into something according more with its wishes. The requirements
for full-time work for certain positions were dropped, thus enabling
most of the physicians with an important private practice to have a
public health position too. In addition, seniority was made one of
the most important factors for any appointment. Although in those
days my approach to these political factors was rather naive, I became aware that the possibilities of getting a good position in the
new career were not very bright. We discussed all this with Simón
Feld—he was undergoing a similar process of conversion to public
health, maybe more painful for a surgeon—and almost at the same
time, we made up our minds to start careers in public health.
Therefore, I made an application for a place in the new School of
Public Health at the University of Buenos Aires and was accepted.

In January of 1961, I left Jachal and its people, those who had learned to trust me, the porteño,[7] and from whom I learned so many things. I left with some sadness, but I was eager to start new activities and to get the necessary technical skills for my new interests. In March 1961, I became a student in the second class of the School of Public Health.[8]

The spirit of the school during that period was remarkable. The class was composed of thirty-one students, physicians, and dentists, most of us in our late twenties or early thirties, all trying to get started in a career in Public Health and willing to learn how to do so. At that time, Argentina only had a handful of academically trained public health professionals, most of them trained in Santiago, Chile, São Paulo, Brazil, or in schools in the United States. The vast majority of the professionals working in the federal or state health agencies had part-time appointments and no formal training, and their view of their public health activities was, with some remarkable exceptions, as a side activity. We, the young and enthusiastic students at the school, were willing to change that order of things, and to modify public health into a technical and established speciality. Our reaction was to follow to the letter all the classic steps in the development of a new profession, without any knowledge of this process; we ascribed a magic power to formal training, and, of course, to the possession of the public health diploma; we started the organization of the professional association; and the like. For us, at that point, state medicine was seen to be the solution to all public health and medical care problems in the country. In that, we were following, without a proper critical analysis, the example of Chile, which had a very different historic, social, and health situation. Chile had a smaller proportion of its population in a middle class and inherited through its German immigrants an ideology of state responsibility. That period was a time of a strong ideology of nationalization of medicine in the public health movement, along with the practice of full-time public health jobs. This ferment generated an ever-widening gap between clinical and public health medicine.

After my graduation from the school, I remained in the double capacity of technical secretary and instructor in health education. The first position was something of an assistant to the dean for academic affairs. The dean and organizer of the school was professor David Sevlever, a member of the small group with academic training in public health, and with long experience in the first attempts made in the country at health planning and in the teaching of preventive medicine. He was a man of a vast and universalistic culture, and was a guiding factor in my future interdisciplinary adventures. My second job was to help the professor of health education, Professor Roberto DePasquale. He was the only faculty member outside the health professions, having a Ph.D. in education, and he also was important in my explorations of other disciplines.

I became very much concerned with the lack of a structured body of knowledge in health education. I was attracted to it by the elements of educational theory, and some references to group dynamics and community organization. Soon I became disappointed with the superficiality of the treatment of these elements, and with the insistence on the use of the mass media. I hesitated in converting myself into a sort of pamphleteer, and I started to look around for other ways to learn useful concepts applicable to the field.

During that year, I was engaged—through a casual encounter with a celebrity in education, Professor Juan Mantovani—in a modest research project with students of the School of Education of the University of Buenos Aires. This circumstance allowed me to get some advice from a young professor there, Norberto Fernández Lamarra. As a result, I enrolled as a special student in a course in pedagogy. The course was heavily influenced by a sociological approach to education, and soon I discovered two things: first, that sociology might offer the theory I was looking for; and second, that despite my painfully gained medical diploma, the other students were much better than I at understanding the lectures and readings. I remember spending long evenings with groups of my fellow students—all ten years younger, mostly women—in an effort to understand ideas so strange to me as those of John Dewey. I discovered that the concrete and pragmatic training in medicine was a heavy ballast in my efforts. Of course, I failed my first examination, and I barely managed to pass the second. But I had learned something, and in the next semester, I registered in a special program of sociology for graduates at UBA.

Gradually, I became more skillful in the intracacies of sociological concepts, and I no longer needed to spend long evenings with my young fellow students in order to have some help in my efforts. There were certain regrets about this, but it was a sign of gaining competence in sociology.

At that period my approach to the social sciences was extremely simplistic. I saw them just as a useful tool to increase the possibilities of health education by developing techniques using some social science concepts, and ceasing to rely on an advertising agency approach. A new member of the faculty of the School of Public Health, Dr. Carlos H. Canitrot, a professor of public health administration with two years of training at the School of Public Health at Berkeley, began to open my eyes to some of the bibliography and to discuss with me the relationships between administration and the social sciences. He actually gave me an informal and tactful training in many things I had ignored.

The following two years—1962 and 1963—were a period of acquisition of new knowledge in the social sciences in the graduate course at UBA, especially sociology at an introductory level, psychology, and social psychology. This included the discovering of some literature in medical sociology. I remember that the first book I got, Samuel Bloom's *The Doctor and His Patient*, took six months to arrive from the United States. I began to achieve an integration of my previous empirical experiences in public health at Jachal, my brand-new theoretical knowledge of public health, and my incipient capacity for the understanding of social concepts. With all that in mind, my definition of medical sociology at that period was still rather simple: to use some elements of social theory—such as culture, social class, role, and status—in order to define and sometimes explain the behavior of people in relation to health and health services. I suppose that my approach was heavily influenced by the classical health education concepts, and, therefore, I still had the common idea of changing the behavior of people in relation to health and medical care through a modification in their levels of information and the acquisition of new attitudes, suitable to the current organization of the available health services. In a word, the people must adapt themselves to what the health services offered. In addition, I had a vague and unstructured idea about the use of the social sciences in the administration of health services through such concepts as group dynamics, the behavioral school of public administration, and the like. My daily contacts with all the levels of the faculty of the school was a sort of postgraduate training in public health that the school did not offer in a formal way.

I became, gradually, a member of an informal group of young faculty who were somehow unhappy with the slow growth of the school and the bureaucratic problems imposed by our dependency on the School of Medicine. The leader of that group was Carlos Canitrot; we worked in several ways—without much success—to improve the academic level of the school, and to gain recognition from the academic authorities within the UBA. One important point is to stress the very special kind of school of public health that this was. The full-time faculty was very small, including only the dean, Canitrot as head of public health administration, another department head (public health dentistry), and a couple of instructors, including myself. The rest had part-time appointments, and they devoted a great deal of their time to jobs in different health agencies, not always related to their teaching activities. We did not have funds for research—a common situation within the university—since we spent almost all our time in teaching activities, the management of the school, and in attempts to improve our very ill-defined position with the School of Medicine. This was a typical pattern of staffing and work at Argentinian universities: mostly part-time faculty, very poorly paid, no money for research, and a highly traditional approach to educational activities.

In 1963, we had an unexpected, short visit from the director of the American foundation the Milbank Memorial Fund. Dr. Alexander Robertson was making a tour of Latin American medical institutions to present to them a new program of fellowships for junior faculty members, the Milbank Faculty Fellowships. Professor Sevlever, Canitrot, and I talked with him, and he encouraged me to make an application for that program. This very short visit—a morning, a lunch, a hasty trip to the airport—was useful in different ways. In the short run, it provided me with some technical and moral support for my activities and my line of thought about an interdisciplinary approach to medicine and social sciences; it opened my eyes to new explorations, and I made new efforts to change the curriculum of the Health Education Section, of which I had become the head. The next year, with the aid of a sociologist, I introduced some hours devoted exclusively to social science and had my first experience with the very cool reception given by physicians to this kind of knowledge. The regulations—all faculty at a medical school were supposed to be physicians—and the budget constraints made that experiment very difficult.

In the long run, the effects of the visit proved to be a turning point in my professional career. That year, I did not make an application, because I was busy settling my private life. This very same year, the school started a new program for the training of intermediate personnel for health and hospital statistics. The new program resulted in an influx of young women at the school, which was, before that, an almost entirely male domain. And an old story was repeated: I married a student, Susana Elena Ravenna, a pretty brunette with a strong and independent character. We married just in the middle of the academic year, to a great scandal of many faculty members who were much more conservative than I ever thought. And I had to adjust my life—our life, from now on—to a new set of responsibilities and activities. It was not easy, not only because of our need to adapt to each other's ways and likes as well as dislikes—for example, to Susana a surgeon was a clearer model of a physician than a public health man—but because of the very peculiar circumstances of my professional life. As a full-time member of UBA and a bachelor living with my parents, it had not been a big problem to be paid once every six months. Now, the rent, the electric and telephone bill, and the food, had to be paid every month. And soon, we were expecting a baby, and that was a big responsibility. We managed, with the aid of Susana's ingenuity and intelligence, and with a great deal of help from her parents and also from my family—especially my sister.

More or less in the middle of all that commotion, Professor Sevlever introduced me to a physician, Samuel J. Bosch. He was asking for Professor Sevlever's support in his application for a Milbank Faculty Fellowship and he got it, as well as the fellowship. He had just given up a successful private practice as a rheumatologist to become a member of a private medical group and institution, Centro de Educación Médica e Investigaciones Clínicas (CEMIC). At the beginning I doubted the honesty and reliability of his commitment to medical education and public health, perhaps because of my experience with private practitioners in Jachal. In any case, after an initial period of distrust, we became very good friends, and started working together in the planning of an experimental program in comprehensive medicine to be initiated the next year. I learned, to my great surprise, that Sandy Robertson had mentioned my name and Canitrot's to Sammy when he, Sammy, was—to use his own expression—"foundation hunting" in New York. It was kind of funny to be unknown in your own country, and to be recommended in New York.

The first contact was the initiation of a very close relationship with Sammy. We worked together in the Comprehensive Medicine Program during that year—1964—and through that program, I became more and more involved in the whole CEMIC operation. The first thing that Sammy did was to help me to prepare an application for the Milbank Memorial Fellowship, with a program to develop the teaching and research in social sciences applied to medicine, both at CEMIC and the school of Public Health. In 1965, the fellowship was awarded after a long selection process.

During 1965, while working in the Comprehensive Medicine Experimental Program, I began to learn much more about the CEMIC operation and Sammy's plans. CEMIC was a private, nonprofit organization, whose general goals were the advancement of medical knowledge and the improvement of the health of the population. It was located in an Internal Medicine Ward in a federal public hospital in the city of Buenos Aires—Sala 20, Hospital Rivadavia. CEMIC had the support of some wealthy people, and in an arrangement that is common in public hospitals, they created a sort of small foundation to improve the equipment and staff of the ward. CEMIC provided outpatient services and hospitalization for an undefined population in internal medicine and its subspecialities. This was one of the teaching units of UBA for the last three years of clinical training of the medical school. The president of the Executive Council of CEMIC was also the professor and head of one of the chairs of medicine. CEMIC had a residency program in internal medicine, one of the first organized in the country. The quality of medical care was high in comparison with the usual standards of public hospitals, and the level of teaching was excellent. The outpatient department was unusually well organized, with scheduled appointments and a day-long operation, in contrast to the two or three hours of morning activities in the rest of public hospitals.

As executive secretary, Sammy was in charge of almost everything. The only full-time senior member, he was loosely supervised by the executive council, composed of prestigious internists with part-time appointments. Soon I became aware that Sammy had big plans for the institution. He had, along with other members of the executive council, been visiting schools of medicine in Latin America and the United States, and also the Health Insurance Program (HIP) in New York and the Kaiser Foundation Prepaid Plans on the West Coast. He was very much concerned with the need to introduce change in the classical teaching of medicine in Argentina, but at the same time he was aware of the necessity of providing the students with a real model of newly conceived health services, to learn and to practice that kind of new medicine.

In summary, his idea was to transform CEMIC into an institution with an enlarged program of medical education, leading eventually to the formation of a new medical school and a program of health and medical care services which would provide a setting for teaching, and at the same time be adapted to the particular characteristics of the city of Buenos Aires. His goal was to connect a program of medical education and a program of medical and health care, having his financial support through a prepaid system.

It was, undoubtedly, a very idealistic project, and maybe it was impractical to think about effecting such a drastic change within a milieu so hostile to change. The medical environment was a powerful and resilient coalition of private practice and superspecialized academic medicine, and the political scene was so unstable and unpredictable that it was difficult to secure enough and lasting support for any long-range program. Nevertheless, and looking in retrospect after ten years of that experience, I still think that it was a sound and imaginative approach to the combined problems of medical education and care in Argentina.

The Comprehensive Medical Program was, apart from its primary teaching objective, a device to change the institution from a classic ward in internal medicine to a small hospital providing basic comprehensive health services. The instructors of the program gradually became involved in the actual operations of services; thus, CEMIC made its first appointments of pediatricians, obstetrician-gynecologists, psychiatrists, a public health nurse, a social worker, a health educator, and so on. During that period, I served as a link to the public health people, and I introduced to Sammy some of my friends and colleagues who became, eventually, important in his ambitious scheme.

An important step was to provide the institution with a sound financial mechanism for the new medical services. For that we had the support and advice of the Kaiser Foundation, through people like Dr. Ernest Saward. A Prepaid Community Health Plan was put into operation in May 1965.

It is outside the scope of this paper to continue describing the CEMIC experience. Sammy Bosch has made a detailed account elsewhere.[9] But it was necessary to give some details in order for the reader to understand the complexity and reach of the program.

Within that framework, I became the head of a health center in a shantytown in the city of Buenos Aires—Villa Mitre—and the head of the brand new Medical Sociology Section—within the Department of Behavioral Sciences, under the leadership of Raúl Usandivaras—along with a full-time sociologist, Héctor Goglio, thus fulfilling my old desire to build up a real multidisciplinary team. The health center at Villa Mitre was initiated as a teaching facility for the Comprehensive Medicine Program. Later, it became an experimental setting for the trial of administrative procedures to operate peripheral clinics, and also to demonstrate that it was possible to intermix such a varied clientele as wealthy ladies from the Barrio Norte and mothers of fatherless families of who knows how many children, living in dwellings made up of tin and cardboard.

The medical sociology section was in charge of an educational program and a research program. With Héctor Goglio, we trained the medical students without any formal program, just responding to their needs in connection with their responsibilities in solving the problems of patients of all sorts of social classes. The villa miseria—the shantytown—was a natural sociological laboratory, and the device of assigning the students actual responsibility for the administrative and clinical tasks was the best educational tool for health administration, statistics, and social science. Each student was responsible, on a rotating basis, for a full day of operations at the center, under direct spervision. A weekly seminar with case presentations, informal meetings, and sessions with Sammy and other clinical instructors were the main teaching activities, and the students learned through the experience of doing. We also had some responsibilities in teaching social science to the Department of Nursing and Social Work.

The research program was connected primarily with the operation of the Prepaid Health Plan. We started to design a continuing study of the membership, monitoring such factors as age, sex, occupation, place of residency, type of institutional membership, socioeconomic status, rate of utilization of the services, diagnosis, and so on. Our intention was to use the membership of the health plan as a closed population, representing, in a way, the urban population of the metropolitan area of Buenos Aires, and to study the possible effects of this new kind of medical care services.

My involvement with CEMIC was almost total. I took a part-time appointment at the School of Public Health, reversing my commitments in order to dedicate more time to CEMIC. One reason for this was pragmatic: CEMIC was a better source of support for our growing family—Andrea Mariana, our first child, was born in July 1964. Another reason was professional: the School of Public Health was in a period of stagnation, due to its position as a part of a conservative medical school. And a third, most powerful reason, was the very special nature of the CEMIC experiment.

Everybody, at least at the professional level, was involved in the three main areas of concern of the institution. For example, and as I already explained, I had service (in my case administration), teaching, and research functions. All were mixed. I had administrative responsibilities as head of the health center, which was also a teaching demonstration for the operation of peripheral clinics and which also involved operational research. The Medical Sociology Section was involved in teaching, but in "real-life" settings, with all the flavor and problems of the actual needs of people, families, and the community; we did not teach about social classes, we were involved with them. And our main research project, the study of the population of the Prepaid Health Plan, was not only an academic study, but a project to help the manager of the plan and the executive secretary make future policy decisions. For everybody the three functions—service (whether clinical or administration-planning), teaching, and research—were closely interrelated, forming a network in which sometimes it was difficult to isolate the components. One important feature of the operation was a weekly meeting among the manager of the health plan, Dr. Carlos J. M. Martini; the hospital administrator, Dr. Omar J. Gómez; Sammy, in his role of director of the medical group; and me, as a sort of sociological umpire. These were very lively meetings, and we discussed every detail of the health plan operation, each participant from his own point of view. Carlos Martini was a sort of representative of the consumer, although we did not use the term in those days; Omar represented the interests of the hospital, and Sammy those of the physicians. We all had a clear concept that the interests of the different groups were in sharp conflict, and that these conflicts should be settled, keeping in mind the primacy of the interests of the patient members of the health plan, that is, our "community." So CEMIC was an environment in which to combine, in a natural way, my academic and service motivations. All this took place between 1965 and 1967.

Meanwhile, I was enjoying the advantages of the Milbank Faculty Fellowship. It soon proved to be much more than a sum of money; it was a whole system of education, through carefully orchestrated encounters with people and institutions.[10] I did have the opportunity to meet, and learn, from people at the fund, like Robin F. Badgley, J. Wendell Macleod, Lowell Levin, Per Stensland, Clyde Kiser, and many others. We went to professional meetings in Latin America and the United States, and we met with the pioneers in the field of our interests. Last, but not least, were the fellows themselves. I met people from Chile, Brazil, Mexico, Colombia, the West Indies, the United States, and Canada, all of them fighting for the same things, all with the same ideology of change in medical education and in health services. I will always remember our "seminars" late in the evenings, when the last guest had left the "Milbank suite," without our coats, our ties loose, and a glass of Scotch in hand, and Sandy presiding. The places differed—Bogota, San Francisco, Buenos Aires, Santiago, Chicago, Kingston—but the spirit was the same.

At this point, it will be good to insert, again, a family note. Our second child, Jorge Pablo, was born in October 1965, exactly forty-eight hours after my arrival from a trip to Chicago, sponsored by my Milbank Fellowship. As always, Susana managed to control all variables, biological and professional, and she waited until I was back. At that point, both of us were working in public health; she was in charge of all medical records operations at CEMIC, and the supervisor of all the receptionists at the ambulatory clinic. The reader will remember that she understood surgeons better—maybe she still does—but after a period of bewilderment about my professional activities, she got into the battle herself. She held her appointment at CEMIC for several years, but was the first victim of the conservative group. With great sorrow, she resigned, under pressure, just before my trip to Pittsburgh. She has never worked again, but she is a close observer of my activities and an energetic and wise critic of them. In addition, she has to cope with all the uncertainties of a rather mobile household. It is not because of the current pressures of the women's movement that I recognize her equal standing as a partner in all our efforts.

Around 1966, Héctor Goglio and I carried out what for us was an important experience. Invited by the director of the Institute of Sociology of the Catholic University of Buenos Aires, we taught a course in medical sociology for advanced students in sociology. It was a new type of challenge, especially for me as a physician, to attempt to teach students of social science about a speciality that, at that time, was almost unknown to them. We had to make a completely new presentation of our traditional material, starting from a new angle, since now we were confronted by a different situation from the traditional one of "selling" sociology to physicians. The response of the students was quite good. Later, some of them got jobs in the field of health—but unfortunately, political factors again intervened, and the director was forced to resign. We had to follow him, losing this unique opportunity of interdisciplinary work.[11]

During that year, I began to look for a place for a year of formal training in medical sociology. The time was ripe for that, with my studies in sociology, both formal and informal, reaching a point at which I could benefit from special training. There were people to take over my different jobs at CEMIC, and then, with the advice of Robin Badgley, I looked into different programs and had the unusual opportunity of visiting a couple of institutions. I chose the program of Ray Elling, at the School of Public Health at Pittsburgh. But before writing about my foreign training, I must comment on some developments that occurred before my trip to the United States, since these were important in setting the stage for the period after my return from abroad.

In 1966, things began to go wrong. A military coup took over the constitutional government, and the policy of the secretary of health toward the CEMIC experiment was reversed. We started to have serious problems with a grant application that we had presented some time before in order to build a private hospital, to enlarge the operations of the health plan, and to gain complete independence from the federal health authorities. At the same time, the new government took over the university in a manner that is almost a tradition in Argentina: a lot of police and some kicking around of students and even faculty. The *tripartito*—students, graduates, and professors—was suspended (it is somehow ironic to note that this system of university self-government was inaugurated by another military government, around 1956, thus fulfilling a long dream of the Movimiento Reformista). Most of the people at the government universities feared a new period of harsh treatment.

In protest, at least in some schools and institutes, including the School of Public Health, faculty resigned en masse. Despite voices of moderation, the resignations were accepted. Therefore, in a matter of weeks several colleagues and I were out of the school. This was a severe blow for us, for the school was an important center of power in the public health system of the country. After this, we suffered long years of isolation from academic centers; the public health movement was split in a bitter and useless power struggle; and, as a consequence, the country lost because of all these negative episodes. For myself, the loss was compensated by a full-time appointment at CEMIC. And to keep some foothold in teaching and research, a private nonprofit institution was founded, Centro de Investigaciones y Adiestramiento en Salúd Púiblica (CIASP), under the presidency of Carlos Canitrot.

In 1967, before I left for Pittsburgh, the situation at CEMIC had started to get out of control. It was clear that there were two groups: one, that I will call the conservative group, was composed mainly of part-time internists, many of them members of the executive council. The other, the innovative group, was composed of the young full-time members of the Medical Group and our public health people. Our formal authority was precarious; only Sammy was in a position of real and formal power, and when his position was also threatened, we knew that things were going wrong. The whole situation can be described as a case in the sociology of or-

ganizations. The broad, loosely defined goals of CEMIC were
shared by all the membership of the institution, but suddenly it
was clear that the meaning ascribed to these goals, and the means
to achieving them, were completely different for the two groups.
The conservative group resented the importance of administration
and the authority given to paramedical and technical personnel. Its
members disliked the Comprehensive Medical Program and its
work at the health center, and named it "medicine of poor quality."
Of course, this is something that should be understood in the light
of the training they had, and the type of private medicine (liberal
profession) that they had practiced for years. All these changes in
the orientation and the priorities of the institution were in
complete opposition in their set of values. For them, our values
were even dangerous—an anonymous pamphlet was circulated
once, accusing me, among others, of being a member of the
Communist party—because we were a menace to the very
foundations of their type of medicine.

In this environment of uncertainty, I left in September 1967 for
Pittsburgh. I had discussed the format of the training period with
Robin, and later with Ray Elling during a short visit he made to
Buenos Aires in 1967. Since I had only one academic year, and for
that period the only degree available was the M.P.H. (which I already had from UBA), we agreed on a special student, postdoctoral
status, including some regular courses along with special tutoring
in certain areas of specific interest to me. This proved to be a wise
decision. I spent no more than 30 percent of my time attending
regular courses, both at the School of Public Health and at the
Department of Sociology, including a weekly seminar with the
students in the Ph.D. program of Social Sciences and Health Services. I spent the rest of my time in tutorial sessions with Ray and
other members of the faculty. I undertook a program of readings in
order to review the major part of the basic bibliography in medical
sociology that I did not have at home. In the second semester, we
began to focus the tutorial and reading activities on problems of the
sociology of organizations and the institutional and political factors
in medical care delivery systems.

I think that such a program tailored to my individual needs and
my future responsibilities at CEMIC was extremely useful. Ray allowed me great flexibility, and with his advice—a rare combination
of expertise and sense of my needs—he was a great help in using
my scarce time to a maximum. I can remember few days that I considered lost, something that would undoubtedly happen should we

have decided on my taking a degree which I already had. Of course, this implied sacrificing the advantages of a foreign diploma. I suppose that I have suffered some inconveniences due to the lack of a nice diploma in English, but I never regret that.[12]

About that period of foreign training, there are a few remarks that I consider important in the training of a Latin American professional such as myself. The first is related to the language barrier. I think that almost any Spanish-speaking student will lose no less than a full third of his working capacity due to his imperfect knowledge of English. As a consequence, some consideration should be given to the length of the period of training; an adaptation stage of some months seems to me very useful to overcome the initial language difficulties, the spatial and social adaptation, and to achieve a working knowledge of the patterns and uses of the institution. After that, a year of full work will be more efficiently used. The better program for the teaching of medical sociology—as well as any person in another specialty in need of foreign training—would be one based in a Latin American country, and with affiliations with foreign centers. The student would spend an initial period in the Latin American country—at least one year—with well-organized visits by members of the affiliated programs. After that, the student would go, if necessary, to any of the affiliated centers for specific work in a research project, under the guidance of bilingual faculty, which is something not so difficult to have nowadays. A permanent program of exchange between centers and projects in comparative research would increase the possibilities of such a program. That would be much better than the traditional fellowship, which in many cases is only just an amount of money to pay expenses, and not a system of training.

During my training period I received letters from Sammy and my friends telling about the worsening of CEMIC problems. The Prepaid Health Plan was growing, but was in the middle of financial strictures that we had forecast in advance, being in relation to a given size of the membership and its demand for services—which were somehow costly due to the small size of the hospital. We knew that due to well-known factors of economy of scale, in a given time the plan would have a deficit. But this, in combination with the total refusal from the federal health authorities to authorize the grant for a new private hospital, was used by the conservative group as a weapon against Sammy Bosch and his policies. When I came back, in June 1968, twenty-four hours after I set foot again in Buenos Aires, I was at Sammy's home, helping him draft his resignation. A month later, I presented my resignation too, and with this, almost all the innovative group at CEMIC was ousted.

The period that followed was very sad indeed. Here I was, with a training almost unique in the country, jobless. I remained like that for six long months, and then I was appointed to the new Latin American Center for Administrative Medicine (CLAM), an international center administered by PAHO through an agreement with the federal health authorities and UBA.

In the next years, I worked with a remarkable group, including Carlos Martini and Omar Gómez, formerly at CEMIC, and Dr. María Teresa Beas, formerly at the School of Public Health. We prepared innumerable drafts for a program of research and teaching in medical care. Due to the manifold problems of getting an international institution off the ground, we had a slow start. Together with officers of PAHO based in Washington, D.C., we prepared a seminar in medical and hospital administration which was given at Buenos Aires. and Lima. A Center of Information and Documentation (CIASP) was organized under the leadership of Carlos Martini. And in 1970, we replicated, with the direction of Jack Elinson from Columbia University, who was on his sabbatical in Buenos Aires, a study of a sociometric measurement of the quality of medical care.[13]

At the same time, I devoted some time to the CIASP operation. We organized several courses in medical care and related subjects; we published a journal, Medicina Administrativa, maybe the only one devoted to medical care in Latin America, under the editorship of Jorge A. Mera, and later, for a year, under my editorship. The group, under the leadership of Carlos Canitrot, was a forum for the discussion of medical care problems and concepts; and despite our isolation, and our lack of resources and political power, CIASP was important in the medical care scene in the country.

But most of the time, I felt deeply frustrated. I think that I never was able to recuperate from the loss of my programs at CEMIC, and prior to that, my ties with the School of Public Health. The growth of CLAM was too slow for our professional needs; Carlos Martini went to England, and I also thought that a period outside the country would be good for healing my wounds. We discussed that idea with Jack Elinson several times, and he was completely against it. But I proved to be a very obstinate subject; and when I got an excellent offer from a new medical school in the United States, he made me another offer, and I went to the Division of Sociomedical Sciences at the School of Public Health of Columbia University in January 1971.

I can assume that at this point the reader is asking himself a very pertinent question: how many times had this man resigned from a position before accomplishing something in it? Too many times; I am the first to agree on that. But I do not know the answer, at least a complete answer, myself. It may rest in some psychological impairment; but, of course, if there were any such problem I would be the last one able to recognize it. Instead, I think that I can also describe a structural problem, related to a state of permanent institutional instability heightened for me personally by the innovativeness of my field and career. This instability is an omnipresent factor in the lives of Latin American professionals, especially the ones without a private practice, those dependent on governmental appointments at different levels. In addition to this, certain positions and roles are very prone to uncertainty; for example, public health was at that time—I do not know about the present conditions—a highly unstable field of work, and sociology was precisely another dangerous area. Both were connected with a strong drive to change things: institutions, techniques, peoples' work and responsibilities, and the like. All these changes were far from welcome by the traditional officeholders, who in our Latin American societies are members, or have the support, of the traditional class in power. A discipline like medical sociology was viewed as potentially dangerous, and even revolutionary. A man like me, coming from a family which was a very recent member of the middle class, without a necessary backing of strong credentials in approved groups, was questionable if not mistrusted. As an example, during the experience at CEMIC, it was necessary for Sammy Bosch to lend me some of his prestige and position, showing at all times that he trusted me, and so on. At a given time, this game became dangerous for himself, and, consequently, the Medical Sociology Section became isolated from the rest of the institution with very little support for its activities.

In contrast, the three years I worked with Jack Elinson at Columbia University were a sort of very long vacation from uncertainty and useless power games. Together, we developed a proposal and got some funding for an exploratory project for the development of a theoretical framework, and a comparative methodology for the study of political decisions in health systems, using the concepts of decision making and power structure. This effort was the culmination of my interests in the study of health systems and policy formation in the health sector. In Jack, and in the Division of Sociomedical Sciences, I found a friend and an environment adequate to this type of highly speculative work. In addition, I taught a seminar "Health Problems and Medical Care in Latin America," and participated in the activities of the Ph.D. program of the division. I benefited from a friendly relation with the members of the division, faculty, students, and staff: Jack, Eric Josephson, John Colombotos, Margary Braren, Meta Nikias, Ann Brunswick, and the people of the Harlem Hospital Evaluation Unit are now, despite the distance, very close friends and colleagues, in a type of relationship that very seldom is achieved in the turbulent environment of Latin American universities.

From another angle, it was also an excellent experience for all the family, despite the initial fear and reluctance regarding the ways of a different country. I never mentioned before, and this is an appropriate time for it, the role of the family in the lives of Latin American professionals. With our particular types of careers, it is a matter of being, from the beginning, a millionaire, or some sort of lay monk, or, otherwise, to have the luck to choose a very intrepid wife. I had that luck, and Susana, bravely, without any knowledge of English, went through the experiences of taking care of a family, in the very different circumstances of life in the United States.

Of course, I moved again. I left behind that American experience, not without doubts and hesitation, but willing to begin to make my way back home, where I feel I still belong. Now, we are back in Latin America, and hoping for the last jump. It is too soon for me to describe the new place in which I am now, and therefore, I will leave this part of my story to the future.[14]

To put an end to this very long account, I would like to make some comments about my current views on sociomedical sciences, or sociosalustics, as Jack Elinson, rather cacophonically, wants to call the field.

The first point is almost of exclusive interest to the Latin American countries; it is about the role of physicians in the development of the speciality of medical sociology. I think, and I know that this is a highly polemical opinion, that sociomedical sciences in Latin America are still too much under the control of physicians. Without qualifying their capacities, I will state my strong doubts about the future of the field if this continues in the same way. I think—and this is my own experience—that in the beginnings of the discipline, in a conservative setting such as medicine, the role of us—sociological physicians, to stress the difference—was clear and even necessary. We were a sort of lost link in the evolution of the discipline, relating both areas and lending to the mixture the blessing of our medical diplomas. But the problem is that those odd lost links are refusing to get lost, and even multiplying. It is understandable that we, the ones already working in the field, will continue to do so, that is easy to accept and even to forgive. But the problem is that it is possible to hear about, and to see in stages of development, programs for the conversion of more physicians into "sociologists," with some years of graduate work. It seems that for some physicians, participation in the field is something more than a temporary phenomenon or a matter of some few academic rarities. I am concerned with the intention to institutionalize the domain of physicians of a field which should be, more and more, in the hands of social scientists. And I think that I can throw the first stone, although by some improbable feat of physics, I may be among the first to be hit by it.

A second point, about the domain and areas of sociomedical sciences, is more general. It is common knowledge that the field of sociomedical sciences evolved more through the necessities of strategy to achieve some approval from the health people, especially physicians, than from a structured theoretical framework. I will not offer such a theoretical framework, but rather an elementary classification in three levels of action. Just by pure chance, my professional career is a good example of the three levels that I see as important in the description of the field:

The level of illness and patients: at this level, concepts derived from psychology, social psychology, anthropology, and microsociology are used. We can call it the "clinical level," since its main applications rest within the areas of patient management and personal health services.

The level of community health: the purpose of this level should be to describe and analyze the phenomena in organizations such as hospitals, professions, and their relationships with the community. Social psychology and sociology, especially sociology of organizations and professions, are useful at this level. This is the "public health" level, which should be useful to administrators and public health people in general.

The level of health systems: here sociology, economics, political science, and social history would work together with interdisciplinary approaches like systems analysis to develop this incipient area which, in my judgment, has a chance to become the most useful application of the discipline. This is the "policy level" that should be used by planners, administrators at the highest levels, and, hopefully, "political" governmental bodies such as legislatures.

Maybe a schematic presentation (see Table 1) will be useful to understand better this organization of the field. Of course, a division like this should be understood in a framework of very fluid and constant references from one level to the others.

The most important question about the sociomedical sciences is how useful the discipline will be to help achieve a better level of health in the general population. I have many doubts about this matter, because of the complexity of processes within health sys-

Table 1

LEVEL	DISCIPLINES	AREAS OF APPLICATION	AGENTS AND INSTITUTIONS
Illness and Patients	Psychology Social Psychology Microsociology	Personal health services; actions in small communities	All the members of the health team in interaction with individuals, families, groups, small communities (emphasis on reciprocity of experiences)
Community Health	Social Psychology Anthropology Sociology	Public health	Administrators and officers of health agencies (other government bodies) at local and regional level. Communities' representatives, in a broad sense
Health Systems	Economics Sociology Political Science Social History Systems Analysis	Policy formulation and implementation	Planners and administrators at high levels (regional, national supranational). Legislators, governmental bodies enacting or effecting policies

tems, their relationships with other sectors of society, and especially with the political processes of government, with respect to the formulation of policies and the allocation of resources among members of different strata. Given the very complex nature of political processes, there is an ever-present doubt in my mind whether more knowledge and information will necessarily result in a better decision-making process for better politics and programs. All these things are subjected to particular sets of values, since they are far from being purely technical matters.

I would like to avoid the usual grandiose last phrase, but I will express my hopes that the field will find a way to be useful in a society which is in great need of redefinitions for the best possible levels of life for all members. For that, the professionals in the field will have to achieve a difficult balance between theory and action, methodology and commitment, technology and values.

NOTES

1. The enrollment of the School of Medicine of the University of Buenos Aires was 9,960 students in 1967 (J. C. García, "Profile of Medical Education in Latin America," *International Journal of Health Services* 1 [1971]: 39–57). The size of each class is variable, between a little less than 2,000 students in normal years, to around 3,000 in the early 1950s, and 10,000 in 1974.

2. Those days, the pattern of staffing emergency services at most public hospitals was based on students of the last years of medical school. There was a chief intern physician for each shift (twenty-four hours). Nowdays, at least in the hospitals of the Municipality of Buenos Aires, the emergency services are staffed entirely by physicians.

3. The School of Medicine is the single central locale for the basic sciences; there are several settings for the clinical years. Today, at the beginning of the third year, the students must choose among several "hospital units" involving a set of clinical subjects and subspecialities, organized around one or two hospitals.

4. It is important to note that the attitudes of young people toward Peron and his party shifted completely. On his return to the country, in 1973, he was actively supported by the student movement.

5. The number of physicians in the city of Buenos Aires is 12,113; that is, 253 inhabitants per physician (National Council for Development, Annual Report, Buenos Aires, 1964). The number of inhabitants per one physician for the whole country is 708.

6. It is difficult for me to offer an explanation about my attitude toward solo private practice. It could be a matter of insecurity; or this same factor could be twisted around and focused in a more favorable light for myself

by saying that I was aware of the need to have supportive personnel and facilities, even in the daily practice, and not only for hospitalized patients. It is a matter of speculation to think what my reaction would be toward clinical medicine in a setting such as a prepaid group practice.

7. Porteño means "from the port"; it is the name used for people born in the city of Buenos Aires.

8. The School of Public Health of the University of Buenos Aires was created in 1958; the first class entered in 1960. It was typical that after so many years without a lasting school of public health—there were previous attempts at the universities of Tucumán and Litoral—two schools were created at the same time; the one at the University of Buenos Aires, and another under the Ministry of Health. Both schools competed for students and funds for several years, until a minister of health closed the School of the Ministry and sent, in twenty-four hours, all the students to the university school, tripling the size of the class in the middle of the academic year.

9. See S. J. Bosch, "An Experiment to Change Medical Education and Medical Care in Argentina," *Social Science and Medicine* 7 (May 1973): 373–86. Also, see S. J. Bosch and J. Segovia, "Enseñando y aprendiendo medicina integrada," *Medicina Administrativa* 4 (1970): 120–131; and J. Segovia, A. Gasullo, and S. J. Bosch, "Evaluación de actitudes en estudiantes de medicina," *Medicina Administrativa* 2 (1968): 168–76.

10. For details about the Milbank Faculty Fellowships, see Per G. Stensland et al., *The Milbank Faculty Fellowship: Preparing Leadership for Change in Community Medicine for the Future* (New York: Milbank Memorial Fund, 1974).

11. The episode at the Catholic University was typical of the general distrust of the more conservative elements of the university scene toward social sciences. A personal episode occurred between the president of the university and the institute, with a swift reorganization of the whole institute, with more conservative, and therefore "safe" faculty.

12. As one of the products of this year, I prepared a paper on the embeddedness of health systems in their surrounding sociopolitical structures. A revised version was published: J. Segovia, "La salud como sistema social," *Medicina Administrativa* 3 (1969): 89–108.

13. The original study is described in M. C. Maloney, R. E. Trussel, and J. Elinson, "Physicians Choose Medical Care: A Sociometric Approach to Quality Appraisal," *American Journal of Public Health* 50 (1960): 1678–86. We made a presentation of some results of the Buenos Aires study. See J. Segovia and J. Elinson, "What Physicians Think about Physicians in Argentina," abstract, *Public Opinion Quarterly* 35 (1971): 3. The Centro Latinoamericano de Administración Médica, Buenos Aires, has two unpublished preliminary reports done in 1971.

14. I wrote this paragraph in 1974, just a few months after my arrival to a new position in a Medical School of a Latin American University. Now, a year later, I am again searching for a new position, which, despite my personal and professional feelings, will be, with all probability, in the North-

ern Hemisphere. It is not an easy task to offer an explanation about why so many Latin American professionals are forced to look for positions elsewhere. Instability, poor opportunities for professional development, a distaste for all the politics and influence games necessary to secure a job may be some of the factors involved. I know that many people will be against this opinion, but it is shared, with the same frustration and sadness, by many of my friends working outside Latin America.

Autobiographical Notes of a Medical Sociologist in Israel

SETTING THE STAGE: SOME PERSONAL NOTES

I am American born and educated and immigrated to Israel in 1949, a year after the new state was established. I have lived in Israel ever since. My decision to settle in Israel was based on a strong Jewish identification and Zionist orientation, first acquired from my parents during my youth and reaffirmed consciously during late adolescence. I was an active participant in the Zionist student movement in college so that the ideal of settling in Israel came as a natural culmination to my upbringing and ideological commitment.

At the time I immigrated, I was in the middle of graduate studies in the Department of Social Relations at Harvard and therefore returned briefly to the United States a few years later to receive my Ph.D., having gathered material for my dissertation in Israel. I can trace my continuing interest in theory and methodology back to my Harvard days and especially to the late Samuel Stouffer who was my thesis supervisor.

While the act of migration required many forms of adaptation on my part, this radical change in setting and culture did not weaken my basic commitment to sociological research. The major reinforcement of this commitment was an immediate invitation upon arrival in Israel to join the staff of the newly established Israel Institute of Applied Social Research. I retained my affiliation with this institute for many years, working as a senior research director until 1968, and have been strongly influenced by Louis Guttman, its scientific director.

Probably because few social scientists were available at the time, I was immediately given the unusual opportunity at a remarkably early stage in my career to assume full responsibility for a large scale study of immigrant adaptation. It will be recalled that during the early 1950s there was mass immigration from a wide assortment of countries to Israel and the institute was asked to research the process and come up with some answers to the many problems involved. I cut my professional teeth on this project, learning by doing everything including the design, building of the research instruments, supervising the interviewing in all parts of the country, coding the data, preparing it for analysis, and writing up the results. I eventually wrote my first book, *Immigrants on the Threshold*,[1] on the basis of this research for which I was awarded the Israel Prize for the Social Sciences in 1965. The field of immigration remains one of my central interests to this day.

My initial entry into the field of medical sociology was not deliberate or preplanned. Neither was it based on a formal preparatory program or specialization. Paradoxically enough, I was doing graduate work at Harvard where Parsons and some of his students were engaged in pioneering work in medical sociology, but somehow I was focused on other areas and was not caught up in this field at the time. Several years went by before I started in medical sociology and by then I was fairly experienced in other specializations which I considered to be my own areas of interest: the sociology of immigration and ethnic relations in Israel.

My substantive training in medical sociology was, therefore, acquired on my own. I simply read extensively in the area. Since I was quickly fascinated by the field and saw in it a number of areas of theoretical interest that appeared to fit my previous sociological interests, this process proved to be an entirely pleasurable undertaking. At this stage I was past my graduate training and had accumulated some experience both in teaching sociology and in carrying out empirical research; this self-training operation therefore proved to be no problem. Nor was there any difficulty in applying familiar research techniques to a new substantive area.

Recognition of this specialty in Israel was rapid and smooth. The academic community is extremely sensitive to developmental trends in other countries and especially to trends in social science. Growing differentiation and specialization in such fields as sociology is expected and approved. I teach undergraduate and graduate students both in the Medical School and in the Department of Sociology of the Hebrew University and hold a joint appointment in the two faculties. It is worth noting, however, that while the specialty is recognized and accepted by both groups, it is far from fully understood by most medical people.

ENTRY INTO MEDICAL SOCIOLOGY

My earliest experience in medical sociology was in 1955 in the area of evaluation of a health education program. My entry was the result of my earlier specialization which was associated with the populations on which the educational program was focused: a number of recently arrived immigrant groups. My experience with research in the sociology of immigration led the health educators to believe that I might be in a position to contribute to a program of research among immigrants on the subject of health behavior.

It is now clear that this bridge served as the critical transit mechanism for my entry into the field of medical sociology; subsequently the joint effect of my own fascination with the material and outside initiative and support served to nurture this interest until it grew into a full-fledged specialization. It is worth mentioning that I have maintained my interest and professional activity in the sociology of immigration and, due to the special Israeli context, have found occasion to join my interest in that field with my undertakings in medical sociology.

This early research undertaking is of some intrinsic interest because it points up a number of satisfactions and frustrations which are in many ways typical of the field. The Ministry of Health, with support from United States funds, planned to set up a demonstration project of integrated regional health services in the Netanya region. This region includes a number of rural communities about which very little was known by those planning the project concerning basic knowledge of health practices or utilization of medical facilities. One of these communities was composed of newly arrived immigrants from Tunisia and another of immigrants from Yemen. Before launching the demonstration project it was felt that an extensive study should be undertaken to gain information concerning the existing attitudes and behavior in the fields of health and sanitation. Such data would make it possible to direct the planned services in terms of real needs of the communities and assist the health educators in focusing their program.

It was planned to follow a classic "before-after" design to evaluate the contemplated regional health services by repeating the survey some time after the program had been in operation.

As noted, the invitation to include me in the project stemmed from an awareness on the part of the Ministry of Health team that the special characteristics of the groups, especially their status as newly-arrived immigrants, required the participation in the project of someone with research experience in the processes of acculturation and adjustment of immigrants. Such awareness indicates a fairly high level of sensitivity to the possible relationship between disease or illness behavior and social processes associated with immigration; it also revealed an understanding of the fact that groups with varying cultural traditions differ in their attitudes and behavior in the health field so that an educational program must be geared accordingly.

The role I adopted on the project was consistent with the professional role I had generally assumed in the past and have largely adhered to throughout my career: I defined myself as a research sociologist whose contribution lay in an analysis of the problems on the basis of empirically observable data with the goal of understanding the processes involved. I did not then, nor do I now, view the decisions based on these findings to be my direct responsibility. Indications on the basis of the analysis as to the probable consequences of certain lines of action are within my realm; alternative courses can be charted with their respective expected results. I have found, however, that when goals have not been adequately defined in advance—which is often the case—clear-cut recommendations become problematic.

The research procedure I recommended and which was adopted in principle was methodologically sound but probably somewhat dysfunctional ultimately in light of the resources it required. I am quite sure that the Ministry of Health officials did not envision the dimensions of the research undertaking I proposed; neither were they entirely aware of the investment it required. In addition to the two rural villages of Tunisian and Yemenite immigrants, we proposed the inclusion of two additional rural villages in the same region in order to expand the cultural range and establish wider baselines for comparison. One addition was a similarly structured rural village of veteran settlers of European origin; the other addition was an Arab village in the region. While they were swept along in the first flush of enthusiasm for the project and were at first able to back that enthusiasm with grant funds, they did not fully consider the implications of the total research undertaking in terms of the resources needed to carry out the project in its entirety.

Two methods of data collection were utilized. One was a survey technique; the other anthropological. The former called for a sample of residents in each village, while the latter involved the addition of two cultural anthropologists to the team to collect data in the villages, and analyze patterns of attitudes and behavior in the areas of health and sanitation. These methods complemented each other and were viewed as jointly necessary to gain a complete picture of the "before" situation.

By hindsight, the fate of this extremely ambitious undertaking should have been predictable. While the "before" study was effectively carried out in all four communities, the "after" part foundered. Due to lack of continued funding, it was impossible to complete the study design. The entire notion of attitude change could therefore not be studied and the data lost much of their scientific interest. The funding of the project was by the United States Technical Assistance Program and it is difficult to assess the specific reasons for the cuts. In part I was probably at fault in planning an overly-elaborate undertaking which, while sound from a research point of view, was probably out of proportion to the total investment planned for the delivery of health care. I wish I could say that I have come with the years to propose more modest research undertakings—but this is not really the case. My preference seems to run consistently to comprehensive research which aims at answering a broad array of questions. In fact I have rather an abhorrence of very limited research which claims to deal with a small, narrow problem—not because I am a grandiose imperialist, but because I have learned that social phenomena and the problems associated with them are immensely complex and require appropriately complex (and often expensive!) research operations if they are to be tackled. My medical colleagues do not always appreciate this and are irritated when I refuse to undertake a "modest survey" or "run a questionnaire" with respect to some quite legitimate problem.

I was quite disturbed at the time because of my feeling that little effort was made by the health education team to utilize the findings of even the first stage of the research. It will be recalled that one goal of the project was to help the health educators focus on salient health problems of the communities in an effort to sharpen their strategy. There is little doubt that much relevant material was available from the first stage of the research and our report attempted to highlight its applicability.[2] However, once the first stage of the research was completed, the health educators showed little initiative in trying to spell out these applications. At the time I had the feeling (which I have experienced frequently since) that the health authorities were more interested in the fact that the research had in fact been done than in utilizing its findings. I was perhaps more naive then than today in my perception of the ostensible goals of the research sponsors and less aware of the other functions which the research may have filled for them, for example, gaining prestige, giving an impression of serious solid work, diverting interest from other policy issues, and so on.

It is also clear that no mechanism was built into the operation to insure a continuing dialogue between researcher and practitioner. Both sides were at fault in failing to incorporate such a structure into the project. Each side operated independently and the result was little contact between the planning stages and completion of the first report of findings. While such a dialogue does not guarantee effective use of research findings, it is probably a sine qua non for all applied research.

MEDICAL SOCIOLOGY AND THE SEMIPROFESSIONS

The Nursing Division of the Ministry of Health invited me to undertake a second research which concerned recruitment to nursing. Israel, like many countries, suffers from a chronic shortage of nursing personnel which stems both from a paucity of candidates to the nursing schools as well as from attrition during training and practice. The research dealt with the first of these problems and attempted to explore motivations for occupational choice among eleventh and twelfth grade high school girls. By focusing on a broad sample of potential recruits and by broadening the framework of the research beyond the nursing context, we were able to pinpoint several of the central motivating components that characterize girls attracted to nursing as compared to girls planning to enter other occupational channels. This approach made it possible to link this study into a wider array of research in occupational sociology and female work roles.

Ever since carrying out this study, I have maintained cordial and collaborative relations with the nursing community. Several of the upwardly mobile nurses have taken B.A. degrees in sociology and a number have gone on for M.A. degrees as well. This has contributed to a common language between us especially in view of the fact that several have taken my course in medical sociology.

In a sense, the research on recruitment to nursing opened the door for this relationship, but I tend to view it more in structural terms as a reflection of the attractions of the social sciences to semiprofessional groups in the health field, many of which are still seeking an acceptable identity. At present, all training for nursing and occupational therapy in Israel is in diploma schools, but there is a plan to launch a baccalaureate program in both fields in the near future by transforming the diploma schools into full academic programs at the Hebrew University of Jerusalem. The leadership in both nursing and occupational therapy is therefore in a somewhat ambiguous status position with feelings running high on the pros and cons of this new program. The academic community of medical sociologists tends to be supportive—especially to the pros—in this controversy and I have therefore been sought out frequently for advice and consultation. In my judgment, our latent function has been to lend some academic aura to these semiprofessionals and ease their entry into their new, as yet insecure, positions in academia. This role has led us into teaching posts in the existing and projected baccalaureate nursing and occupational therapy programs.

What is striking—although perhaps not unique in Israel—is the ease with which medical sociologists have been accepted by the semiprofessions in medicine as compared to the profession itself. Clearly we are functioning at a different relative status position in the two cases and the traditional elitism of medicine works to our disfavor. Even within that profession the medical sociologist is generally most accepted by the lower ranking specialties.

SHIFT IN INITIATIVE

The next major research effort in this field was undertaken at my own initiative. The shifting of the initiative to me rather than it coming from one of the health care organizations or health policy bodies resulted in a realignment of goals and rewards as well as a differently structured array of problems.

I decided to seek funding for a project which was tailor made to satisfy several of my long-standing interests: development and refinement of sociological theory by means of research in a medical context; and attempting to understand a central problem of health care. The research undertaking we designed answered both of these needs and we were fortunate to obtain funding for a number of years. The study concerned latent functions of a medical care organization with particular reference to the problem of overutilization of ambulatory clinic facilities by the insured population. On a theoretical level we were interested in an exploration of Merton's concept of latent functions of social institutions and particularly in an attempt to obtain empirical evidence for the theory. Our approach to the health problem, that is, the overutilization of clinic facilities, proposed that it could be best understood in terms of the latent functions of the institution for its clients. The hypotheses tested focused on the extent to which high utilization rates could be explained by clients' desire to "enjoy" the latent functions of the medical care institution in addition to, or in lieu of its manifest functions. From our viewpoint, the research problem focused squarely and simultaneously on both a theoretical problem and a medical care issue which was of central concern to the health authorities. Indeed there has long been a feeling in health circles in Israel that overuse of clinic facilities has an adverse effect on the quality of medical care.

Furthermore, the client populations selected for study consisted of several groups of immigrants, thus providing us with a further opportunity to continue our long-standing interest in problems of immigrant adjustment and acculturation. In this research, the medical care institution was viewed as a socializing agent, "representing" Israeli society to immigrants, while the latent functions were hypothesized to be particularly salient to immigrants in light of their special needs.[3]

From a structural point of view, it is of some importance to note that the study was carried out with the unreserved approval of Kupat Holim, the major medical insurance scheme in Israel.[4] There was formal approval on the part of the top administration to interview people sampled from lists of Kupat Holim members; data from physicians working within the system were obtained through a series of regional meetings organized in various parts of the country with the assistance and cooperation of the regional directors of Kupat Holim. Viewing such research as a generally positive thing and perceiving no obvious threat to itself in the undertaking, the institution gave its formal blessing to the project.

At the same time, the entire research initiative remained ours and the medical care organization felt no responsibility for the study. While it was willing to go along with us on the assumption that the problem was of general interest, it felt no commitment—and in fact made no investment in the study since all financing was from outside sources.

There is little doubt that this structural factor accounts to no small extent for the subsequent lack of interest of the medical care organization in the findings of the study. There was little response from it when the findings were published. Our own preoccupation with the sociological concepts and implications of the latent functions caused our formulation of the research findings to be heavily sociological. They were not spelled out in terms of applied findings but—as noted earlier—in terms of understanding of the specific problem of overutilization of clinic facilities. There is undoubtedly a gap between an understanding of why and under what circumstances a problem exists and attempting solutions to it. In the present case, this gap was not adequately bridged.

It is worth noting that our research team, while weighted heavily with two medical sociologists,[5] included a prominent medical man as well.[6] The latter played an active role in the course of the study in preventing the social scientists from committing errors of medical judgment, in providing insight in analyzing the data, and in maintaining liaison with the medical care organization. The research therefore cannot be said to have suffered from isolation from the realities of medical practice. At the same time his formal affiliation was with the Medical School and not with the organization responsible for delivery of medical care. While he enjoyed cordial relations with the latter, he was not identified with it in any formal sense. Furthermore, his dominant interests were in research rather than clinical practice. His research in the area of medical care was at the time from the vantage point of an academic outsider.

An analysis of this project highlights the dilemma of the medical sociologist who is motivated by the two goals previously referred to: contributing to sociological theory and understanding health problems. Undoubtedly much of this dilemma focuses on the relative weight placed on these two goals. Many academic sociologists tend to formulate their findings in terms of concepts that are not meaningful to practitioners.

Central to understanding this dilemma is the structural framework under which the research is carried out. In Israel, the realities of research sponsored by medical care organizations (and this is no less true of other public service organizations), are that pressures are often put on the sociologist from a number of directions and these may prevent him from delivering an optimal professional performance. Most problematic is the material pressure expressed in terms of the resources allotted for the research; research funds allotted by government or other public bodies tend to be restricted and minimal, thus pressuring the sociologist to produce findings in a relatively short space of time and with minimal facilities. Many academically oriented sociologists find this type of pressure unconducive to fruitful, rewarding work. There are also the familiar pressures to produce unambiguous, clearly applicable findings. Here the sociologist is caught on the horns of a sub-dilemma: on the one hand the state of the social sciences does not always permit him to formulate such findings, and neither is the sociologist well equipped to do so; on the other hand, the political realities of the sponsoring organization may be such that the findings he does produce are "wrong" or "inappropriate" in terms of the needs and internal conflicts of the sponsor.

Looked at from a more positive view, however, it would appear that sponsorship of a research undertaking by an organization responsible for medical care is a sine qua non for any real use of the sociologist's findings. It is a necessary but not sufficient condition. Without a feeling of identification and commitment to the research as well as a specific investment—either in funds or in manpower and facilities—there is little chance that the medical care organization will take the research findings seriously. The history of our own project described above bears witness to this pattern.

The strategy followed in our own case is undoubtedly a much more comfortable one for many sociologists; however, as noted, it does little to assure that anyone will take the findings to heart or put them to any use. In terms of keeping the medical sociologist fairly happy in carrying through on his theoretical interests, outside sponsorship of research through grants is generally less demanding in terms of time and the need for specific, directly applicable findings. At the same time a new generation of socially aware sociologists may feel that this comfort is rather a luxury in societies with major medical problems to which social scientists could perhaps make a real contribution.

SHIFT IN AFFILIATION

This brings me to my current and possibly most ambitious research undertaking in the field of medical sociology: a study of the socialization patterns of health professionals. To no small extent the choice of this subject was associated with an invitation to join the Faculty of the Hebrew University–Hadassah Medical School in its Department of Medical Education in 1968. At the same time my own interest in this field stemmed from the earlier study previously described in which the focus was on patterns of community practice. Having learned something about the style of practice and of the kinds of nonmedical needs associated with it, we were led to an interest in how professionals are "produced": what factors in the selection or training process result in one style of practice or another? How are the values and orientations of medical professionals associated with specific elements in their socialization process? While there is a growing literature focusing on medical socialization, the growing concern with health-team practice seemed to make a cross-occupational perspective worthy of exploration.

Clearly the above are questions which bridge a number of classical areas in sociology: occupations, professions, and adult socialization. Quite a number of theoretical issues of the research mesh into these areas so that it is of central interest to me on purely sociological grounds. At the same time these issues are of major concern to educators of health professionals who are increasingly concerned with the kinds of professionals produced by socializing institutions and with curricular factors which may effect eventual style of practice. We have therefore structured what appears to be an optimal research situation which satisfies both the social scientist and the practitioner.

Thinking ahead to potential applications of our research findings, I tend to be somewhat more optimistic than with the latent functions study essentially because of my structural location *within* the system. Since the project is still ongoing, only time will tell whether this optimism is misplaced or exaggerated. It would be myopic to imagine that a social scientist could be central in the decision-making power constellation of a medical school; nevertheless there is a difference in being inside rather than outside the system on which the research focuses.

Appreciating the importance of this research, the Medical School faculty provided seed money to get the study off the ground. The research involves a longitudinal study of students undergoing socialization for four health professions: medicine, dentistry, pharmacy, and nursing. Beginning in 1969, a study was made of the pool of applicants to these professions and an analysis undertaken of the implications of the selection procedures. These classes have been and will continue to be under regular observation by a team of social anthropologists and sociologists who study the socialization process by means of interviews, questionnaires, and observation of informal interaction. Interviews with all levels of faculty and teachers provide an additional dimension to the analysis of these data. Shortly after initiating the project I was fortunate in obtaining more substantial funding from a foreign grant so that the project could be expanded in range and depth.

The perspective on professional socialization could be greatly expanded by comparative, cross-national research in this field. Together with a number of colleagues, I have recently been exploring the possibilities for such an undertaking, possibly under WHO sponsorship.[7] Such research would address itself to the following socially important issues: Are different systems of medical education producing similar or different types of practicing physicians in terms of level of performance, style of practice, orientation to patients? And what factors in the various systems of medical education are producing these similarities or differences? Quality and style of medical practice vary from country to country and such research can shed light on some of the factors which may be responsible for these differences.[8] Such an undertaking is both ambitious and expensive and we have not yet succeeded in getting it underway. However, I am much attracted to the possibility of cross-national research because of its theoretical interest and because of the opportunity it provides for a sociologist in a small country to feel part of a broader community of scholars with similar interests.

Joining the faculty of the Medical School introduced a new dilemma for me although it is a familiar one to medical sociologists: teaching behavioral science to medical students. Since my past teaching had been largely in the Sociology Department, my experience was in teaching motivated, interested students. Even when I have taught medical sociology in the Sociology Department (as I have for the past several years), the course was an elective for advanced undergraduates or graduate students. Clearly such a teaching situation assures a motivated audience and I have always enjoyed the teaching experience.

Teaching medical students represents another problem entirely. While the program of teaching the behavioral sciences is still fairly new at the Hebrew University–Hadassah Medical School, several issues and dilemmas are already clear. Although the faculty seems outwardly convinced that behavioral sciences are a necessary part of the curriculum, and have allocated it substantial teaching time, most of the staff are not really clear just why this has been done. Partly, no doubt, this school which is sensitive to styles and trends in current medical education in Western countries is impressed by what it sees done in up-to-date medical schools in other countries. Intuitively many sense that teaching behavioral science to medical students will help them "understand" their future patients and instill in them a more humanitarian approach. Clinicians on the faculty tend quite naturally to press for clinically oriented teaching—a style which is not always congenial to many academically oriented social scientists. In fact, my own experience in teaching and past research does not really lead me to feel entirely comfortable with this style of teaching.

Insofar as the Israeli medical students are concerned, time will tell which style of teaching is most effective with them. By and large they are currently less caught up than some of their contemporaries in other countries in the great social issues of the society. Partly because of the pressures of army and reserve duty, partly because of an absence of overall alienation from the dominant values of the society, Israeli students appear to be somewhat narrow in their orientations and strongly career oriented. However, awareness of social issues in medicine is growing and I sense increased sensitivity among students to these problems. Many such "styles" reach Israel a few years after they have been widespread in the United States and Western Europe, so we may yet ride a wave of active concern with sociomedical issues.

As in other countries, medical students are heavily caught up in the natural, "hard" sciences. This pattern stems to no small extent from self-selection into the pool of applicants as well as from selection processes of the medical school itself. Furthermore, the curriculum is otherwise composed exclusively of courses in the natural sciences during the early years when behavioral sciences have been introduced. The presence of the behavioral sciences in the curriculum during this period can have two contrasting effects and we do not know which is dominant: it can appear "soft" and "garbagey" to many hard-minded young people who prefer the more specific, unambiguous style of the natural science approach; conversely, it can appear as a welcome relief to human-oriented students who feel overwhelmed by the heavy diet of natural sciences during the early years when they have no other contact with "people-oriented" problems. One of the most surprising responses we have heard from first year medical students is a positive appreciation of the behavioral sciences course because it is the only course they take that year that deals directly with medicine!

What is increasingly clear to me is the fact that teaching behavioral science to medical students requires a rather different set of skills and motives than those to which most sociologists have been socialized and for which they have been rewarded in other teaching contexts. There are many frustrations involved so that a much stronger level of commitment is required: one must be really convinced, for one's own reasons, that it really *is* important for medical students to learn something about the behavioral sciences. Otherwise the frustrations will probably prove too great.

ON BEING A WOMAN SOCIOLOGIST

Finally a word on being a woman sociologist. I must be one of the few such persons to whom this has posed very few problems. To some extent I have been lucky but certain factors in the picture reflect structural features of the Israeli social system. The critical key undoubtedly lies in my rather special husband, who, well before the liberationists' crusade, realized that my personal fulfillment and happiness lay in realizing my professional interests and ambitions. (Is this good fortune—or good selection?) Since he himself occupies a strong and respected professional position (in environmental health) at the university and since he is a remarkably secure person, he has not viewed my activities as competitive. While I carry the central responsibility for running the household, he has been willing to help out with household chores or with family obligations which have never been perceived by him as demeaning or fated to be performed exclusively by women. As an example, this has expressed itself in his taking over the management of the family when I have traveled abroad for professional conferences and consultations. I cannot deny some "educational" efforts on my own part, but he has never shown resistance to sharing these jobs. Furthermore, he has always been flexible and supportive at times of strain or conflict between family and career.

We have three daughters who have come quite naturally to accept my strong work interests. I do not honestly believe that they have been deprived and perhaps they have gained by having as their female role model a person strongly committed to an intellectually exciting program of activities which I have attempted to share with them as they became old enough.

This picture would not be complete if I did not admit that I have been fortunate in all of my work situations, from the time I arrived in Israel and took over the first study of immigration, in having independence and flexibility in setting my own hours. With the exception of classes or specific appointments, I have never been bound by a rigid program. This has made it possible for me to work fewer hours when the children were very young and to spend afternoons with them while filling in my professional obligations at odd hours at home and during the evenings. My first book was written entirely at home—between the births of my first and second child! My husband's obligations also require him to work several evenings a week and since we are not great social butterflies, we have both come to enjoy these patterns which complement each other.

An additional factor which is coming to characterize fewer and fewer countries but which still exists in Israel, is the availability of good household help. I have had the remarkable good fortune to employ the same housekeeper for over eighteen years. That is a record by anyone's standards! She has helped most skillfully with all the children from their infancy and with maintaining the house for this entire period. We have never been affluent, but two salaries have been sufficient to allow us the luxury of this full-time help as well as additional baby-sitters when needed. Frankly, I dislike housework and have become skilled in many shortcuts which reduce the burden of such tasks but I have learned over the years not to feel guilty about this. While our housekeeper is married with children of her own, she is a much-loved part of our own family. Again, I truly do not believe that our children were deprived by this arrangement. The opposite is more likely: in an era of isolated nuclear families, the personal and consistent relationship they developed with our housekeeper was supportive and enriching.

I would be less than honest if I were to say that I never felt any role conflict or guilt. This has diminished as the children matured and I developed more and more conscious mechanisms to deal with it. Bear in mind that I grew up during the heyday of the womens' home-oriented magazines, well before the liberationists raised their voices. But ever since graduate school I have been committed to a career in sociology and in those years this was considerably more deviant than it is today. The children were all born in Israel where the cultural context was comparatively supportive: it is normative in Israel for women with higher education to work, there were reasonably good nursery schools in the community, and it was entirely acceptable to send even three year old children.

To some extent my personal good fortune is idiosyncratic since Israel certainly does not represent a paradise of equalitarianism for women. Despite the newness of the society, it shows many traditional sex role patterns with respect to job allocation, wage levels, self-perception and levels of expectation among women and girls, stereotyping by men, expectations and streaming in the schools, and task allocation in the home. As already described, I somehow skirted most of these. Perhaps because of the relatively high academic level on which I worked, I have rarely felt sex-oriented discrimination in wages or in attitudes. Paradoxically, my first real awareness of this problem came in my most recent position as a professor in the faculty of medicine where women are conspicuously absent, especially in senior clinical posts and in critical power positions of faculty committees. I have felt—perhaps for the

first time—that the top level clinicians' view of a senior ranking
woman may be somewhat jaundiced. However, I may be wrong on
this—it only reflects a feeling and has rarely expressed itself in
anything more concrete. It is, however, worth reflecting that my
chances for attaining influence in the faculty body are likely to be
small since I am both a woman and a representative of a "soft"
science. This doesn't really bother me since my interests tend to be
in research rather than in power—although the cynics will surely
suggest that this attitude is a form of sex-bound "sour-grapeism."

AN OVERVIEW

Looking back at this stage, I am more than ever convinced that
the field of medical sociology is rich in problems of major substantive interest and these overlap into many areas of classical sociology. From the point of view of its content, I find the area of increasing interest.

Living in Israel has sharpened my sensitivity to the close association between social research and current, occasionally urgent, social problems. My professional work has been continually stimulating because it was frequently carried out in response to the needs
of policymakers grappling with a pressing issue. I have already
noted that the applied follow-up of such research was not always as
complete as one might wish, but this has not diminished my
awareness that I am frequently called on to help "deal with" an
urgent national problem.

The most recent example of this was a request from the Ministry
for Absorption of Immigrants for a study of the absorption of newly
arrived immigrant physicians from the Soviet Union. Here is a
project that neatly bridges my two big sociological interests: immigration and medical sociology. Background work preparatory to
launching this study required a comparative analysis of the two
systems of medical education as well as of the structure of the two
delivery systems. On the basis of this analytic comparison, we have
been able to formulate hypotheses concerning processes of absorption of these professionals in Israel. It has also been necessary to
draw on sociological research concerning the adjustment of other
immigrants to Israel from the Soviet Union. I naturally view this
research as a contemporary extension of Mark Field's earlier work
in this field.[9]

Many of the dilemmas characterizing the field of medical sociology are essentially the same as those that typify other areas of

applied social research. We are probably not as unique as we would like to think. The problems and strains encountered by the medical sociologist do not stem essentially from the *medical* aspects of the setting but rather from the position of the research sociologist in a structure which is seeking applicable answers to practical problems. Such settings place a burden on the academically oriented social scientist who may not always be prepared or willing to provide such answers; there may be pressure for more rapid and specific solutions than he can supply. Furthermore, the latent goals of the sponsor may not be concerned at all with the answers which the social scientist is so diligently seeking but rather with quite different rewards with which the research endows the sponsor. Our experience with research both inside and outside the field of medical sociology has often showed this to be the case.

Our specialization will continue to be populated by two types of scientists: those whose interests focus more heavily on a basic understanding of the underlying sociological processes involved in a given social or medical problem; and those who prefer to focus more specifically on applications of findings and solutions. Both roles are needed and legitimate; personal factors will push individuals to prefer one over the other; however, I think it will be increasingly unacceptable to completely separate the two. I myself have gained many of my rewards from the elegance and sociological fruitfulness of such analyses, but still enjoy feeling that my research has some relevance to ongoing social problems. The delicate balance between these two orientations explains much of my personal history.

NOTES

1. Judith T. Shuval, *Immigrants on the Threshold* (New York: Atherton, 1963).

2. Judith T. Shuval, *Attitudes and Behavior Concerning Health and Sanitation* (Jerusalem: Israel Institute of Applied Social Research, 1955).

3. Judith T. Shuval, Aaron Antonovsky, and A. M. Davies, *Social Functions of Medical Practice* (San Francisco: Jossey-Bass, 1970).

4. Ibid, pp. 6–9.

5. Professor Aaron Antonovsky and me.

6. Professor A. M. Davies, chairman of the Department of Medical Ecology at the Hebrew University-Hadassah Medical School.

7. World Health Organization, Regional Office for Europe, "Proceedings: Working Group on the Selection of Students for Medical Education," mimeographed (Copenhagen: WHO-EURO, 1971); and World Health

Organization, "Summary Report of the Advisory Group on the Sociology of Professional Training and Health Manpower," mimeographed (Geneva, 1972).

8. Judith T. Shuval, "Some Issues in Cross-National Studies on Socialization of Medical Students," in *Methods in Cross-National Socio-Medical Research*, ed. M. Pflanz and E. Schach (Stuttgart: Thieme, 1976), pp. 36–42.

9. Mark G. Field, *Doctor and Patient in Soviet Russia* (Cambridge: Harvard University Press, 1957); and idem, *Soviet Socialized Medicine* (New York: Free Press, 1967).

My Path to Medical Sociology

MAGDALENA SOKOŁOWSKA

I graduated from high school (*gimnazium*) in June 1939, and in September was to enter the National Institute of Theatre Arts in Warsaw to study acting. But on the first of September the war broke out and on the third German troops were already in my town in Upper Silesia. This part of Poland was promptly incorporated into the "Reich," whereas a piece of central Poland with Warsaw and Cracow became the so-called "General Government." At the beginning, prior to the mass deportation of the Polish population from the "incorporated territories," it was possible to escape to the General Government area and I was lucky enough to do so. In November 1939 I found myself in Warsaw.

I was seventeen, the only child of a well-off family of the intelligentsia, for the first time on my own. What to do? All secondary and higher schools were closed down. Nazis were not interested in producing an educated stratum of Poles. They allowed only the primary schools and a few vocational schools to function. Among these there was a two-and-a-half-year nursing school of the Polish Red Cross. Since it had a dormitory and I had nowhere to live, I decided to enter this school. I did not care a bit for a nursing career. In any case long-term plans were uncalled for, as the whole city firmly believed that the German occupation of Poland would last no longer than a few months. Nobody would even dream that the nightmare would last for six years.

In June 1942, I received my license as a registered nurse. At the same time I passed examinations after a two-year course at the Medical Faculty of the Underground Warsaw University. There was an excellently organized system of secret secondary and higher education in Warsaw which embraced a large number of young people. I got in with the help of a professor who taught at the nursing school.

It is hardly possible to explain here how this system—or rather several systems—worked. However, a few words at least should be said about the kind I participated in. It was established by Dr. Jan Zaorski whose name should be remembered forever. I have no idea how he managed to get permission for opening of an official school called "School for Medical Help Personnel." It was located in the part of a building belonging to the Warsaw University whereas other systems of the underground education in Warsaw took place in private houses. All university buildings were occupied by German troops and the main library was transformed into a stable. From the windows of our class we could see horses. The immediate proximity of hundreds of Germans in uniforms made our place grim; we were surrounded on all sides by them. The formal program of the school had of course nothing to do with what was really taught there, and what was in fact almost a complete curriculum required in the Polish medical schools for students of the first two years. It was a dangerous game. But our professors did not show any fear. They continued to lecture, calm as ever, during the sounds of shots, during loud songs of the German troops, and during the visits of German authorities. The topics became quickly changed then into something appropriate for the "help personnel." Names of these professors are well known in the Polish medicine: Loth, anatomist; Czubalski, physiologist; Przełecki, biochemist; Kapuscinski, physicist; Elkner, histopathologist. Three of them perished in Auschwitz.

Today it is difficult to understand how I managed then to finish simultaneously the nursing school and a two-year medical curriculum. It was due to the aid of several people to whom I am much indebted. For instance, I did not fully realize at the time that my participation in the secret medical training endangered the entire nursing school. The director of the nursing school was fully aware of it, but she never said "no" and pretended not to know what I was doing. And during the duties in hospital while my colleague nurses answered patient's calls instead of me, I was allowed to sit somewhere in the corner and to study. And my future husband, himself a medical student working as a hospital attendant, put much effort in to knocking into my head the basic concepts of physics and chemistry, while wondering that I could be so ignorant. The reason for my ignorance was that in high school I did not pay much attention to these disciplines, being convinced that I would never have anything to do with them. Our school awarded each year a national prize for the school theatre; my receipt of it one year had provided me with a very convenient excuse to avoid mathematics and natural sciences.

During these years in Warsaw I still thought about the theatre. I read a lot, looked for contacts with theatre people and got popularity as a manager of the theatre in the nursing school. However, against the background of what was going on in the country, the idea that the stage might be my life career seemed strangely unreal, in contrast to nursing and medicine. But I discovered that I disliked the hospital. I was attracted to social nursing and medicine which meant working in a health center and visiting people in their homes. One could not help the people much professionally. Hunger reigned in Warsaw and medical supplies were very scarce for the Polish population. However, the people loved for us to come. I learned a lot then about how they lived, what is real poverty and what is real courage, taken for granted, without big words for it.

The life and work of Dr. Tomasz Judym, the idealistic, socially minded physician from before World War I, played a great role in my attraction to social medicine. He is a hero of the past in Stefan Zeromski's novel, *Homeless People*, but his life and work continue to excite interest as if he were alive. He is a very popular person in Poland. The third generation already, my children's generation, is still heatedly quarreling and debating this figure. Is a happy personal life a barrier to altruistic work? Was Judym right to reject his love, the pretty and wise Joasia, a teacher, who could have been his best partner and companion? More than thirty years ago, in high school, I was literally ill while reading this book. It returned to me with double force during the war.

The terror raged. A chance for my survival was the forced labor in Germany. I was sent there in 1943. I worked first as a domestic in Bavaria and then as a sanitarian at a hospital for mentally ill in Vienna.

After the Red Army entered Vienna in April 1945, I enrolled in the University of Vienna Medical School for the third year curriculum. I was unable to present the necessary documents certifying to my first two years in the underground school of Warsaw, but was admitted as a member of the Austrian Resistance Movement.

At the beginning of 1947 I returned permanently to Poland and entered the newly-established Medical School in Gdansk (Danzig) on the Baltic. I received my physician's diploma in 1949. This was the second diploma issued by that school. The school suffered from a severe lack of staff and I had a free choice of a place to work. To everyone's surprise, I picked one that enjoyed rather a low prestige: the Department of Hygiene where I began to work as an intern. I was already sure that I wanted social medicine as my life career and it was centered in Poland at the time in departments of hygiene. I worked there for four years and received the degree of Doctor of Medicine on the basis of a dissertation on the influence of density of housing on the occurrence of scarlet fever in Gdansk (there had been an epidemic of that disease about that time).

In the early 1950s I moved to Lodz, Poland's second largest city, a textile center called "The Polish Manchester." My husband, a doctor, had been transferred there, to the Central Military Hospital. I began to work in an Institute of Industrial Medicine, where I remained for about seven years and attained the position of department head. I consider my main achievement in this period the organization of a model post of the industrial health service which arose in Poland at the time and of which I was one of the pioneers. In the large textile combine, where I was the medical director, a team of some score of specialists in the field of industrial health was trained: doctors and nurses of various specialties. We introduced there, among other things, a modern health care system for women employed in industry and for the first time in the country gynecological preventive examinations on a mass scale.

The majority of workers at this textile combine were women, mainly married women and mothers. I myself was married and a mother, but it did not occur to me to occupy myself with those women's family environments. Our model of industrial health care, to whose establishment I contributed myself and which was conducted by our team, concerned itself exclusively with the workers and only at the plant. The influence of the home on the physical and emotional health of the working women we discovered indirectly: by observation of various phenomena manifested at the place of work. It dawned upon us gradually that the source of these phenomena and various kinds of "troubles with women" at the workplace lay outside the factory, in the women's homes. We therefore proceeded to systematically differentiate in our investigations between the women's role as workers—heretofore our subject of interest—and their vaguely defined family-household role. It turned out then that women's higher absenteeism due to sickness, for instance, was not due to the situation at the place of work but to conditions in the household. I thus began to interest myself in that remote environment beyond the reach of the industrial physician and generally little investigated by medical doctors.

I worked like mad. This was a period of Poland's intensive industrialization, of the first six-year-plan, and sometimes called the period of "the cult of the individual." The industrial combine where I worked, the largest in Lodz, was named after Joseph Stalin. Today the various plants of the combine bear the names of eminent Poles or of the places of heroic battles. I worked to realize a socialist model of the industrial doctor, codirector of the plant who is concerned not only with the workers' ill health but with the broadly conceived conditions of work and social facilities as a member of the managing collective—in a word, as a model physician-public activist. This required almost constant presence in the enterprise, participation in endless meetings, conferences, confrontations, actions. I moreover desired to win the confidence of the people employed in this combine and this entailed first of all being a good doctor.

Besides all that there was my home. My husband was a neurosurgeon. He built up, organized, and directed a neurosurgical department at the military hospital. He gathered together with great difficulty modern equipment, trained a team, and made complicated brain operations. He often stayed away from home for several days at a time, since he was afraid to leave patients after an operation, and returned home terribly tired. We had two small children. I realize only now what a difficult childhood they had and I am surprised that they have no complaints on that score. We counted every penny, for we did not earn much. Both our posts were in the relatively low-income category, as compared with the earnings of doctors practicing individual clinical medicine. We had a cold, dark, damp apartment, heated by coal stoves. We had to carry pails of coal to the fourth floor from the cellar of a neighboring staircase. The longest lasting domestic help was a rather good but deaf farm woman who instead of taking the children out for a walk, took them to church. I was not prepared for the wife and mother role. In the high school from which I graduated just before the war, the probability of getting married and having children some day did not occur to us. Our models were very special. Our school was named after *Emilia Plater*, the famous woman heroine of the nineteenth century who dressed as a man, was a colonel, fought, and perished in an uprising against czarist Russians. Alternatively, we could perhaps be one more woman candidate for the Nobel Prize, like our famous countrywoman Maria Curie Sokołowska. Then came the war and it was impossible to think of entering the wife and mother roles. Nor was my husband prepared for the roles of husband and father. We were very young when we got acquainted at the beginning of the war. We lived through it together and the varied trials and tribulations bound us strongly together. After the war we could not cope with the family roles which in the difficult living conditions were overshadowed by our professional roles. We were like two race horses pulling in different directions. Absorbed in creating a social macrostructure, we destroyed our own microstructure. I am now able to express this situation in a scholarly way as befits a sociologist. Then, I saw only the progressive process of disintegration of my marriage and I could not, and perhaps did not want to, resist it.

The price I paid for my professional career was rather high. I have asked myself many times whether I would pay such a price if I could start all over again and with my present experience. The question remains unanswered; I simply do not know. I lost much and gained much, and then—the values lost and those gained are qualitatively different and incomparable.

The second half of my career commenced in New York. I arrived there in 1958; it was like arriving on another planet. It was a family reason which brought me to the United States, but our Ministry of Health agreed to my extended stay, long enough to finish the program of studies for the Master of Public Health degree at Columbia University School of Public Health. In addition I received my regular salary for one year. It would have been impossible for me to stay in the United States without this kind of help from the ministry.

For several weeks I was in a state of cultural shock. I was never previously in the West. I had been a pretty dogmatic industrial physician in the Polish People's Republic. I knew English only so much that I was able to read and more or less to understand the industrial medicine literature. I never spoke with the English-speaking people, and also never with Americans. During the first weeks in the school, I did not understand a word of what people said to me or to each other. Everything sounded to me like inarticulated gibberish. Fortunately, Professor Rosen, the unforgettable George Rosen, knew German. Moreover, the teaching system was entirely different. In Poland I had never written examinations; here there seemed to be nothing else and it was always necessary to write something. I was unable to answer such tests, and was lost in the flood of materials received (these were called "aids"—nice help!). The school did not make special allowances for foreigners who were expected to know English. All students were obliged to cover the same reading matter in the same allotted time: daily several hundred pages of scientific text—a mere trifle!

Examinations too had to be completed within the same time. I could never manage on time, particularly with the long answers required by Jack Elinson. He rewarded me with the invariable mark, C, explaining that the answers were pretty good, but unfortunately not all questions were answered. My worst experience was with statistics. I could never cope with them in Polish, let alone in English. Sometimes looking at those tables thickly covered with hieroglyphics I came to the conclusion that I was chasing butterflies, that I would never finish that school.

There were many foreigners but few Europeans. I was a strange animal, the first student in the history of the school from Eastern Europe, from a Communist country "behind the iron curtain," and therefore had to hold the banner high. This was a good period in my life. There was nothing to do but to study. What a pleasure that was! Besides, I strolled about New York, about the city which is not a city in the European sense. New York is not like Paris, Rome, Leningrad or Warsaw. New York is a world in itself, either hated or loved, depending upon whether a person swallows its potions or not. I certainly did. And if for any reason I could not live in Warsaw, I would like to live in New York, no matter how dirty it is.

The school underwent basic changes at the time. I understood later that I hit on a period of transformation of the concept "public health" in the United States, when its traditional natural science base was being reoriented to include its social and behavioral aspects. In practice this was manifested in the presence of sociologists as graduate students in "my" course, leading to the degree, Master of Public Health. Here I came into contact with sociology students for the first time. I distinctly remember when a sympathetic, tall gentleman, Irving Silverman, took the floor in a discussion. I knew enough English by that time to more or less understand what was spoken. But this time I understood nothing and turned to my neighbor, an American M.D., and asked, "Will you please explain me what it is all about?" "Ah, if I only knew," answered my physician colleague, "he is a sociologist. I don't understand anything either."

Other contacts with sociology came about because, already at that time, this school employed sociologists as faculty. Jack Elinson conducted for the first time a seminar on the methodology of social surveys, which seemed very interesting. Previous commitments were slipping; my notes on occupational health were long since covered with dust. Also at that time, in the unforgetable home of Bohdan and Nela Zawadzki, a meeting place of Poles from Poland in New York, I met a group of Polish sociologists who were in the

United States on a Ford Foundation grant. These were: Maria Os-
sowska, Andrzej Malewski, Stefan and Irena Nowak, and Adam
Podgórecki. Contact with them exerted a great influence on my
personal and professional life.

I did not return to Lodz, I was through with industrial medicine
and changed my place of residence. I now lived in a suburb of
Warsaw in the house of my mother, the sensitive and wise guardian
of my children during my absence. Thanks to her, the children had
a family home and developed well. They furthermore attended a
school directed by an unusual man. The school was a small building situated in the woods and my children felt well there.

Then I looked for work. My desire was to conduct epidemiological research in the area of cardiovascular diseases. I had been involved at Columbia in a study of this kind and I wanted to do the
same in Poland. But in 1960 Poland did not occupy itself with this
problem and the term "epidemiology" was related only to the
study of acute communicable diseases. I was received by the Minister of Health who congratulated me on my Columbia University
diploma but actually did not know what to do with me. And I
wished to do research. Accidentally I discovered from the
sociologists I met in New York that a post was open at the Institute
of Philosophy and Sociology under the Polish Academy of Sciences. Without further thought I applied and was accepted as "ad-
junct" (which roughly corresponds to assistant professor) in the
Department of Sociology of Work.

The Polish Academy of Sciences is a prestige research institution
supervised and financed by the Presidium of the government, an
independent agency, a kind of a ministry of research. It is organized along two lines: one is the General Assembly composed of the
members of the academy who are appointed from among the prominent professors of the country; the second line includes six operating research departments corresponding to the main spheres of scientific study—the Department of Medical Sciences and the Department of Social Sciences among them. Each department super-
vises its research institutes which are the main working bodies of
the academy. The Institute of Philosophy and Sociology is the
biggest within the Department of Social Sciences; it now has some
two hundred research workers. It is composed of two branches,
philosophical and sociological, under one director. The director is
either a philosopher or a sociologist with the other type as vice
director. The main task of the institute, as of the whole academy, is
to carry out basic research according to the National Research Plan.

Although most of the senior staff members are involved in teaching as well, mainly at Warsaw University, teaching is not our obligatory task.

How did I ever get a job there? Only later it became clear to me that I hit on a very special period of development in Polish sociology. In the early 1960s the "applied" areas were being pushed in which the practical meaning and utility of sociology could be relatively easily shown. A few people without a sociological background and degree were awarded sociological posts: an engineer, a lawyer, an economist, and me, a physician. All of us held degrees corresponding with the Ph.D. level, for instance, I had a Doctor of Medicine degree. A degree at this level was a condition for us to be hired. According to Polish law, such degrees entitle one to get the highest scientific degree, docent, in any discipline, not necessarily the original one. At the present time almost all of us "outsiders," docents of sociology, have been appointed professors and are heads of several sociological units and teams. Now, however, only people with formal sociological training get research jobs in our institute.

Looking back, I sometimes wonder how I conceived my role in that first period of work at the Institute of Philosophy and Sociology. It seems that I wanted to acquire first-hand information on social factors harmful to health and to transmit, as quickly as possible, the information to medicine. I was a physician and considered that everyone ought to be interested in and help realize such a noble aim. I had a very vague idea of the aims of my institute and to be frank I did not care too much.

It was not necessary for me to travel to America to experience cultural shock. For over twenty years I had been under the influence of the medical subculture. Now, I entered into a kind of new dimension which I could not even name. Ignorance gave me the courage to begin work there. I found myself in the main current of the academic sociological community, in the milieu of eminent Polish humanists.

Everything was strange to me. There was no work discipline. Everybody came and went at will. Some did not show themselves at all at times, saying that they were working. The first day I reported at the institute at 8:00 o'clock in the morning, but only scared the charwoman.

The highest professor was addressed in the familiar form and one did not rise in his presence. The first time I did so he also rose and finally asked if we cannot sit down, for his legs hurt. But I was a

nurse and a doctor and I knew how I should behave in the presence
of superiors. The atmosphere of the institute confused me. I was
never sure when my colleagues were serious and when they were
joking. And I felt that they made fun of me. I did not understand
much of what they were talking about, although they spoke Polish.
They were eloquent, spoke fluently, and it seemed to me that the
words kept rolling out of their mouths. In medicine, I was regarded
as a good speaker; here I sat like a wall fixture. I was similarly
silent only once in my life: when I first arrived in New York.

I did not understand what my sociological coworkers did besides
talk. They constantly repeated the magic word "studies," often pre-
fixed by the adjective "empirical," as if examination could be
nonempirical. Their studies involved writing which was their main
work. When they said that they were working, that meant they
were writing. And they wrote as they talked: much, lightly, and
smoothly. In medicine it was possible not to write at all, or, if so,
rarely, and then only the shortest texts. Medical journals published
articles of only a few pages. Here one always wrote and only articles of at least twenty or so pages counted. I found it hard to write;
my texts were always too short, too laconic, inadequately elabo-
rated, and the editors advised me to "get out of your braces."

They were comradely. At the beginning I received the most aid
from Adam Podgórecki who advised me how to start to study sociology, which books to read and which seminars to attend at Warsaw University. I slept, ate, and walked possessed by sociological
texts, while Adam and his colleagues determined how much I
learned. This was devilishly hard, much more difficult than public
health in English. I remember that they tried to explain the meaning of the concept, environment, to me. I could not for the life of
me grasp that it could have any meaning other than the one I knew.
I could not comprehend that for the sociologist, environment is not
a natural "Umwelt," place where the individual lives, but the
sociocultural reality in which the individual appears simultaneously as subject and object; that the social environment is also in
the hospital, not only in the patient's home and that it is made up
of people. Most difficult was the switch to the structural way of
thinking, to the comprehension that the basic concept of social
structure is composed of people as socially formed beings. I finally
grasped the essence of the distinctness and specifics of the
sociological approach and it appealed to me very much. How plas-
tic is the picture of mobile society and how much it differs from the
static, one-dimensional population! Sociology appears easy to be-

ginners who gradually become more and more confused. At first I too saw little difference between the sociology of medicine and social medicine.

I wrote my first book. It originated in the following way. It was already clear that my task was to help develop a field of sociology which was to become somehow widespread in the sociological community. As already noted, in the early 1960s various applied sociologies were fashionable in Poland and a physician who also wanted to "sociologize"—of course on the theme of medicine—was welcomed with outstretched arms. I wanted to begin with establishing, for some important social problem, an association between biological and medicopathological variables on the one hand and social variables, on the other. I decided on the subject of women's work and health, since I was occupied with this question as an industrial doctor. The book *Socjomedyczna Charakterystyka Pracy Kobiet (Sociomedical Characteristics of Women's Work)* was accepted in 1963 as the basis for the degree of Docent of Sociology.

There was one medical person with whom I could speak the old medical language, a person to whom I could report what was going on at my new place of work, with whom I could share my thoughts, ideas, problems. Professor Brunon Nowakowski was still alive. It would require much space to outline the contributions of this eminent representative of preventive medicine in Central Europe. Pioneer in the science of occupational hygiene, and creator of the Polish school in this field, director of the Institute of Occupational Health in mining and heavy industry, author of 114 scientific works, including seven books and textbooks, in the fields of industrial medicine and hygiene, nutrition, and epidemiology. Rich and variegated are the attainments of this experimental investigator, public leader, teacher and educator, distinguished for his modesty and inner independence. He was already retired, but his work increased instead of diminishing; his mind was lively and supple and he declared a desire to study sociology in his old age. He was a frequent visitor at the Department of Sociology of Work where I was attached. He participated in preparing the book *Industrial Doctors*, a unique collection of personal documents, and was coeditor of it, with Adam Sarapata, chairman of the Department of Sociology of Work, and myself. This book was published in 1965. This aging, soft-spoken, reserved, somewhat stiff but always erect gentleman became very popular at the institute.

I shall never forget the following incident. I was to stand oral examination for the degree of docent, during the meeting of the

Scientific Council of our institute, in the presence of eminent members of the council. Professor Nowakowski arrived in Warsaw from Katowice—where he lived—the evening before my exam and I took him to his hotel. He generally just said good-bye and went to sleep, but this time he looked at me and granted, "Hmm. Is my colleague afraid of tomorrow? Well, let's go and relax." In a few minutes we found ourselves in a large coffee shop. The orchestra was playing, the dance floor was full of young people. He again looked at me discretely and said: "I am sure you will make it. Shall we dance?" Before I could recover from surprise the professor rose, bowed with old-fashioned gallantry, let me to the dance floor and paying no attention to the sensation we made—and to be truthful, to the music—we danced a tango.

On 22 November 1965, he wrote: "You have the ability to practice social medicine enriched by sociology as well as to follow the sociology of medicine as a social phenomenon. You are fortunately aided by being a doctor-sociologist and a sociologist. This duality should be maintained. Such a position on the borderline of two systems of thought affords exceptional possibilities which it is impermissible to waste." This was the professor's last letter.

When I now look back over the road I followed and helped to fashion since Professor Nowakowski passed away, I come to the conclusion that while I have always aspired to attain the duality which he wrote of, I am as far from it now as ten years ago. Of course, much depends on the definition. If this duality is defined as the cooperation of physicians and sociologists at joint meetings, conferences and discussions, then we can note great progress. Certain changes have also taken place in the training of medical and sociological students. Furthermore, sociologists are now employed and are part of research teams in several research institutes supervised by the Ministry of Health. They also work in the country's various medical schools and in services such as psychiatric hospitals and rehabilitation centers. The number of scientific publications written by sociologists in medical journals as well as the number of works on medical themes in sociological journals and books have considerably increased. Sociological-medical subjects are popularized by the mass media. Many factors have contributed to this. Among these, undoubtedly the establishment in 1965 of the Medical Sociology Department at the Institute of Philosophy and Sociology was important as was the Section on Medical Sociology of the Polish Sociological Association established in 1964. These organizations acted as catalytic agents. All this was to the good. But what I have in mind and what has not yet been achieved is "the contact of systems of thought" according to Professor Nowakowski.

I have no excuse for not myself achieving this theoretical rapprochment such as barriers on the side of the institute or that I was tied up with the research plan. Both consecutive directors of the institute, Adam Schaff, a philosopher-professor, and Jan Szczepański, a sociologist-professor, are known for their support of a new scientific idea, for pushing the initiatives of their collaborators. It is a characteristic trait of our directors that research plans and bureaucratic necessities are realized in a way which leaves a research worker enough time and—what is perhaps more important—enough financial support to do what he or she really wants to do. As a matter of fact I had some difficulties in getting used to this special laissez-faire approach. It is a negation of the authoritarian attitude, one is not commanded, "do this" or "don't do that." This approach enables, rather, a friendly discussion, shows competently several sides and objectives and leaves the final decision to the investigator.

Back to the problem of divergence or lack of convergence in medical and sociological theory. It appears to me that replacing the word "medicine" by "health" and/or "sociology" by "behavioral sciences" does not help much. It rather complicates the situation which is complicated enough without broadening the terms of the relationship. It seems to me that it makes no difference whether one discusses health or medicine in relation to the system of the sociological thought, because it is human biology one has in mind, neither health nor medicine. I think that it will be possible eventually to conceptualize the links between social structure and man's biological equipment, including genetics, neurophysiology, and/or psychophysiology. In other words, I can envision the development of theoretical concepts encompassing society and the normal human traits including biological traits. I hardly see a need here for the practical medical knowledge, for clinical sciences, even if they are called "health sciences".[1]

This is an exciting study area but not for us. In my opinion the United States is the only place where at the moment conditions are favorable for the development of such knowledge. Europe, both West and East, has presently rather limited chances for competition in this area. Whereas we cannot contribute much to the study of biological aspects, there would be an intriguing opportunity for us to study the social part of the linkage, in other words to look fc: the hypothetical similarities, differences, or perhaps some unique characteristics due to the different social system. This would be, of course, not "medical sociology" but what is sometimes called "social biology" (I prefer the name "biological foundations of the social life"). I know that general sociologists at our institute and also at Warsaw University, particularly the team studying changes in the class and stratum structure, would strongly support the idea of introducing a biological thread in our research. But that would necessitate shifting onto an entirely new track.

Perhaps an integrated medical-sociological (or sociological-medical) theory cannot develop because of the lack of people equally competent in both sociology and medicine? As for me, the twenty years I spent in medicine left a permanent mark. Organizational work, administration is easy for me, writing comes hard. I am a better empiricist than thinker. I face obstacles in theoretical thought which I shall probably never overcome. This is certainly why I rate theoretical works so highly, for instance, those of Eliot Freidson.

One is either a medical doctor or a sociologist. I, at least, see no possibility of cultivating that dualism in daily practice. The aims of the sociologist are different than those of the physician, even if he or she is chiefly an investigator. George Reader, Manfred Pflanz, Mervyn Susser, John Cassel, John Stoeckle consider themselves doctors, although not a few sociologists would be content to be as versed in sociology as they are. I consider myself a sociologist. I work in an institution the principal aim of which is to conduct basic sociological research, to gather systematic knowledge on Polish society. This is a far cry from health care, and from the social causes of disease as the main center of interest. I have been thinking in such categories only in the last six or seven years. Previously I had felt myself a physician and considered it a matter of course that I was serving medicine. I participated in investigations directed by medical doctors, acted as consultant to officials and posts of the health service at various levels and of various types, and conducted research for the purpose of solving problems designated by physicians. This was a particular kind of sociology in medicine, a mixture of public health and isolated, singular sociological variables geared to the needs of clinical and rehabilitation centers, since they were the first to request cooperation.

The organization of the Institute of Philosophy and Sociology at that time favored this style of work. It was composed of a number of loosely connected centers of various applied sociologies whose main groups of reference were outside the institute. My group of reference was medicine.

In the early 1960s there was no other approach to medical sociology in Europe, both East and West, except through medicine. This has exerted a definite influence on the manner of pursuing medical sociology. For example, several people of the first generation of European medical sociologists have a definite aptitude for organizational work and the ambition to create a "school," which is not so common among general sociologists, at least at the present time. Such people, I think, are well suited to the development of a discipline in its initial period. It should be borne in mind that contrary to other branches of sociology, it was necessary to start medical sociology from the foundation, and to create an environment, a climate, an organizational framework, workshops, and so on.

With regard to writing books, it seems to me that medical sociologists, at least in Europe, face greater difficulties than general sociologists. As for me, apart from other factors, in the 1960s I could not cope with the American model of medical sociology which then dominated the world—within the framework of American sociology. As a physician, I could not rid myself of a feeling of responsibility to my colleagues to whom that model was not understandable and of little practical use, especially since I was then unable to demonstrate the utility of some concepts, Parson's sick role, for instance. In Poland some additional factors contributed to this situation, because in the early 1960s sociology was not recognized in Polish medicine. Students were taught the fundamentals of Marxist philosophy in an oversimplified form and the normative aspects of what was called "organization of the health service." I was unable then to write a book for physicians based on American sociology and I did not know how to write a book for sociologists.

In 1965, I started work on the book *Badania socjologiczne w medycynie (Sociological Studies in Medicine)*. It was issued in Warsaw in 1969, as a collective work published under the auspices of the Research Committee of Medical Sociology of the International Sociological Association and a four member editorial committee of physicians and sociologists from Great Britain, Sweden, the German Democratic Republic and Poland. The book contains contributions of authors from European countries, for the first time both East and West. The studies were selected according to a carefully worked out scheme and depicted the state of European sociology applied in medicine, that is, the fields where sociologists are in a position to provide certain sociotechnical directives. The volume's message to health personnel was to be unafraid of sociology, that it is a useful and interesting field. Its model of sociology was rather social than sociological, and medicine was viewed more as a biological than a social phenomenon.

In 1968 the Institute of Philosophy and Sociology underwent a basic change of its operating principles. Separate units ceased to exist and topical studies were discontinued. Three large teams were created, dealing with theory of the socialist society, class and strata structures, and development and social change. This was an attempt to turn our interest from the various "applied" areas to the theory. And this was the Marxist theory. Soon complex studies were initiated with the intention of building a platform on which two principal problems designated by the National Research Plan would be studied: evolution of the structure of the socialist society and transformation of consciousness; and expected changes of consumption patterns, of cultural needs, and of the system of values of Polish society. For the first time since the establishment of the institute in 1957, the Polish society at large became the focus of study and survey samples amounted to several thousand people. The institute was appointed to act as the countrywide coordinating agency and took direct responsibility for elaboration of a great number of issues related to these principal research problems. The former sociology of medicine under a new name, Social Problems of Health, was included in the class and strata team's area of concentration. Health was incorporated in both study directions: as the correlate of structure and as a social and cultural value.

I distinctly remember this period. It had a profound influence on the further development of our sociological-medical unit. Actually only then the sociological approach started to develop in our studies of health, illness and medicine. And then I became fully aware of my sociological identity.

The situation of our unit was quite different from that of other of the institute's departments. The change in its organization and operation left the majority of my colleagues in the institute rather unhappy, at least for the time being, because they had to drastically change their studies, approaches, methods, goals, and so on, and to adjust to quite new requirements. But our small unit had neither its own body of accumulated knowledge and special scientific achievements nor any well-established, long-lasting working tradition. We had nothing to lose, rather everything to gain.

Suddenly it became clear to me that the main goal of my activity was not medicine and health service but knowledge of society. Of course, *also* medicine and health service, but indirectly, in the process of transformation and application of this accumulated knowledge for the improvement of functioning of real social institutions. The basic task and specific contribution of our unit was to enrich knowledge of society by information about its "medical" or "health" sphere. It was a dramatic change of my goals and "reference group": from doing for medicine to knowing society. The question arose of how to incorporate "health" into the macrosocial studies described above, as they were undertaken by our institute. We had no ready-made patterns for such an approach. American medical sociologists in academic institutions published much less on health than on illness and properly speaking, not on illness as such but, as Eliot Freidson called it, on "behavior surrounding disease" diagnosed by doctors,[2] irrespective of the professional foundation for such diagnoses which sociologists did not question or investigate, considering themselves incompetent in this sphere. This was perhaps due to the particular esteem enjoyed by medical doctors in the United States where they are regarded as experts of the highest category whose evaluations are final and not to be questioned. And this approach spread over the world. The result has been that sociologists either uncritically accepted diagnostic-clinical assessments or rather avoided all investigations of this kind. Hence it appeared that medicine is an exceptional sphere of social life governed by specific laws proper only to itself. A vicious circle thus arose: since health and disease was excluded from sociologists' sphere of interest, or a medical way of looking at these phenomena was accepted, no sociological orientation could develop. And because of lack of such an orientation, medical phenomena were expressed as formerly in categories which left unclear their social effects.

Such an "alien body" could not be a part of the studies planned in our institute. All sectors of the social life under study were to be expressed in sociological categories, which are alternative to the professional: legal, technical, economic, for instance. Medicine was the only sector where such alternative categories did not exist. What to do? We decided to approach "disease" functionally, to pay relatively little attention to its professional name (diagnosis) and to concentrate on its consequences, that is, on the changed human functioning. I know of only one slightly similar type of approach involving a population at large, namely, some definite investigations carried out in the framework of the National Health Survey in the United States.

I spent the academic year 1971–72 in the United States as a visiting professor of sociology at Southern Illinois University (SIU) at Carbondale where I taught an undergraduate course on Social Change in Polish Society (stratification, women's roles and social position, the educational and health systems) and a graduate seminar on the sociology of medicine. During that autumn I was in an unremitting rapture gazing at the wall of trees shimmering with all shades of sharp yellow-orange-red colors. I still sense the pungent sweet smell of grass and flowers and hear the loud song of crickets in the pervasive quiet of those nights. In the complete darkness glowed from afar the lighted windows of the university library like a lighthouse at sea. I hope Herman Lantz and other colleagues from SIU will forgive my writing such foolishness.

I spent the winter and spring in New York at "my" School of Public Health at the Division of Epidemiology, headed by Mervyn Susser. Also I was a frequent visitor of the Division of Socio-Medical Science under the direction of Jack Elinson. In the spring trimester I was invited by Eliot Freidson to conduct a graduate seminar called "Introduction to Medical Sociology" at New York University in the Department of Sociology. I pinched myself from time to time to make sure I was not dreaming, that I really was teaching there.

If I had to state in a few words what impressed me most in the United States, in the professional sphere, I would say the changes transpiring in medicine. I well remember the dean from the University of Missouri Medical School. He was a general practitioner—something unheard of! And he declared that he needs a sociologist like, air, water and food. "I must have a sociologist," said he, "to disagree with me."

Back in Poland in the academic year 1972–73, I started teaching undergraduate sociology at Warsaw University. I had taught in previous years too, but medical students in medical school (in Poland medical schools are not related to the universities). That previous work was more in the vein of "sociology for doctors" than "sociology in medicine." I considered, and still consider, that sociology and psychology should be regarded as basic disciplines for medicine on a par with the other basic sciences traditional in medical education. Sociology must be integrated for this purpose with the main stream of the medical curriculum and occupy as important a position as physics, chemistry, or biology. From the very beginning of their training, the students ought to be exposed to both systems of thought: of the natural sciences and the humanities. This is not yet the case in Poland. The words "for doctors" in the phrase "sociology for doctors" signify that the lecturer selected, arbitrarily, those elements and concepts of sociology he considers particularly useful for medical men. The lecturer must hence be versed in both sociology and medicine, since he or she must supply relevant examples from the area of medicine.

But the course I teach the sociological students is a quite different matter. This is a survey course of the sociology of medicine and a seminar for the master's degree in this area. The goal is to direct future investigators of society and social practitioners to fields where sociological analysis has been overlooked by or completely unknown to young sociology graduates. The lectures are composed of two parts; medicine for sociologists and the sociology of medicine. Recently the lectures started to be attended by a group of medical students from the Warsaw Medical School.[3]

I have not enough time and this is my major problem. In the United States and also in Great Britain there are a lot of people working in medical sociology. And many of them are writing books. There are so many books! In my country the situation is different. We are a tiny sociological-medical group and except for myself this is a very young group. The people are excellent I think, and also very nice, but they need a few more years to study, to concentrate on one particular problem, to receive their degrees.

There are few books. My sociological students have no written materials on medical sociology, let alone textbooks. Not many of them read English, but in any case American and British books should not be their only source of written knowledge. Also, there is virtually nothing for medical students and I keep prolonging my contract, more than four years, with a medical publisher for a text book of sociology. There is neither "sociology," "behavioral sciences," nor anything of this kind for nurses, and I am still approached in this matter. (I taught nurses until recently.) And research—my most important task? Until now we studied mass processes and my collaborators are complaining that they are fed up with our seemingly permanent macroapproach: society at large, health, and epidemiology. They yearn for microsociology, the community, the family, the individual illness, psychosocial variables. One coworker has confided that she could occupy herself with social differentiation of mortality in macro, but only under the condition that she would be able to investigate simultaneously the processes of individual dying and death. The young people are right. That side of medical sociology is almost entirely untouched by us. And several other important questions as well.

Nevertheless, or just because of such continuing challenges, life is beautiful, very beautiful indeed.

NOTES

1. The theory of social stress also fits in here though it is "pathological." Its study involves little of traditional clinical medicine and is developing within quite a different framework.

2. The terms "illness" and "sickness" do not exist in the Polish language.

3. In the Institute of Social Medicine at the Warsaw Medical School there is a newly established laboratory of sociology headed by one of "my" M.A. graduates from the Warsaw University. The teaching of sociology in the medical school is concentrated in that institute.

Becoming and Being a Medical Behavioral Scientist

ROBERT STRAUS

It is characteristic of human societies that most people, even friends and relatives, like to be able to identify each other in terms of clearly defined roles that carry some readily recognizable expectations and responsibilities. People who do not fit into usually prescribed roles tend to be called mavericks, a term originally applied to unbranded calves, but now generally used to describe individuals who can not be classified according to prevailing social molds and who initiate an independent or innovative course of activities.

Although my personal life has been relatively conventional, I began my professional career as a "far out" maverick and have become less unconventional over the past thirty years only because others have gradually assumed the same kinds of cross-disciplinary, cross-professional activities in which I have been engaged.

By professional degrees I am a sociologist, but virtually all of my activities since early graduate school have been related to health and medicine. After receiving the Ph.D. in sociology at Yale University in 1947, I spent six years with a university appointment in applied physiology, three and a half years in preventive medicine, then joined the planning staff of a university medical center and, since 1958, have chaired the Behavioral Science Department in the College of Medicine at the University of Kentucky. Throughout this period, there has been a concentration of research interests in the problems of alcohol and other dependency behavior, and in processes of patient care.

Why did I first become a sociologist and then follow a maverick's commitment to the health-medical segment of society?

To explore this and other factors it is usual to indulge in some introspection about one's childhood. Here I am reminded of a quotation originating, I think, with Christopher Morley: "Remembered impressions of childhood are under suspicion. It is difficult not to interpolate into them significances we became aware of later."

Health and medicine loom quite significant in my childhood memories, though not then pertaining to my own future. On my mother's side, a great uncle had been a physician whose impact on both family and community I constantly heard discussed. A maternal uncle had become a renowned pediatrician who pioneered in research on poliomyelitis with Rhesus monkeys. He also supervised my own infant care via correspondence and I still have the prescription blanks with his handwritten directions concerning my diet through infancy. Throughout my childhood, perhaps because it was assumed that my older brother was destined to become a physician, I never recall thinking of a medical career for myself.

Shortly after I was born, my mother began twenty-five years of voluntary service devoted to the well-being of patients in the New Haven Hospital. She pioneered in the field of diversional therapy for sick children, gave her time, energy, and love to children in the hospital, developed techniques which led to the first book on the subject,[1] and finally helped expand her personal voluntary efforts into a major professional program.

My father's budding legal career was interrupted by service in World War I and after the war he turned to teaching high school mathematics. During the next thirty years, he became a man loved and appreciated by so many that even twenty years after his death I still encounter people who remember how he helped or inspired them or profoundly influenced the lives of a son or daughter or friend.

Both of my parents read widely, were much more interested in their deeds than in public recognition or appreciation, and both had high moral standards and simple personal needs and demands. Both suffered prolonged and painful terminal illnesses, yet continued to give of themselves until near the very end, my mother in 1948 and my father in 1953.

My own childhood in New Haven seems average and uneventful in memory. I gradually developed the habits of an overachiever at school, and the self-destructive persistence of an ambitious but totally incompetent athlete. The former, not the latter, led to admission by Yale.

The Yale of pre–World War II was a mixture of social, athletic, and academic life. However, my own circumstances quickly narrowed in on the academic. Yale society was still dominated by old prep school ties which excluded a student with the combined stigmas of a New Haven home address, a public high school preparation, and a non-WASP background. Still the would-be athlete, I went out for lacrosse and managed to damage a knee which has plagued me ever since. Despite the "good life" atmosphere, the real impact of Yale for me lay in the great teachers who were available to all who sought their courses. After my first year, every course I took was selected for the man who taught it rather than the subject. Thirty years earlier, my father had been impressed by the dynamic sociologist, Albert G. Keller. I enrolled in the last class that Keller taught. Although he had become politically anachronistic and bitter, Keller was a superb teacher of disciplined learning. A sociologist who really believed that his subject was the science of society, Keller insisted that his students know something of biology and he had little patience with petty arguments over what was legitimate to each of the competing social science disciplines. He stressed the development of rigorous thinking about the phenomena of human life. He inspired habits of thinking and of writing that have contributed to my own work style and to what I try to teach. I majored in sociology because this gave me the greatest freedom to wander broadly to other courses. I took every course available from a German scholar, Carl Schreiber. My interest in railroads led to Kent Healy's course on transportation economics. Psychologist Robert Sears, then early in his career, introduced me to a comprehensive review of the prevalent theories of individual behavior. Sociologists James G. Leyburn and Raymond Kennedy solidified my interest in their field, and provided an opportunity to sit at the feet (literally, one evening) of Bronislaw Malinowski. Malinowski's functional theory of behavior has profoundly influenced my own conceptual notions. And, like most Yale undergraduates, I took the physiology course in "applied sex," taught by Howard W. Haggard, never dreaming at the time that Haggard would be my first department chairman when I entered the academic marketplace.

Bright college years for the class of 1944 were cut short by the events of December 7, 1941. The knee injury kept me from a desired Naval commission, so I enlisted in the Army reserve and plugged away to finish as much college as possible before the call to active duty. When the call came, two and a half years after my matriculation, I had managed to finish three academic years plus a couple of extra courses and a senior thesis. This was enough for a degree in December of 1943, and election to Phi Beta Kappa, notice of which reached me while encased in the grease and grime of a rifle range. My Army career was unglorious, nonheroic and ig-nominious. An obstacle course at Camp Lee, Virginia proved too much for the knee and when reinjury on an icy street in Washing-ton, D.C. put me in Walter Reed Hospital, occupying a bed which was badly needed for the wounded of Salerno, I was discharged as too "weakkneed" for military service.

On St. Patrick's Day of 1944, I returned to New Haven and a job with the Connecticut Post-War Planning Commission. In the fall of 1944, I entered graduate school at Yale. The sociology graduate program at Yale, in the fall of 1944, had few students and a rare opportunity to know and be known by some gifted teachers. Selden Bacon (later my employer, coauthor, colleague, and lifelong friend) carried the tradition of Keller's disciplined thinking to the teaching of criminology and social problems. A brilliant conceptualist, Bacon insisted that his students critically evaluate and identify their evidence, and reason from facts to relevant conclusions. Leo M. Simmons introduced me to the excitement and fruitfulness of life history material, took me with him to conferences in the De-partment of Psychiatry, encouraged me to take anthropology courses, and later directed my dissertation. Maurice R. Davie, loved by all for his gentleness and wisdom, chose to make an example of me and to prove that a student could complete a Ph.D. in the de-partment in just three years. Of great significance was the influence of a visiting professor from Columbia, Bernhard J. Stern. I consider Stern the unchallenged "father" of medical sociology. Many years before "medical sociology" was seriously identified at all, Stern in-spired excitement for the opportunities which the study of medical systems provided for testing and extending sociological theory and the ways in which the social scientist could reinterpret the history, clarify the processes, and even predict the future of medicine. If ever a sociologist deserved more and received less recognition from his profession, it was Bernhard Stern.

In January 1945, I met my wife-to-be, Ruth Dawson, who was then working in the Physiology Department at the Yale Medical School. Within two weeks, we were spending so much time in courtship that her job and my graduate work received short shrift until we were married in September 1945. This magnificent woman has so totally shared and supported all of my life since 1945 that the "I" in this essay should almost always read "we." Ruth was born in Ottawa of Scotch-Irish and Kansan stock, grew up in Hartford, went to college at Vassar, worked in New York City and, as far as I am concerned, she came to New Haven just so that we could meet.

In the summer of 1945, Selden Bacon offered me part-time employment with the then developing Center of Alcohol Studies at Yale. The job was to explore what could be learned about the use of alcohol by homeless men. Not only did this opportunity lead to my first publication ("Alcohol and the Homeless Man") in 1946, but it provided the beginnings of a study of institutional dependency which has been a major research interest ever since, and has recently culminated in the publication of a twenty-seven-year prospective life record.[2] This job also launched my career in the study of alcohol problems and indirectly as a medical sociologist.

"Alcohol and the Homeless Man" might have been my doctoral dissertation had it not been for some idealistic or pragmatic notions about keeping my job and my academic program as separate as possible. However, with the inspiration of Stern and the encouraging direction of Simmons and Davie I decided to study the history of public medical care in the United States in a search for conditions universal to the entry of governments into the health care field. The resulting manuscript, "The Evolution of Public Medical Services in the United States," completed the Ph.D. in 1947. It was eventually revised for publication by the Yale University Press as *Medical Care for Seamen* (1950), so entitled partly because merchant seamen have played a prominent role in the origins of public medical care, and partly because a fund for Merchant Seamens' Studies, managed by Leo Simmons, subsidized the book's publication.

Job opportunities in 1947 were available in a metropolitan department of sociology, a medical school department of public health, and in Yale's Department of Applied Physiology. For pure excitement, stimulation, and opportunity, there seemed to be no choice but to remain at Yale. Howard W. Haggard, famed physiologist and medical historian, had assembled in his Laboratory of Applied Physiology, one of the few truly interdisciplinary groups in the academic world. Physiology, pharmacology, biochemistry, medicine, psychiatry, psychology, anthropology, law, economics, biometrics, education, and theology were all represented and a sociology group was headed by Selden Bacon, one of my most stimulating teachers. By 1947, most of the department's resources were being devoted to the study of alcohol and its associated problems. For six years, in the emerging Center of Alcohol Studies, I had a rare opportunity to learn from and share with men and women from varied disciplines, all looking at the same phenomena from different perspectives, and most looking for some common and meaningful conceptual frameworks. Of particular value was the influence of Bacon, E. M. Jellinek, Mark Keller, and Raymond McCarthy. They taught me much and they eased the transition from a student to a professional colleague. Although teaching during the six years at Yale was limited to the annual Summer School of Alcohol Studies, a semester substituting for Bacon in sociology, and some bits and pieces, the research opportunities were magnificent. There were studies of skid row drinking, the life history of an alocholic, the functions of early specialized alcoholism clinics, the personal diary as a research technique (with Italian-Americans), drinking among some occupational groups and, most significant, the study (with Bacon) of drinking patterns and attitudes and related behavior among college students in the United States.[3]

The years at Yale were not completely restricted to alcohol studies. My dissertation on medical care was revised and published in 1950. That year, I also met William R. Willard, a physician who was then associate dean of the Yale Medical School and chairman of the Connecticut Governor's Commission on Health Resources. Vacation and moonlighting time was devoted to some staff work for the commission and when a change in governors made the commission lameduck and fundless, Dr. Willard and I wrote the final report as a way of achieving personal closure. This was in early 1951 and shortly thereafter Dr. Williard was called to Syracuse as dean of the State University of New York's Upstate Medical Center.

Another vacation-moonlighting opportunity came in 1952 from Milton J. E. Senn, pediatrician, psychiatrist, and director of Yale's Child Study Center. Dr. Senn and others had succeeded in persuading the Connecticut legislature to create the Child Study and Treatment Home to provide institutional treatment for severely emotionally disturbed children. Although provided with an operating budget, the home had no capital funds for construction of a facility. In preparation for another appeal to the legislature, some precise studies were needed to delineate the nature and magnitude of the problem in Connecticut, the unmet needs of these children as seen by various professional groups, and the ways in which other states were approaching the problem. Some part-time activity led to the offer of a half-time job as "superintendent" of the nonexistent institution with the primary responsibility for planning the facility, estimating staffing and budget requirements, searching for a suitable site and interpreting the needs to the legislature. A half-time leave from Yale permitted me to take on this job for a year and to benefit from close association with Milton Senn and with Helen Case Foster, a wise, talented, and dedicated woman who chaired the agency's Board of Trustees.

Work for the Child Study and Treatment Home followed a decision to move from the alcohol studies field and from Yale with the completion of the *Drinking in College* manuscript, estimated for the spring of 1953. The decision was based in part on a desire to explore the then emerging field of medical sociology more broadly, in part in the realization that a longer tenure with the Yale Center might lock me into the alcohol field, and in part in a personal desire to broaden my geographic horizons from the New Haven area, which had been my hometown, the only place where I had attended college, and the site of my first major job. In the summer of 1952, I was offered and accepted a position with Dr. William R. Willard in Syracuse to be effective in June of 1953. In retrospect, the academic year 1952–53 was rugged indeed with two half-time jobs which both had full-time demands and a determination to finish *Drinking in College* before departing for Syracuse. We finished the book in part because the Yale Press set up a production line and had some chapters in page proof, others in galley, and others being edited while the last ones were still being written.

The years in New Haven devoted to alcohol studies, beginning with part-time studies of homeless men in 1945 and ending with the publication of *Drinking in College* in 1953 were also the first eight years of my marriage. Ruth worked during the first year and then we had our first-born, Robert James, followed in two year intervals by Carol Martin and Margaret Dawson. We planned number four, John William, to arrive six months after our move to Syracuse. This is an appropriate point to pause in the professional history and talk of Ruth and the children. In New Haven, and again in Syracuse, Ruth gave the children and me her major attention and devotion, keeping her active mind and creative abilities stimulated with a variety of volunteer activities. By the early 1960s, volunteerism was tasting like exploitation, the children were needing less continuing attention, college tuitions were approaching, and Ruth decided that it was time to reestablish a career. She studied the new math and the education courses necessary for teacher certification and for several years now has been a very committed teacher of high school mathematics. Our oldest son, Jim, from an early age, apparently set his heart on following grandfather and

father to Yale. He graduated cum laude, married, survived three
years as a Marine officer including a stint in the South Pacific, fa-
thered two daughters, has completed law school at the University
of Chicago, and is launching a law career in Louisville. Carol, the
first to marry and to present us with a grandchild, is now a com-
puter programmer. Peg went the medical route and is now a nurse,
married to a pharmacist. Bill is an Earlham College student, committed to becoming a biologist. We have been blessed so far that all
seem to have found their way through the maze of nonidentity and
uncertainty that plagues so many of their generation.

Back to career, the move from a primarily research post at Yale to
Syracuse brought the surprising assignment from Dean Willard to
devote full time to developing a teaching role in the medical
school. Dr. Willard had appropriated three hours a week of
curriculum time primarily from anatomy and given it to new departments of psychiatry and preventive medicine. The school was
steeped in tradition and inertia. The reception given a sociologist
who had been hired on hard money and given someone else's
curriculum time, ranged from skepticism to overt hostility. There
were a few friends, most of them like myself, brought in by the
dean.

For me, the Syracuse years meant learning how to live in a medical community, experimenting with meaningful ways to teach relevant things to medical and nursing students, resisting invitations to
cut my own throat by studying things that could not be studied,
and learning to live with students who were constantly reminded
that their own pressures and difficulties with traditional courses
were partly due to the dilution of curriculum time and of their own
efforts by things like the social sciences. Informally, with a cluster
of other mavericks on the faculty I collaborated to teach some
committee-type courses and to share research interests. This collaboration provided opportunities to sit in on the teaching of many
other departments. For nearly three years, I regularly attended
rounds in internal medicine, collecting case material, which helped
make sociology relevant. There was also a chance to extend my
major research interest in institutional dependency to recidivist patients of the affiliated Veterans Administration Hospital.

Aside from teaching and research, I also spent considerable time
working on staff studies for Dr. Willard. This provided opportunities to visit numerous other medical schools and to become
identified with several then crucial issues in medical education
and medical school administration. Also, my past work in the al-

cohol field provided continuing opportunities for consulting and lecturing.

In our teaching at Syracuse, we experimented with an overview course which we called "Health and Society;" we sent students out to meet and follow families (but found that many were so distressed by the demands of the role that they rejected the value of the experience); we met with small groups, discussing issues of current interest in medicine (which often could not compete with examinations in anatomy); and we provided opportunities to discuss students' personal problems and questions of self-identity and insight. Despite the initial hostile environment, we had made many close friends among the faculty of different departments and we felt so optimistic about the future that Ruth and I sold the old house we had initially bought in Syracuse and built a new one which she designed for a family of four young children in a neighborhood of young parents.

Then suddenly, one June evening in 1956, our lives changed abruptly. Dr. Willard dropped by the house to indicate that he had been invited to head the development of a new medical center at the University of Kentucky, in Lexington. He spoke wistfully of the many opportunities associated with starting from scratch and said that his only hesitation in accepting lay in his sense of obligation to those whom he had brought to Syracuse. With some trepidation, I told him he had no obligation to me, whereupon he said that if he decided to go, he hoped I would go with him.

The Syracuse years ended with such little warning that for several weeks I was actually both teaching in Syracuse and working in Lexington. In retrospect, the Syracuse years were not easy, but they provided for much personal growth, they provided a tough acculturation to the medical culture, and they provided a base of ideas just begging to be tried out with a fresh start. While in Syracuse, I also enjoyed the success of Drinking in College, chaired for one year the Upstate Sociological Society, participated in several community health surveys, made some enduring friendships, lost a parent and gained a son, and weathered a rugged climate which has made Lexington, even in winter, seem like paradise.

While I still pretended to debate the decision of a move to Lexington, several old friends warned that I would be off the beaten track and might quickly be forgotten professionally. Kentucky had such a backwoods stereotype that Lexington was not widely recognized as a progressive community closely tied to the outside world by four airlines and as quickly reached from New York and

Washington as are New Haven and Syracuse. The early years of planning in Lexington demanded much travel to look at facilities, seek ideas and recruit faculty from other medical schools. An average of twenty-five trips yearly established in the planning years has been maintained as planning has given way to consulting and committee membership.

William R. Willard was an innovator in Syracuse when he provided regular budget positions for first one, and then several, social scientists at a time when, nationally, most social science in medicine was looked on as purely experimental and to be supported by grants or foundations. When he went to Lexington, Bill Willard's planning staff included one other physician, an economist, a statistician, and a sociologist. His ambition was to develop medical education and education for other health professions which would be in the forefront of ferment, would anticipate inevitable changes, and would be particularly well geared to meeting the needs of the university, community, state, and region. With an initial five million dollar appropriation symbolizing the support that would be necessary, the backing of Governor A. B. Chandler and new University President Frank Dickey, thirty-nine acres of land, and some scattered basement offices, our planning staff settled in. An architect had been engaged and we were immediately under pressure to complete our program planning geared to objectives so that we could stay ahead of and give direction to the architect. With a statement of Dr. Willard's broad philosophy of medical education as a guide, we scattered out and, during the first few months, visited more than half of the medical schools in the country, talking about curriculum modifications, examining innovations in laboratory and teaching resources, and discussing the relationship between architecture and patient care in hospitals and clinics. Our key questions were: "What would you design differently if you had the chance, and why? What changes do you want to make and what are the barriers to change? Who are the exciting young people in your organization whose talents you can't yourself absorb?" In center after center, we met with deans, chairmen, faculty at all levels, nurses, students and, sometimes, with patients. Our first task was to relate program to architecture, but all the while we looked for good people as well. My own role during the first year and a half was not directly that of a sociologist, but I was bringing the perspective of one who was trained as a sociologist to the task of raising questions, interpreting answers, and thinking constantly about the relationship between program objectives, people behaving in groups and spatial arrangements. Our staff conferences often started at six in the morning and our evenings often ended very late. For several months, my wife and children stayed in Syracuse, selling our house and finishing half a school year. Finally, just before Christmas of 1956, we moved to Lexington which, after eighteen years we now identify as home.

While we were moving from New Haven to Syracuse to Lexington, the field of medical sociology was germinating, taking roots and sprouting foliage. The year after I received my degree at Yale, August B. Hollingshead joined the department there and soon entered his collaborative relationship with Fritz Redlich, a psychiatrist. Other graduate students, including Jerome K. Myers and Albert Wessen did dissertations in the health-related field and a concentration in faculty strength and interest in medical sociology was emerging which eventually led to one of the early training programs for medical sociologists. During my middle year at Syracuse, a small group of medical sociologists was convened at the national sociology meetings by A. B. Hollingshead to explore ways of exchanging experiences and better identifying common interests. An informal committee on medical sociology was established with Hollingshead as chairman and me as secretary. For the next several years, we circulated an annotated membership roster among an increasing number of self-styled medical sociologists and others with common interests. After my move to Lexington, the Russell Sage Foundation provided some support for this activity, Sam Bloom took on the secretary's role, and eventually the committee became one of the first sections of the American Sociological Association. The Section on Medical Sociology has probably been the association's most vital specialty group. It has undertaken several projects of professional significance around both medical and graduate education, sponsored assumption by the association of the *Journal of Health and Social Behavior* (initiated by E. Gartly Jaco as the *Journal of Health and Human Behavior*), and has sponsored an important study of the behavioral sciences in medical education. I was privileged to serve as chairman of the section for the year 1967–68.

Back in Lexington, in 1956, several objectives began to emerge for capitalizing on the opportunities offered by starting from "scratch." We hoped to minimize the fragmentation of knowledge by facilitating communication and cooperation between disciplines and departments. We designed an excellent central library, "conjoint" teaching laboratories, and a curriculum with numerous multidisciplinary courses. We planned many facilities (study cubicles, lounge, showers, twenty-four hour snack bar) specifically for students to help them make maximum use of their time and encourage them to feel that the medical center was designed to meet their needs. We called for a "patient-oriented" hospital and clinics, and hoped to implement these goals in part through numerous architectural provisions, designed to facilitate exemplary patient care. Special attention was given to the design of space which would support comfortable communication between patients and staff and would protect patients from communications which might be distressing or an invasion of their privacy or dignity. Several conference rooms were built on each hospital floor so that teaching could be removed from its traditional bedside and the corridor settings. Studies of hospitalized patients' needs for services were made by medical economist Howard Bost and biostatistician Alan Ross (both among our closest friends) providing a basis for planning the first teaching hospital specifically designed to provide progressive care (intensive, general, and minimal), a concept which quickly became quite standard hospital practice throughout the country.

Since we hoped to gear programs to the special needs of the area, sociological research was logical and necessary. Thomas R. Ford undertook a study of demographic data pertaining to the health of the population,[4] and John H. Mabry, who had first joined us in Syracuse in 1955, came to Lexington to begin studies of patterns of response to illness in both rural and urban areas of Kentucky. Ground was broken for the first phase of medical center construction in December 1957, and gradually activities of the original planning staff turned from those of generalists to specialists. My own assignments were in the areas of educational policy, curriculum planning, and staff recruitment. Another wave of trips was made to other medical centers seeking ideas on new curricula and scouting for key faculty in many disciplines. As lists of potential candidates for various jobs were accumulated and priorities established, we began inviting people into Lexington, often in pairs, for several days. This activity involved our entire families as our wives took turns entertaining our guests and conducting tours of the community. Those months are now a haze of stimulation and exhaustion.

Medical behavioral science was not forgotten during this period. We reviewed our experiences in Syracuse and sought the views of others who were now employed as sociologists or anthropologists at other medical schools. Clearly psychiatry and preventive medicine were giving leadership to introducing behavioral scientists into medical faculties. But, in most such programs, the impact of the behavioral scientist was limited to something within a particular department. In addition, turnover among social scientists in medicine was rapid and it was clear that many schools were having difficulty satisfying social scientists and many social scientists were having difficulty finding satisfying jobs in medical settings. Again, Dr. Willard demonstrated his innovative courage by creating the first department of behavioral science in a college of medicine. He reasoned that by giving the behavioral sciences departmental status, he could attract and hold a competent and secure faculty; behavioral scientists could participate in the decision making and power play of the school along with those of other disciplines; and the behavioral sciences could be identified as basic to all fields of medicine.

A nucleus of faculty already existed in the planning staff and the Department of Behavioral Science was officially created by the Board of Trustees of the University of Kentucky in 1958. By creating a department early in the formative stage of a new school, it was possible to eliminate questions of legitimacy which have posed barriers to the development of behavioral science in many established schools. Some behavioral scientists were there before most other faculty came; they chaired and served on key committees and even played a major role in the recruitment of others. The behavioral sciences were an integral part of the philosophy, objectives, and curriculum of the school.

In addition to developing the Department of Behavioral Science, my personal activities in 1958–63 continued to involve carryover responsibilities from the planning staff. I was offered the opportunity to be an associate dean (instead of a department chairman) and, in opting for the department role, agreed to serve in a transitional period as coordinator of academic affairs. Initially this meant curriculum planning, establishing the admissions program, and providing for the handling of student services. In 1959, our first five department chairmen constituted a curriculum committee which met two days a week and an admissions committee which met on a different two days. At the same time, we were recruiting other chairmen and our own staffs, planning our departmental teaching, requisitioning equipment, and engaging in liaison activities within the university and with other medical health agencies in the area.

In addition to developing a department and serving to help get the academic programs of the college launched, a new set of demands on my time had emerged. In 1958 I joined a grant review committee for the National Institute of Mental Health and this began thirteen uninterrupted years of service on a series of research grant study sections and training grant review committees which entailed frequent trips to Washington and to site visits throughout the country. In 1959, I joined the board of the newly established Cooperative Commission for the Study of Alcoholism. For two years I served on an executive committee charged with selecting key personnel and launching the commission's task of overviewing the field. From 1961 to 1963, I served as chairman of the commission and remained a member until the commission's task was completed in 1967.

The teaching programs of the Department of Behavioral Science were formally launched in the fall of 1960 when the University of Kentucky admitted its first medical school class. In addition to presenting our own "Health and Society" course, we participated in courses on "Communication and Interviewing," "Human Growth and Development," and in a clinical conference for first year students designed to emphasize the interrelatedness and applicability of basic science concepts and knowledge. Because of the school's then radical curriculum, most of the students, like most of the faculty, seemed to accept behavioral science and the several conjoint courses as reasonable innovations for a new school. In retrospect, these students were quite kind for we subjected them to what now seems like a very dull and not always relevant barrage of lectures into each of which we tried to cram a whole course topic from sociology or anthropology or psychology.

In the fall of 1961, I was carrying a heavy personal teaching load, still serving as coordinator of academic affairs and chairing the Cooperative Commission of the Study of Alcoholism, plus saying "yes" to innumerable requests to be a speaker in a variety of substantive areas. In October we had our first accreditation visit from the Joint Committee of the American Association of Medical Colleges and the American Medical Association. It had been my task to put together all of the exhibits for the Accrediting Committee, arrange the schedule for their four-day visit, and make sure that things went smoothly. I left Lexington on the same plane with most of the accreditors and flew to California to chair a meeting of the Cooperative Commission in Palo Alto. I had become proud of the fact that my frequent trips to the West Coast could be accomplished by leaving Lexington after work, putting in two or three days on the Coast, and then flying back at night and being in my office by mid-morning. On this particular trip, several years of personal neglect finally caught up with me. Arm pains on the Coast were denied until they became more severe enroute home where my good friend and magnificent physician Edmund Pellegrino grounded me for a month. Dr. Pellegrino, our first professor of medicine at Kentucky, was a constant source of support for the behavioral sciences and for me personally. When he left us to undertake the demanding and exciting task of creating a new medical center for the State University of New York at Stony Brook, there was a void that no other man could fill.

With Ed Pellegrino's skillful care and counsel, I was able to define a mild coronary episode as a potentially life-extending experience with the major treatment the cultivating of hygienic living—that is, recognizing when I am pushing myself beyond the limit and having the courage to decide that some things are not necessary.

As the stàffing capacity of the Medical Center grew, the role of Coordinator of Academic Affairs was reduced in scope and ended with my chairing the Curriculum Committee through 1962.

In retrospect most of the really innovative phase of curriculum development and program planning at Kentucky preceded the arrival of students and patients. During the planning years, there was time to look, discuss, debate, read, write, and, most of all, think expansively. During this period most of the people who joined us were attracted by opportunities for innovation and were oriented to change. But as the various dates for implementation of educational and patient care programs arrived, there was enormous pressure to get the job done. Less and less time was devoted to recruitment according to the original "student-oriented and patient-oriented" philosophy, objectives, and commitment to change. More and more, staff were hired who defined their job at Kentucky as it had been defined where they had previously worked. Gradually, the spirit of experimentation and innovation was eroded as pressures to put the show on the road mounted. Although the College of Medicine, in national perspective, has been recognized for many "firsts" (Kurt Deuschle's Department of Community Medicine and our program in behavioral science are just two examples), I have had to make a substantial personal adjustment to compromise with many of the "ideals" for programs of education and patient care which we envisioned as attainable realities in the planning days. Probably the most significant factor in changing the weighting of values which determined our directions of development was the national investment in research which dominated medical schools during the 1960s. The research dollar dictated many decisions regarding staff recruitment, time and effort allocation, and space utilization. The more recent shift in national goals toward the facilitation of education for health personnel and health care delivery makes currently relevant in the 1970s many of our planning ideas of the 1950s, some of which fell short of achievement in the 1960s.

One day in March 1963, a call came from Dr. Robert Felix, then director of the National Institute of Mental Health, requesting a "drop everything" trip to Washington. There he had assembled seven men (four psychiatrists and three social scientists) coincidental with President Kennedy's message to Congress calling for nation-wide programs in comprehensive community mental health. Dr. Felix asked this group, under the chairmanship of Dr. Francis Braceland, to recommend guidelines for the implementation of a national program of support for community mental health centers. In thirteen months, we met nineteen times in a most exciting adventure in planning for social policy. Ironically, just after the report was completed, Dr. Felix left Washington to become dean of the Medical School at St. Louis University. Although his departure limited the impact of our effort, the time and sacrifice by families that this job involved was made personally worthwhile by the close associations with other committee members and the intensive exercise in planning for social policy.

In the meantime, in Lexington, the opportunities for the behavioral sciences were expanding beyond our fondest dreams. Our teaching was extended into the colleges of Nursing and Dentistry and subsequently into Allied Health Professions and Pharmacy. Graduate students began seeking us out and we initiated an informal graduate specialization in medical behavioral science. A training grant from the National Institute of Mental Health for course work in human behavior in the medical school helped expand our faculty. Another training grant provided stipends for graduate students and enabled us to formalize the graduate Concentration in Medical Behavioral Science in collaboration with the Departments of Sociology, Anthropology, and Psychology. The Department of Behavioral Science has grown to ten full-time positions with several others joint-appointed from the main campus or related institutions. It has been a wonderful group of colleagues who have, for the most part, been secure in themselves and respected by each other.

By design, we have limited the number of behavioral disciplines we have tried to cover and have sought some depth in each. Alan Ross, my colleague from the planning staff, selected our department as his base for biostatistics and, until he moved to Johns Hopkins in 1964, was a constant source of support and strength. His role as "alterchairman" has, in recent years, been filled by sociologist Eugene Gallagher, who directed the department while we were on sabbatical leave. Other full-time faculty have included anthropologists Marion Pearsall (1958–present); Thomas Weaver (1964–67); Anthony Colson (1969–71); H. Jean Wiese (1972–present); psychologists David Marlowe (1959–61); Melvin J. Lerner (1961–70); Ronald C. Dillehay (1964–66); John V. Haley (1964–present); Judith Archambo (1970–present); Donald McVarish (1966–72); Russell A. Jones (1971–present); sociologists John H. Mabry (1958–63); Basil Sherlock (1961–62); David S. Hall (1965–69); Philip M. Moody (1968–present); Thomas F. Garrity (1970–present); Roland P. Ficken (1972–74).

Within the Department of Behavioral Science, the format of our teaching program has been modified on several occasions, although the basic objectives have remained quite constant. In 1960, and still in 1974, we see our objectives as contributing to a broadening of the perspective from which the student views the dimension of medicine and with influencing his *ways of thinking* about human behavior, health care delivery, and the hierarchy of values he places on the relevance of behavioral and biological phenomena in relation to health and disease. We try to make meaningful a unifying concept of behavior and a frame of reference for relating the health-medical systems of behavior with such other systems as family, religion, government and economics, and an appreciation of the tendency for pathology to occur in clusters or for "problems to beget problems."

Our ways of teaching have changed greatly. We began with sixty lectures, each covering an enormous topic. Soon we supplemented lectures with some seminars, then added more seminars and some laboratories, and now we teach "Health and Society" in the form of topical seminars which the students select and which emphasize their own involvement in learning and teaching each other. We hit a particularly gratifying note with the entering class of 1972 when more than 75 per cent of the students evaluated most phases of the course on the "plus" side of a scale and only about 10 per cent found fault. Rising enrollment in other courses has justified staff expansion.

In the extracurricular area, the intensive work on the Braceland Committee and the Cooperative Commission of the Study of Alcoholism was followed with a rare privilege in 1966 to serve as chairman of the National Advisory Committee on Alcoholism. This group was appointed by Secretary of Health, Education, and Welfare John Gardner at the direction of President Johnson to provide advice for the Department of HEW and the entire federal enterprise regarding both long and short range strategies for dealing with the problems of alcohol. My three year chairmanship was highlighted by the development of an "Interim Report" which contained numerous recommendations since enacted into federal policy and action. One more Washington assignment as chairman of the Health Services Research and Development, Research Training Study Section, ended in the summer of 1971 when I resigned, impressed with the necessity to cut back a travel schedule which had crept up to eighteen trips in six months.

It is appropriate here to mention a strong personal philosophy of "chairmanship" which I have become committed to over the years. Because of the general goodwill and mutual trust that has prevailed, we have always been able to talk through our decisions in free and open discussion and generally reach a consensus. Voting has been used only when required as a "form" but never merely in connection with parliamentary process. From the department and my numerous experiences in chairing committees and commissions, I have come to treasure this process. Formal rules of order, when used in groups like departments or committees, serve to block free discussion, limiting it to motions, amendments, or amendments to amendments which, as often as not, do not pertain to the crucial issues. In recent years, whenever I chair a committee I seek the group's agreement to savor motions and use the formal process only after full and free discussion has identified for all concerned what ideas are relevant and how the group's opinions are distributed. This approach not only facilitates group decision making processes but also avoids forcing some group members to be "losers" for they do not have to commit themselves until the outcome is fairly predictable. At the first meeting of the National Advisory Committee on Alcoholism in 1966, my seventeen colleagues agreed to follow this procedure and I cannot recall any other group in which I believe people listened to and heard each other's views more effectively while formulating numerous important recommendations for social policy.

In 1968, after twenty-one years of academic life, and twelve years at Kentucky, we took our first sabbatical leave. With a NIMH research fellowship, we spent the entire year in New Haven where Jerry Myers and Sandy Hollingshead arranged an ideal situation. Professional stimulation, lots of contacts with students, time to think and retread, were icing on a cake which enabled me to pull together more than twenty years of work and interest in institutional dependency. The manuscript, *Escape From Custody*, was completed in first draft form and includes an unusual twenty-seven year prospective history of Frank Moore.

I first met the man I call Frank Moore in the summer of 1945 when he was one of the 203 participants in my study of "Alcohol and the Homeless Man." Frank's unusual intelligence, self-insight and interest in my studies led to the establishment of a friendship and association which has continued through twenty-seven years. In 1948 we published Frank's life history (based on his first forty-four years) and since that time, through occasional visits and more than three hundred letters, we have made a prospective record of Frank's institutional living, alcoholism, and struggle to escape from dependence on custodial living. This remarkable and tragic man has provided a document (published as *Escape from Custody*) which seems to have no counterpart in the social science literature.

The sabbatical year ended with summer (1969) visits to programs and people in five European cities. This was followed, in the fall of 1969, by another European trip to serve at a WHO conference on the behavioral sciences in medical education.

Returning to Lexington in the fall of 1969, my hope for a continued writing spree was dashed by an assignment to conduct a "self-study" of the College of Medicine—a half-time task for a year. After that I was able to finish *Escape from Custody*, to prepare a monograph on "Alcohol and Society," and a thinkpiece called "Departments and Disciplines: Stasis and Change."[5] Aside from these projects there have, over the years, been continuing involvements with several smaller research ventures. Some of these have been published; some have been geared to specific problems in the Medical Center; many have been in association with the work of my graduate students.

The Concentration in Medical Behavioral Science has now produced ten completed Ph.D.'s with another eight in the dissertation writing state and, at the moment, we have nearly twenty students taking courses and research training with us. We have also had an assortment of postdoctoral students who have come to the department to supplement their medical backgrounds, and there have been a host of visitors, for from a day to several weeks duration, who have come to Lexington to see our department or study with us. Many of these associations have led to continuing and valued friendships. A proposal for a doctoral program in Medical Behavioral Science for health professionals is now pending university approval.

Before closing this review, it is appropriate to ask the question, "What about sociology, and how over the years have I retained or lost my identity and associations with the field of my major training?" In the first stretch at Yale, my contacts with the Sociology Department were quite tangential. I did some substitute teaching, maintained friendships with some of the faculty, but identified primarily with applied physiology. When I went to SUNY, in Syracuse, the sociologists of Syracuse University were most hospitable and gracious, both socially and professionally. After I left New Haven, the relationship with Sociology at Yale became closer, for by this time the department had formalized a medical sociology program and I was invited back several times to meet with their planning group and lecture about the role of sociology in my medical school setting. Yale Sociology could not have been more generous or gracious when I returned in 1968 as a visiting fellow. In Kentucky, the relationship with sociology began on a most cordial note and has remained that way ever since. When the Department of Sociology first heard that Dr. Willard was planning to bring a sociologist with him, they offered help in making the university and the community attractive for me. On my first visits, Howard Beers, Lee Coleman and Tom Ford, and their wives, helped us to get acclimated and feel that we had true friends. Furthermore, Sociology immediately offered me a joint appointment with carte blanche to participate in the way I chose in the affairs of the department. My first "Society and Health" course at Kentucky was taught in 1957 under the auspices of Sociology and much of my graduate teaching since that time has been identified with the Sociology Department. Similar hospitality and arrangements have been extended within the Departments of Anthropology and Psychology.

How much am I able to keep up to date and to think like a sociologist? I think that the answer depends on one's perspective. As a methodologist, I am a strong advocate of case study and experimental designs. I have not been able to maintain competence in survey research although I advocate much greater attention to instrument design than I see in many contemporary training programs. I am trying to encourage more students and young colleagues to become involved in longitudinal research. Conceptually, I am particularly interested in social change, deviance, and dependency. For anyone who tries to become multidisciplinary and to span administrative and academic activities and substantive fields like alcohol problems, dependency behavior, and patient care, it is impossible not to be spread too thinly. Unquestionably, I think more as a behavioral scientist and less as a sociologist as the years go by. The gap would be greater if it was not for the harmonious tie with sociology departments and the retreading sabbatical year at Yale. My goals are to remain able to identify relevant sociological theories to test in my health-medical studies and teaching, and to recognize opportunities to extend sociological theory when they arise in my work or that of my colleagues or students. But I am not looking for recognition as a sociologist, per se.

I do want to become a more competent behavioral scientist, and here, for many years, I have faced the dilemma which heavy involvement in administration poses for any academician. Over the past fourteen years, I have repeatedly declined opportunities to be considered as a candidate for positions in academic administration including those of vice president, provost, and dean of medical, graduate, and arts and sciences colleges. I sincerely believe that the administration duties of a department chairman are the most that can be compatible with retention of my usefulness as a teacher and investigator, and with my personal strengths and weaknesses.

Yet, if I know myself, I realize that some variety has been an important spice in my professional life. Currently, I am serving on the first Behavioral Science Test Committee of the National Board of Medical Examiners (who would have dreamed just about ten years ago that behavioral sciences would now be one of the substantive areas on which aspiring physicians must pass examinations?), on the Committee on Alcoholism and Drug Dependence of the American Medical Association, and on the Study Commission on Pharmacy, under the inspiring chairmanship of John S. Millis. I am also chairing a Task Group on Health Sciences Education for the Kentucky Board of Public Higher Education. My associations with organized medicine at the scientific level have been rewarding and mutually respectful. When I received the Faculty Scientific Achievement Award of the Kentucky Medical Association in 1966, I believe this was the first such recognition to a behavioral scientist.

Upon rereading this sketch, I realize that my first job with the Connecticut Post-War Planning Board in 1944 was prophetic of the years to come. The post–World War II planning activities of the early 1940s provided early opportunities for social scientists and other professionals to become involved in applying their research and theory to planning for social policy. Much of my own professional career has been involved directly or indirectly with social planning—with alcohol problems for over twenty-five years, for Connecticut's Health Resources in 1950–51, for emotionally disturbed children in 1952–53, for community mental health in 1963–64, and for medical education and patient care intensively between 1956 and 1963 and again at the present time. Today, my concern with problems of alcohol has expanded to other drugs and dependency behavior, and interests in planning for the future of health services has been revitalized.

Where do we go from here? For any man past fifty, this is a common question. If I know myself, I would say that my ambitions from this point on are intrinsic; rather than for power, I wish there were fewer committee assignments and less mail and paper pushing. I try to have teaching come first; paper pushing comes next, and there is never enough time, and thinking and writing, the two activities which require concentrated periods of uninterruption, often seem to come last. Midst the joys and rewards and continued stimulation of a busy life, I shall continue to indulge in that yearning for more time for reflection.

NOTES

1. Alma F. Straus, *Keep Busy* (New York: G. P. Putnam's Sons, 1937).

2. Robert Straus, *Escape from Custody* (New York: Harper and Row, 1974).

3. Robert Straus and Selden Bacon, *Drinking in College* (1953; reprint ed., Westport, Conn.: Greenwood Press, 1971).

4. Thomas R. Ford, *Health and Demography in Kentucky* (Lexington: University of Kentucky Press, 1964).

5. Robert Straus, "Alcohol and Society," *Psychiatric Annals* 3 (October 1973, special issue); idem, "Departments and Disciplines: Stasis and Change" *Science* 182 (November 1973): 895–98.

Contributors

JACK ELINSON is professor and head of the program in sociomedical sciences at Columbia University. This program, which he inaugurated, brings the various social sciences (predominantly, but not restricted to, sociology) to bear on problems of health and health care. His work has dealt with the quantitative estimation of community health care needs, comparison of medical and sociological perspectives in conceptualizing illness, sociometric evaluation of the quality of medical and hospital care, and the development of sociomedical health indicators. He has completed studies on the Hunterdon County experiment, a university medical center-sponsored rural group practice; career attitudes of physicians and nurses as a part of health manpower studies in Puerto Rico; and the measurement of quality of care by examining where and how physicians seek care when they are patients. He is currently engaged in research on the antecedents and consequents of teenage drug behavior. He has held a number of important professional positions including the Council of the Medical Sociology Section, American Sociological Association. In 1975, he became chairman of this section.

RAY ELLING is professor of sociology and coordinator of the Program in Cross-National Studies of Health Systems in the Department of Community Medicine and Health Care at the University of Connecticut Health Center and professor in the Department of Sociology. He received his M.A. in sociology from the University of Chicago and his Ph.D. in medical sociology from Yale University. He served (1971–73) as chief of the Behavioral Sciences Unit and later chief scientist (sociologist) in the Program in Development of Health Services of the World Health Organization at Geneva. He has done studies of patient participation in care for rheumatic fever, organizational support (hospitals), and examined problems of coordinating competing occupational groups and complex organizations in regional health services systems. A recent research monograph (with Russell Martin), *Health and Health Care for the Urban Poor*, examines health problems and health care behavior among residents of a largely black, Puerto Rican section of Hartford. An edited volume, *Comparative Health Systems*, appeared in June 1975 as a supplemental issue of the journal *Inquiry*. He was elected and served as secretary-treasurer of the Medical Sociology Section, American Sociological Association, 1968–71.

MARK FIELD is a professor in the Department of Sociology at Boston University. He is also an associate of the Russian Research Center and lecturer on sociology in the School of Medicine, and a visiting lecturer at the School of Public Health at Harvard University. His M.A. was in Regional Studies and his Ph.D. in Social Relations (Sociology) from Harvard. He has published a number of works on the health system of the Soviet Union. His research interests cluster around the health systems of industrial societies, on the degree to which and ways in which these systems face common demands and problems and show a tendency toward a convergence of structures. He has begun work on a comparative study of six nations (the United States, the Soviet Union, France, Japan, Great Britain, and Sweden). Related areas of interest are health manpower, primary care, specialization, and the delivery of health services. He has served in recent years as chairperson of the Medical Sociology Research Committee of the International Sociological Association.

ELIOT FREIDSON is professor and chairman of the Department of Sociology at New York University. His M.A. and Ph.D. were in sociology from the University of Chicago. His research has included work on public opinion and the media, patient referral networks, colleague control in group practice, and professional organization and ideology. Major works include *The Profession of Medicine: A Study of the Sociology of Applied Knowledge* and *Professional Dominance: The Social Structure of Medical Care*. He has held numerous important positions in sociology. Among them are: chairperson of the Committee on Publications of the Society for the Study for Social Problems; editor of the *Journal of Health and Social Behavior*; chairperson of the Medical Sociology Section of the American Sociological Association; and chairperson of the Medical Sociology Research Committee of the International Sociological Association.

MARGOT JEFFERYS is professor of medical sociology and joint director of the Social Research Unit in the Department of Sociology of Bedford College at University of London. She received a B.Sc. in economics from the London School of Economics. Her research has centered on issues of social policy as regards the provision of health care with specific concern for problems of health and social services personnel, smoking, health behavior of employed women compared with those in housework, selection of medical students, and care for the physically handicapped. Her current research interests include tension and conflict in national health systems seen historically and comparatively; and at the more microcosmic level, conflict and decision making in general practice in Britain; pre- and post-M.D. education; and women in health occupations. Recent publications include *People-oriented Health Services* and *The Menopausal Syndrome*. She has served in a number of positions of importance to the development of medical sociology including the Council of the Medical Sociology Research Committee of the International Sociological Association.

YNGVAR LØCHEN is professor of Sociology and chairperson of the Institute of Social Science at the University of Tromsø. His M.A. and Ph.D. are from the University of Oslo. He has taught in the School of Medicine at the University of Oslo and continues to teach medical students as well as sociology students at his present university. In 1967–68 he was a visiting scientist at the National Institute of Mental Health at Bethesda, Maryland. He has done research on the social organization of a mental hospital with special attention to the diagnostic culture—"cases" versus "persons," and so forth. His current interest is in the role of science in society. He has served as vice chairperson of the Central Committee of the Norwegian Research Council and now holds the chair of this important group advising the government on science policy. Recently he traveled with a group of Norwegian scholars to look into the medical care system in China.

HANS MAUKSCH is recently (1977) returned to his professorship at the University of Missouri after serving as executive officer of the American Sociological Association. Prior to this he served as professor and chief of the Section of Behavioral Sciences in the Department of Community Health and Medical Practice, and as director of the Graduate Training Program in Medical Sociology in the Department of Sociology at the University of Missouri-Columbia. For a number of years he was dean of liberal arts at the Illinois Institute of Technology. He received his M.A. and Ph.D. in sociology from the University of Chicago. His research includes studies of professionalization in nursing and social interaction in the hospital among staff and between staff and patients. More recently his research interest has focused on the development of family health care. He has held national offices in a wide range of associations including those of sociology, medical sociology, nursing, and engineering.

YVO NUYENS is professor of Medical Sociology and chairperson of the Department of Sociology and director of the Research Group for Medical Sociology in the Sociological Research Institute at Leuven University. He is also extraordinary professor in medical sociology at the Medical School of Antwerp University. His M.A. and Ph.D. in sociology were from Leuven University. His research has centered on the sociopolitical aspects of health care organization, health and illness behavior, mental health, and health occupations. A short monograph of his describing and analyzing the Belgian health care system was recently published. He serves on the Council of the Medical Sociology Research Committee of the International Sociological Association.

JORGE SEGOVIA is an associate professor in the Department of Community Medicine at University of King's College in Halifax, Nova Scotia. He was a Milbank Faculty Fellow during 1965–70. He received his M.D. and M.P.H. from the University of Buenos Aires. He took courses in sociology at the University of Buenos Aires and was a postdoctoral student in the Social Sciences Unit of the Graduate School of Public Health at the University of Pittsburgh. He has served as a medical officer for preventive medicine in a rural region of Argentina, as head of the medical sociology section and of a shantytown health center included in an experimental group practice in Buenos Aires. His research includes work on urban poor mothers' understanding of summer diarrhea, what physicians think of physicians in Argentina, and a conceptual statement of health as a social system. He is a founding member of the Argentine Public Health Association and served as general secretary of the executive council, 1965–67. He is a member of the American Sociological Association.

JUDITH SHUVAL is an associate professor in sociology and medical education at Hebrew University in Jerusalem. Her M.A. and Ph.D. in sociology were received from Radcliffe College, Harvard University. She is recipient of the Helen De Roy Prize of the Society for the Study of Social Problems, and the Israel Prize for the Social Sciences for her book, *Immigrants on the Threshold*. In addition to work on the health and health care behavior of immigrants, she has done research on selection to and socialization in medical education. She has served as a consultant to WHO and holds a number of positions in scientific associations including the Executive Committee of the Israel Sociological Association, the Israel Council for Demographic Problems, and the Executive Committee of the Israel Council for Art and Culture.

MAGDALENA SOKOŁOWSKA is professor of sociology and chairperson of the Medical Sociology Section of the Institute of Philosophy and Sociology of the Polish Academy of Sciences in Warsaw and she belongs to the industrial health service in Poland which developed after World War II. From 1951 to 1958 she was medical director of the textile industry's amalgamation in Lodz. Dr. Sokołowska received a physician's diploma in 1949 and doctor's degree in 1951 from the Medical School in Gdansk; in 1960 she earned her M.P.H. from the Columbia University School of Public Health, followed by a docent degree in sociology from the Polish Academy of Sciences in 1963. Current research interests include health in social stratification and styles of life of Polish society, sociology of disability and rehabilitation, and changing sex roles. Among her major publications are *Sociomedical Characteristics of Women's Work; Health and Society;* and *Fraunemanzipation und Sozialismus: Beispiel von Volksrepublik Polen.* She is regional editor for Eastern Europe of the journal *Social Science and Medicine.* She is a member of the Executive Committee of the International Sociological Association and the vice chairperson of the Research Committee on Medical Sociology of this association.

ROBERT STRAUS is professor and chairperson of the Department of Behavioral Science at the University of Kentucky College of Medicine. He received his M.A. and Ph.D. in sociology from Yale University. His first teaching position was in the Syracuse Medical School, one of the first such positions held by a sociologist. He was one of the original planning staff of the new college of medicine at Kentucky. His major research interests are in alcohol problems, institutional dependency, and processes of patient care. His major publications include *Medical Care for Seamen, Drinking in College, Alcohol and Society, The Nature and Status of Medical Sociology,* and *Escape from Custody.* He has served as associate editor of the *Journal of Health and Human Behavior* and the *Quarterly Journal of Studies on Alcohol.* He has held a number of important positions in scientific associations including chairperson of the Medical Sociology Section of the American Sociological Association, and chairperson of the National Advisory Committee on Alcoholism.

INDEX OF NAMES,
INSTITUTIONS, AND PROGRAMS

Dahrendorf, R., 68
David, James A., 37
Davidson, G. E., 63
Davie, Maurice R., 312–13
Davies, A. M., 279
Davis, Fred, 207
Davis, Michael, 52
Davis, Milton S., 40
Department of Applied
  Physiology, Yale University,
  313
Department of Behavioral
  Science, University of
  Kentucky, 321–22, 324–25
Department of Clinical Medicine
  and Health Care, University of
  Connecticut, School of
  Medicine, 73–74
Department of Community Health
  and Medical Practice,
  University of Missouri, 205
Department of Community
  Medicine and Health Care,
  University of Connecticut, 75,
  78–79
Department of Hygiene,
  University of Gdansk, 292
Department of Patient Care
  Research, St. Luke's Hospital
  (Chicago), 195–96, 198
Department of Sociology at the
  Hebrew University of
  Jerusalem, 272, 282
Department of Sociology,
  University of Leuven, 213, 216,
  225, 228–30
Department of Sociology of Work,
  Warsaw University, 299
Department of Social Affairs of
  Norway, 183
Department of Social Relations,
  Harvard University, 92, 94, 99,
  113, 271
DePasquale, Roberto, 250
Deuschle, Kurt, 323

Dewey, John, 250
Dickey, Frank, 318
Dikemark Hospital, Norway,
  166–67, 170–73, 183
Dillehay, Ronald C., 325
Division of Sociomedical Sciences,
  Columbia University School
  of Public Health, 262–63
DIVO, 61
Djukanovic, V., 78
Dohrenwend, Bruce S., 39
Doll, Richard, 147
Douglas, Dorothy, 74
Dubin, Robert, 32
Duhl, Leonard, 64
Duncan, D., 52
Dunnell, Karen, 146
Durkheim, E., 64

Edinburgh University,
  Department of Public Health,
  147
Eichhorn, Robert, 37
Einstein, Albert, 26
Elinson, Jack, 25–45, 262–64,
  295, 306
Elinson, May, 42
Elling, Ray, 40, 47–87, 221, 228,
  258, 260
Europa Institute at the Free
  University of Berlin, 102
Evan, W. M., 67
Evans, Lester, 195

Family Health Maintenance
  Demonstration, 118–20, 125
Feld, Simon, 244–46
Feldman, Jacob, 121–22
Felix, Robert, 324
Ficken, Roland P., 325
Field, Mark, 79, 90–114, 218, 286
Fink, Ray, 37
Firth, Raymond, 148